123.00

Understanding and Dealing With Violence

WINTER ROUNDTABLE SERIES

This book series is based upon the annual Winter Roundtable on Cross-Cultural Psychology and Education, convened each year by the Counseling Psychology Program at Teachers College, Columbia University. Inaugurated in 1983, the cross-cultural Winter Roundtable is the longest running, annual, national conference in the United States that specifically focuses on cultural, racial, and ethnic issues in psychology and education. Volumes in this series have their origin either in themes of Winter Roundtable conferences or in research developments in cross-cultural and multicultural psychology and education that reflect the goals and vision of the Winter Roundtable.

Volumes in this series . . .

1. Addressing Cultural Issues in Organization,
edited by Robert T. Carter

2. Promoting Diversity and Social Justice:
Educating People From Privileged Groups,
by Diane J. Goodman

3. Understanding and Dealing With Violence,
edited by Barbara C. Wallace and Robert T. Carter

Editors

Barbara C. Wallace
Teachers College, Columbia University

Robert T. Carter
Teachers College, Columbia University

Understanding and Dealing With Violence

A
Multicultural
Approach

WINTER ROUNDTABLE SERIES

SAGE Publications
International Educational and Professional Publisher
Thousand Oaks ■ London ■ New Delhi

Copyright © 2003 by Sage Publications, Inc.

For information:

Sage Publications, Inc.
2455 Teller Road
Thousand Oaks, California 91320
E-mail: order@sagepub.com

Sage Publications Ltd.
6 Bonhill Street
London EC2A 4PU
United Kingdom

Sage Publications India Pvt. Ltd.
B-42 Panchsheel Enclave
Post Box 4109
New Delhi 110 017 India

Printed in the United States of America

Library of Congress Cataloging-in-Publication Data

Understanding and dealing with violence: A multicultural approach/
Barbara C. Wallace and Robert T. Carter, editors.
    p. cm. — (Winter roundtable series; 3)
Includes bibliographical references and index.
ISBN 0-7619-1714-4 (C) — ISBN 0-7619-1715-2 (P)
   1. Violence-Psychological aspects. 2. Oppression (Psychology)
3. Prejudices. 4. Identity (Psychology) 5. Respect for persons. 6. Violence-
Prevention. I. Wallace, Barbara C. II. Carter, Robert T., 1948- III. Series.
HM1116 .U53 2003
303.6—dc211
                              2002013219

02 03 10 9 8 7 6 5 4 3 2 1

Acquiring Editor:	Margaret H. Seawell
Editorial Assistant:	Alicia Carter/Vonessa Vondera
Production Editor:	Diana E. Axelsen
Copy Editor:	Gillian Dickens
Typesetter:	C&M Digitals (P) Ltd
Indexer:	Rachel Rice
Cover Designer:	Janet Foulger

Contents

Foreword

"Violence begets violence."

Wallace and Carter have compiled a significant volume that underscores the importance of each of us understanding the many facets of violence, including racism, prejudice, discrimination, sexism, heterosexism, classism, ethnic cleansing, physical and sexual assault, verbal assault, terrorism, war, hate messages, hate crimes, racial profiling, police brutality, and many other acts of inhumanity that exist. The authors of the book's chapters have many outstanding and powerful things to communicate, and I believe that most readers will continue to reflect on the written material long after reading each chapter. The contributors are quite skillful in blending their scholarly and personal perspectives throughout. The words and messages in each of the chapters are so profound that most individuals will find it difficult to read more than one chapter at a time without taking the opportunity to digest it fully.

Among the first of its kind, this book will fill a substantial void in the multicultural mental health and education literature by offering unique and timely perspectives related to various forms of personal and interpersonal violence. I am also especially pleased by the social justice dimensions that are either implicit or explicit in each chapter. In particular, the chapters' authors consistently underscore the point that violence in all of its forms is damaging not only to individual persons but also to many components of the affected system(s). They almost uniformly assert that violence in any manner should not be tolerated because it contributes to a cycle or system of abuse that is ongoing until deliberate and concerted efforts are made to end this cycle.

Wallace and Carter's book challenges us to identify constructive ways to resolve or at least address conflicts that could lead to violence in some way. Living in a multicultural society such as the United States and even the world further tests our ability to recognize and affirm the values and experiences of others as valid, even if we do not personally agree with others' ways of being. Nonetheless, it is important to note that to view one's worldview or experience as "absolute truth" is to negate and potentially pathologize other worldviews or experiences. This phenomenon, in fact, may lead to many types of intentional or unintentional violence.

Wallace and Carter's edited volume is destined to serve as a primer to mental health clinicians, educators, clergy, social service personnel, students, and even community members and activists in their quest to combat violence in its numerous forms. This book is a "must-have" for anyone who is even remotely interested or affected in a small way by some type of violence. Especially in light of the terrorist events that occurred in the United States on September 11, 2001—and, indeed, other terrorist events that may occur on a daily basis in countries throughout the world—I would conclude that some form of violence has affected nearly every living being. I am grateful to Wallace and Carter for their vision and perseverance in bringing this book to fruition. I am certain that you will feel similarly after reading this volume—a work that, I predict, will be a seminal contribution to many areas of social science and education.

Madonna G. Constantine, Ph.D.
Associate Professor of Psychology and Education
Department of Counseling and Clinical Psychology
Teachers College, Columbia University

Preface

After the violence of September 11, 2001, it was as if the world had stopped. Indeed, the production process involving this book halted as well, and a global community contemplated the devastating impact of violence. Those here in New York City, in particular, as well as across the expanse of the United States, faced the individual and collective task of fully absorbing the repercussions of violence as well as realizing that things will never be the same. This is the nature of the traumatic impact of violence—a universal experience of trauma that is ever so intimately known all too well by all too many around the globe.

How are we to understand and deal with personal and social violence? This book answers that question, providing timely and much-needed answers at a time in American history when more individuals may be asking that question and seeking answers than ever before.

In the aftermath of the terrorist attacks on September 11, 2001, immigrants are being rounded up, interviewed, arrested, detained, incarcerated, and deported. Some institutions are extending "racial profiling," as it is known when practiced against Blacks, to those who appear to be Islamic or Saudi Arabian, and bias crimes against such individuals have proliferated as one repercussion of the violence of September 11, even as one battle after another rages on distant lands. As Constantine reminds us in her Foreword, "violence begets violence." So how do we go about the task of stopping the cycle of violence?

Because the new millennium brings new demographics suggestive of an increasingly diverse society in the United States, as well as a diverse global community, what is needed is an approach to violence that appreciates the social, cultural, and historical context in which violence occurs. This kind of an approach to violence may be called multicultural in design. Thus, this edited volume introduces a multicultural approach to violence to the social sciences—as well as to the fields of psychology, education, and religion—that represents a viable approach to understanding and dealing with contemporary social and personal violence. Indeed, literally any member of the global community who seeks to understand violence and practical ways of dealing with it will find a practical tool for their use in this handbook.

The multicultural approach to violence that this edited volume presents may itself be situated within a social, cultural, and historical context. The idea for this book arose around the planning of the 15th annual Teachers College Winter Roundtable on Cross-Cultural Psychology and Education in 1998. The roundtable has evolved from a pioneering conference setting for the discussion of cross-cultural counseling issues in psychology in the early 1980s to an annual national conference known for excellence in bringing together leading researchers, scholars, and practitioners in the areas of diversity and multiculturalism.

Robert T. Carter, coeditor of this volume, has been the director of the conference for more than a decade. His leadership and vision of the conference have resulted in the roundtable expanding to include a focus on diversity and multiculturalism in education, going beyond the original focus primarily on cross-cultural counseling psychology. Since 1993, I have used the roundtable as an annual vehicle for presenting my thinking on the area of violence from a multicultural perspective. Over the years, I have developed a comprehensive theory of violence that accommodates both visible as well as invisible violence, seeks to end all forms of violence and oppression, and addresses damage done to identity. This edited volume allows me to present this comprehensive theory of violence as a psychology of oppression, liberation, and identity development, introducing the volume with this multicultural approach to violence in Chapter 1.

What follows in subsequent chapters are the contributions of individuals who presented papers at the 1998 roundtable conference when the theme was "Understanding and Dealing With Personal and Social Violence." Robert T. Carter asked me to provide leadership in selecting invited speakers who were experts in this area, as well as in organizing an edited book project on the same conference theme. Beyond what selected presenters shared at the conference, a few additional chapters were solicited from individuals who were not presenters at the roundtable but, nonetheless, have much to say of value.

As a foundation in building a viable approach to violence that is multicultural and also expands the frontier of the field of cross-cultural psychology and education, it is hoped that the groundwork has been laid through this edited volume on which subsequent research and scholarship may stand. In addition, the "diverse and different other" within any society on any continent will find within this book important theory, research, and scholarship that effectively guide psychologists, educators, policymakers, religious leaders, community members, perpetrators, and victims or survivors of violence toward healing. Healing is required on the level of individuals, families, communities, organizations, professions, society, and the global community. The "diverse and different others" who are members of varied regional, national, and international communities will find in this book a practical tool to use in forging social justice movements that will improve the quality of their lives. Ideally, they will be supported if not accompanied by varied professionals working as equals alongside them who are willing to share their power, empower the oppressed, and take social action for social justice.

The goal of this edited volume is to radically transform the personal and social lives of the "diverse and different" who have been historically oppressed, as well as transform the dynamic interplay between the oppressed and oppressor so that all can realize their highest potential and self-actualize the creation of positive identities. The goal of the volume is to also promote the work of ending all forms of violence and oppression, or man's inhumanity to man. This goal may seem idealistic to some. But any mission that is destined to take a considerable amount of time to complete requires a clear vision. Thus, the stated goal represents articulation of the vision, whereas this book is just one foundation stone placed on the path toward fulfilling the mission. Indeed, the book may inspire many to place their foot on that path and to take social action for social justice, as well as forge social justice movements for the liberation of the oppressed. It is hoped that future research and scholarship will attest to this prediction.

But, today, in the aftermath of September 11, 2001, attacks and the regional, national, and international forms of violence reigning around the globe, a desperate humanity yearning to be free calls out for this book, and the volume responds through delivery of the kind of handbook that can direct social justice movements for their liberation. In addition, the voices of those who died on September 11 and in countless other atrocious acts of violence that still haunt a global community some days, months, years, decades, and centuries later collectively rise from the realm of spirit, asking us all to dedicate our energies to bringing an end to all forms of violence and oppression. Toward that end, this volume responds to a collective chorus of voices calling for well-reasoned, nonviolent efforts and offers a practical handbook for ending man's inhumanity to man.

—Barbara C. Wallace

Acknowledgments

Barbara C. Wallace acknowledges the many members of her extended family: Nana Okomfohene Korantemaa Ayeboafo for her spiritual service, editorial assistance, love, and support, as well as Cynthia, Uriel, Tersh, Adrienne, Ramsey, Kippie, and Isabella for their foundation of love, support, and good times. Not to be forgotten are Asuo Opare and Menu Opare, Ivonne Miranda, Dr. James Rosado, and Mensa Atta. Teachers College family includes Marsha Streeter and Cynthia Green, as well as a host of many others, including many beloved students. Spiritual family includes Nana Asuo Gyebi, Nana Asi, Nana Anima, Nana Oparebea, Boafo Tigare, Suapem, and my dear friend of many years, Jesus. And not to be forgotten are my ancestors, going back to the very beginning of time.

Robert T. Carter would like to acknowledge many as well: He acknowledges and expresses his gratitude for the dedication and diligence of Barbara C. Wallace in "shepherding" this project from beginning to end, as well as the contributors to this edited volume for their thoughtful, insightful work and their courage in sharing their experience and cutting-edge work in the area of violence.

He would also like to acknowledge the staff from the annual winter roundtable conference and those people who support the winter roundtable from around the country. Acknowledgments must also go to the people at Teachers College who support the annual conference, as well as the union staff and professional staff who provide invaluable assistance from various offices around the college. Finally, he acknowledges his wife, Adrienne, and his family.

This book is dedicated to the memory of all of those who transitioned as a result of one of the many manifestations of violence and oppression, whether an atrocity, genocide, torture, trauma, war, hate, a bias crime, gun violence, police brutality, or any other form of man's inhumanity to man. It is also dedicated to those who are still living and willing to dedicate their lives to the eradication of violence and oppression. May this handbook guide the process of professionals and community members working alongside each other to bring about a world in which all can peacefully live and fully self-actualize an identity—regardless of how they may be perceived from the perspective of another as a "diverse and different other."

Part I

Understanding and Dealing With
Violence Through a Psychology of
Oppression, Liberation, and
Identity Development

1

A Multicultural
Approach to Violence

*Toward a Psychology of Oppression,
Liberation, and Identity Development*

BARBARA C. WALLACE

A multicultural approach to violence considers multiple cultural
variables that operate in the origin, manifestation, and dynamics of violence on the level of the individual, family, organization, and
society while appreciating both historical and sociocultural influences. Hence, these multiple cultural variables may be derived from
the social context or from the personal characteristics and experiences
of those either perpetrating or being victimized by violence.

This means we must consider the experiences of the oppressed
and the oppressor when the form of "diversity or difference" at issue
may take any one or more manifestations. This also allows for us to
consider the experiences of oppression when an individual has created and self-defined himself or herself as possessing literally any
identity—even one that is a composite of multiple identities—as he
or she will be respected in evolving that unique identity, be allowed
to self-determine what it is and should be called as an identity, and
may share perceptions and conceptualizations regarding those
kinds and forms of oppression to which he or she has been subjected. What is needed and offered is a kind of generic or global

understanding of violence and oppression that can be applied to literally any instance of social injustice.

This volume's multicultural approach to personal and social violence examines the broad dimensions of violence as it occurs on multiple levels involving multiple systems. On the level of the individual, multiple cultural influences include race, ethnicity, gender, sexual orientation, ability/disability status, religion, class, socioeconomic status, education, background, and experiences. Literally, any attitudes, beliefs, traditions, and practices that are passed on from group member to group member and from generation to generation may constitute a cultural influence. Or one may be the first to create that identity, perhaps in one's generation or contemporary social environment, even as one may then connect with others who embrace that identity for themselves, as well. Any one individual may, therefore, claim multiple cultural influences on his or her self-concept, identity, beliefs, attitudes, feelings, behaviors, and overall consciousness. For example, one might be an African American, Jewish, gay, disabled individual from a middle-class background who is currently affluent with a graduate-level education. Any of these multiple markers of identity, whether readily perceived by others or not, may serve as a trigger for others to target an individual for the experience of institutionalized racism, prejudice, discrimination, and even overt visible violent attacks. The bottom line is that the "diverse and different other" may be subject to overt and covert violence. The multiple levels and systems on which we focus within the multicultural approach to violence go beyond that of the individual to include family, community, and the larger society in the United States, as well as an international community linked by war, refugee and exile experiences, telecommunications, and frequent immigration and travel. This encompasses societal institutions and organizations, such as academia, professions, medical centers, community clinics, government agencies and laboratories, churches, synagogues, mosques, social settings, the retail industry, corporations, the criminal justice system, and the Internet and media—all of which reflect the realities of contemporary personal and social violence. This book strives to empower readers to be multiculturally competent change agents who can effectively engage with diverse community members on a national and international scale to end violence and promote healing.

Understanding and dealing with violence means acknowledging the social context, as well as historical and/or contemporary forms of oppression. The social context is full of institutions that foster contemporary forms of oppression, effectively perpetuating personal and social violence. Much harm is done through institutionalized violence and oppression.

Institutionalized violence and oppression may be defined as the presence in organizations, as well as its leadership and members, of patterns of behavior, ways of thinking, and emotional responses to "diverse and different others" who are made to feel unwelcome, unaccepted, and disrespected within the institution as a result of a multiplicity of factors—such as white privilege, white domination, prejudice, discrimination, racism, sexism, classism, ageism, heterosexism, homophobia, and the perpetuation of invisibility and disregard for people with disabilities. The result of institutionalized violence and oppression is that those exposed to it may suffer unfavorable work conditions, lower pay, patterns of not being promoted or retained, firings, unfair treatment, stress reactions, health problems, emotional pain, and cognitive distress, and they may behave in a variety of ways that specifically reflect the impact of being a target of hate, anger, and the many manifestations of institutionalized violence listed above.

Historically, disadvantages have accrued for those who have suffered from institutionalized violence and oppression. This disadvantaging has taken many forms for enslaved Africans, Native Americans, women, immigrants, people with disabilities, and gay, lesbian, bisexual, and transgender people. Long periods and eras of oppression involving discrimination and even accepted and legally sanctioned forms of violence against members of these groups are a part of that history. The legacy of institutionalized violence, oppression, and historical disadvantaging has direct links with persisting contemporary forms of oppression, including white privilege. Considering these factors means fully appreciating the social context for violence. The approach to violence that is taken, therefore, allows us to draw links between historical factors, prevailing practices that are rooted in history, and contemporary manifestations of violence.

Once one appreciates how the manifestations of violence and solutions to violence have everything to do with a social context rampant with the realities of oppression, a call for social justice and advocacy work on behalf of the oppressed follows logically. Activists for social change may benefit from the multicultural approach to violence, as their engagement in the change process is essential. Psychological and educational organizational consultants are needed who have a multicultural perspective that appreciates the manner in which oppression and covert violence may operate on multiple systems levels, including the level of the individual, family, community, organizations, professions, and society overall. However, it is important to increase the knowledge of all professionals in varied fields, as well as members of a global community, because professionals and community members need to work in partnership to end the multiple manifestations of violence.

As the introductory foundation chapter for establishing the nature and dimensions of a multicultural approach to violence, this chapter will present the following: (a) the psychology of oppression and liberation in order to foster understanding of the impact of the U.S. culture of violence, (b) graphic symbols to codify the dynamics within a psychology of oppression and liberation, (c) what it means to enter the inner worldview and self-structure of the oppressed and the oppressor toward articulating a psychology of identity development, (d) the psychology or pedagogy of liberation for the plight of internalization, and (e) seven steps for transforming personal and cultural paradigms, illustrating the central role of carefully structured dialogue.

The Psychology of Oppression: Understanding the Impact of the U.S. Culture of Violence

One might begin with a case in point to understand why a psychology of oppression is needed in many parts of the world that have languished in the aftermath of enslavement, colonialism, and centuries of institutionalized racism and multiple forms of oppression against the "diverse and different other." For example, the United States is a culture of violence that represents a good starting point for introducing the psychology of oppression.

The U.S. culture of violence has been defined as a way of life, behaviors, beliefs, practices, and traditions that are taught and transmitted from group member to member and from generation to generation regarding the use of physical force, displays of power, and the spreading of misinformation and myths. Moreover, this transmission of practices and traditions regarding violence occurs in such a way that historically traumatic events profoundly shape and impact what is transmitted to different cultural group members and across generations (Wallace, 1993, 1996). This definition of the culture of violence includes the historical destruction of Native American civilization, the existence of the slave trade, violence against many newly arrived immigrants, and the codified degradation of African Americans. It also includes subsequent forms of more contemporary institutionalized racism and historically sanctioned discrimination and violence, especially as practiced against people of color, providing the overall context for clients' lives in the United States (Wallace, 1993, 1996). Perhaps somewhat less pronounced in societal discourse is a focus on historically sanctioned discrimination and violence against a number of marginalized and oppressed groups. These include persons with disabilities and gay, lesbian, bisexual, and transgender individuals, in addition to those with any "diversity or difference" typically disdained in society. As a result of beliefs about these "diverse and different others" being transmitted from group member to group member, one may speak of societal members' possession of conditioned cognitions. These conditioned cognitions, or learned thoughts, involve the learning of stereotypes to effectively spread misinformation and myths. Possession of conditioned cognitions reflects socialization influences from the larger culture, mass media, and family, religious, and ethnic groups to which individuals belong. Cognitions guide behavior, so that individuals may draw on their conditioned cognitions as they engage in behavioral practices and traditions, such as directing physical violence against members of ethnic, racial, gender, class, sexual orientation, and other varied "different" groups. It is within this cultural context that psychologists, educators, and community members have experienced socialization processes within varied settings and institutions within the United States. The media, the Web, and international telecommunications allow for the transmission of beliefs about "different" persons, as well as stereotypes, across national and international borders.

A Broad Definition of Violence

Violence is defined as delivering physical blows (with or without weaponry), displaying and misusing one's power, or bombarding a person with destructive misinformation and myths so that, in effect, an assault occurs either on a person's physical body or to the self-concept, identity, cognitions, affects, and consciousness of the victim of violence (Wallace, 1993, 1996). This definition permits an evaluation of the role that psychologists, educators, and community members may unwittingly play when they have unconsciously and unintentionally perpetrated an assault, negatively impacting the self-concept, identity, cognitions, affects, and consciousness of a fellow human being, client, research participant, or student. Indeed, any individual, family, community, or societal member needs to go well beyond a keen awareness of the reality of overt physical violence or violence perpetrated with weaponry such as handguns. It is essential that we all become aware of how invisible, covert violence typically precedes the manifestation of visible overt violence. Invisible covert violence may actually set the stage and create conditions for the manifestation of overt physical violence. Moreover, even where invisible covert violence reigns, a substantial assault has been perpetrated, nonetheless, on others. The damage done is significant and quite destructive, and it can be measured in terms of the insidious, often enduring impact on the self-concept, identity, cognitions, affects, and consciousness of the victim of violence.

To establish the approach set forth in this volume as multicultural, we need an approach to understanding that is sensitive to how members of historically marginalized and oppressed groups end up experiencing both covert and overt forms of violence. The knowledge base offered in regard to personal and social violence needs to permit understanding the painful, disillusioning, and unfortunately typical experiences of oppressed and marginalized people in the United States who are diverse and from varied multicultural groups. An in-depth examination of invisible covert violence permits fostering this understanding and establishing a sufficient knowledge base for this purpose, as this chapter seeks to demonstrate.

From the broad definition of violence that guides the compilation of scholarly work and research to be presented in subsequent chapters in this volume, it follows that all forms of violence must be exposed and rejected. This includes any invisible covert violence that psychologists and educators (whether when counseling others, engaging in research, or teaching) may also perpetrate in their respective work and settings. This violence encompasses the negative impact and damage done to the self-concept, identity, cognitions, affects, and consciousness of a client, research participant, student, or community member. Assuming the responsibility to do no harm in

Table 1.1   The Psychology of Oppression

Given an actor A, who has been socially conditioned to feel superior, and an actor B, who is deemed to be inferior, the psychology of oppression acknowledges the following dynamics:

1. The projection of negative and low expectations, as well as stereotypes from the spreading of misinformation and myths:

$$A \Rightarrow B$$

2. The practice of domination and hierarchical authority by a controlling superior seeking to subjugate one deemed inferior:

$$\frac{A}{B}$$

3. One feeling superior talks down to another as though he or she is inferior in one-way communication:

$$A \sim\!\Downarrow B$$

our work with clients, research participants, students, and community members means that we must not engage in invisible covert violence, suggesting the need for the training presented in this chapter.

Graphic Symbols to Codify the Dynamics Within a Psychology of Oppression and Liberation

Graphic, symbolic concepts may be of value in increasing psychologists', educators', and community members' understanding and knowledge of the importance of avoiding the perpetration of invisible covert violence. These graphic symbols also serve to codify the dynamics within a psychology of oppression (see Table 1.1), as well as those dynamics within a psychology of liberation (see Table 1.2). The goal is to avoid three ways of perpetrating invisible covert violence: (a) the projection of negative and low expectations, (b) the practice of domination and exercise of hierarchical authority, and (c) verbal communication wherein a dominant superior talks down to a subordinate inferior. This knowledge may potentially stop the cycle of individuals (e.g., counselors, researchers, teachers, and community members) who role model and condition the next generation to follow them in perpetrating invisible covert violence.

Table 1.2   The Psychology of Liberation

Given an actor A, who has been socially conditioned to feel superior, and an actor B, who is deemed to be inferior, the psychology of liberation recommends the following:

1. Create *reciprocal recognition*, or create a new dialectic in which each enters the worldview of the other and discovers the "other" with an attitude of genuine respect and acceptance:

$$A \Leftrightarrow B$$

This means transforming $A \Rightarrow B$ to $A \Leftrightarrow B$.

2. Create a *nonhierarchical state of equality*, wherein a relationship based on equality, freedom, justice, and the conditions for all reaching their full human potential prevail:

$$A = B$$

This means transforming A/B to $A = B$.

3. Create a *free-flowing dialogue among equals*, or a two-way mutual exchange of words in an authentic form of communication:

$$A \approx B$$

This means transforming $A \sim\!\Downarrow B$ to $A \approx B$.

Avoiding Projection of Negative and Low Expectations: Transforming $A \Rightarrow B$ to $A \Leftrightarrow B$

If practitioners project negative and low expectations or stereotypes on community members, individuals, research participants, or students, then they engage in violence (Wallace, 1994, 1995). This act of projection occurs when salient stimuli or markers of identity are perceived. These serve as triggers when skin color, race, ethnicity, gender, class, sexual orientation, disability, class, status, or some other "diversity or difference" is perceived. Merely perceiving someone's identity status may trigger the projection of negative and low expectations. The act of projection is represented by the following formula: $A \Rightarrow B$. This formula captures the prevailing cultural paradigm and the abusive power relationship wherein A, any actor, imposes on B, another actor, his or her cognitions (thoughts) that correspond to stereotypes, negative images, misinformation, and myths possessed by A about B. Training to be a multiculturally competent psychologist or educator—whether functioning specifically as a counselor, researcher, or teacher within a variety of settings—rests on learning how to create new relationships captured in an alternative symbolic formula, $A \Leftrightarrow B$. In this case, a genuine, authentic relationship prevails when power is mutually shared and new knowledge is gained by both A and B regarding the "diverse and different other," as each are mutually enriched, empowered, and enhanced by the interaction. Freedom, equality, and possibilities for each to reach their highest potential are opened up by creative dialogue and interaction under this alternative paradigm of $A \Leftrightarrow B$. Taylor (1994) offered the term *reciprocal recognition,* which captures the new dialectic recommended in the formula $A \Leftrightarrow B$.

Avoiding Domination and Hierarchical Authority: Transforming A/B to $A = B$

Plainly stated by hooks (1995), "This is a white supremacist culture" and "white supremacy is rooted in pathological responses to difference" (p. 27). The U.S. culture of violence has trained citizens in pathological responses to difference, and far too many counselors, researchers, and teachers need to acquire the new knowledge of how to avoid the unacknowledged practice of domination and hierarchical authority. Greene (1988) analyzed this domination in Melville's (1856/1952, pp. 255-353) short story "Benito Cereno," which focuses on Captain Delano's misunderstanding of his relationship with his Black body servant Babo. According to Greene (1988), Captain Delano "cannot acknowledge even for a moment his own nation's, his own state's complicity in the violence against Black people; he cannot acknowledge the place of domination of others in the search for freedom" (p. 45) associated with the opening of the New World. Melville reminds us, according to Greene (1988), of what was overlooked by great reformers such as Dewey, Steffens, Jane Addams and Justice Brandeis—"not only the sense in which nature abhors slavery, but the sense in which a free society (and its citizens) are morally endangered by unacknowledged mastery, by domination of every kind" (p. 46).

At the beginning of the 20th century, Du Bois wrote that "the problem of the Twentieth Century is the problem of the color line" (Kenan, 1995, p. xxxi). Updating this dictum, Canon (1995) asserted that the "problem of the twentieth-first century is the problem of the color line, gender line, and the class line" (p. 25). Going one step further, this dictum may be extended to include *the line* (/) drawn to subjugate those with unpopular sexual orientations, a disability, any "diversity or difference," or any human. The problem can be conceptualized as one of unacknowledged domination and hierarchical authority in all forms that foster oppression. The symbolic formula summarizing the line drawn (/) or all forms of domination is A/B, capturing the generic problem of a line drawn to subjugate and oppress *any* human. The formula conveys how A subjugates and denies the basic humanity of B; it captures how many people repeatedly and compulsively assert the privilege of acting in the role of the dominant superior, A, by placing B in a subordinate position as the inferior—to be controlled and dominated. The central problem facing our nation is summarized through this formula. The formula also conveys the central problem confronting professionals in the fields of psychology and education.

The question arises as to how these practitioners may end the process of denying the basic humanity of clients, research participants, students, and all diverse members of varied communities who are effectively oppressed by the practice of unacknowledged domination and exercise of hierarchical authority. A solution to A/B is suggested in $A = B$, an alternative formula wherein a relationship of equality, freedom, and justice and the conditions for all reaching their full human potential prevail. The goal of interpersonal relationships reflecting a *nonhierarchical state of equality*—a term put forth by Taylor (1994)—is recommended by the $A = B$ formula.

Support for a nonhierarchical state of equality is not a denial of real power. It cannot be denied that the counselor who possesses professional training and degrees, the researcher who pays a fee or provides access to a service, or the teacher who ultimately gives out a final grade each has real power. However, it is important for those with power to avoid engaging in the unacknowledged practice of domination and exercise of hierarchical authority, which serve to oppress clients, research participants, and students. Indeed, when those with power correctly wield it, the result may be that both the wielder and those impacted by the correct use of power will grow substantially toward their highest potential in a creative process. Storey (1994) argued that in the field of cultural studies, Michel Foucault (1979) has made the greatest impact in recent years; Foucault does not see power as a "negative force, something which denies, represses, negates; for Foucault, power is a productive force"

(Storey, 1994, p. 105). Power "produces reality" and "rituals of truth" (Storey, 1994, p. 105). Heyward (1993) critiqued the misuse of power as follows:

> I was learning that this mutual authenticity is the root of all that is genuinely moral, creative, liberating, whether in teaching, pastoral work, or psychotherapy. I was also learning that this mutually empowering connection does not contravene, or deny, the systemic/institutional power-differential between teachers and students, counselors and client, doctors and patients. I was learning that, in our professional work, our good intention and depth of caring are not enough. I was learning that we who teach, preach, or counsel need to be mindful of the ways in which power is shaped systematically and structurally in our professions. . . . We should try to be always in a process of giving this power up responsibly, with the help of our friends and colleagues, letting it be transformed by the power of mutuality. . . . *For a priest, teacher, or therapist either to refuse to accept her power or to refuse to let it be transformed and thereby given up is potentially abusive.* The basic ethical question for healing professionals is how to embody our institutional power in such a way that it is transformed into mutually creative energy between us and those who seek our help. (pp. 183-185)

Heyward's (1993) liberation theology perspective and critique are consistent with Ivey's (1995) suggestion that "a liberation psychotherapy must, of necessity, criticize hierarchical Platonic epistemology" (p. 59). Heyward's (1993) work offers a potential guide in fostering evolution in the fields of psychology and education. Power can be transformed into a mutually creative energy, but dialogue remains a vital tool in this process. However, dialogue must be critically examined for whether it fosters freedom or also serves to oppress.

Avoiding Talking Down to Another as Though He or She Is Inferior: Transforming $A \sim\Downarrow B$ to $A \approx B$

The act of conveying the perception that one is superior and another is inferior occurs on a daily basis when words are spoken, especially aloud. In *Black Skin, White Masks*, Fanon (1967) exposed the dynamic of how a superior talks down to an inferior in an "automatic manner" and, in this process of "classifying him, imprisoning him, primitivizing him, decivilizing him," makes the Black man angry (p. 32). This form of violence that is also perpetrated by counselors, researchers, and teachers has been captured and described so well by Fanon (1967):

> A white man addressing a Negro behaves exactly like an adult with a child and starts smirking, whispering, patronizing, cozening. It is not one white man I have watched, but hundreds; and I have not limited my investigation to any one class but, if I may claim an essentially objective position, I have made a point of observing such behavior in physicians, policeman, employers. (p. 31)

The dehumanizing experience of being talked down to as though one is a child is also a display of power that does harm, constituting an act of violence and appropriately evoking the rage of the one abused. A symbolic formula, $A \sim\Downarrow B$, captures the moment of violence when a superior, A, talks down to an inferior, B, engaging in abusive communication involving a one-way delivery of verbal messages. A suggested formula, $A \approx B$, depicts a two-way mutual exchange of words, an authentic form of communication—a *free-flowing dialogue among equals*. This must replace the abusive communication that enrages those who are talked down to as though they are inferior ($A \sim\Downarrow B$).

Far too many clients in treatment, members of the populations from which researchers have drawn the participants they study and write about in publications, and students in classrooms have felt implicitly placed in an inferior position by language. Community members who have interacted with the physicians, police officers, and employers of which Fanon (1967) speaks also possess intimate knowledge of the rage that can be evoked when spoken down to as though one is inferior. It is extremely important to understand the difference between dialogue that serves to foster oppression and the recommended free-flowing dialogue among equals. Freire's (1970) remarks are helpful in this regard:

> Dialogue is thus an existential necessity. And since dialogue is the encounter in which the united reflection and action of the dialoguers are addressed to the world which is to be transformed and humanized, this dialogue cannot be reduced to the act of one person's "depositing" ideas in another, nor can it become a simple exchange of ideas to be "consumed" by discussants. Nor yet is it a hostile, polemical argument between men who are committed

neither to the naming of the world, nor to the search for truth, but rather to the imposition of their own truth. Because dialogue is an encounter among men who name the world, it must not be a situation where some men name on behalf of others. It is an act of creation; it must not serve as a crafty instrument for the domination of one man by another. The domination implicit in dialogue is that of the world by the dialoguers; it is the conquest of the world for the liberation of men. (p. 77)

Again, the correct use of power in dialogue emerges as a creative process. Taylor (1994) explained how dialogue can foster human development:

> This crucial feature of human life is its fundamentally *dialogical* character. We become full human agents, capable of understanding ourselves, and hence of defining our identity, through our acquisition of rich human languages of expression. . . . But we learn these modes of expression through exchanges with others. People do not acquire the languages needed for self-definition on their own. Rather, we are introduced to them through interaction with others who matter to us—what George Mead called "significant others." The genesis of the human mind is in this sense not monological, not something each person accomplishes on his own or her own, but dialogical. (p. 32)

Psychologists and educators, whether working as counselors, researchers, or teachers, may either be "significant others" who foster self-definition and the search for truth or perpetrators of invisible covert violence who corrupt the use of human language and damage the self-concept, identity, cognitions, affects, and consciousness of others. Community members who interact with psychologists, educators, physicians, police officers, employers, and each other similarly need to appreciate the negative impact of invisible covert violence when the use of language is corrupted in this manner.

In sum, *reciprocal recognition, nonhierarchical equality* (Taylor, 1994), and a *free-flowing dialogue among equals* are introduced as new concepts critical to a successful paradigm shift toward a set of values that can guide our standards of conduct with "the different and diverse other" in the new millennium. These concepts establish what it means to possess multicultural competence. These three concepts and the symbolic formulas that correspond to them also serve as a key part of the psychology of liberation because following them will constitute bringing to an end the dynamics of oppression. These three principles, summarized in simple graphic formulas, increase the knowledge of professionals, paraprofessionals, and community workers and may foster the attainment of new cognitions ($A \Leftrightarrow B$, $A = B$, and $A \approx B$). Acquiring these new cognitions or thoughts is central to the production of new behaviors in interacting with the "diverse and different" that reflect multicultural competence, permitting an end to violence and oppression.

Entering the Inner Worldview and Self-Structure of the Oppressed and the Oppressor: A Psychology of Identity Development

However, oppression is a concept that must be fully understood. The knowledge base of professionals should also expand to include a full understanding of the experience of being oppressed. Entering the worldview of the oppressed and gaining knowledge of the concepts put forth by the oppressed in their attempt to describe their own experience seem vital to the task of producing multicultural competence in professionals and ending oppression. Of course, this also necessitates entering and understanding the inner worldview of the oppressor. This entails learning something about the inner self-structure and identity of the oppressed. This understanding will form the basis of the psychology of identity development, even as we must also understand the identity development of the oppressor.

A New Self-Psychology or Identity Development in the Oppressed and Oppressor: $A(B) = B(A)$

By fostering an understanding of the concept of oppression, as well as the inner worldview, inner self, and identity of those socialized in our culture of violence, we effectively advance a new self-psychology of the oppressed and the oppressor. Or, it can be thought of as a new psychology of identity development in the oppressed and oppressor (see Table 1.3). The formula $A(B) = B(A)$ is introduced to advance this new self-psychology of the oppressed and the oppressor, as well as their identity development.

I am reminded of a statement often used in a joking manner to remind individuals of the way in which the slave and the master

Table 1.3   The Psychology of Identity Development

Identity Development for the Oppressor/Superior

Via societal conditioning, an identity and concept of self for A has been created based on the following cognitions:

$$A \Rightarrow B, A/B, \text{ and } A \sim\Downarrow B$$

Identity Development for the Oppressed/Inferior

Via societal conditioning in an oppressive environment, an identity and concept of self for B has been created based on the following cognitions:

$$A \Rightarrow B, A/B, \text{ and } A \sim\Downarrow B$$

Interdependence: Self-Definition and Identity of A in Relation to B and B in Relation to A

The self-definition and identity of A stand in relation to the societal value placed on B. Also, the self-definition and identity of B stand in relation to the proclaimed value of A in society. This suggests a state of interdependence. A and B are each equally dependent on each other for one's definition of self, as symbolized by

$$A(B) = B(A)$$

became intertwined and even intimately interdependent in their identity: "We sick Massah" (N. Korantemaa, personal communication, July 2000). Imagine a slave approaching his master in the morning, finding the master to be sick in bed, assisting his master, and then declaring the situation in this manner: "We sick Massah." Slavery produced a situation in which the identity of the slave and the master was such that what one felt, the other could express as his or her own state or condition. For when the master was sick, the slave could articulate it as a shared state or condition, given their intertwined and interdependent identity and state of being. Each was equally dependent on the other, in many ways. We referred earlier to Greene's (1988) analysis of *domination* of the master over the slave in Melville's (1856/1952, pp. 255-353) short story "Benito Cereno," focusing on Captain Delano's misunderstanding of his relationship with his Black body servant Babo. Another aspect of this relationship that stands out in Melville's short story is how Captain Delano so intimately depended on his servant each morning to be shaved, get dressed, and have his boots shined.

Meanwhile, the slave depended on the master to be fed. Such intimate interdependence allows for the master to enter and become a part of the self-structure and identity of the slave and for the slave to enter and become part of the self-structure and identity of the master—so that the slave could profess on a morning when it was appropriate, "We sick Massah." Indeed, the master might need and even depend on the perceptual and observational capacities of the slave to fully grasp the reality that they did not feel well that morning, as evidenced in moving more slowly and being harder to shave, dress, and feed from the perspective of the slave.

In addition to that of master and slave, many identities are impacted in their development by the existence of opposing positions of one deemed superior and another deemed inferior, as each stand in relation to each other and thereby gain distinct value and meaning. In this regard, Sedgwick (1990) discussed the epistemology of the closet—known all too well to gays, lesbians, and transgender individuals who are oppressed by the walls of closets—and also used A and B to symbolize the two positions under discussion. Sedgwick carefully considered the relationship between any symmetrical binary oppositions in our culture, such as the categories of heterosexual and homosexual, which is applicable to our discussion of that between the oppressor and the oppressed:

> . . . first, term B is not symmetrical with but subordinated to term A; but, second, the ontologically valorized term A actually depends for its meaning on the simultaneous subsumption and exclusion of term B; hence, third, the question of priority between the supposed central and the supposed marginal category of each dyad is irresolvably unstable, an instability caused by the fact that term B is constituted as at once internal and external to term A. (pp. 9-10)

The fact that term B is constituted as at once internal and external to term A suggests yet another symbolic formula. This concept may now be introduced, following the prior formulas discussed in this chapter, as a state or condition in which $A(B) = B(A)$. This begins to serve as a good introduction to the complexity of the relationship between the oppressed and the oppressor, between the one allegedly superior and the one conditioned into the role of the inferior. Living in a social context that makes one invisible or provides distortion in mirroring back to the oppressed disdained "self" results in a complex internalization process for the oppressed. However, the experience of one deemed superior, specifically in relation to others deemed inferior, also impacts the self and the identity development of the superior—suggesting a parallel complex internalization process.

It is important to fully understand the damage done from *bombarding a person with destructive misinformation and myths so that, in effect, an assault occurs to the self-concept, identity, cognitions, affects, and consciousness of the victim of violence*—specifically when one is living in a social environment dominated by the oppressor. Yet, one must ultimately also appreciate how, at the very same time, the individuals who define themselves as superior are simultaneously undergoing an identical process. The superior oppressors participate in and suffer from bombardment with destructive misinformation and myths about their superiority and others' inferiority, so that, in effect, damage also occurs to the self-concept, identity, cognitions, affects, and consciousness of superiors/oppressors.

In this way, the symbolic formula $A(B) = B(A)$ captures quite well the reality of *both* the oppressor and the oppressed being in somewhat comparable (equal) states of damage from covert invisible violence, even as most might agree that the potential risk is greatest for the oppressed inferior in position B. After all, the invisible and covert violence done to both in terms of cognitions and consciousness, as well as self-concept and identity and affects, is more painful to the oppressed and can lead to quite painful and destructive overt, visible violence being unleashed *on the oppressed.* However, many individuals who have caught themselves in the act of possessing a cognition that is equivalent to destructive misinformation and myth often feel deep, intense pain over knowing they have bombarded another with it and potentially engaged in an invisible assault. In this manner, some would argue for equivalency in how the oppressed and oppressor suffer and how all of humanity suffers whenever anyone is oppressed, is deemed inferior, or becomes the target for invisible covert or visible overt violence. Both the oppressed and the oppressor may be viewed as in need of healing from socialization processes or freedom and liberation from the cycle of oppression and violence.

The voice of the oppressed raised in response to this destructive set of conditions typically also begins the process of both the oppressed and the oppressor gaining freedom, as well as healing from the damage done from invisible violence, following Freire (1970), as we shall see. This moves us toward an analysis that can be seen as the psychology of liberation. When the oppressed begin to raise their voice, we enter their inner world, hear their worldview, and typically hear about the impact of misinformation and myths with which they have been bombarded. This allows us to understand how damage is done to their self-concept and identity, causing pain.

Bombardment With Misinformation and Myth: Invisibility and Distortion in Mirroring

Ellison, in his 1952 book, *Invisible Man*, introduces the concept of invisibility and distortion in mirroring, inviting the reader to enter the worldview of the millions of African Americans oppressed in the United States:

> I am an invisible man. . . . I am invisible, understand, simply because people refuse to see me. . . . I have been surrounded by mirrors of hard, distorting glass. When they approach me they see only my surroundings, themselves, or figments of their imagination indeed, everything and anything except me. (p. 3)

To perpetuate the myth that the African American is invisible in society is to engage in an insidious covert form of violence. Ellison's (1952) words, from the perspective of one oppressed, go a long way toward describing the experience of being the target of the projection of negative and low expectations while conveying the resultant sense of invisibility. Meanwhile, the misinformation and myth that one is invisible in the society bombards one; this negatively impacts identity, self-concept, affects, cognitions, and consciousness. A damaged self and identity result from internalization of myths and misinformation. To state that "I am invisible" reflects internalization of an assault and a state of having a damaged self-concept and identity. Yet, it also acknowledges the reality of being invisible to oppressors in society, insofar as they do not mirror or reflect back to the oppressed any kind of accurate image or perception in regards to the actual identity of the oppressed.

In support of attention being paid to these concepts, Taylor (1994) noted the following:

> The thesis is that our identity is partly shaped by recognition or its absence, often by the *mis*recognition of others, and so a person or group of people can suffer real damage, real distortion, if the

people or society around them mirror back to them a confining or demeaning or contemptible picture of themselves. Nonrecognition or misrecogniton can inflict harm, can be a form of oppression, imprisoning someone in a false, distorted, and reduced mode of being. (p. 25)

However, if the oppressor defines his or her superiority on the basis of the existence of an inferior, then the oppressor also ends up internalizing the image of the inferior as a basis for an identity. The identity of the superior stands in antithesis to the inferior and gains meaning based on the inferior's very existence. The superior creates a society based on bombarding all members with the misinformation and myth that the oppressor is superior, the only visible and legitimate group, and the only group to be valued. The superior is also bombarded with misinformation and myth about the inferiority, invisibility, and debased status of other "inferiors."

Meanwhile, feared images of these "diverse and different others" are, nonetheless, internalized and harbored as something horrible, buried deep within the superior. These images are hidden away because they are considered too awful to see the light of day— remaining held in some invisible space within. What is introjected and internalized may be a disdained image, discounted as meaningless, yet it is inside, nonetheless. For the oppressor, this is captured as $A(B)$, suggesting how the identity of A stands as superior in relation to something that is their internalized knowledge of the inferior, B—an image held inside, even as it is disdained. Yet, this debased set of images—all the oppressed and disdained people in that society—serves as the contrasting set of conditions and cognitions that establish the superiority of A.

The oppressor also regularly represses, buries, and actively takes advantage of opportunities to eject and project these images on the "diverse and different other." Images of the disdained inferior, secretly harbored within as a part of their "dark" or "shadow side," are also ejected and projected on those available "diverse and different others" who are encountered in society. The one that society "says" is superior then has the urge to fight or flee from the "diverse and different others" that society also "says" are inferior. The disdained inferior is now the container for the contents of the superior's dark or shadow side that were projected onto all inferior "different others." What is disdained and debased in the different other and also within the self is ejected and projected onto the "diverse and different," taking the form of negative and low expectations, as well as stereotypes. Most important to appreciate is how what is ejected and projected by superiors is their own internalized, disdained part of themselves, their own inner image of personal inferiority. They then get rid of "it" in each interaction in which they can project that inferior inner self-image on the disdained "diverse and different other" in society. In this way, the superior needs the presence of some external inferior in society to eject from their inner world and project on societal inferiors those typically well-hidden inner feelings of inferiority. "Superiors" thereby maintain feelings of superiority. Unfortunately, the *damage done to the "superior,"* in the process, includes *having a false sense of self,* one that never adequately integrates and comes to terms with what is feared, disdained, disliked, and rejected that actually lies within. If what is problematic inside is seen as easily locatable in the disdained "different other" and thereby never located as the problematic, feared part of the inner self, the opportunity and challenge in working toward being whole and integrated are missed. One's dark or shadow side is never adequately embraced as something that can see the light of day and be accepted as a part of one's own inner, inevitable duality as a human and divine being.

Social Responsibility in Articulating One's Oppression: First Step to Potential Dialogue and Creating a New Identity

This analysis helps to promote fuller comprehension of the real predicament and problems inherent in embracing white privilege. This emergent self-psychology of the oppressor resonates with explanations of the narcissistic self. Thus, when the slave declares, "We sick Massah," it is also a comment on the inherent pathology of narcissism, white privilege, and oppression of inferiors. The resulting "inner state of being" of "self" for oppressor and the oppressed can be declared as sick, in terms of the psychopathology of obscene narcissism and a stance of white privilege that requires an inferior who is deprived. Or, an empathic self-psychology of oppression can guide liberation from this condition.

Declaring "We sick Massah" is the first step taken by the oppressed in clarifying the experience of a close interdependence that inherently sustains the two intimately interrelated positions of inferior and superior. This first step can also be seen as the beginning of a process of liberation. Going beyond the limitations of this one statement, the point to be made is that the oppressed have a socially responsible role in declaring the nature and state of being inherent in oppression and subjugation. The socially responsible role of articulating the experience of oppression also brings the hope of liberation for both the oppressed and the oppressor.

Ellison (1952) suggested that the oppressed play a socially responsible role in articulating their experience of oppression:

> I must come out, I must emerge. . . . And I suppose it's damn well time. Even hibernations can be overdone, come to think of it. Perhaps that's my greatest social crime, I've overstayed my hibernation, since there's a possibility that even an invisible man has a socially responsible role to play. "Ah," I can hear you say, "So it was all a build-up to bore us with his buggy jiving. He only wanted us to listen to him rave!" But only partially true: Being invisible and without substance, a disembodied voice, as it were, what else could I do? What else but try to tell you what was really happening when your eyes were looking through? And it is this which frightens me: Who knows but that, on the lower frequencies, I speak for you? (pp. 567-568)

Ellison (1952) played a socially responsible role in giving voice—on behalf of a collective—to what is the common experience of an entire group of people or anyone injured from the violence of invisibility, distortion in mirroring, and being the recipient of false, negative projections. Whether the experience of a person of color, a woman experiencing sexism, a person with a disability, or a gay, lesbian, bisexual, or transgender person or the oppressor, Ellison (1952) indeed may speak for a collective of oppressed and marginalized voices. By potentially making conscious for all—the oppressed and the oppressor—that it is no longer acceptable to be oppressed, silent, and hidden away as invisible in some dark place (hibernation), the possibility exists for both the oppressed and the oppressor to begin to heal. This is akin to becoming whole, progressing in identity development, moving toward creation of a new self reflecting integration of one's good and bad inner parts, attaining liberation, and reaching their respective highest potential. For if the oppressor cannot keep the oppressed invisible and hidden, the oppressor's own corresponding dark side may not be as easily kept repressed and invisible in their own inner self. What was happening when the oppressed was invisible includes how the oppressor was also being kept from wholeness, insofar as their own shadow side, their own dark side, did not have to be integrated or actively contended with in the light of day. Instead, projections of the dark, shadow side could be placed on the different other, and the disdained inner self was thereby never embraced by the oppressor. The development of the self toward wholeness and integration was hindered.

Through this articulation of his experience of oppression, one might also suggest that Ellison (1952) begins the process of ending oppression, taking steps toward his own liberation. "Liberation is praxis: the action and reflection of men upon their world in order to transform it" (Freire, 1970, p. 66). Ellison violates the oppressor's preferred guide for the behavior of the oppressed—remaining silent and accepting the state or condition of being oppressed. Hence, if one is a psychologist or educator—as well as if one is a client, research participant, student, community member, or individual from any oppressed group—one needs to embrace the concept Ellison (1952) puts forth of having a socially responsible role to play. This involves the important task of giving voice to one's experience of oppression. This means speaking up. This means speaking one's truth, even speaking one's truth to power—as embodied in those oppressors who must hear the truth of what it is like to be oppressed and the demand for that oppression to end. For Freire (1970), speaking up is a critical step in transforming an oppressive reality and finding liberation. It is the first critical step in leading the oppressed and the oppressor to freedom, wholeness, an integrated self, and moving toward one's highest potential. Raising one's voice and speaking the truth regarding one's experience are the first step toward potential dialogue, as well. Only such an act of giving voice to one's experience can create the potential for dialogue between the oppressor and the oppressed. Such an act also serves to redefine one's identity, as one can now be conceived as resisting one's oppression or as creating a new identity as a defender of one's self or a new identity as a social activist seeking social justice.

In turn, former oppressors and/or current oppressors (including psychologists and educators who, in their roles as counselors, researchers, and teachers, may have once also practiced $A \Rightarrow B$, A/B, and $A \sim\Downarrow B$) must absolutely respect the moment when the oppressed exercise their social responsibility and speak out about the experience of being oppressed. It becomes critical to truly "hear" about their experience of sustaining injury; these are injuries to the self-concept, identity, cognitions, affects, and consciousness. One may thereby witness the birth of new selves, the creation of a new healthier identity, and the beginning of one being made whole—as well as moving not only the individual but also the larger society toward healing and integration. Societies divided by "difference" may now begin to heal.

At the very same moment, former or current oppressors' own disdained inner parts of the self see the light of day. Their dark shadow side can now be faced in the light of day, and the possibility of moving toward an integrated self exists.

A Caution on the Role Reversal: A Potential Pitfall Postinternalization of the Oppressor

We must also consider the implications of $A(B) = B(A)$ wherein even the psychologist, educator, or community member—as instances of $B(A)$—who is from a marginalized, oppressed, and "inferior" group has internalized the oppressor and identified with them (see Table 1.4). One implication is that these individuals can then mimic the behavior of the oppressor even though they are members of oppressed groups, engaging in a *role reversal* (Wallace, 1996). The role reversal involves taking on the behavior of the oppressor, even doing a perfect imitation of the oppressor's violent ways and striving to engage in and maintain the oppressor's practices and traditions of violence and oppression. Hence, a part of the training of psychologists, educators, and community members from historically oppressed and marginalized groups needs to include a process of fostering awareness of the presence of the oppressor within $(B(A))$ and the possibilities of acting out the role behavior of A as well. The traditionally oppressed may now reverse roles and act out the role behavior of their oppressor, revealing how they are in essence $B(A)$, having an internalized oppressor who can guide them in replicating the behaviors of the oppressor.

It is hoped that one who is $B(A)$, a member of a historically oppressed and marginalized group who has engaged in a *role reversal* and acted out the behaviors of the oppressor with other oppressed persons (as $B(A) \Rightarrow B$, $B(A)/B$, and $B(A) \sim\Downarrow B$), can also attain the level of being a *former* oppressor. This can be achieved by virtue of training in multicultural sensitivity and competency. This

Table 1.4   The Plight of Internalization for the Oppressed and the
Role Reversal

Plight of Internalization for the Oppressed and Abused

Psychologists, educators, and community members, if from a
marginalized, oppressed, and "inferior" group, may have internalized the
oppressor. Also, in dysfunctional family life, abused and oppressed
children, B, may come to internalize their abusive, oppressive, parental
authorities, A. As adults, these "adult children" from dysfunctional
families also constitute a state of $B(A)$, harboring inside their former
abusive, oppressive parents. This state of harboring the internalized
oppressor/abuser inside is symbolized by

$$B(A)$$

Role Reversal in the Behavior of the Oppressed as a Result of
Internalization

Psychologists, educators, and community members, if members of
oppressed groups, and former abused children are able to imitate the
behavior of the oppressor or parental abuser, engaging in a *role reversal.*
The oppressed/abused, B, may now reverse roles and enact the role
behavior of their oppressor/abuser, A, revealing how they are, in essence,
$B(A)$. They may enact the behaviors of the oppressor with other oppressed
persons, based on the guiding cognitions of

$$B(A) \Rightarrow B, B(A)/B, \text{ and } B(A) \sim\!\Downarrow B$$

again suggests attaining a new consciousness based on the cogni-
tions of $A \Leftrightarrow B$, $A = B$, and $A \approx B$, with a corresponding set of behaviors that are suggestive of multicultural competency and freedom
from engaging in oppression and violence.

Former oppressors—whether from group A or B, whether having or currently embodying $A(B)$ or $B(A)$—need to listen to the voice
of the oppressed, for it is the key to the liberation of all. For, as
praxis, following Freire (1970), former oppressors need to deeply
and genuinely reflect on what they hear the oppressed saying as a
necessary step in helping to transform reality and produce liberation
from the cycle of violence for both the oppressed and the oppressor.

The Psychology or Pedagogy of
Liberation for the Plight of Internalization

Having knowledge of how $A \Rightarrow B$, A/B, and $A \sim\!\Downarrow B$ represent the
socially conditioned cognitions that guide the interpersonal behavior

Table 1.5   Psychology of Liberation From the Plight of Internalization: Integration of the Internalized "Other" and Creation of a New Self

---

Liberation for the Oppressed/Abused, B: Integration of (A) to Create a New Self (CNS)

Any oppressed/abused person suffering from internalization of the oppressor, $B(A)$, can attain to the level of being a *former* oppressor and create a new self (CNS), new identity, or concept of self. Survivors of oppression or abuse can integrate the oppressor, A, they have internalized, into their self-structure, creating a new identity or concept of self, C, symbolized as

$$B + (A) = CNS$$

Liberation for the Oppressor, A: Integration of (B) to Create a New Self (CNS)

Similarly, being in a state of $A(B)$, oppressors suffering from narcissism or a false sense of superiority and privilege, which is coupled with a well-hidden sense of inferiority, can also seek to integrate the inner inferior sense of self or the dark side of themselves that they harbor inside. They, too, can become *former oppressors*. This process of integration can result in the creation of a new self (CNS), new concept of self, or new identity that is much more realistic and humanistic, being symbolized as follows:

$$A + (B) = CNS$$

---

of many citizens in the U.S. culture of violence and professionals in the fields of psychology and education, we must fully understand how a part of the experience of the oppressed includes the ongoing struggle with also having internalized $A \Rightarrow B$, A/B, and $A \sim\Downarrow B$. If one is oppressed and therefore has internalized the oppressor ($B(A)$), by virtue of that same socialization process, one has also internalized a whole set of cognitions ($A \Rightarrow B$, A/B, and $A \sim\Downarrow B$) on which notions of superiority and inferiority are based. Hence, we must discuss a psychology of liberation or pedagogy of liberation that results in the creation of a new self or identity. This is summarized in Table 1.5.

The plight of internalization has been described by numerous writers. Freire (1970, p. 31) offered the view that freedom requires the oppressed to eject the internalized image of the oppressor and any adopted guidelines while attaining a new autonomy and responsibility. These negative guidelines to be abandoned are captured in $A \Rightarrow B$, A/B, and $A \sim\Downarrow B$. The oppressed must confront the reality of internalizing the oppressor as $B(A)$, which Freire explained as follows:

The central problem is this: How can the oppressed, as divided, unauthentic beings, participate in developing the pedagogy of their liberation? Only as they discover themselves to be "hosts" of the oppressor can they contribute to the midwifery of their liberating pedagogy. As long as they live in the duality in which *to be* is *to be like,* and *to be like* is *to be like the oppressor,* this contribution is impossible. The pedagogy of the oppressed is an instrument for their critical discovery that both they and their oppressors are manifestations of dehumanization. (p. 33)

A dimension of this dehumanization is the state of "internalization" of "inferiority" (Fanon, 1967). Fanon (1967) began his book, *Black Skin, White Masks,* with a quote by Aime Cesaire from *Discours sur le Colonialisme:* "I am talking of millions of men who have been skillfully injected with fear, inferiority complexes, trepidation, servility, despair, abasement" (p. 7). Freire (1970) summarized the predicament as follows:

The oppressed suffer from the duality which has established itself in their innermost being. They discover that without freedom they cannot exist authentically. . . . They are at one and the same time themselves and the oppressor whose consciousness they have internalized. The conflict lies in the choice between . . . ejecting the oppressor within or not ejecting him. . . . This is the tragic dilemma of the oppressed. (pp. 32-33)

The formula $B(A)$ captures the duality established in their innermost being. Meanwhile, the consciousness of the oppressor, which they have also internalized as a set of guiding cognitions, is captured in $A \Rightarrow B$, A/B, and $A \sim\Downarrow B$; these three socially conditioned sets of cognitions may permit the oppressed to replicate the behavior of the oppressor, as well as allow them to accept dehumanizing treatment as the norm and standard in society, given these internalized beliefs.

But based on my experience working with adult children from dysfunctional families who were abused, victimized, and oppressed by abusive, violent parents, the psychology of liberation or the pedagogy of liberation at which the oppressed arrive has included, by necessity, *accepting and integrating the presence of the oppressor—not ejecting the oppressor.* Integration of the oppressor or abuser harbored within, as a result of internalization and identification with the aggressor, can result in the creation of a new self (CNS) or new identity. The resulting pedagogy of liberation resolves the problem of the plight of internalization, insofar as one works hard to accept the presence of the oppressor within yet seeks to control affects, behaviors, and cognitions that follow from the state of $B(A)$. An example of a behavior that must be controlled and transformed is engaging in a role reversal and adopting the violent, oppressive behaviors of the oppressor. Indeed, in many cases, the process includes sensitive recognition that one may have already engaged in a role reversal and enacted the behaviors of the oppressor and that this is what must be given up—including giving up chemical dependency, domestic violence, physical abuse of one's own children, sexual abuse of others, and general verbal abuse of multiple others.

A Psychology and Pedagogy of Liberation for the Individual, Family, Community, and Societal Levels

In this manner, it is necessary to go beyond a consideration of the cultural level and also consider family-level socialization influences on what we internalize. Individuals can never liberate themselves completely from those whose love and care shaped them early in life, yet a person can come to understand and "thus get some control over the influence of our parents" (Taylor, 1994, p. 33). This is consistent with the pedagogy of liberation that I discovered in working with women recovering from chemical dependency in the sacred circle of the group in counseling. The goal was control of a number of compulsive behaviors and interpersonal dramas, as well as improved regulation of affects, self-esteem, impulses, interpersonal behavior, and general self-care. Yet, how did these women arrive at having to face the task of realizing that they could not eject the oppressor who was their own internalized abusive parental figure but had to learn control over the legacy of their influence?

Internalizing Oppressors in Dysfunctional Family Life

When the social and economic realities of daily coping with the stressors that accompany family life in the U.S. culture of violence are appreciated, one may analyze how some families gradually cross a thin line into dysfunction (Wallace, 1996, p. 38). Immigrants and migrants who initially coped in extraordinary fashion may eventually degenerate into neglectful, abusive, alcoholic parents with whom their children identify under the influence of a powerful parental socialization process. Exposure to parents stressed to extremes helps to create the next generation of parents who may also end up chemically dependent and abusive to a new generation, their own children. Wallace (1996) elaborated on how "if you know the trauma, you can figure out the drama" (p. 189), explaining that adults may enact a behavioral drama that involves repetition of the basic interactional pattern that was experienced as traumatic for them as children. However, once these children become adults, there may be a *role reversal* wherein those adults now take on the former behavior of their parent and place a new object—their own child—in the position that they once occupied themselves as a child. Through the process of socialization in a family, an abused and oppressed child (B) may come to internalize their abusive, oppressive, parental authorities (A) who created tyranny and chaos within family life (often because their own impoverished, stressed, or immigrant status included the experience of being B, or oppressed in the larger society). As adults (B), these adult children from dysfunctional families also constitute a state of B(A). They have internalized the abusive, oppressive parents (A), even though they themselves were once abused, oppressed children, as B. They are now in a state of B(A), harboring their former abusive, oppressive parents inside.

The once abused, oppressed children grow up into abusive, oppressive adults who are now capable of unconsciously and unwittingly oppressing their own children. Wallace (1996) explained how clients once abused as children now, as adults, engage in splitting, regression, and projection and reenact an old behavioral drama that effectively places a child born in a new generation in the role of the abused and oppressed victim (Wallace, 1996). Again, they face the task of integrating the abuser harbored within and creating a new self (CNS) or identity.

Any liberating dialogue in a nonhierarchical therapeutic relationship should not only foster perceptions in clients that become a motivating force for their participation in their own liberation but also reveal how the oppressor, once disdained in childhood, actually lives within and can emerge through a role reversal (Wallace, 1996). Children once assaulted and abused may now stand as adults who engage in the abuse and oppression of children in a new generation. The internalized oppressor must be identified and integrated—not technically extracted—as a therapeutic process of self-liberation. It is more technically accurate to state that they must accept and integrate their inner state of being—harboring inside or having internalized their abusive, oppressive parents through identification. They must also integrate this part of themselves (A) and move toward creation of a new self of their own making, perhaps based on selective identifications with warm, nurturing, empathic role models of their choosing—often their mentor, friend, counselor, teacher, or psychologist.

Internalizing Oppressors Within the Larger Society

Moving from the level of family socialization processes back to that of the larger society, individuals also abused or victimized at the larger community level may also internalize and identify with the aggressor during interpersonal violence. The possibility exists that an individual abused or victimized, B, by an aggressor who overpowered him or her, A, may now harbor inside an image of that aggressor so that B(A). As a result, the potential exists for B to also engage in a role reversal and perform the violent behaviors of A. Whether at the family level or community level or through larger societal-level socialization processes, the goal of this book is to promote a process whereby those oppressed and victimized on any level *do not* perpetuate a cycle of violence continuing generation after generation, sustaining our culture of violence. The goal is freedom from oppression, including freedom from a role reversal wherein one takes on the cognitions and role behavior of an oppressor, victimizer, abuser, or assaulter of any kind—whether a parent, a community gang member, or a person guilty of a bias crime as a racist, sexist, or a homophobic, for example.

Freedom From the Oppressor

Going back to the larger societal level, Freire (1970) further indicated that this freedom "is acquired by conquest, not by gift. It must be pursued constantly and responsibly" (p. 31). For "through self-liberation, in and through the needed, just struggle, the oppressed, as an individual and as a class, liberates the oppressor, by the simple fact of forbidding him or her to keep on oppressing" (Freire, 1995, p. 99). Given socialization processes in the fields of psychology and education and the tradition of using books such as this one in training, perhaps by increasing knowledge in professionals and paraprofessionals of the experience of oppression, an individual who has engaged in oppression in the past may find liberation from the cycle of perpetrating acts of covert invisible violence and passing on these practices to the next generation of professionals. Similarly, when psychologists and educators in their roles as counselors, researchers, and teachers work with clients, research participants, students, and community members, possibilities exist for fostering freedom for both the oppressed and for oppressors.

Implications

Knowledge and understanding gained by any through education and training, such as through this book, may translate into counseling interventions, prevention activities, treatment, research, and teaching strategies that break the cycle of oppression and foster freedom. This needs to occur on the level of the individual whose consciousness, affects, cognitions, self-concept, and identity must be healed from the consequences of experiencing oppression, as well as from the experience of being an oppressor. Psychologists and educators may also embrace the task of healing the consciousness, affects, cognitions, self-concept, and identity of individuals who may be members of families with similar needs for healing, as well as those of community members and societal group members at large.

A Graphic Training Guide for a
Psychology and Pedagogy of Liberation

In this regard, Figure 1.1 provides a graphic training guide for psychologists, educators, or any individual, family, or community member aspiring to actively deal with the consequences of socialization in our culture of violence, seeking to promote healing and liberation from oppression and violence. The bottom half of the figure summarizes the task of shifting beliefs and attitudes away from the view that the status quo is acceptable and "all is well," depicting how invisible covert violence reigns in our society and its organizational settings, as the tension and violence graphically depicted capture. Actually, the actors, A and B, need not be gesturing or in a stance to suggest overt violence because in many societal and

NEW CULTURAL PARADIGM:

Sustain freedom via 1) reciprocal recognition; 2) non-hierarchical equality; and, 3) a free flowing dialogue.

⇑

7. Celebrate liberation.

⇑

6. Create reality.

⇑

5. Expand consciousness.

⇑

4. Produce new behavior, using inner and outer dialogue to refine it.

⇑

3. Produce new cognitions.

⇑

2. Reflect perception of contradictions; create cognitive dissonance.

⇑

1. Listen actively; attune to affects; hearing another to speech; empathic mirroring.

⇑

Through dialogue, any two actors, **A** and **B**, foster the (upward ⇑) evolution of personal and cultural dialectics (civilization) toward establishment of a new cultural paradigm, following the seven steps above.

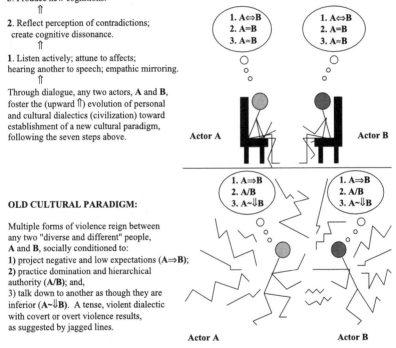

OLD CULTURAL PARADIGM:

Multiple forms of violence reign between any two "diverse and different" people, **A** and **B**, socially conditioned to:

1) project negative and low expectations (**A⇒B**);

2) practice domination and hierarchical authority (**A/B**); and,

3) talk down to another as though they are inferior (**A~⇓B**). A tense, violent dialectic with covert or overt violence results, as suggested by jagged lines.

Figure 1.1   Power of Dialogue Via Seven Steps in the New Paradigm Versus the Reign of Overt and Covert Violence in Tense Dialectics Under the Old Paradigm

organizational settings, it is more typically just invisible covert forms of violence that reign.

However, historically as well as in contemporary times, within the U.S. culture of violence, an overt violence of the kind depicted in Figure 1.1 has been all too common. In any case, it is when any two actors, A and B, whether professionals or community members, internally possess the common conditioned cognitions of $A \Rightarrow B, A/B$, and $A \sim\Downarrow B$ that their interpersonal dialectic is tense and violent— whether covertly or overtly so. The training that sought to increase knowledge is also summarized in the bottom half of Figure 1.1, as it depicts how both actors A and B, the oppressor and the oppressed, have internalized conditioned cognitions of $A \Rightarrow B, A/B$, and $A \sim\Downarrow B$. These conditioned cognitions serve as a guide for interpersonal behavior, permitting violence. In the top portion of Figure 1.1, both actors A and B, having transformed their personal paradigms, reflect internalization of the new cognitions $A \Leftrightarrow B, A = B$, and $A \approx B$. These new cognitions serve as a guide to interpersonal behavior, permitting actors A and B to sit face-to-face, as equals, and engage in a civil dialogue in a counseling, research, teaching, or one of many other community settings. The context now exists for an effective form of communication to occur that is free of violence. But specific skills are necessary for effective communication or productive dialogue to transpire, suggesting the need to transmit skills in this part of the chapter.

Dialogue: Seven Steps for Transforming Personal and Cultural Paradigms

The combination of recommended skills holds the promise of creating new cognitions; producing new behaviors and, ultimately, an expansion in consciousness; and sustaining a new cultural paradigm based on the principles of reciprocal recognition, nonhierarchical authority, and a free-flowing dialogue among equals. The following seven steps, which are also summarized in Figure 1.1, suggest the hope for evolution in the fields of psychology and education. These steps codify the essence of a pedagogy of liberation or a psychology of liberation through the transformative power of dialogue while also spelling out in detail the specific skills necessary for success in dialogue and in actualizing the process of individuals becoming free of past dramas of oppression and violence. A detailed description of the seven steps within the pedagogy of liberation or psychology of liberation follows:

    1.   During dialogue with "different others," *actively listen*. Discover how the process of listening to another permits this person

to open up and disclose information. This is the process of *hearing another to speech* (Heyward, 1993). Discover how being listened to also leads you to open up and disclose information. While listening to another and talking in a dialogue, *attune to affects*—both your own inner affects and those that you sense the other person is feeling. Strive to experience a *genuine empathy* as you attune to the affects of another. Engage in careful reflection on that dialogue and those affects to which one has attuned, moving on to the task of mirroring those affects or feelings perceived back to the other person and also meanings heard when you were listening. The cumulative process of deploying these skills may be thought of as *empathic mirroring* (Wallace, 1991, 1996). Thus, empathic mirroring may be defined as the skill of listening to another person, attuning to his or her inner affects or feelings, and striving to sense what that person is feeling inside, as well as ever so gently holding up a mirror and reflecting back to that person what you sense he or she is feeling inside. Yet, as we shall see in Step 2, a component of empathic mirroring also involves listening to the individuals' whole story and grasping their cognitions or thoughts while paying special attention to contradictions in their thoughts, as well as searching for contradictions between their thoughts and what they describe as their behavior through their story.

2.   During dialogue with others, pay special attention to the moment when you perceive any contradictions in what you hear them saying. *Reflect with empathy your perception of any contradictions* in what another is saying. These are contradictions between their cognitions or between what others are saying or believe and their behavior. Typically, this creates a state of *cognitive dissonance,* and accompanying *affects or feelings arise* about the apparent contradictions, creating a moment of profound insight. The emerging affects to which you attune may then be reflected back to the person and discussed in a continuing dialogue. Similarly, in dialogue, one may have contradictions in one's own cognitions or between cognitions and behavior pointed out. In either case, the new awareness of contradictions may lead to a consideration of a range of inconsistencies within one's inner self, family, and larger culture, as other insights are experienced in either a continuing dialogue or in private reflection. One may reflect on possessing the cognition "I do not want to be oppressed" and how this stands in contradiction to personal behavior of engaging in oppressive acts against others.

3. As a result of experiencing new perceptions, especially as they involve new knowledge of one's own contradictions or thoughts and behavior, *the production of new cognitions* follows (e.g., $A \Leftrightarrow B$, $A = B$, and $A \approx B$, or "I should never have been treated like that" and "I should not treat others in that fashion"), replacing old conditioned cognitions (e.g., $A \Rightarrow B$, A/B, and $A \sim\Downarrow B$, or "Being treated like this is the way it is in our society" and "I am justified in treating others in this fashion").

4. The perception of contradictions (i.e., cognitive dissonance in Step 2), the subsequent state of affect, and the production of new cognitions (Step 3) produce motivation to *engage in new behaviors.* New behaviors are created and refined through practice, and inner and outer dialogue may be used as new behavior is practiced and refined (Wallace, 1996). *Carefully constructed self-talk or affirmations (inner dialogue) guide and strengthen the performance of new behavioral strategies* (Wallace, 1996)—for example, repeating new cognitions such as "I should not treat others in that fashion" or "I am creating new patterns of relating with others." Tailored self-talk, especially that which begins with "I am" and specifies the desired behavior or outcome one would like to manifest in reality, is particularly powerful. Repeating this carefully tailored self-talk or affirmations, especially aloud, allows a person to experience the power of the spoken word, as what is spoken aloud (external dialogue), over and over and again; this tailored self-talk serves to help manifest the desired reality. Beyond self-talk that occurs aloud, it can then be repeated silently within (internal dialogue with the self). Suddenly, new patterns of relating are being created and observed by the individual, as evidenced by what this person made a determination to create and actually did create or manifest in reality. A state of personal empowerment results, as the level of personal confidence to perform new behavioral strategies (self-efficacy) increases and facilitates successful maintenance of behavior change over time.

5. Expansion in consciousness results directly from (a) a new awareness of inner affects and the moment they arise, (b) the ability to focus on and perceive contradictions in one's cognitions or between cognitions and behavior and to process the feelings that arise from being in a state of cognitive dissonance, (c) the production of new cognitions and the internal and external rehearsal of cognitions in dialogue, and (d) the production of new behavior that is

then observed, monitored, discussed with others, and also refined and maintained by using inner dialogue. The capacity to self-observe increases dramatically as a result of these four steps. As one's ability to attune to inner affects, self-observe, and direct both inner cognitions and outer behavior increases, one effectively makes what was once unconscious (affects, contradictions in cognitions, contradictions between cognitions and behaviors) a part of his or her conscious awareness—effectively and progressively expanding the domain of consciousness.

6. The ability to produce and maintain new cognitions and behaviors, as well as the overall expansion in consciousness, results in a state of empowerment, including the ability to *create reality*. An individual emerges, feeling empowered to create reality. As a result, Foucault's (1979) experience of power follows for that individual— "power produces; it produces reality" (p. 194; see also Storey, 1994, p. 105). Because of the prior steps, one does indeed know how to manifest desired outcomes because new cognition or thought can lead to the design of tailored self-talk, and the external and then internal repetition of this self-talk, as vital dialogue with the self, serves to keep thinking focused on the desired outcome and also produces behavior and the overall reality consistent with that tai-lored self-talk. Indeed, individuals following these steps, including the use of carefully designed and tailored self-talk, know how to produce outcomes or produce reality. This may be called *manifesta-tion* or creating reality.

7. If Steps 1 through 6 are followed, an individual may reach Step 7 and experience what has been articulated as the vision of Fanon (1963, 1967), Freire (1970, 1995), Heyward (1993), Ivey (1995), and many others—the celebration of liberation and freedom from oppression. Both the oppressor and the oppressed are liberated. The celebration of liberation and freedom follows from the ability to cre-ate reality. The new reality created reflects a new cultural paradigm that will be maintained through the practice of reciprocal recogni-tion, nonhierarchical equality, and free-flowing dialogue among equals. Most important, the maintenance of freedom and liberation demands a personal and cultural praxis that is free of all forms of violence. As Fanon (1967) concluded in *Black Skin, White Masks*, it is important for us to work out new concepts and remake humanity anew.

These seven steps hold out hope for the fields of psychology and education and for community members contending with oppression and violence. These steps, being dependent on the power of dialogue—both that occurring between individuals and as internal and external dialogue delivered by any individual to his or her inner self—may potentially transform the historical dynamics in the organizational settings in which psychologists and educators work. There is also the potential to transform the impact of having internalized oppressors or having functioned as an oppressor who engages in problematic behavior.

Conclusion

This chapter has introduced the concept that the United States is a culture of violence that effectively socializes and conditions members in how to sustain this culture through beliefs, traditions, and practices regarding violence that are passed from group member to group member and from generation to generation. In addition, a broad definition of violence was introduced that encompassed and explains both invisible covert violence as well as overt visible violence. Most important, this chapter has begun to illustrate the nature of a multicultural approach to violence by focusing on the experience of oppression from the perspective of members from a variety of historically marginalized groups. Symbolic concepts were introduced to reveal the nature and forms of invisible covert violence, focusing on the projection of negative and low expectations, hierarchical domination, and talking down to others as though they are inferior. In addition, the manner in which both the oppressed and the oppressor suffer from bombardment with misinformation and myths, resulting in internalization processes and damage to identity, was symbolized graphically and discussed. A pedagogy of liberation was introduced that depends on the process of dialogue, a process requiring specific skills described in seven steps that lead to liberation and freedom from oppression. Central concepts—reciprocal recognition, nonhierarchical equality, and a free-flowing dialogue among equals—are suggested as essential to establishing and maintaining a new cultural paradigm in our society, our organizations, and in our personal lives that is conducive to creating and maintaining freedom from oppression. In this manner, this chapter has moved toward a new integrated psychology of oppression, liberation, and identity development.

As an introductory foundation chapter, this discussion has been important in establishing the nature of the multicultural approach to personal and social violence introduced through this edited volume. The novel concepts and unusual approach to personal and social violence taken in this volume are refreshing to those who have been frustrated by attempts to discuss, investigate, and theorize about violence without adequately taking into consideration how historical factors and continuing socialization work to create a dimension in the field of violence that is inextricably linked to the problem of oppression of historically marginalized groups. The resulting multicultural approach established in this introductory chapter lays the foundation for the authors and researchers who, in subsequent chapters, present their research and scholarship that also reflect a multicultural approach to one or another contemporary manifestation of violence.

It can now be taken as foundational knowledge, established in this chapter, that beyond the physical violence that distresses us so and still calls for a multiculturally sensitive approach, there is also a rationale for understanding the experiences of those who suffer both visible and invisible forms of violence. This may include research and scholarship on those who may either perpetrate or suffer from hate crimes; transgender individuals who are targeted for violence and require us to expand our notions of gender; the experiences of African American adolescent males in urban settings, women rape victims, or Japanese and Asians who are victims of hate crimes; and traditional males in need of leadership training in light of today's multicultural and diverse society.

These topics and others will be presented in this volume with multicultural sensitivity and competence by the researchers and scholars who contribute something invaluable, as the field of violence expands to include the first volume to take a multicultural approach to violence. Collectively, the volume seeks to foster the kind of paradigm shift in the fields of psychology and education that is suggested in this chapter, as society moves toward liberation from oppression via praxis and a pedagogy that is made and remade by the oppressed and those with whom they engage in transformative dialogue.

2

Identity Development for "Diverse and Different Others"

Integrating Stages of Change, Motivational Interviewing, and Identity Theories for Race, People of Color, Sexual Orientation, and Disability

BARBARA C. WALLACE

ROBERT T. CARTER

JOSÉ E. NANIN

RICHARD KELLER

VANESSA ALLEYNE

Racial identity theory has been validated in research and has been applied to interpersonal interactions, such as group dynamics and systemic processes, including those in organizational and educational settings. Racial identity models have evolved to include all racial groups in the process of developing racial and cultural consciousness. Within racial identity theory, all racial groups are equally valued. Consistent with trends in psychology that value positivism (Seligman & Csikszentmihalyi, 2000), racial identity theory views multiracial and multicultural differences as a source of strength and enrichment to the overall social context (Carter, 2000).

In this manner, relative to identity development theories for sexual orientation and disability, one might argue that racial identity theory for Blacks, people of color, and Whites is more advanced, is better grounded in research, and has found broader application, constituting a theory that is continually evolving and being refined to meet contemporary needs. The knowledge and insight obtained through this process of evolving and refining racial identity theory may help foster evolution and refinement of other identity development theories, such as those addressing sexual orientation and disability identity development.

But there is an alternative view. Linton (1998) suggested clear benefits to the field of multiculturalism—and we would suggest to racial identity theory, specifically—if there is consideration of how "group cohesion, culture, and identity form when there is no intergenerational transmission of culture, as with most lesbian and gay, and disabled people" (p. 93). Thus, simultaneous consideration and analysis of racial, people of color, sexual orientation, and disability identity development theories may be beneficial to each specific area, as well as to the overall field of training in multicultural competence.

The field of training in multicultural competence surely needs to be refined. Wallace (2000) suggested that even those well versed in the field of multicultural training need to consider placing greater emphasis on gay, lesbian, bisexual, and transgender studies, as well as disability studies. The fundamental issue is whether students are being prepared to assist in ending the oppression of all humankind and to teach and work for social justice, regardless of the "difference" encountered. Thus, Wallace contended that there is a need for a greater emphasis on linguistic diversity and related immigrant issues (see Torres-Guzman, Chapter 9, this volume), as well as spirituality in multicultural training (Emmons, 1999; Miller, 1999). Multicultural training, which is based in theory, research, and practice models for a range of "diverse and different others," holds great promise for adequately preparing psychologists and educators to meet the needs of increasingly diverse communities and societies. The field may even need to move toward a more generic and all-encompassing theory of identity development for "diverse and different others" that may be applied to literally any new identity that may emerge in society. In this way, an identity development theory for the "diverse and different other" may find broad application in meeting the national, international, and global needs of individuals and communities seeking healing in the aftermath of colonialism, enslavement, genocide, persecution, ethnopolitical conflict, and war. More specifically, the healing needed involves addressing the damage done to individual and collective identity.

Exactly what constitutes multicultural sensitivity and multicultural competence for psychologists, educators, and community members seeking to respond to the call to engage in social justice work around the nation and globe? The answer to this question continues to be clarified and expanded on in contemporary literature (Sue et al., 1998; Wallace, 2000). This chapter extends this knowledge base for training psychologists, educators, and community members in how to be multiculturally competent social change agents—by evolving and refining identity development theories of race, people of color, sexual orientation, disability, and the "diverse and different other" in general. The goal is to forge identity development theories for the broad range of "diverse and different others" so that this book can meet contemporary and evolving needs in the new millennium.

The need for this chapter's extension and refinement of identity development theory also arises from the social context. This sociopolitical context, with roots in historical factors, involves how wounds to individual and collective identity are sustained in violent cultures. For example, Chapter 1 highlighted how society socially conditions people within the U.S. culture of violence by constantly exposing them to covert and overt forms of violence. Given this culture of violence and the broad definition of violence guiding this volume, this chapter seeks to prepare psychologists, educators, and community members for the task of healing wounds to damaged identity by assisting individuals who are "diverse and different others" in moving toward more positive identity statuses—because of exposure to violence.

The social context also includes a reality in which there is a health care revolution. The next wave of change for psychology and mental health includes facing a mandate to accomplish most treatment goals within short-term therapy or brief interventions (Kiesler, 2000). However, cognitive-behavioral treatment alone need not dominate. Identity development theory can guide very specific interventions designed to improve affective, behavioral, and cognitive coping, as this edited volume and chapter seek to demonstrate. Thus, if psychology and the field of mental health care take seriously the continuing evolution and refinement of the field of identity development, then identity development theory (also as a component of the psychology of oppression, liberation, and identity development) will be acknowledged as a valued source for interventions to be deployed within the health care revolution. But the interventions must be deployable within the context of short-term or brief treatment. Thus, this chapter integrates stages of change theory (Prochaska & DiClemente, 1982; Prochaska, DiClemente, & Norcross, 1992) and motivational interviewing (Miller, 1995; Miller & Rollnick, 1991)—as an example of a brief intervention finding wide application—with identity development theory, to create a short-term or brief intervention. The goal is to be able to deploy motivational interviewing or motivation enhancement techniques to move people through stages of change, or through identity statuses, so that they attain progressively more positive identity statuses— healing wounds to identity from violence, in the process.

Thus, this chapter introduces the integration of multiple strands of theory and thought to create a short-term or brief intervention for the "diverse and different other" that can heal wounds to damaged identity from violence. The integration of the following is presented in this chapter: (a) identity development theory for race and people of color, sexual orientation, and disability; (b) the psychology of oppression, liberation, and identity development; (c) stages of change theory; and (d) motivational interviewing as a brief intervention that moves people through stages of change. This integration of theory should result in the introduction of a brief intervention that holds promise for effectively addressing the mental health needs of those with wounds to identity due to racism, homophobia, heterosexism, and violence perpetrated against people with a disability, as well as all those who are the varied "diverse and different" around the globe. The goal is to create a sufficiently comprehensive guiding theory of identity development for the varied population of the "diverse and different" that effectively informs practice—whether this practice is short-term therapy or a brief intervention delivered by multiculturally competent psychologists, counselors, educators, peer-to-peer community counselors, or community outreach workers.

What May Be Gained From
Integrating Racial Identity Theory?

The identity development models for Blacks, people of color (Africans, Latinos, Asians, Native Americans, and some immigrants), and Whites comprise three separate models with several distinct racial identity statuses. These statuses are viewed as an aspect of personality, reflecting both individual and collective group resolution of identity issues. Thus, racial identity may be seen as including the influence of affects, behaviors, and cognitions, as may be surmised from Carter (2000) and remaining consistent with Wallace's (1996) preference for focusing on the "ABCs." These ABCs, or affects, behaviors, and cognitions, relate to one's membership in a racial group. Thus, it may be important to consider affective, behavioral, and cognitive responses to one's identity, whether it is one's racial, sexual orientation, or disability status. In this manner, we arrive at one core component to how identity will be approached in this chapter. This involves the first key question: What are an individual's ABCs, or affects, behaviors, and cognitions, in relation to his or her identity status?

Racial identity theory has also found that sociopolitical history impacts not only identity status, including the current social position of people with that identity, but also expression of that identity (Carter, 2000). Thus, a second key question, which could be applied to all instances of identity formation, may be the following: What is the impact of historical influences and the current social climate on how that identity may find expression by an individual?

In addition, racial identity theorists have found that racial identity is not about distinct stages; rather, the statuses operate all together, and an individual has all of the statuses available and present in his or her personality structure but to varying degrees and at different points in personality development. As it turns out, at any given point in time, one or more statuses may dominate. Certain affects, behaviors, and cognitions also may dominate at certain points in time, whereas other affects, behaviors, and cognitions may dominate and find primary expression at another point in time, even as the potential continues to exist to express yet other affects, behaviors, and cognitions that reside within the person as central components of past or potential dominant statuses. Yet it has also been said that a "person can develop sequentially from a less differentiated, externally derived, and less mature status to a more internally based, complex, and differentiated mature status" (Carter, 2000, p. 876). Thus, we arrive at a third important question: At what dominant status do we find any one individual negotiating identity development for race, sexual orientation, or disability, and what affects, behaviors, and cognitions are finding dominant expression at this time—even as other affects, behaviors, and cognitions have held sway in the past and may emerge again in the future? A fourth question arises from racial identity theory, which may be applied to all instances of identity development: What is the nature of the sequential progression that individuals are negotiating, or what identity status is currently dominant, as they move over time from a less differentiated, externally derived identity to a more differentiated, internally based, more mature, and complex identity?

What May Be Gained by Integrating the Psychology of Oppression, Liberation, and Identity Development?

The psychology of oppression, liberation, and identity development (see Wallace, Chapter 1, this volume) emphasizes preparing psychologists, educators, and community members to work for social justice and heal wounds to damaged identity from socialization in a culture of violence that has impacted a range of "diverse and different others." This leads to the fifth question: Is the theory describing the sequential progression that individuals are negotiating—as they move from a less differentiated, externally derived identity to a more differentiated, internally derived identity—capable of being applied to literally all "diverse and different others" so that theory guides social justice work on behalf of all oppressed humanity? A sixth question arising from the psychology of oppression, liberation, and identity development would be as follows: Is the theory of identity development capable of not only healing wounds to damaged identity but also supporting individuals toward attaining a differentiated, mature, altruistic, and internally based identity so that they become autonomous workers for social justice in individual- and/or collective-level liberation movements, attaining personal liberation and a consciousness in which all forms of injustice become intolerable?

What May Be Gained From Integrating Motivational Interviewing Principles?

Actually, the idea for this chapter was born in Barbara Wallace's office at Teachers College, where she met with Vanessa Alleyne and José Nanin and explored integrating stages of change theory and motivational interviewing with theories of identity development for race and sexual orientation. At that time, Wallace asserted that the racial identity theory that Carter (2000) had systematically advanced, along with others, would be further enriched by adding considerations of the "timing" of movement across a sequential path of identity development. Specifically, considerations of timing led to a seventh question: Does the theory for identity development address issues of "timing" or how to expedite (through delivery of a brief intervention) the length of time that it takes to move sequentially from a less differentiated, externally derived, and less mature identity toward a more differentiated, internally based, mature, and complex identity status?

Issues of "timing" are central to the field of chemical dependency, given the work of Wallace (1991, 1996) and others (Miller, 1995; Miller & Rollnick, 1991). People with chemical dependencies—who may be *suddenly externally motivated* by employment, family, or the criminal justice system to become nonusers—have benefited from brief interventions designed to quickly resolve crises associated with their identity of being *active illicit chemical users*. It seems logical to extend those brief motivational interventions—designed to move chemical users along a sequential identity developmental process as quickly as possible—to identity development theories in general, such as those for race, sexual orientation, disability, and all "diverse and different others."

Drawing on Wallace's (1991, 1996) clinical work in the field of chemical dependency, we have aimed to move clients in crisis from an *externally derived identity* as nonactive people in recovery from addiction—*under supervision* of parole or probation—to an *internally derived identity* that values their *own choice* in embracing a new lifestyle that no longer includes active illicit chemical use. Clients end up having a progressively and sequentially more differentiated, more complex, and more mature identity status as people in recovery from addiction who are quite different at multiple points in time. They may be observed undergoing an identity transformation as they move sequentially from the first day they stop using to 3 months, 6 months, and 1 year after they stop using illicit chemicals. An identity transformation may also be observed when they relapse or return to chemical use—whether for a day, months, or years—as well as when they are externally forced or internally decide to terminate illicit chemical use yet again. Thus, the element of "time" and issues of "timing" can enhance identity development theory and the selection of treatment interventions for "well-timed" delivery, in addition to influencing the selection of treatment goals to be established for specific points in time—such as at 1, 3, or 6 months from the onset of treatment.

Motivational interviewing (Miller, 1995; Miller & Rollnick, 1991) and motivational enhancement techniques, such as Wallace's (1991, 1996) empathic mirroring, have been used to assist clients in actualizing progressively more positive identity statuses, helping them resolve their ambivalence around "using" or "not using" illicit chemicals and alcohol. These techniques are also finding application in reducing the harm associated with use when total abstinence is not chosen as the treatment goal (Denning, 2000; Marlatt, 1998). Wallace (1996) asserted that both motivational interviewing and empathic mirroring restore hope and instill a sense of empowerment in helping people take steps toward change, as both create readiness to change through four components:

1. *empathy,* or being empathic and not confrontational as you elicit a client's concerns about an issue or problem;

2. *cognitive dissonance,* or pointing out discrepancies in the client's thinking or between thoughts and behavior;

3. *mirroring,* or reflecting back to the client, after intensive listening, what he or she is saying and feeling;

4 *self-determination,* or asking the client what he or she thinks should be done about the issue or problem of concern to him or her and about possible next steps to take—even as you may assist the client, through a decisional balance exercise, in (a) reviewing the pros and cons, as well as the costs and benefits, and (b) helping him or her generate a menu of options from which to select the next step(s). These techniques, in combination, serve to move people through stages of change toward taking action, expediting the rate at which they enter a state of readiness to change.

Thus, it seems logical to ask an eighth question: Can the kind of brief motivational interviewing or motivation enhancement interventions, in vogue in the field of chemical dependency, be applied to identity development theory to enhance sequential movement along identity statuses or expedite progressive movement across identity statuses?

Motivational interviewing (Miller, 1995; Miller & Rollnick, 1991) and empathic mirroring (Wallace, 1991, 1996), as brief interventions, may move an individual from one identity status to another even when that individual had no prior intention to work on his or her identity on a specific issue. Indeed, some may critique motivational interviewing or motivation enhancement techniques as being somewhat manipulative because they appear effective in moving individuals toward taking action on their identity, issue, or problem; prior to the brief intervention, however, no intent to change or take action was observed. However, the technique of motivational interviewing is nonauthoritarian, using a nonhierarchical approach; it is consistent with this volume's intended value orientation, which is to avoid perpetrating domination and hierarchical control. Instead, motivational interviewing respects individuals' absolute needs to be and feel free. Motivational interviewing elicits individuals' own concerns about their identity, issue, or problem as a way of getting them to think about the next steps to take, given their concerns. Also, a menu of options can then be reviewed with these individuals, so that at each step, they remain free to choose their future actions and never feel told what to do, talked down to, or harshly confronted. Instead, at the heart of motivational interviewing is the skillful art of bringing people face-to-face with reality, given their concerns and state of being. Their concerns and state of being are gently reflected back to them with great empathy, so that motivational interviewing emerges as a form of dialogue that can empower individuals to take action on issues of concern to them. In addition, the actions taken are of their own choosing, given their free will and exercise of that free will in selecting which actions to take from a menu of options. In fact, the seven steps of effective dialogue—as presented in Chapter 1 by Wallace and summarized later in this chapter within the first column of Figure 2.1, under the psychology of oppression, liberation, and identity development—incorporate motivational interviewing and empathic mirroring. These steps also focus on pointing out contradictions between one cognition and another that a person possesses or between one cognition and some aspect of the individual's behavior—creating cognitive dissonance, arousing emotion, and serving to enhance motivation to take action. This is how motivational interviewing (Miller & Rollnick, 1991) and empathic mirroring (Wallace, 1991, 1996) work, in essence, as motivation enhancement techniques.

Motivational interviewing or motivation enhancement techniques have been demonstrated to be highly effective as brief interventions (Miller et al., 1995) that serve to get people moving toward taking action and engaging in behavior change, given an issue or problem. As a brief intervention, research suggests that motivational enhancement techniques serve to expedite the process of individuals moving from one identity status (not thinking about an issue) to another (thinking about an issue) to yet another (determining to do something and then actually taking action on an issue).

Thus, this raises a ninth question: Does the theory of identity development give rise to an intervention style that is nonhierarchical, permitting individuals to explore their own concerns about their identity, issue, or problem as a way of getting them to think about next steps to take, as well as the available menu of options for changing their affects, behaviors, and cognitions—with individuals, at each step of the brief intervention, feeling absolutely free to self-determine their future actions and *not* being told what to do, talked down to, or harshly confronted?

What May Be Gained by
Integrating Stages of Change Theory?

Much may be gained by integrating stages of change theory (Prochaska & DiClemente, 1982; Prochaska et al., 1992). Prochaska and DiClemente (1982) introduced the stages of change theory, allowing an assessment for whether a person is in one of several stages and revolutionizing treatment outcome research, as well as how interventions delivered are "tailored" to match the stage in which a person may be found. Usually, these stages are best appreciated within the context of also considering the kind of interventions that are appropriate for delivery at that given stage. For example, Miller and Rollnick (1991) discussed the stages of change and the likely motivation-enhancing interventions suitable for use at each stage. Meanwhile, we also follow Wallace (1996) in considering individuals' affects, behaviors, and cognitions as vital correlates of their identity status in explaining the stages of change. In what follows, some comments will be added that are consistent with the psychology of oppression, liberation, and identity development, even as the essence of the stages will emerge as Prochaska and DiClemente (1982) originally conceived them.

Precontemplation Stage. Individuals are not even thinking about changing their affects, behaviors, or cognitions with regard to the issue or problem that has been brought to their attention. Providing information and education or increasing their awareness may serve to move them to the next stage of contemplation.

Contemplation Stage. Individuals are thinking about changing their affects, behaviors, or cognitions with regard to the issue at hand or problem situation. This stage is marked by ambivalence and potential confusion. For individuals to move beyond just thinking about the issue, they may need to weigh the pros and cons and the benefits and costs in a decisional balance exercise, as well as review a menu of options.

Determination/Preparation Stage. Individuals have made a determination that something needs to be done and that some potential action must be taken, and so they make preparations to take action or to change their affects, behaviors, and cognitions.

Action Stage. In this stage, individuals have actually begun to take steps or take action in regards to the issue or problem. There is evidence of active engagement in the process of expressing new affects, performing new behaviors, and possessing new cognitions. Individuals feel, act, and think differently, evidencing real change. Individuals are considered as being in the action stage when change has been pursued, or the issue or problem has been addressed, for a period lasting up to 6 months.

Maintenance Stage. When change has been pursued or the issue or problem has been addressed for a period more than 6 months, individuals enter the maintenance stage. Changes made in the areas of affect, behavior, and cognitions are enduring or lasting over time—in this case, beyond a period of 6 months, maybe going into one or many years. Even the affects, behaviors, and cognitions may be changing in a direction suggestive of positive growth. In the maintenance stage, there is evidence of practice effects that occur over time. The ability to express new affects, behaviors, and cognitions continually improves over time, becoming more refined and effective. Individuals (a) can feel and express a broader range of affects with greater ease, clarity, and confidence, being able to engage in healthy affective coping; (b) may evidence some strengthening of behavioral coping skills, a greater repertoire of successful coping behaviors, and an enhanced sense of being able to be effective in taking action on the issue or problem—as increased self-efficacy; and (c) can cognitively cope with greater sophistication, being able to demonstrate creative problem solving, verbal assertiveness, and reasoning abilities that permit realistic decision making and good judgment.

When the maintenance stage becomes progressively longer across years—or the period of time when change has been pursued or the issue or problem has been addressed begins to accumulate to the point that one or many years have gone by—individuals may be said to be moving toward self-actualization or fulfillment of their highest potential. This means that their affects, behavior, and cognitions may begin to reflect the highest and most valued characteristics for individuals with that particular issue or problem. This includes values associated with those considered the most self-actualized, altruistic, or humanistic in our society.

Relapse Stage. Highly consistent with the introductory discussion about identity statuses—specifically with regard to how individuals have all of the statuses available to them, but usually only one or more statuses are dominant—it is possible that the identity status associated with an earlier time in life may emerge again. A person may have a relapse or return to prior affects, behaviors, and cognitions associated with that period when he or she was not thinking about changing or addressing an issue or problem. Thus, a person may, for example, return to being an active user of illicit chemicals, even after months or years of actualizing a predominant identity status as a nonuser. This would constitute a relapse, or a return to a prior identity status.

Also, an individual may not be using chemicals, which technically means that he or she is in the action or maintenance stage. But this individual may be thinking about or contemplating the use of chemicals. Perhaps he or she has even made a decision to use at a point in the near future, having made a determination to use chemicals. Perhaps this person is even preparing for that relapse or return to a prior identity status. This illustrates how one can, within a complete cognitive schema, be in possession of multiple identity statuses—a user, a nonuser, or one preparing to use illicit chemicals— even though only one identity status may *appear to be predominant* at a given time. Consistent with this, recent research suggests that the stages need to be viewed as more of a continuum than discrete stages (Joseph et al., 1999) because individuals often endorse items suggestive of possessing cognitions congruent with being in more than one stage, even though one stage may predominate. In follow-up research, one could analyze data for shifts in the proportion of items that are being endorsed under a primary stage and thereby would be able to determine sequential progress in the change process.

The stages of change theory also conveys the cyclical nature of change. For example, research with cigarette smokers found that most individuals cycle through the stages of change three to seven times, averaging four times when they stop smoking (Miller & Rollnick, 1991; Prochaska & DiClemente, 1982). Thus, this theory contributes to the concept of regressive and progressive movement, or movement around a wheel so that one may cycle around many times and eventually exit when change is stable over many years. Others offer the imagery of an upward spiral (Wallace & Ayeboafo, 2001), so that with each relapse and then return to action, there is evidence of pursuing change for what is now the second or third or fourth time, as well as evidence of a process occurring on a higher level. This reflects the progress made in prior periods of contemplation, determination, action, and maintenance in establishing certain patterns of affective, behavioral, and cognitive coping. One is enriched by knowing what it means to have a powerful trigger in the environment provoke relapse, regression, or abandonment of the change process. One is then able to take this as some new vital information into the next future attempt to change. Thus, a spiral begins to convey both "going around the cycle again" but moving on a somewhat higher level each time one "goes around."

This leads to the presentation of a 10th question: Can the theory of identity development—even as it appreciates that an identity status that appears to be dominant may have been preceded and at any time may be followed by the manifestation of a different dominant identity status—be integrated with the stages of change as we move toward a more general identity development theory for all the "diverse and different others"? An 11th question arises: Can a more general theory of identity development based on stages of change theory be presented for application to a broad range of "diverse and different others," permitting consideration of how any individual may (a) not be thinking about his or her identity (precontemplation), (b) thinking about his or her identity (contemplation), (c) determining or preparing to work on his or her identity (determination/preparation), (d) actively working on his or her identity (action), (e) maintaining progress in working on his or her identity (maintenance), or (f) having returned to a less differentiated or prior identity status (in relapse)?

What May Be Gained From Integrating Sexual Orientation Identity Theory?

As shall be seen when we review sexual orientation development theory later in this chapter, there will be times when an individual in the identity development process may become a target of a bias crime, hate crime, or violent attack or even may be at risk for suicide. The dangers and risks involved in making progress in the area of sexual orientation identity development may mean that we do not want to expedite the process through a brief intervention. Instead, because of the risks of homicide, suicide, and life-threatening injuries, we may need to abandon some of the goals of a brief intervention and provide lengthier and more frequent treatment as an ethically appropriate response. Bongar et al. (1998) presented the standards of risk management with suicidal patients, whereas Connors (2000) discussed psychotherapy with those who engage in self-injury. However, identity development theory augments these approaches with a multicultural approach to violence so that multiculturally competent psychologists, counselors, and community peers may provide adequate support for individuals who are moving through an identity development process that may need to proceed at its own self-regulated pace. Thus, a 12th question may be posed: Can the theory of identity development adapt to the reality that "relapse" may mean aborting the identity development process as a result of one's murder or suicide or as a result of a real or perceived threat of physical injury and death, while a brief intervention goal must be abandoned when a person is recovering from violent assault, is suicidal, or is engaging in self-harm or self-injury?

What May Be Gained From Integrating Disability Identity Theory?

Disability identity theory is invaluable for reminding us that any psychologist, educator, or community member may arrive at the point when the bottom line must be declared. In the field of disability studies, this bottom line is that the focus should be on the social environment and how it must change, including the attitudes and behaviors of professionals and community members who create the social climate and institutional policies. The focus should not be on how the individual should be changed. Thus, the 13th question is as follows: Can we recognize and submit to the reality that at times the pertinent issue is not the individual's identity status, including what can be done to promote progressive sequential movement across identity statuses for that individual, but how to forge social justice now by putting all of our energy into changing an intolerable social context?

Guiding Questions for Revising Identity Development Theory and Creating the "Diverse and Different Other" Identity Theory

What is gained by integrating racial identity theory; the psychology of oppression, liberation, and identity development; the stages of change and motivational interviewing; sexual orientation identity development theory; and disability identity development theory? The 13 questions in Table 2.1 may guide the creation of a more general theory for the identity development of "diverse and different" others.

The question arises as to what happens when considerations from a particular identity development theory are integrated with elements of the psychology of oppression, liberation, and identity development, as well as with the stages of change and motivational

Table 2.1   Questions to Guide Development and Refinement of Identity Development Theories for All "Diverse and Different Others"

---

1. What are an individual's ABCs, or affects, behaviors, and cognitions, in relation to his or her identity status?
2. What is the impact of historical influences and the current social climate on how that identity may find expression by an individual?
3. At what dominant status do we find any one individual negotiating identity development for race, sexual orientation, or disability, and what affects, behaviors, and cognitions are finding dominant expression at this time—even as other affects, behaviors, and cognitions have held sway in the past and may emerge again in the future?
4. What is the nature of the sequential progression that individuals are negotiating, or what identity status is currently dominant, as they move over time from a less differentiated, externally derived identity to a more differentiated, internally based, more mature, and complex identity?
5. Is the theory describing the sequential progression that individuals are negotiating—as they move from a less differentiated, externally derived identity to a more differentiated, internally derived identity—capable of being applied to literally all "diverse and different others" so that theory guides social justice work on behalf of all oppressed humanity?
6 Is the theory of identity development capable of not only healing wounds to damaged identity but also supporting individuals toward attaining a differentiated, mature, altruistic, and internally based identity so that they become autonomous workers for social justice in individual- and/or collective-level liberation movements, attaining personal liberation and a consciousness in which all forms of injustice become intolerable?
7. Does the theory for identity development address issues of "timing" or how to expedite (through delivery of a brief intervention) the length of time that it takes to move sequentially from a less differentiated, externally derived, and less mature identity toward a more differentiated, internally based, mature, and complex identity status?
8. Can the kind of brief motivational interviewing or motivation enhancement interventions, in vogue in the field of chemical dependency, be applied to identity development theory to enhance sequential movement along identity statuses or expedite progressive movement across identity statuses?
9. Does the theory of identity development give rise to an intervention style that is nonhierarchical, permitting individuals to explore their own concerns about their identity, issue, or problem as a way of getting them to think about next steps to take, as well as the available menu of options for changing their affects, behaviors, and cognitions—with individuals, at each step of the brief intervention, feeling

absolutely free to self-determine their future actions and *not* being told what to do, talked down to, or harshly confronted?

10. Can the theory of identity development—even as it appreciates that an identity status that appears to be dominant may have been preceded and at any time may be followed by the manifestation of a different dominant identity status—be integrated with the stages of change as we move toward a more general identity development theory for all the "diverse and different others"?

11. Can a more general theory of identity development based on stages of change theory be presented for application to a broad range of "diverse and different others," permitting consideration of how any individual may (a) not be thinking about his or her identity (precontemplation), (b) thinking about his or her identity (contemplation), (c) determining or preparing to work on his or her identity (determination/preparation), (d) actively working on his or her identity (action), (e) maintaining progress in working on his or her identity (maintenance), or (f) having returned to a less differentiated or prior identity status (in relapse)?

12. Can the theory of identity development adapt to the reality that "relapse" may mean aborting the identity development process as a result of one's murder or suicide or as a result of a real or perceived threat of physical injury and death, while a brief intervention goal must be abandoned when a person is recovering from violent assault, is suicidal, or is engaging in self-harm or self-injury?

13. Can we recognize and submit to the reality that at times the pertinent issue is not the individual's identity status, including what can be done to promote progressive sequential movement across identity statuses for that individual, but how to forge social justice now by putting all of our energy into changing an intolerable social context?

interviewing. The result may be a new, integrated theory of identity development. Such integration is presented for identity development theories for the Black race and people of color, the White race, sexual orientation, and disability in the four sections that follow, respectively.

A New Integrated Racial Identity Development Theory for Blacks and People of Color

Carter (2000) summarized the five statuses for Blacks and people of color together, even as some differences between the two groups require specification. Here, people of color are considered to be

Africans, Latinos, Asians, Native Americans, and some immigrants. The five statuses pertinent to these groups are as follows:

1. Preencounter (Blacks) or Conformity (people of color)

2. Encounter (Blacks) or Dissonance (people of color)

3. Immersion-Emersion

4. Internalization

5. Internalization-Commitment (Blacks) or Integrative Awareness (people of color)

These five statuses can now be integrated with stages of change theory; elements of a psychology of oppression, liberation, and identity development; and motivational interviewing.

Preencounter or Conformity: Precontemplation Stage

In the Preencounter (Blacks) or Conformity (people of color) status, the person adheres to an external self-definition, having attitudes and preferences for the dominant race and culture. There are negative attitudes toward one's own race and culture. These individuals tend to experience social rewards for their acceptance of the dominant worldview. This is the equivalent of the precontemplation stage. Individuals in this stage may benefit by being asked if they have any concerns about their experiences in society, or about the experiences of any other members of society, as a way to stimulate their thinking. Given their concerns, they may be asked about next steps they might take. They can also be assisted in generating a menu of options from which they can select one thing they might do or at least are thinking about doing in the future. They may also benefit from information about the dynamics and psychology of oppression, liberation, and identity development to understand the experiences of some oppressed members of society about whom they may have expressed concern.

Dissonance or Encounter: Contemplation and Determination/Preparation Stages

The Encounter (Blacks) or Dissonance (people of color) identity status is characterized by the experience of challenges to one's externally derived beliefs. The individual has affects and cognitions that reflect confusion and conflict in regards to his or her own group and the dominant racial group. This state of confusion and conflict begins a process of discovery and learning about himself or herself as a racial person. This may be considered a stage of contemplation. This means there may be considerable ambivalence, and the individual can benefit from empathy, reflective listening, and having contradictions in cognitions and behavior gently pointed out and underscored for him or her. This creates cognitive dissonance; emotion may be aroused, and the result may be movement toward resolving the contradictions, thereby leading to the creation of new cognitions. The first new cognition or thought may be a determination that something needs to be done, as the individual prepares to take action. This is when the person enters the determination stage. Also, new affects, behaviors, and cognitions may also result as a result of empathy, reflection, and mirroring, as well as from the creation of cognitive dissonance on the part of the psychologist, counselor, educator, or community member deploying motivational interviewing or empathic mirroring. The individual may also be supported in generating a list of the pros and cons, as well as the costs and benefits, of taking a specific action as part of a decisional balance exercise; this will assist him or her in actually moving toward taking action. This helps the individual further resolve ambivalence and confusion and move toward taking action.

Immersion-Emersion: Action Stage

In the Immersion-Emersion stage, Blacks and people of color take action, becoming deeply involved in discovering their own racial-cultural heritage, even as this involves two phases:

1. obsessive preoccupation or immersion in one's group and culture, moving from having externally derived information for one's identity to acquiring information for himself or herself, so there is internally generated information and knowledge for one's identity; and

2. integration of one's new internally meaningful identity into his or her overall personality structure, being able to acknowledge strengths and weakness of one's group and the role played by one's group in society.

The dominant culture and race have been rejected, and immersion in one's own culture has followed, permitting development of an internal definition of the self.

This stage is the equivalent to the action stage, spanning at least 6 months. The individual can benefit from continuing empathy, reflection, and mirroring, as well as from the creation of cognitive dissonance, especially as he or she seeks to integrate parts of himself or herself. This means, following Chapter 1 of this volume, integrating the internalized oppressor and replacing it with the creation of a new self. Most important, what comes to dominate is a new identity of the individual's own creation that is internally based and meaningful to him or her versus a prior sense of self and identity that was externally derived. The new self reflects integration of a person's new identity, as well as prior aspects of the self or personality. Therapeutic support over many months (6 months of the action stage) can play a vital role in helping a person attain integration of components of the self structure and creation of a new self and identity, whether it comes in short-term therapy or from supportive dialogue with a teacher, friend, mentor, or peer in the community. Supportive, constructive dialogue may help an individual to strengthen his or her commitment to the changes he or she is making through taking action, and this may need to continue for quite some time into the future.

Internalization: Maintenance Stage

For Blacks and people of color, the Internalization stage represents having attained stability in the new self structure or identity that has been created by successfully integrating their new internally meaningful identity with prior aspects of their personality. The individual is secure in using internal criteria for self-definition because he or she has been doing this for more than 6 months (we also consider this to be equivalent to the maintenance stage). Because this stage may last from 7 months to many, many years, self and identity development proceed so that the individual's commitment to race and culture gets progressively stronger, as does his or her sense of pride and self-fulfillment. An individual in this stage may benefit from empathy, reflective listening, and mirroring back to him or her the new emergent affects, behaviors, and cognitions, so that this person's new sense of self becomes stronger and stronger. Again, any source of empathic support and quality dialogue will assist in this process, whether with a psychologist, counselor, teacher, mentor, or friend or through one's own inner self—as through journaling or writing poetry.

Suggesting balance and empowerment, the individual in this stage is capable of accepting the reality of that dominant society within which he or she may have to function while taking pride in and valuing his or her own racial or cultural identity and group. There is ideological flexibility, psychological openness, and self-confidence in regards to one's race and culture in both interpersonal and group encounters. Because this stage lasts for many years, the result may be ever increasingly complex internal processes involving the individual's ability to attain to a sense of peace, altruism, and concern for all of humanity and his or her right to freedom and self-determination. Self-actualization and fulfillment of one's highest potential may follow from years of progressing toward a more complex and internally meaningful identity. Spiritual development is also likely, including the ability to engage in selfless or altruistic acts on behalf of others and humanity, given one's possession of spiritual values that guide behavior. One is most likely to be an effective social agent for social justice on behalf of humanity, given attainment of this identity status. The role of therapists, psychologists, teachers, mentors, friends, and peers is critical in this stage because when individuals finally create themselves in ways that benefit themselves and society the most, they need reflection, mirroring, and validation that what they "are" and "are finally doing" is, indeed, on target. This allows them to further strengthen their sense of self and know when they are peaking or "riding the crest of the wave" or self-actualizing their highest potential.

A New Integrated Racial Identity Development Theory for Whites

Following Helms (1995), Carter (2000) summarized white racial identity development as involving the following identity statuses:

1. Contact
2. Disintegration
3. Reintegration

4. Pseudo-Independence

5. Immersion-Emersion

6. Autonomy

These statuses may also be integrated with stages of change; a psychology of oppression, liberation, and identity development; and motivational interviewing.

Contact: Precontemplation

For Whites, this is also an externally derived identity status in which one holds the view that race has little or no personal or social meaning, whereas personal effort is seen as producing the rewards one experiences in life. The status quo, including white privilege, is seen as acceptable, even though some people may be unable to perceive how they participate in white privilege or the status quo. A colorblind philosophy may be adhered to, and the individual receives social support for accepting the dominant worldview. This contact identity status for Whites is a stage of precontemplation. The individual may be asked about concerns about anything transpiring in society, or within that person's own world or experiences, to get him or her moving in considering what may be transpiring as the status quo. The individual's affects, behaviors, and cognitions should be reflected or mirrored back to him or her, including any contradictions between one cognition and another or between a cognition and a behavior. For example, on one hand, you are concerned about hungry children, yet you do not engage in social action on their behalf. Next steps may also be explored, given the person's concerns. The individual can generate a menu of options from which he or she can select at least one "next step" that can be taken on his or her concern. This kind of dialogue may move the individual into the stage of contemplation, or disintegration.

Disintegration: Contemplation Stage

The White individual experiences a great deal of emotional conflict, confusion, and ambivalence as he or she contemplates the contradiction that "people are people," even though racial inequalities also exist. The individual may have an interaction that produces an awareness that others believe he or she should be respecting the existence of racial inequalities, yet the individual still feels a continuing alliance with other Whites. The individual may benefit from empathic dialogue that engages him or her around any concerns about racial inequalities, potential next steps that could be taken, and the creation of a menu of options for at least one step the individual might take. The individual's confusion and ambivalence need to be worked with, as reflection and mirroring serve to point out contradictions in his or her thinking, as well as between thoughts and behavior, potentially creating cognitive dissonance and moving that person to the next identity status or the one beyond that.

Reintegration: Contemplation Continued but Drawing the Wrong Conclusions

In the contemplation stage, one weighs different sides of the issue and may endorse one side of the problem or issue at one time but then may endorse the other side at other times—reflecting deep ambivalence that often takes time to resolve. Defenses may also be deployed at different times in the contemplation stage, so that one's cognitions reflect intellectualization, rationalization, denial, inflation and grandiosity, or poor reality testing. Such dynamics are in operation in white racial identity, as we consider the stage of Reintegration.

In the Reintegration stage, the individual seems to conclude that if racial inequalities do exist, then Whites deserve the benefits they receive and are superior because other non-Whites must not be exerting sufficient will or effort to receive benefits. The person who thinks about his or her race this way and the benefits he or she enjoys will receive a lot of reinforcement and support for having views about white superiority. A powerful event may be required to move a person away from this racist identity status, in which he or she contemplates the issue of white identity but draws the wrong conclusions—from the perspective of what is needed to create a nonoppressive society that no longer constitutes a culture of violence. Exposure to multicultural education may lead to an examination of the individual's beliefs about race and culture, potentially leading to movement to the next identity status. The individual could benefit from empathic, nonhierarchical dialogue that ascertains concerns about himself or herself or others in society who may suffer, such as children. Next steps may also be explored, as well as the creation of a menu of options for next steps. The pros and cons, as well as the costs and benefits, of the status quo may be considered through the decisional balance exercise. Most important, contradictions in an individual's thinking versus his or her behavior need to be reflected back to that person, creating cognitive dissonance, the emergence of feelings, and an increased chance of moving toward taking action. Information and education on multicultural issues may assist a person in drawing more appropriate conclusions as he or she continues to contemplate the issues.

Pseudo-Independence: Contemplation Continued— Drawing the Right Conclusions and Entering the Determination Stage

A White individual in the Pseudo-Independence identity status continues to contemplate the issues but finally makes the right determination. This determination is that racism should be abandoned, and the individual needs to go about the task of developing a nonracist identity. In addition to all guidance that any person in contemplation can benefit from, the individual in this identity status now needs validation and reinforcement in dialogue that this is a good idea, perhaps by pointing out how it is consistent with other values that this person has expressed as part of some other part of his or her personality.

Immersion-Emersion: Action Stage

An individual in this identity status is now actively pursuing self-exploration and discovery by working to internalize a personally significant understanding of his or her own race. The core question asked of the self that is indicative of taking action is the following: "Who am I racially, and who do I want to be?" An individual may also take action by seeking out historical information about acts of oppression and violence, as this knowledge replaces the misinformation and myth spread in society's culture of violence. One discovers how to be proud of oneself and one's race without being a racist. An individual also may take action by finding ways to address or tackle racism and oppression as it flourishes in contemporary society. This may be considered the action stage, which covers up to 6 months and allows for considerable transformation to occur. The individual in this stage seeks out historical and other information and can benefit from receipt of such information. Psychologists, teachers, mentors, friends, or peers in the community can assist individuals in strengthening their new identity with empathy, reflective listening, and mirroring back to them their own affects, behaviors, and cognitions.

Autonomy: Maintenance Stage

When a person has been taking action for more than 6 months (perhaps for 1, 2, or many years), working on and nurturing his or her new internalized meaning of Whiteness, and maintaining a state of being in which he or she does not oppress people or support others who act on white privilege, that person is successfully in the autonomy identity status. This individual's affective, behavioral, and cognitive change process is successfully enduring over time, so that there is no evidence of engaging in cultural, institutional, or personal racism. Again, such individuals also need empathy, reflective listening, and, most important, validation and reinforcement, as well as encouragement in speaking their truth and sharing it with others. These individuals need to be encouraged to spread their message and potentially serve as role models to stimulate movement across identity statuses for other Whites still subscribing to and engaging in racism, violence, and oppression. Whites in autonomy are important to social justice movements because their willingness to work toward ending all forms of violence and oppression signals hope for all of humanity that radical transformation is indeed possible; former oppressors can join the formerly oppressed and work alongside them in creating a society in which all can realize their full potential. Indeed, a White person who attains to the status of autonomy and is able to maintain it over years and decades creates a life in which he or she is realizing his or her full potential.

A New Integrated Identity Development Theory for Sexual Orientation

As with race, sexuality is one of many personal factors used to express and identify one's self. Yet in our society, one's sexual identity is, by default, assumed to be heterosexual. Anything nonheterosexual (i.e., being gay, identifying as gay or "queer," being partnered with someone of the same sex, etc.) is not fully or at all accepted. Thus, the violence that results from this nonacceptance can hinder a person's sexual identity development. To reiterate, Wallace (1996) offered a definition of violence that is inclusive of not just the delivery of physical blows but also acknowledges the socialization of a person with misinformation and myths so that, in effect, an assault occurs either on a person's physical body or to the self-concept, identity, cognitions, affects, and consciousness of the victim of violence. People who are nonheterosexual have been and are consistently dealing with all levels of violence. Antigay violence in our society is on the rise, as exemplified by the printing of "newspaper ads sponsored by the religious right claiming gays can be 'cured,' and the beating death of Matthew Shepard" in October 1998 (Horowitz, 1998, pp. 29-30).

Internalized homophobia is defined as "the hostility of gay men or lesbians toward their own homosexuality"; *heterosexism* describes "heterosexuals' [culturally and individually manifested] prejudices against lesbians and gay men, as well as the behaviors based on those prejudices" (Herek, 1996, p. 102). The acceptance and proliferation of such oppressive norms by a nonheterosexual person is a form of self-violence: Believing myths and misconceptions about one's sexual identity as told by the White heterosexual male majority is a direct assault to one's developing positive self-concept. The internalized oppression can also lead to violence against others because people can misplace their anger, sadness, and frustration by acting out against others (e.g., rape, gay bashing). Sometimes, that misplaced anger and frustration may be directed toward the gay or lesbian person's own partner. Domestic violence in gay and lesbian relationships may exist as a manifestation of one or both partners' self-loathing of their sexual identity; the behaviors can "range from name calling to homicide" (Klinger & Stein, 1996, p. 809). Resolution of such interpersonal and intrapersonal conflicts is integral for progression through further stages of sexual identity development.

To understand how violence can affect the sexuality development of nonheterosexuals, we must consider the stages of sexuality identity development and the multiple points along the stage continuum where the impact hinders progress. Stage-oriented models of sexual identity formation have been formulated by a number of researchers, including Cass (1979), Coleman (1981-1982), and Troiden (1989). Blumenfeld (1997) has provided a comprehensive overview of these models.

Among the models formulated to help us understand the development of sexual identity, Cass's (1979) model is inclusive of the intricate processes that take into account the psychosocial impact of sexual identity development. This model traces the circular process of sexual identity development via six stages: identity confusion, identity comparison, identity tolerance, identity acceptance, identity pride, and identity synthesis. These stages incorporate one's psychosocial processes, including coping mechanisms and social reactions to one's identity.

The Prestage Process or Precontemplation Stage

Within Cass's (1996) model, the prestage process entails understanding the self as belonging to the majority group of heterosexuals and recognizing the stigma of nonheterosexual status. An individual in this precontemplation stage should be respected and accepted for who and where they are at this stage in identity development. Information may be provided that serves educational or consciousness-raising purposes.

Prestage Process Equivalent to the Contemplation Stage

Conflict arises within the self as individuals observe how they relate to people of the same and opposite gender in fundamentally different ways. This is the beginning of a contemplation stage. This conflict or recognition of "difference" serves as an epiphany and prepares individuals for movement into the first stage of sexual identity development. Empathy and support as well as reflective listening may be provided, in addition to education and information.

Identity Confusion: Contemplation Stage

Identity confusion is the equivalent of the contemplation stage. In this first stage of sexual orientation identity development, a person feels different from others. As a result, a person feels alone and confused, dealing with the "impact on personal interchanges of labeling one's own behavior as 'lesbian' or 'gay'" (Cass, 1996, p. 234) or as bisexual or transgender. There is not much discussion of one's sexuality in this stage. The dissonance caused by the realization of one's nonheterosexuality causes trauma and turmoil. It is necessary to note that for women prediscovering or just discovering their lesbian or bisexual identities, much silence about the dynamics of female sexuality has already had an effect on gender identity development; they have been predisposed to the notorious notion that female sexuality and sexual identity development are an invisible phenomenon or a "shameful secret" (Eliason, 1996, p. 4). Extreme forms of self-inflicted violence can thus occur. In discussing Cass's (1996) model, Blumenfeld (1997) noted how violence against oneself via suicide can be a common occurrence in this stage, especially among adolescents. Individuals need empathy, support, reflective listening, creation of cognitive dissonance, and monitoring for suicidality and other destructive behaviors.

Identity Comparison:
Contemplation and Determination Stages

Identity comparison, the second stage in Cass's (1996) model, primarily entails feelings of ambivalence, whereby individuals rationalize or bargain with their sexual identity. This is the contemplation stage that also typically leads to individuals entering into the determination stage as they prepare to act in some way. There are still feelings of solitude, yet some may choose to express their identity on different levels, ranging on a continuum from "passing" as heterosexuals while living with nonheterosexual feelings to viewing themselves and their behaviors as unwelcome and wishing to modify both (Blumenfeld, 1997). The fear of externally inflicted violence can be the basis for their ambivalence. Fear of being ridiculed, physically violated, or even killed can exacerbate the feeling of needing to hide their true sexual identity. Individuals may perceive a need to protect themselves from harm by ensuring that they are not "found out" or perceived as nonheterosexual. Resolution of the ambivalence in this stage is essential for progress into later stages. Some individuals in this stage may feel forced to accept their nonheterosexual identity and yet hold "extreme levels of self-hatred that may lead to suicide or self-mutilation" (Cass, 1996, p. 239). Individuals in this stage need empathy, support, reflective listening, creation of cognitive dissonance, and monitoring for suicidality and other destructive behaviors.

Identity Tolerance: Action
Stage With Risk of Entering Relapse Stage

The third stage, identity tolerance, finds the person on a journey to social relationship building with others of similar nonheterosexual identity and experiences so as to overcome loneliness and isolation (Cass, 1996). This constitutes an action stage in which there is considerable risk of relapse, given the surrounding culture of violence. Negative contacts with others may cause a *relapse* to behaviors and experiences that cause alienation and inhibition from expressing one's true sexual identity. Positive experiences with others can assist a person with the development of a more acceptable self-identity and commitment to that identity (Cass, 1996). Psychologists, teachers, friends, peers, and community members can play a vital role in creating such positive experiences through constructive dialogue and supportive, loving actions. The effect of violence in this stage can be detrimental because it may cause individuals to revert back or relapse into earlier stages of nonresolution of their sexual identity issues. A review of studies by Berrill (1992) found that "a median of 44% of [gay and lesbian] respondents had been threatened with violence because of their sexual orientation" (Herek, 1996, p. 103). It is reported by Levine (1998) that to deal with the stigma propagated by mainstream society, "gay men often withdraw from the larger society and restrict their social life and primary relation to other gay people" (p. 40). If positive experiences with others instill a sense of affiliation to a nonheterosexual community, people may find it self-efficacious to overcome the effects of the inflicted violence and move on to further acceptance of their true sexual identity. Thus, empathy, support, acceptance, reflective listening, and creation of cognitive dissonance to strengthen commitment to action are very important. Social action to create a safe environment for gay, lesbian, bisexual, and transgender individuals is also vitally needed.

Identity Acceptance: Maintenance
Stage With Risk of Relapse

Identity acceptance is a stage in which one continues to contact and build relationships with other nonheterosexuals (Cass, 1996). Acceptance of one's identity is evident, yet "the inner sense of self as lesbian or gay is still tenuous" (Cass, 1996, p. 244). But if this process has been occurring for more than 6 months, then we can consider this the maintenance stage, as this challenging work on the self continues. A firmer sense of self is created when individuals can selectively disclose to others their sexual identity. They can still experience violence in this stage if they find people in their circle who are not accepting of nonheterosexuality. Some may react by not disclosing their identity and by internalizing the homophobia and heterosexism experienced in such a situation. Herek (1996) explained how antigay hate crimes represent an attack on the victim's gay identity and community, affecting feelings about herself or himself as a gay individual and toward the gay community. People may feel vulnerable to attack and that their sexuality can be a source of danger. If they are actually attacked, then internalized homophobia may reemerge or may be intensified. So, a risk of relapse exists in this stage, too. Individuals need social activism, as psychologists, educators, and community members work to change the social context and increase safety for nonheterosexuals, in addition to all that prescribed for those in the maintenance stage.

Identity Pride: Maintenance Stage

The final and fifth stage of identity pride may be achieved after successful completion of the previous four stages, suggesting a maintenance stage. Here one perceives the world as "them and us" vis-à-vis a newly developed dissonance between an "increasingly positive concept of self as lesbian or gay and an awareness of society's rejection of this orientation" (Blumenfeld, 1997, p. 9). Anger toward and the devaluing of heterosexuals and their institutions (e.g., marriage, gender roles) are common, as well as self-empowerment and a feeling of increased safety as one becomes more of a member of the nonheterosexual community. One "comes out" and discloses sexual identity on an increased level. Activism against social and institutionalized homophobia and heterosexism is not unusual in this stage. It may cause a person to be more visible as a nonheterosexual and more vocal about the positive aspects of this sexual identity. This increased exposure in society can seem threatening to many who do not believe that nonheterosexuals should have such a presence or voice and who may feel a need to react in violent ways with behaviors ranging from the public condemnation of homosexuals as sinners and demons (e.g., Reverend Jerry Falwell's admonishment of television star Ellen DeGeneres) to acts of murder (e.g., Matthew Shepard). Furthermore, institutionally sanctioned acts of violence based on cultural heterosexism include the deficiency of antidiscrimination laws for gays and lesbians. Other examples include the military's "don't ask, don't tell" policy on homosexuality and the continuation of sodomy laws in many U.S. states (Herek, 1996). As with the stage above, individuals need the professionals and peers in their lives to assist in the pursuit of social justice through taking social action to end violence and oppression against nonheterosexuals.

Identity Synthesis: Maintenance Stage

The last stage, identity synthesis, emerges as one feels less separatist and acknowledges increased unity with supportive and trustworthy heterosexuals. This is also still within a maintenance stage, suggesting how the internally based identity status may evolve and become more complex and differentiated over many months or years. The intensity of the anger and frustration caused by experiencing homophobia and heterosexism is diminished but not absent (Cass, 1996). A nonheterosexual identity (e.g., "gay," "lesbian," "dyke," "queer," etc.) is perceived as part of one's personality and humanness and extends into one's social relationships with heterosexuals and nonheterosexuals. Society, on the other hand, may condemn this positive self-identity via varied acts of violence already discussed and institutional acts of violence, as in the denial of permission for same-sex marriages. Infliction of violence on someone who is developing or has developed a more complete sense of sexual self-identity can be injurious to the oppressor as well as the oppressed. One example of this is provided by Sullivan (1999, p. 57), who talked about how people demeaned and objectified in society often develop an aversion to their tormentors—even feeling hate.

Relapse Stage: Aborting the Identity Development Process

Even though relapse was mentioned in the action and maintenance stages above, it is worth adding our own formal relapse stage. Relapse as a stage in sexual orientation identity development should have a place of importance and prominence because it informs us about the ways in which this particular identity formation process is distinct and meaningful, especially when there is no generational transmission of culture, no family support and familiarity with this identity process, and no societal support of this identity. One must appreciate how the entire identity development process can end in relapse or even can abort the development of a gay, lesbian, bisexual, or transgender identity. Terror, fear, reality testing, and judgment that death is possible can be considerable barriers to identity formation and expression. Violence or threat of violence on someone who is transgressing the developmental stages of sexual identity via Cass's (1996) model, described earlier, can be traumatic and detrimental to progressive movement through the stages and cycles. Klinger and Stein (1996) stated that the mere awareness of antigay violence can give a nonheterosexual person, whether attacked or not, a "heightened sense of vulnerability about and reluctance to disclose sexual orientation" (p. 804), in addition to creating or exacerbating other psychosocial problems. As noted, acts of violence can also be inflicted by oneself and directed toward oneself; suicide aborts the entire identity development process and is, unfortunately, very common among gay youth (Wells, 1999).

The New York City Lesbian and Gay Anti-Violence Project reports how a "hunting phenomenon" exists in the city, wherein "a group of young men leave their home and travel to an area they believe has a lot of gay people with the specific [premeditated] intention of beating up someone who's gay" (Horowitz, 1998, p. 33). This type of social atmosphere can encourage anyone who is in the process of developing a nonheterosexual identity to stay hidden in the closet, exhibit concepts of oneself that are false, and behave in ways that violate one's own true self-concept. It has been documented that the "stigmatization of homosexuality fostered harsh social sanctions designed to isolate, treat, correct, or punish gay men" (Levine, 1998, p. 20). Lesbian women and bisexuals are not immune to oppression either. Certainly, persons of transgender experience suffer as well (see Hill, Chapter 5, this volume).

It is critical to be aware of the devastating impact that violence can have on one's sexual identity development, as well as the resources that exist in one's community to assist someone who is oppressed in such a way. Fortunately, resources do exist to support individuals who are negotiating stages of sexual identity development. Psychologists, educators, and community members who read this book need to be a part of that resource network and respond to the urgent need to engage in social action to forge social justice for nonheterosexuals, as well as bring an end to the violence that often results in the identity development process being aborted, often via suicide. Note that for no other identity development theory mentioned thus far has suicide been mentioned as a risk, nor has a relapse that forces individuals to abandon their own internally based authentic identity. Thus, this highlights a unique set of challenges associated with negotiating sexual orientation identity development. This underscores the urgent need for a queer social justice movement. Fleshman discusses this queer social justice movement and spiritual violence in Chapter 3 (this volume).

A Comment on Developing Multiple Identities

When faced with the evolution of multiple levels of identity, those who are oppressed based on race, ethnicity, culture, gender, disability, or sexual orientation and identity have even more to battle and overcome. For example, Díaz (1998) has researched the impact of ethnocultural scripts on the safer sex behaviors of gay Latino men; he stated that the "machismo message" given to Latino men who are exploring their sexuality "does not allow much space for the kind of caring and nurturing that is needed for the negotiation of safer sex between sexual partners" (p. 78). More disturbingly, the author informs us that the reality for most Latino gay men includes how their homosexuality is "culturally accepted (or rather tolerated) only if it is not mentioned or talked about and not labeled as such" (Díaz, 1998, p. 61).

As an additional example, among communities of African descent, homosexuality is seen as a "rejection of cultural values or as a form of social deviance that brings shame to the family" (Scrivner, 1997, p. 237). African American men may demoralize and defame others like them because of a "false sense of masculinity" and male sexuality, and they may think less of other African American men if they have sex with others like them (McClean, 1997, p. 214). The nature of the oppression and violence against nonheterosexuals, the risk of being violently attacked and resorting to suicide, and the possibility of negotiating multiple identities must be appreciated. This means that the challenges for nonheterosexuals are daunting indeed, requiring psychologists, educators, and community members to bring extra sensitivity and awareness to their dialogue with the gay, lesbian, bisexual, and transgender community.

A New Integrated Identity Development Theory for People With Disabilities

Following Wallace's definition of violence (see Chapter 1, this volume), clearly the community of people with disabilities, similar to other stigmatized populations, has had violence perpetrated against it throughout history. This creates the contemporary challenge of identity development for people with disabilities. Some introductory historical background seems essential before presentation of a suggested new integrated identity development model for people with disabilities. For, as we shall see, changing the social context will be a central recommendation in fostering identity development for this group, suggesting a need to thoroughly understand the sociohistorical context.

Historical Background

In ancient Sparta, disabled children were left on the mountainside to the mercy of the cold night or wild animals. "Other cultures, closer to the present day, condoned the smashing of infant sculls against stones or trunks of trees when children were strange, worrisome, or unwanted" (Warren, 1985, p. 201). The infamy of the Holocaust is most closely associated with the murder of 6 million Jews. However, the world has overlooked the fact that the Nazis also exterminated more than three quarters of a million people identified as disabled through compulsory sterilization and mass genocide (Disability Holocaust Project; see www.dralegal.org).

Such flagrant and massive acts of overt violence are rejected and abhorred by the collective American psyche, being found incompatible with the rules and norms of a modern and democratic society. We believe that such events could never have happened in America. However, through the 1930s in the United States, laws restricted marriage by persons with intellectual disabilities and required them to be sterilized and institutionalized (Ferguson, 1994). In its majority opinion in *Buck v. Bell* (1927), the U.S. Supreme Court upheld a compulsory sterilization law in which Justice Oliver Wendell Holmes Jr. wrote, "Three generations of imbeciles are enough." Segregation of persons with disabilities into institutional life grew throughout the first part of the 20th century, from 9,334 institutionalized persons with mental retardation in 1900 to 68,035 people who were in institutions in 1930 (Scheerenberger, 1983).

The Contemporary Social Context

In our attempt to distance ourselves from this shameful state of affairs in our collective past, we might cling to the belief that similar events could not take place in the United States today. Although limited statistical information exists pertaining to the criminal victimization of people with disabilities, the available data suggest that persons with developmental disabilities have a 4 to 10 times higher risk of becoming crime victims than persons without a disability. Concurrently, children with any kind of disability are more than twice as likely as nondisabled children to be physically abused and almost twice as likely to be sexually abused. The nature of the assault on the identity of crime victims with disabilities can be understood through professional reports from the crime victims field. These reports characterize crimes against people with disabilities as often extremely violent and calculatedly intended to injure, control, and humiliate the victims (Bulletin #97-BF-GX-K022, 1998).

Covert violence against persons with disabilities, though less obvious, is even more pervasive. Literature on life outcome variables for people with disabilities describes both the nature of the assault on the identity and the life circumstances resultant from these assaults. The most well-known act of social violence against people with disabilities is related to employment. Notwithstanding the passage of the Americans with Disabilities Act (ADA) of 1990, which prohibits discrimination on the basis of disability in all aspects of employment, both a pre-ADA Harris Poll in 1986 and a post-ADA Harris Poll in 1994 indicate that two thirds of persons with disabilities are unemployed. During the same interval, there has been an increase in the proportion of people with disabilities without jobs who want to work, from 66% to 79% (LaPlante, 1997). According to LaPlante, Kennedy, Kaye, and Wenger (1995), only 27.8% of working-age Americans with disabilities are employed, which is in sharp contrast to the 76.3% of those without disabilities.

This high unemployment rate contributes to the economic disadvantage that persons with disabilities experience. Within the working-age population, 30% of people with disabilities live below the poverty level compared with 10.2% of those without disabilities. Persons with disabilities who are able to maintain employment earn only 63.6% as much as their nondisabled counterparts.

Persons with disabilities are more likely to live alone and less likely to engage in intimate partnerships. Similarly, when disability occurs in a family, it coincides with an increase in marital strain and is likely to contribute to marriage dissolution (LaPlante, Carlson, Kaye, & Bradsher, 1996).

These realities reflect often subtle discrimination that may be experienced as covert violence by persons with disabilities. Remaining in a disadvantaged, compromised, and disenfranchised state in a world that refuses to acknowledge or change such violence puts the identity of a person with disability at risk for further attack.

What are the mechanisms of this covert violence against people with disabilities? When considering assault and its impact on the identity of a person with disability, violence starts with the negative attitudes of people without disabilities. There is evidence to support how negative attitudes toward persons with disabilities are learned early in life through socialization in our culture of violence, and these attitudes remain consistent throughout the life span. Diamond (1994b) found that children without disabilities between 3.5 and 5.5 years of age negatively evaluated their peers with disabilities. In a study of acceptance of classmates involving kindergarten children, Diamond (1994a) reported that nondisabled children expected a significantly higher level of prosocial behavior by their counterparts with disabilities to accept them. In Doddington's (1994) study of 99 thirteen- to fourteen-year-olds not experiencing disability, negative perceptions and feelings about the disabled population were found. This study indicated that these perceptions may be tied to various media representations of people with disabilities. A study of 427 undergraduate and graduate students showed a lack of knowledge and understanding concerning individuals with disabilities and their rights and further showed a significant correlation between this lack of knowledge and negative attitudes (Pitman, 1994). Negative attitudes and stereotypes about individuals with disabilities exist in everyday interactions, unless an individual without a disability has had a personal experience with a person with a disability or some type of sensitivity training to mitigate against these negative perceptions (Barret, 1993).

Urgent Need for Multicultural Sensitivity in Professionals

The predominantly negative experiences are encountered in relationships with a variety of contextual settings and the full range of level of intimacy. In a world where interpersonal interactions can be overwhelmingly negative, individuals with disabilities might hope that at least their treatment by professionals is indicative of sensitivity and understanding. Unfortunately, however, evidence suggests that this is not the case. For example, a study by Handler (1994) reports that persons training in the medical professions demonstrate low expectations of individuals with disabilities unless a sensitization element is included in their training. Persons with disabilities face difficulties in dealing with other professionals whom they meet in everyday life, including law enforcement officers (McAfee, 1995).

Assaults on Identity

Two alternative sets of expectations that drive attitudes toward persons with disabilities can be observed: Either low expectations and negative attitudes occur, or they are replaced by expectations of extraordinary achievement and overwhelming competency (Hafferty, 1994). In either case, findings suggest that these historically rooted characterizations reduce disabilities to just physical impairments—along with minimizing and trivializing the importance of social, historical, and contextual factors—in an effort to displace the source of difficulties from social and environmental to individual origins. This displacement, which is manifested in blaming a person with disability for the disability and demanding that this person resolve any and all his or her disability-related difficulties, exemplifies an assault on identity.

Another assault on identity is the requirement placed by society on people with disabilities to regulate their affect (Olkin, 1999, p. 77). The required regulation most often includes elevation of cheerfulness and attenuation of anger. Olkin (1999) summarized H. Gallagher's description of the mandated cheerfulness in his *FDR's Splendid Deception* (1985) as follows: "We (nondisabled) will let you (the disabled) live and work among us, provided that you never make us unduly aware of your disability or its attendant difficulties, and provide that you at all times appear cheerful" (p. 77).

In her discussion of anger attenuation, Olkin (1999, p. 78) stated that expression of anger by people with disabilities is not socially tolerated because it contradicts the expectation that people with disabilities should remain grateful. Thus, their expression of anger is characterized as individual pathology, lack of adjustment, and failure to be appropriately socialized.

Yet another psychosocial act of violence against people with disabilities is the negative nature of interpersonal communications with their nondisabled peers. A partial explanation for these negative encounters includes the discomfort and uncertainty during the interaction reported by persons without disabilities (Davis, 1961; Kleck, Ono, & Hastorf, 1966). These subjective reports have been supported by an objective measure of emotional arousal (Kleck et al., 1966). Additional findings indicate that, while interacting with a person with disability, nondisabled individuals exhibit less variability in their behavior, express opinions less representative of their actual belief, gesture less, and even end the interaction sooner than they do when interacting with persons without disabilities (Kleck, 1968; Kleck et al., 1966).

Interactions seem to improve when a person with a disability reduces the discomfort and uncertainty in an interaction through the use of self-disclosure (Goffman, 1963; Hastorf, Wildfogel, & Cassman, 1979; Thompson & Seibold, 1978; White, Wright, & Dembo, 1948). Thompson (1982) reviewed eight studies about self-disclosure by persons with disabilities and concluded that nondisabled individuals reacted more positively toward persons with disabilities who engaged in self-disclosure and even more positively when the information revealed pertained to their disability. In fact, persons without disabilities preferred that persons with disabilities disclose about their disability, even when the act of disclosure made them visibly nervous (Evans, 1976; Hastorf et al., 1979; Mills, Belgrave, & Boyer, 1984).

Nondisabled persons may believe that individuals who talk about their disabilities may be comfortable with their disabilities, so the nondisabled persons feel more comfortable as well. In their research, Hastorf et al. (1979) concluded that when persons with disabilities disclose something about their disability, persons without disabilities like them more than when they do not disclose. However, Thompson and Seibold (1978) found little support for this claim, arguing that disclosure does reduce tension levels and uncertainty of nondisabled persons but does not increase their acceptance of persons with disabilities. The finding on acceptance is based on a single encounter, and acceptance of a person with a disability might only develop through multiple encounters. Braithwaite (1985) has suggested that disclosure about one's disability may be an important factor at the beginning of relationships as a means of reducing discomfort and uncertainty. The availability of disability as a topic of conversation also reduces self-focused attention on both sides of interactions between persons with and without disabilities, which has also been shown to improve these interactions (Fichten et al., 1996).

Braithwaite (1985) argued that, from the perspective of people without disabilities, it is difficult to disagree with these conclusions. These conclusions, however, make an implicit assumption that the results of self-disclosure are equally beneficial for both sides. The person with a disability does benefit from the improvement of interaction, yet the function and outcome of revealing private information for interactants with disabilities may not always be positive. The cost of the disclosure includes reduced control of one's own private information, which is also linked to indicators of psychological well-being such as identity, self-esteem, and sense of autonomy (Braithwaite, 1985).

Finding the Most Appropriate Approach to Disability

As we consider the tasks of understanding and healing the damage done to the identity of people with disabilities within the U.S. culture of violence, we should keep in mind that psychology primarily trains practitioners to intervene on the personal level rather than intervene to alter the environment (Linton, 1998). Psychology in general has traditionally focused attention on "the personal qualities of those defined as having or being the problem," and, as a result, the policy derived from that research addresses "person fixing rather than context-changing" (Trickett, Watts, & Birman, 1994, p. 18).

Two major schools of thought exist that attempt to understand the lives of persons with disabilities and the impact that a disability experience may have on an individual's identity. The first has been called the medical model of disability. This traditional view of disability is thought to be a natural extension of the diagnosis and treatment of various medical conditions that may lead to disability. The medical model is primarily a deficits model that describes an individual with a disability as having less resources, less capacity, and less competence than individuals not experiencing disabilities.

This model has been used in the medical professions, in helping professions, and in education, specifically in special education. The primary focus of this model is to identify or diagnose differences in abilities as a loss of function or an impediment to function. The utility of this scheme is that it identifies barriers to full and independent function and thus is a starting point for considering barrier removal and the development of alternative skills and strategies. The drawback of this scheme is that it contributes to negative perceptions of persons with disabilities, locates the source of disability-related concerns *within* the disabled population itself, and limits responsibility for change to the disabled population and experts in disability-related fields.

The second model, known as the social constructionist model of disability, has been developed in reaction to the limited location of responsibility for social and environmental change, which the medical model places on persons with disabilities. This model has developed in conjunction with the growth of the disability rights movement and the emergence of the field of disability studies. The social constructionist model emphasizes the role of environmental factors in the disability experience. This model shifts the location of disability-related concerns away from the population with disabilities and describes disability as a condition that may exist given a specific interaction between a person and environment. The advantage of this model is that it facilitates the perception that individual differences contribute only a partial understanding of the disabled experience. The society at large bears some responsibility for disabled experiences as they may result from historical, social, contextual, and environmental factors imbedded within the choices of the dominant culture. The drawback of this scheme is that it deemphasizes those disability experiences that do not originate in social environmental choices but that are the manifestations of the objective reality of disability.

Despite contributions by various scholars who urge a move away from the traditional medical model to the social constructionist approach in the understanding of the disability experience (Pfeiffer, 1995; Scofield, Pape, McCracken, & Maki, 1980), the medical model remains the standard. This model describes life outcomes for persons with disabilities through theoretical models of adjustment to disability.

Stages of Disability
Identity Development: Adjustment

Livneh (1986) attempted to synthesize 40 models of adjustment to disability and defined the following stages of adjustment:

1. initial impact, consisting of shock and anxiety substages;

2. defense mobilization, which encompasses the substages of bargaining and denial;

3. initial realization or recognition, which includes the subcategory of mourning or depression in addition to that of internalized anger;

4. retaliation or rebellion stage, often referred to as externalized anger or aggression;

5. reintegration or reorganization, which is further subcategorized according to its cognitive (acknowledgment), affective (acceptance), and behavioral (final adjustment) components.

The lack of a clear consensus describing the number, duration, order, and exclusivity of stages can be observed in the variations presented by numerous researchers (Blank, 1957; Cholden, 1954; Cohn-Kerr, 1961; Dunn, 1975; Falek & Britton, 1974; Fink, 1967; Shontz, 1965; Vargo, 1978). Furthermore, a universally accepted theoretical model of adjustment to disability would only enable us to classify or diagnose an individual with a disability but would not give us insight into the factors that permit movement through or across stages. Attempts to measure adjustment to disability through stage models fail to achieve satisfactory psychometric properties and remain dubious with respect to utility (Livneh & Antonak, 1990).

A Call to Change the Social Context

Considering the tendency of psychology toward "person fixing" rather than "context changing," it may be useful for psychologists and training programs to include materials from disability studies that, in contrast, are focused on the external variables: the social, political, and intellectual contingencies that shape meaning and behavior. This more comprehensive approach to understanding persons with disabilities unites intrapersonal and environmental factors acknowledging both the possibility of individual maladjustment or pathology as well as covert and overt violence perpetrated on the identity of persons with disabilities, which may lead to enhanced therapeutic outcomes. We need to consider that damage to the identity of people with disabilities has much to do with being made invisible in society, being placed in institutions, or being denied access to varied opportunities within society. Hence, healing the damage done similarly has much to do with changing the social systems, social policy, and intellectual analyses that have historically and may, in contemporary times, perpetuate damage to the identity of people with disabilities.

Thus, it is recommended that psychologists, educators, and community members spend more time addressing and changing the social context through social action that seeks social justice for people with disabilities, making sure they possess multicultural sensitivity. This may be more important than supporting individuals with disability through stages of change toward progressively more positive identity statuses. However, this chapter's presentation of a generic model of identity development for all "diverse and different others" may serve purposes of also facilitating the healing of wounds to identity for some categories of people with disabilities.

Toward an Identity Development Theory for All "Diverse and Different Others"

An identity development theory for all "diverse and different others" is proposed in this section, drawing largely on the psychology of oppression, liberation, and identity development introduced in Chapter 1 by Wallace (this volume). In particular, the identity development component of this theory finds necessary elaboration in this section.

Table 2.2 shows how old socially conditioned cognitions and thoughts—consistent with the old cultural paradigm, or the prevailing culture of violence—are held by both oppressors and the oppressed, or actors A and B, respectively. As a result of having these cognitions, affects and behaviors follow that serve to sustain a culture of violence—or the old paradigm. One can also see how the oppressed, or actor B, is capable of the same affects and behaviors as the oppressor as a result of processes of internalization $(B(A))$. This

Table 2.2   Old Cognitions and Identity Development Under the Old Cultural Paradigm

Actor A Thinks	*Actor B Thinks*
1. $A \Rightarrow B$ (projection of negative and low expectations)	1. $A \Rightarrow B$
2. A/B (domination and hierarchical authority)	2. A/B
3. $A \sim\Downarrow B$ (talking down to another as though inferior)	3. $A \sim\Downarrow B$

Multiple forms of invisible and/or visible violence reign between any two "different" people, A and B, cognitively conditioned or brainwashed to think in the following manner: (1) to enact $A \Rightarrow B$ or project negative and low expectations or stereotypes and negative labels on the "diverse and different other"; (2) to enact A/B or practice domination and hierarchical authority, consistent with traditional European American notions of superiority and inferiority; and (3) to enact $A \sim\Downarrow B$ or talk down to others as though they are inferior.

Actor A (who has white privilege, is not disabled, and is heterosexual) thinks the following:

1. I have every right to project negative and low expectations on actor B because actor B is inferior and therefore should not gain access, should not receive opportunity, and is not valued.
2. I have every right to practice domination and hierarchical authority because I am superior and actor B is inferior.
3. I have every right to talk down to actor B as though he or she is inferior because I am superior to actor B.

Actor B (who is the "different other" in society and of a devalued race, a person with a disability, or homosexual, bisexual, or transgender) reflects internalization of the oppressor:

1. $B(A) \Rightarrow B$
2. $B(A)/B$
3. $B(A) \sim\Downarrow B$

Actor B thinks the following:

1. I know about stereotypes, by virtue of cognitive conditioning and brainwashing from living in this society, and I may also project negative and low expectations on myself or others who are "different."
2. I know about the practice of domination and hierarchical authority because I have been cognitively conditioned and brainwashed by this society into knowing about who is superior and inferior, as well as where I and other "diverse and different others" fit into this schema.
3. I know about how the inferior can be talked down to, and I may accept being talked down to, not challenge it, or talk down to other inferior "different others."

Old cognitions and corresponding affects of hate and disdain lead to behaviors of overt and covert violence under the old paradigm. Those with damaged identity engage in violence.

is why we may observe Black police officers engaging in police brutality, Black-on-Black homicide, and gay men battering their gay male partners. The socially conditioned cognitions and corresponding affects of hate and disdain lead to behaviors of covert and overt violence on the part of oppressors and all who take on the role behavior of the oppressor. Change is needed.

Change is manifested under a new cultural paradigm in which there is freedom from oppression, as shown in Table 2.3. Former oppressors now possess new cognitions and corresponding affects that guide healthy behaviors, including taking social action and participating in social justice movements. They have integrated their internal sense of inferiority and no longer need an inferior on whom they can project their internal disdained parts, having moved on to create a new self (CNS).

Table 2.4 illustrates how those formerly oppressed now find freedom from oppression and violence in a new cultural paradigm as their new cognitions reflect creation of a new self (CNS). This new identity reflects healing from the damage sustained under the old paradigm, as they have integrated that internalized oppressor and now allow the creation of a new self, new cognitions, and new affects to guide their behavior.

In this manner, Tables 2.2, 2.3, and 2.4 serve to elaborate on the psychology of identity development for the "diverse and different other," making the psychology of oppression, liberation, and identity development introduced in Chapter 1 by Wallace more complete. However, Figure 2.1 (pp. 88-89) goes a step further in integrating several strands of theory to forge a new approach to identity development theory for "diverse and different others."

The first column in Figure 2.1 shows the seven steps of dialogue in the psychology of oppression, liberation, and identity development (moving from the bottom [Step 1] up to the top [Step 7]) for fostering the upward evolution of personal and cultural dialectics in a new paradigm that replaces the old culture of violence and oppression. This dialogue is based on the use of empathic mirroring and the elements of motivational interviewing, which include the use of empathy, reflective listening, creation of cognitive dissonance, and creation of new cognitions (reciprocal recognition, nonhierarchical authority, and free-flowing dialogue). These new cognitions have corresponding new affects (acceptance, respect) and lead to the production of new behavior that is free from overt and covert violence.

(Text continues on p. 87)

Table 2.3   New Cognitions and Identity Development for Actor A in a
             New Cultural Paradigm

Actor A Thinks	Actor B Thinks
1. $A \Leftrightarrow B$ (reciprocal recognition)	1. $A \Leftrightarrow B$
2. $A = B$ (nonhierarchical equality)	2. $A = B$
3. $A \approx B$ (free-flowing dialogue)	3. $A \approx B$

Actor A integrates the internal B and creates a new self (CNS), overcoming narcissism, internalized inferiority, and a false self:

$$A + (B) = CNS \text{ symbolizes new identity attained}$$

Actor A thinks the following:

1. Through the practice of reciprocal recognition, I listen to "different others," interact with them, and recognize who they are, entering their worldview. I get to know them and accept and respect who and what they are. I move beyond tolerance so that, even if I disagree with their ways, I respect them and support their right to be without the experience of oppression. I will help ensure their access to opportunity and the experience of social justice.

2. Through the practice of nonhierarchical equality, I do not feel superior to "different others," nor do I view them as inferior. In all interactions, a feeling of equality as human beings should prevail, even as access, opportunities, and accommodations may need to be *tailored* in organizations and society to meet the needs of all.

3. Through the practice of a free-flowing dialogue among equals, there are no longer patterns whereby those with white privilege dominate conversations and talk down to others as though they are inferior. Free-flowing dialogue among equals means that spaces are created in which those who are perceived and treated as equal raise their voices to be heard and are listened to, and all are able to respond and participate in the dialogue. Such dialogue allows for learning about others and entering their worldview, and it provides a basis for an informed reciprocal recognition of each other. By communicating with others in a free-flowing dialogue, I also continually speak up to make sure I experience social justice and that there is change in the professions, in organizations, and in society as whole. I use dialogue to continually raise my voice and forge social justice to end the oppression of all of humanity. This allows me to be an advocate for all who have been oppressed or may ever suffer oppression.

New cognitions and corresponding affects of acceptance and respect lead to behaviors of civil dialogue and peaceful coexistence under the new paradigm. Dialogue, social action, and social justice movements permit healing the damaged identity on individual and collective levels. Social action and social justice movements create freedom from violence and oppression for all community members.

Table 2.4   New Cognitions and Identity Development for Actor B in a
New Cultural Paradigm

Actor A Thinks	Actor B Thinks
1. $A \Leftrightarrow B$ (reciprocal recognition)	1. $A \Leftrightarrow B$
2. $A = B$ (nonhierarchical equality)	2. $A = B$
3. $A \approx B$ (free-flowing dialogue)	3. $A \approx B$

Actor B integrates the internal A, overcomes internalization of the
oppressor, becomes a survivor of oppression, and creates a new self (CNS):

$$B + (A) = \text{CNS symbolizes new identity attained}$$

Actor B thinks the following:

1. Through the practice of reciprocal recognition, I no longer feel invisible, invalidated, or slighted. I feel validated and respected for who
   and what I am. I am able to accept and love myself, having had the
   beauty of who I am reflected back or mirrored to me. I feel that my
   worldview and experience is valid, real, and worthy of appreciation.
   I am coming to know that there are others who may be different
   from me who can see me for myself and reflect myself and my
   "differences" back to me in an unbiased, nonhateful, nonjudgmental
   manner. I feel more empowered to be who I am and to go on to
   self-determine how I want to live.
2. Through the practice of nonhierarchical equality, I am no longer
   made to feel inferior to others, nor do I feel inferior. I feel competent,
   worthy, and able to engage in self-determination and the creation of
   my own reality, including my preferences for living, thinking,
   behaving, and feeling. Feeling equal to others, as a human being,
   I may nonetheless demand that which will ensure social justice and
   effectively end my former state of oppression by those who
   presumed themselves to be superior to me.
3. Through the practice of free-flowing dialogue, I am listened to,
   actually heard, and respected for possessing my own, perhaps
   unique, worldview. I am able to communicate my needs, preferences,
   and that which I feel is needed to ensure my personal experience of
   social justice and to effectively end the negative impact of others
   who have or may still attempt to oppress me. By communicating
   with others in a free-flowing dialogue, I also continually speak up to
   make sure I experience social justice and that there is change in the
   professions, in organizations, and in society as whole. I use dialogue
   to continually raise my voice and forge social justice to end the
   oppression of all of humanity. This allows me to be an advocate for
   all who have been oppressed or may ever suffer oppression.

New cognitions and corresponding affects of self-acceptance and
self-respect, as well as validation through the mirroring of others, lead to

behaviors of civil dialogue and peaceful coexistence under the new paradigm. Dialogue, social action, and social justice movements permit healing damaged identity on individual and collective levels. Social action and social justice movements create freedom from violence and oppression for all community members.

This serves to effectively create a brief intervention that moves both former oppressors and the oppressed toward an expansion in consciousness and an ability to create reality through social action and social justice movements. To the extent that success is attained through social action and social justice movements and a new reality is created as the prevailing social context, then all may celebrate liberation from oppression. However, this application of empathic mirroring and motivational interviewing also serves to move people through stages of change for identity statuses.

Thus, the second column in Figure 2.1 shows the stages of change in affects, behavior, and cognitions that are central to any process of identity development for "diverse and different others." Starting at the bottom, the techniques of empathic mirroring and motivational interviewing allow people to move through the stages of change—precontemplation, contemplation, determination, action, and maintenance—including the possibility for some to experience a relapse stage. If there is a relapse, the use of empathic mirroring and motivational interviewing may stimulate movement yet again through the stages of change, helping people to take action on manifesting and then maintaining a healthy identity status or creating a new self. As suggested, the core aspects of creating a new identity or new self involve a process of changing affects, behaviors, and cognitions at each progressive, sequential stage of change. It should be noted that the maintenance stage reflects increasingly refined affective, behavioral, and cognitive coping skills. Once one is able to create reality, these refined skills are consistent with the self-actualization and realization of one's highest potential. Some spiritual schools of thought would equate this with being a co-creator with the divine because one is assisting in bringing about world conditions aligned with a divine will and loving vision for humanity, creating and sustaining a new Golden Age. As a result of this kind of co-creation with the divine, one attains the highest states of consciousness, a state of divinity, and is able to practice altruism by

Psychology of Oppression, Liberation, and Identity Development	*Stages of Change in Affects, Behavior, and Cognitions*	*Identity Development for All "Diverse and Different Others"*
Sustain freedom via reciprocal recognition, nonhierarchical equality, and a free-flowing dialogue.	Motivational interviewing and empathic mirroring stimulate movement after any relapse or sustain growth.	Identity serves humanity and guides social justice work, ending global violence and oppression.
↑	↑	↑
7. Celebrate liberation.	Highest states of consciousness, divinity, and altruism attained.	Identity is "at one" with one's divine plan.
↑	↑	↑
6. Create reality.	Instead of or including relapse, movement toward full potential, self-actualization, and self-determination as a co-creator with the divine.	New identity, worldview guide creation of reality.
↑	↑	↑
5. Expand consciousness.	Maintenance or substantial time spent actively engaged in rehearsal of new affects, behavior, and cognitions with refinement of repertoire from 7 months to several years, establishing lifetime change.	An evolving identity gains strength and internal value as a new worldview.
↑	↑	↑

4. Produce new behavior using inner and outer dialogue to refine it.

Action or making changes in affects, behavior, and/or cognitions, practicing and learning for 3 to 6 months.

One actively addresses identity issues.

↑   ↑   ↑

3. Produce new cognitions (1. $A \Leftrightarrow B$; 2. $A = B$; 3. $A \approx B$).

Determination or some recognition of need to change affects, behavior, and/or cognitions.

Decision made; societal view of one's identity does not work.

↑   ↑   ↑

2. Reflect perception of contradictions; create cognitive dissonance.

Contemplation or some thoughts about making a change in affects, behavior, and/or cognitions.

Societal view of identity is questioned.

↑   ↑   ↑

1. Listen actively; attune to affects, hearing another to speech, and empathic mirroring.

Precontemplation or not thinking about making a change in affects, behavior, and/or cognitions.

Identity is a societal view of one's self.

↑   ↑   ↑

Through dialogue, any two actors, A and B, foster the (upward ⇑) evolution of personal and cultural dialectics in a new paradigm.

Through motivational interviewing and empathic mirroring, (⇑) movement occurs through stages of change, as individuals, professions, organizations, and society progress.

Through societal conditioning, the "different" suffer assaults to identity.

Figure 2.1   Integrating Theory for a New Approach to Identity Development

engaging in selfless acts that serve humanity and even allowing oneself to be used as an instrument by divine forces.

The third column in Figure 2.1 presents identity development for all "diverse and different others" who benefit from the seven steps of dialogue or the use of empathic mirroring and motivational interviewing as they move individuals through stages of change so that their affects, behaviors, and cognitions progressively change. Meanwhile, as a result of these elements, identity undergoes a systematic transformation, and movement occurs as follows:

1. Initially, there is the societal view of self (precontemplation).

2. The societal view of self is then questioned (contemplation).

3. A decision is made that the societal view of self does not work (determination).

4. One then actively addresses identity issues (action).

5. When this work on identity issues has been going on for more than 6 months, evidence of an evolving identity gaining strength and greater internal value may be observed, as individuals now present a new more mature worldview that is meaningful to them and guides their lives, giving them purpose and direction.

6. As months and years go by, the new identity and worldview guide the creation of reality.

7. The individual emerges with an identity that is consistent with his or her divine plan or what divine spiritual forces would want the individual to self-actualize, as he or she now functions in a reality where freedom from violence and oppression may be celebrated.

8. The identity of the individual has evolved to the point where it serves humanity, as he or she may be relied on to be used as instruments of spiritual forces and the divine to be effective in social justice work, ending all forms of global violence and oppression.

Conclusion

This chapter introduced the integration of multiple strands of theory and thought to create a short-term or brief intervention that can heal wounds to damaged identity from violence for the "diverse and different other." The theory integrated included (a) identity development theory for race, sexual orientation, and disability; (b) the psychology of oppression, liberation, and identity development; (c) stages of change theory; and (d) motivational interviewing and empathic mirroring. The result of this integration is a brief intervention that holds promise for healing wounds to identity due to racism, homophobia, heterosexism, and violence perpetrated against people with a disability, as well as a global community of "diverse and different" others. It is hoped that the final product will serve as a sufficiently comprehensive guiding theory of identity development for the varied population of the "diverse and different" that effectively informs practice. This practice may be short-term therapy or a brief intervention delivered by multiculturally competent psychologists, counselors, educators, peer-to-peer community counselors, or community outreach workers.

Dialogue, ideally incorporated into the repertoire of those psychologists, educators, and community members who read this book and as taught to others, emerges as a powerful tool. If one carefully adheres to the elements of empathic mirroring and motivational interviewing detailed in this chapter, as well as introduced in Chapter 1 by Wallace, then hope for humanity may reside in all of us. This means that the goals of changing our selves and our professions, organizations, societies, and global community are realistic and attainable.

Part II

Understanding and Dealing With Hate,
Hate Crimes, and Hate Violence

3

Understanding and Dealing With Spiritual Violence

Preaching, Testifying, and Gandhi's Satyagrapha *as Tools in the Queer Social Justice Movement*

KARLA FLESHMAN

I t must be understood that "diverse and different others" are spiritual beings, and many have had their spirits damaged. This damage has even come from hate-filled messages delivered from ministers, pulpits, and religious institutions. Often, these messages have also been delivered and/or reinforced by parents, elders, community members, politicians, members of the media, and peers. This chapter classifies these messages as spiritual violence, providing a definition of this concept. The chapter makes an important contribution to this edited volume, described as a handbook for psychologists and educators. For, on a near daily basis, psychologists and educators encounter youth in the community and school setting at risk for substance abuse, dropout, running away, and suicide because of an emergent gay, lesbian, bisexual, or transgender (G/L/B/T) identity. Thus, it is important that the audience of readers understands the nature of the spiritual violence—as a frequent contributor to the manifestation of painful and destructive behaviors among gay, lesbian, bisexual, and transgender youth. Professionals similarly need to bring the same understanding to interactions with adults who have suffered spiritual violence across their lifetimes, given their sexual orientation identity.

Beyond acquiring understanding, ways of dealing with spiritual violence must also be discussed, especially as educators, psychologists, policymakers, ministers, and varied community members may need to become social activists who are able to confront, challenge, and transform the oppression and spiritual violence that daily assaults G/L/B/T youth and adults. Indeed, social activists for bringing about social justice for the queer community must recognize that, just as an era for bringing about racial equality predominated in the second half of the past century, this century will bring G/L/B/T equality through a queer social justice movement.

As a call for educators, psychologists, policymakers, ministers, and community members to begin to actively promote such equality and social justice for the queer community, this chapter will offer the following: (a) an approach to understanding and dealing with spiritual violence that is based on the use of preaching, testifying, and Mahatma K. Gandhi's *satyagrapha* (principles of nonviolence) as tools for use in a queer social justice movement; (b) a powerful story that serves as classic Christian testifying about a historic day in the queer social justice movement when those who engage in spiritual violence were confronted, using Gandhi's *satyagrapha*; and (c) the text of an actual sermon I delivered to a G/L/B/T congregation that served to heal their wounds, promote understanding of spiritual violence, and offer a prescription for dealing with that violence. Discussion of these three topics will form the three main sections of this chapter.

Understanding and Dealing
With Spiritual Violence

The approach to understanding and dealing with spiritual violence presented in this first section of the chapter begins with a definition of spiritual violence, as well as spiritual abuse. Moreover, the reader is assisted in entering the worldview and daily experience of G/L/B/T youth and adults, fostering understanding of that which goes beyond common name-calling, verbal abuse, and taunting, given the nature of spiritual violence. In terms of how to deal with spiritual violence,

I offer and discuss an approach that I have taken that uses preaching as a defense against violence. I explain how preaching as an act of resistance can inspire others to take action against oppression and evil. In addition, storytelling—or testifying, as it is called in the Christian tradition—is discussed as a tool for dealing with violence. Also, Gandhi's *satyagrapha* is described as an important tool in any viable nonviolent social justice movement, such as that needed for the queer community. Through discussion of these tools, it is hoped that a viable approach to understanding and dealing with spiritual violence emerges from this first section of the chapter.

Spiritual Violence and Spiritual Abuse

Spiritual violence occurs when any word spoken or deed committed against another wounds the spiritual psyche of that person, especially when the intentions of the abuser are to attack an aspect of the one being abused that is unchangeable (i.e., sexual orientation, race/ethnicity, or physical ability). If one understands name-calling as verbal abuse and hitting as physical abuse, then spiritual abuse occurs when the acts of name-calling and hitting are erroneously interpreted and conducted under the auspice of God's approval.

Spiritual violence is the worst kind of violence. Spiritual violence takes place in many diverse communities within and beyond the gay, lesbian, bisexual, and transgendered community. Unfortunately, spiritual violence is not a new phenomenon. As children, all of us learned of the power of words to hurt, even as the will and word of God may not have been evoked as sources of approval for that verbal abuse. When I was a child, it was not uncommon to hear on the playground, "Sticks and stones may break my bones, but names will never hurt me." In reality, sticks and stones often hurt less than the name-calling, and physical wounds tend to heal at a much faster pace than bruised feelings, battered spirits, and damaged identities. This is especially true when the words used to abuse drill into the very core of one's being. And when the voices that hurl the words of hurt come from the very ones who are supposed to love unconditionally, the damage may become unbearable to a fragile, developing spirit. Thus, it is no surprise that adolescent G/L/B/T often resort to suicide, especially when the expectation of unconditional parental love is replaced with the harsh reality of condemnation of their emergent homosexual orientation. Words are the worst kind of sticks and stones because they can and often do penetrate to the heart and break the spirit of a child (of God). This type of violence is spiritual violence.

Although many of us from varied backgrounds may recall incidents that led to the common defensive refrain of "Sticks and stones may break my bones, but names will never hurt me," we may need a more graphic image to understand what happens to a gay child or adolescent being victimized by spiritual violence and spiritual abuse. Picture yourself as the one being bullied by a kid who acts as if you are nothing more than scum on a shoe. The bully is calling you names as two cronies stand on either side laughing at you. Just then the bully pokes a finger to your chest and says, "I am going to beat you up, you little *sissy!*" What do you do? Do you beg for mercy? Or do you attempt to run? Do you try to reason or just accept the approaching blows, wondering if somehow you deserve to be beaten?

What if you are well past adolescence when you find yourself facing a bully of a different kind? This one does not necessarily want to physically punch you but rather chooses to use a pulpit to pronounce judgment and damnation on your very soul. Words that wound the soul are the minister's weapon of choice to belittle and berate you while compelling others, including your own parents, into believing that God does not love you. All of a sudden, being seen as scum on a shoe seems a better option because at least scum may have an acceptable purpose and existence. After all, what "good" purpose does a self-avowed, practicing homosexual have to offer society anyway? At least that is what some people think. Especially given the messages of hate delivered regularly on Sunday mornings from pulpits around the United States.

Every day, queer people face bullies and a barrage of hate-filled speech from politicians and preachers alike. As a direct result, many have left the church thinking and believing that God turned away from them the moment they declared their sexual orientation. What should gay, lesbian, bisexual, and transgendered youth and adults do in the face of real and perceived rejection and violence? Do they beg for mercy? Or run away? Do they try to reason with their oppressors or just accept the abuse?

Preaching as Defense and Resistance Against Violence

Where does help come from for queer men and women? Where is the queer social justice movement that offers an alternative chorus of activist voices, serving to counter the spiritual violence done against gay, lesbian, bisexual, and transgendered youth and adults? I can only speak for myself when I say that my help comes from the Lord. I have also served as part of a delegation that experienced one of the most historic days of the queer social justice movement in recent history, as I will discuss in the second section of this chapter. I choose to defend myself against all acts of violence with a life of faith, my *own* voice, and the Word of God. I am a preacher. I choose to counter church-sanctioned violence by accessing the very avenue of support that many preachers proclaim that I have no right to as a Christian lesbian. I choose to turn to God for guidance and the Bible for inspiration as I seek to understand why a society is torn apart over whether or not God loves queer people for how God created them. I preach in the hope that other queer folks may come to discover that hate does not have the last word. Preaching, for me, has become my avenue of resistance against bullies and hate-mongers.

Christine Smith (1992), in her book, *Preaching as Weeping, Confession, and Resistance,* speaks about the very act of preaching as a most powerful way to address the "radical evil that can dominate our everyday reality" (p. 4). Radical evil is another name for oppression. Oppression takes place on both the micro and macro level of society. From the playground bully to systems of violence, persons are denied their inalienable rights to the pursuit of life, liberty, and happiness because of their age, race/ethnicity, gender, socio-economic status, religion, physical ability, or sexual orientation.

In the face of such oppression, preaching can become a conduit of change and an avenue of radical transformation. As one who is to bring into tension the ways of the world and the ways of God, the preacher takes the words and deeds of the community and holds them up to the Word of God so that the people of God may face both judgment and grace. The preacher is to resist the temptations of popular culture and a tradition of oppression by turning to the Spirit of God for inspiration and instruction. Smith (1992) offers the following in this regard:

> To affirm preaching as resistance is to suggest that preaching is not only about the hearing and receiving of good news, but that it is an act that must enable and sustain persons to be good news in the larger world. To affirm preaching as resistance is to encourage the faithful community to be about God's redemptive activity in

> the world in concrete, particular ways . . . to suggest that preaching
> is resistance is to invite members of the religious communities to
> oppose the occupying power of evil in our world and to place their
> lives in the stream of those who are working for change. (p. 6)

The result of preaching serving as resistance, a conduit for change, and an avenue for radical transformation may be that a community of listeners emerges mobilized for action. Preaching may inspire potential social activists who can work for social justice for queers, as well as for all those oppressed by radical evil. Thus, preaching is one way to combat evil and violence, especially if preaching has been misused as a tool to transmit evil and violence. The preacher is supposed to be guided by the Spirit of God as she or he delves into the Word of God, seeking inspiration and insight into today's world. Truth be told, preaching has the potential to be a highly subjective exercise with respect to what the *preacher* wants to say rather than what *God* is calling her or him to say to the congregation. To counter this potential harm, standards of accountability are put into place. Some, but not all preachers, choose their standard to be the life ministry and message of Jesus Christ. Other standards are to be found in contemporary spiritual leaders such as Martin Luther King Jr. and Mahatma K. Gandhi.

This standard of following who Jesus is, was, and will be again requires that one take seriously the question, "What would Jesus do?" What would this son—who was created out of wedlock, was birthed into a religious/cultural minority community, and came out of a rural peasant family and an oppressed nation-state—do and say to an outsider today? The answer may be found in the Gospels, *the good news.* Jesus of Nazareth never turned people away or treated them as if they were anything but precious in God's sight (see Meeks, 1989). Whether they were female (Luke 10:38ff) or of a different race or ethnicity (Mark 7:26ff), physical ability (Matthew 8:1ff), religion (John 4:7ff), age (Mark 10:13ff), or sexual orientation (Matthew 8:5ff), Jesus' message was simple: "Love God and neighbor as yourself with your entire mind, body, and spirit" (Luke 10:25ff). This is the standard that preachers are to follow today. Love should guide preaching. Instead, hate-filled messages often proliferate from pulpits. Imagine a preacher proclaiming, "God hates fags!"

Hate-filled rhetoric is unbecoming for people who call themselves Christian, especially if they are preaching from any pulpit. Oppressive words and deeds are unbecoming and unacceptable by anyone toward anyone, especially from Christians who profess to follow the teaching of Jesus Christ. When radical evil and oppressive realities try to cause people to submit to slavery, then the ones who are called to be a voice in the wilderness, with God leading the people to freedom, need to preach messages that resonate with the life ministry of Jesus Christ.

Storytelling as Testifying About a Historic Dialogue

Storytelling within the context of the Christian community is often referred to as *testifying*. The testimony that follows in the second section of this chapter is about a historic dialogue that took place October 23, 1999, in Lynchburg, Virginia. This dialogue was between those who engaged in spiritual violence and a delegation that sought to bring an end to that practice of spiritual violence, especially as it had been regularly targeted against gay, lesbian, bisexual, and transgendered persons.

My story and the testimony it provides also come in the form of a sermon that I preached on October 31, 1999, at the Metropolitan Community Church of Philadelphia—a Christian church that has a special ministry to the gay, lesbian, bisexual, and transgendered community of Philadelphia, Pennsylvania. This sermon appears as the third section of this chapter, illustrating the power of testifying and how preaching can serve as an act of defense and resistance against violence. This illustrative sermon also represents my voice in the wilderness, as God leads people to freedom. At the same time, a story is told, as I sought to describe what happened in Lynchburg, Virginia, at the Thomas Road Baptist Church where Reverend Jerry Falwell is senior pastor. Through testifying, sacred space for healing and transformation becomes possible for those who gather to praise God. Thus, testifying as storytelling about a historic dialogue must be appreciated as a viable way to deal with spiritual violence. In addition to preaching, testifying must be recognized as an important tool in the queer social justice movement, given the need to identify ways to deal with spiritual violence.

Gandhi's Teaching of *Satyagrapha*: The Soulforce Mission

Gandhi's *satyagrapha* must also be valued as a tool in the queer social justice movement. But what is *satyagrapha*? And what is Soulforce?

> Soulforce is named for Gandhi's teaching of *satyagrapha*, Gandhi's term for "truth force" or "soulforce," which he defined as a plan of action that developed inner lives while working to transform society. These soulforce principles guide many nonviolent justice movements, including Martin Luther King Jr.'s fight for racial equality. ("Soulforce, Inc. Organization Backgrounder," 1999; see also Branch, 1988; Merton, 1964)

Persons who follow the principles of Soulforce believe that violence begets violence. Thus, the only way to stop violence is to refuse to participate in the violence of fist, tongue, or heart. The only way to promote healing and reconciliation is through nonviolent, passive resistance by speaking the Truth in love through word and deed. My story of a historic day in the queer social justice movement, to follow in the next section of this chapter, reflects utilization of *satyagrapha* as an important tool in this movement. As we shall see, the group of social activists who traveled to Lynchburg, Virginia, that historic day constituted participants in "The Soulforce Journey." This journey was about speaking the Truth in love to Rev. Falwell and those who were watching television, listening to the radio, and reading the newspapers about this historic weekend. Consistent with the *satyagrapha* principles that are needed to guide any effective nonviolent social justice movement, the mission of Soulforce during the weekend in Lynchburg was as follows:

1. To help end the suffering of God's lesbian, gay, bisexual, and transgendered children

2. To help change the minds and hearts of religious leaders whose anti-homosexual campaigns lead (directly and indirectly) to that suffering

3. To be guided in our every action by SOULFORCE—the principles of relentless nonviolent resistance as lived and taught by M. K. Gandhi and Martin Luther King Jr.

4. And in the process of bringing hope and healing to our society find redirection and renewal of our minds and spirits. ("Soulforce, Inc. Organization Backgrounder," 1999)

As we shall see through my story of that historic day, the tool of *satyagrapha* is a powerful one, indeed. It provided important direction to the Soulforce delegation that traveled to Lynchburg, Virginia.

My Story: The Anti-Violence Summit in Lynchburg, Virginia

Given my analysis of the power of storytelling, testifying, and the practice of *satyagrapha* as important tools in the queer social justice movement, I offer in this section of the chapter my story of how events unfolded on one historic day in that movement. Spiritual violence certainly existed prior to October 23, 1999. However, for those of us present that day in Lynchburg, Virginia, at the Thomas Road Baptist Church for the "Anti-Violence Summit" between the Reverend Mel White and the Reverend Jerry Falwell and their respective 200 hundred delegates each, the phrase *spiritual violence* became a part of the vocabulary of the Soulforce delegation. On that weekend, an ecumenical network of volunteers committed to teaching and applying the Soulforce principles of nonviolence on behalf of sexual minorities was led by Rev. Mel White. The intent of Rev. Mel White and the Soulforce delegation was to meet Rev. Falwell to say the following: "Your often false and inflammatory rhetoric against gay, lesbian, bisexual, and transgendered (G/L/B/T) persons is causing irrefutable harm to the body, mind, and spirit of God's beloved children." We came to say, "Enough is enough" through the action of nonviolent resistance. Yet, as a delegation composed of what might be called social activists for change, propelling the queer social justice movement, we were guided by spiritual principles of nonviolence that have long guided the actions of others like us.

Relationship Rebuilding Through Dialogue

This historic meeting between Rev. White and Rev. Falwell culminated after years of relationship rebuilding between the two pastors. Rev. White is a Christian minister, filmmaker, and author of several books, including his personal story titled *Stranger at the Gate: To Be Gay and Christian in America,* published in 1994. Rev. White was once also a ghostwriter to several evangelical Christians, including Billy Graham (*Approaching Hoofbeats*), Pat Robertson (*America's Date With Destiny*), and Jerry Falwell (*If I Should Die Before I Wake* and *Strength for the Journey*). When Rev. White finally accepted himself as a gay man, after years of prayer, psychotherapy, exorcism, and electric shock, his former evangelical Christian friends disappeared from his side ("Soulforce, Inc. Organization Backgrounder," 1999).

This act of abandonment and the antigay rhetoric that followed could be called spiritual violence. Imagine if your friends turned away from you after you dared to be honest about how God created you as a sexual and spiritual being. It happens every day to countless numbers of men, women, and children.

The words of violence flung at God's children are harmful and hateful no matter how loving the original intent. This is true and valid evidence of radical evil, at least from the perspective of Rev. White and those of us who traveled to Lynchburg to meet with Rev. Falwell. Rev. Falwell is the founder and chancellor of Liberty University, senior pastor of the Thomas Road Baptist Church, and the founder of the now-defunct Moral Majority. He is also known for his very outspoken and long-held view of condemnation against G/L/B/T persons. In the past, he has been known to say,

> These perverted homosexuals who absolutely hate everything that you and I and most decent, God-fearing citizens stand for . . . these deviants seek no less than total control and influence in society, politics, our schools and in our exercise of free speech and religious freedom. ("A Brief Sample of Jerry Falwell's Toxic Rhetoric," 1999)

No matter how loving the intent, the former words of Rev. Falwell and others who speak such violence can and often sting the soul like a poisonous viper causing the beating heart to arrest, whither, and die. The weekend between Rev. White, Rev. Falwell, and the 400 hundred delegates was an opportunity for those of us who were part of Rev. White's Soulforce delegation to engage in dialogue, saying to Rev. Falwell and his people, "There has to be another way for you to be faithful to your Christian belief without disrespecting and doing harm to our respective faith traditions, spiritual beings, sexual selves, and the lives of our friends and families." During this weekend, many of us gathered and found our actions of loving resistance toward those who once perpetrated violence against us as a time of cathartic healing. For one of the best ways to defeat the effects of spiritual violence is to face the abuser within the context of a supportive nurturing and loving community. Even God knows that it is not good for a person to be alone. By gathering together to reclaim our individual and collective self-worth as a community of gay, lesbian, bisexual, transgendered, and straight allies, we were able to shake the shackles of spiritual violence. By gathering together to speak out against acts of violence, we were able to strengthen our own spirits while simultaneously bringing attention to the world that enough is enough.

The sermon that follows is a culmination of the emotions, insight, and wisdom I gained through life experiences; from the exchange that took place among the Soulforce delegation; and from dialogue among those who affirm G/L/B/T persons as God's beloved children and those who do not. May you find the sermon that follows in the next section to be a source of spiritual renewal to your mind, body, and spirit, even as it illustrates how the tools of preaching, testifying, and practicing *satyagrapha* as deployed in Lynchburg, Virginia, are key elements of the queer social justice movement.

My Philadelphia Sermon

"WE CAME BEARING GIFTS": MATTHEW 5:43-44; 22:34-40

I AM WHO I AM, I AM WHAT I AM
IT DOESN'T MATTER HOW, IT DOESN'T MATTER WHY
THERE'S NO ONE TO BLAME
THE TRUTH NOW IS CLEAR, I STAND WITHOUT FEAR
YOU CAN KNOW MY NAME
FOR I AM NOT ASHAMED.

—Night and North (1998) (Used with permission by V. Night and D. K. North.)

We came to Lynchburg without shame—gay, transgendered, lesbian, bisexual, and straight allies came to meet Rev. Falwell and his people with our heads held high knowing no shame! We came bearing gifts—T-shirts, ceramic angels, Hawaiian leis, and oil lamps—like the wise people who came to the baby Jesus. We came to share our many cultures and our diverse lives with those whom we once called enemy.

. . . And each of us in the delegation came with the greatest gift that we had to offer: the gift of ourselves—our lives, our love—to share with persons we hoped to call friends.

Some refused to meet with us or eat with us. A few met us with bridled hostility, and some met us with fear and trembling in their eyes. However, many more still met us with the peace of Christ, which surpasses all understanding and all differences. For, Jesus says, "Love your enemies and pray for those who persecute you" (Matthew 5:44) (Meeks, 1989). Yes, many of the members of Thomas Road Baptist Church and Liberty University once saw us as enemies as we once saw them as the enemy. *Some* may still see transgendered, bisexual, lesbian, and gay men as enemies, but so many more were changed by this rag-tag group of visitors who were composed of many faith traditions and all sexual orientations. Dare I say with hope that some enemies became friends on both sides in Lynchburg?

And what made it possible for those of us who traveled to Lynchburg, VA, to meet with our "enemies"? What made it possible for them to meet with us? Well, I can only speak for myself, and my reason is as simple and as complex as the Greatest Commandments. When asked, "Teacher, which commandment in the law is the greatest?" Jesus responded, "'You shall love the Lord your God with all of your heart, and with all your soul, and with all your mind.' This is the greatest and first commandment. And a second is like it: 'You shall love your neighbor as yourself.' On these two commandments hang all the law and the prophets" (Matthew 22:36-40) (Meeks, 1989). It is that simple and that complex.

So you see I went to Lynchburg loving God. I went loving myself. I went showing love to my Fundamentalist, Baptist neighbors. Love is simple, but Love is also complex and hard—maybe even too hard sometimes.

How many of us have found it hard at one time or another to love our neighbor, love ourselves, or even to love God with all of our heart, our soul, and our mind? How many have found it especially hard when we are told time and again that God doesn't love us? When we are told that God does not love us because we are not straight enough, not White enough, Black enough, male enough, not thin enough, not rich enough, able-bodied enough, or even Christian enough? How many of us were told that we are unworthy sinners going to hell? How many of us at one time or another have seen God as the Enemy and the One to fear because of *these* messages?

And just who told us that God didn't love our *wicked* ways? (Whatever that meant.) Who told us this unkind stuff anyway? Well, they were our neighbors, our families, and our churches. And they preached a message in which we were to fear God and repent. They perhaps spoke out of love, but maybe their brand of love wasn't the right kind because fear—perfect fear (of God)—casts out love, my friends. They shared *their* understanding of God and the Bible out of love, *but* they didn't understand how you or I could have a different understanding or experience with God and God's love. Our neighbors, families, and churches told us through "good" intentioned words and deeds that they loved us, but not all good intentions are truly good or loving. If you hear enough "conditional" love statements about God long enough, you may actually start believing the stuff, especially if there is no person or church present to counter those messages with a truth-filled message about the God of Love.

Too many people who went to Lynchburg and too many people who have graced this church have already had experiences where they sought the bread of love and received instead a stone of hurt. The intentions of our neighbors, families, and churches were probably—mostly—meant to be good at least from their perspective, but that didn't mean it wasn't harmful to our soul, mind, or body. I have witnessed good-intentioned folks like the members of Thomas Road Baptist Church blast their messages into a person's very soul, and as I gazed into the eyes of that child of God I saw a deep pain and a numbing fear. Have you ever seen that haunting look? I have witnessed the hurt of rejection screaming from every pore of a person who carries their body as if it has been dejected by the very One who created it. Haven't you seen this haunting hurting image? Perhaps you have seen such a person and, perhaps, in your very own mirror? I say that some things are simply not kind or truthful and shouldn't ever be said. And some intentions, no matter how good, are not loving and not of God!

Who here knows what I am talking about? Who here has had this experience? What words or deeds have caused your body to ache? Caused your soul to cry out in pain? Caused you to bow your head in shame? What has been done unto you that is not of God? I call that stuff the lack of true love! In Lynchburg, we named this type of good-intentioned ill will: *spiritual violence*. When cliches such as "love the sinner, hate the sin" are said to you, it is spiritual violence. When words are shouted at you such as "faggot," "fatso," and "freak," it is spiritual violence. When someone shouts at you, "Turn from your sinful ways or the fires of hell will consume you," you are experiencing spiritual violence. Why? Because they are wrong! God doesn't make any junk and God doesn't throw anyone away! When someone says, "You must believe in God the way I understand God," "You must call God what I call God," "You must worship God the way I worship God"—that, my friends, is spiritual violence.

For no one person or one church has the cornerstone on how to worship or how to know God. No one person or church has the elite privilege to sit at God's right hand. And, most importantly, no one person or one church dictates who God loves for how God created them—not Rev. Jerry Falwell, not Thomas Road Baptist Church, not even Rev. Mel White, myself, or the Metropolitan Community Church. No one dictates your worth and your place in this God's great creation.

***

You know, I find it almost too fitting that one year ago, I found myself wrestling with the very stuff that I am preaching about today: God, the Greatest Commandments, and the call to love one's enemies. I found myself in the midst of a controversy between people who were trying to dictate not only what I was to believe but what others were to believe about me and queer people in general. One year ago, I was being persecuted for being an out Christian lesbian who dared to follow the guidance of the Holy Spirit and preach a sermon at my local seminary.[1] I preached a sermon that called on my friends, neighbors, and the church to stop the violence against gay, lesbian, bisexual, and transgendered people, particularly against the most vulnerable: queer youth. And, subsequently, I received a backlash for my bold proclamations that God loves gay kids and that the church needed to stop its sanctioned spiritual violence against the queer community. I guess I shouldn't have been surprised by the response and the struggle that ensued.

Nonetheless, in the midst of it all, I found loving my enemy—my neighbor—almost impossible. I found myself wrestling with who was right and who was wrong, as I struggled to shake off the shackles of spiritual violence. I did not want to like my enemy, let alone love my enemy. And, so, as I sat by a mountain stream in the North Georgia mountains, praying—or rather, yelling to God—I found myself in need of being honest with how I felt about the folks who were causing me pain. I found that I needed to be honest with myself and God. As I was yelling out my pain to God, I found myself being honest with God by saying, "I want to hate, but God you call me to a higher way! You call me to love them!"

Yes, one year ago, I almost turned to hate. I could taste the bile of hate preparing itself to cover my heart in bitterness and rage as I almost started down a path that would hurt only my soul. But instead of hating, I cried out to my God in anger and pain. And God heard my prayer. One year ago, as I was saying the Lord's prayer and as I got to the words "forgive us our sins as we forgive those who sin against us," I felt myself letting go of the ill will that I harbored in my soul. I felt the Holy, Healing Spirit of God wash over me and fill me with love again—love for God, for myself, and, yes, love for, even and especially, my enemy.

Does this act of forgiveness make me noble? No, because it was the right thing to do. It was a justice thing. And it was an act of healing. It was of my desire to forgive, but it was God who helped me break free. As my heart broke free from bitterness, anguish, depression, I was freed up for love. Forgiving and letting go freed me up for love. Letting go of the hate that you harbor against another—even if the feeling stems from injustices incurred—is not only the right thing but the healthy thing to do because it cleanses your own soul and opens you up to God's love. Letting go of the hurt that you harbor against yourself leads you down a path of renewed love and revived life. And when you are feeling God's love, no words or deeds can bring you down. In fact, when you are filled with God's Healing Spirit, you may feel yourself compelled to seek out those who are still hurting even if it means going to places like Thomas Road Baptist Church, the street, or even in your own family! As an act of loving justice, you may find yourself helping the hurting ones find healing and true love. Love is simple when it is of God and from God.

Jesus didn't simply call us to love our enemies because we should or could but because we must for our own sake. Loving God with all we got while honoring the Divine, the Divine within ourselves, and the Divine in each of our neighbors is the healthiest thing we can do for our own mind, body, and soul. I realized a year ago that I needed God to help me heal, and I needed God to help me hope. I needed to feel God's love—true love—because perfect love casts out fear! I needed God-love then, I needed it in Lynchburg, and I need it here today and everyday. It is knowing that God loved me first, created me out of love, and calls me to love that I know no matter what is said to me, I need not be afraid. The next time someone shouts, "You are not straight enough," "You are not thin enough," "You are not rich enough," "You are not able-bodied enough," "You are not Christian enough," I know that I will be okay. For

I AM WHO I AM, I AM WHAT I AM
IT DOESN'T MATTER HOW, IT DOESN'T MATTER WHY
THERE'S NO ONE TO BLAME
THE TRUTH NOW IS CLEAR, I STAND WITHOUT FEAR
YOU CAN KNOW MY NAME
FOR I AM NOT ASHAMED.

—North and Night (1998)

I pray to God this day and every day that each of you may say the same. Amen.

Conclusion

May this testimony of God's power in the midst of a community of faith that sought to heal and build up relationships speak to your own mind, body, and soul. May you, the reader, find healing from spiritual violence. May you find yourself moved to become an instrument of love and truth to others who are as diverse as God's great and varied creation. For the task of ending spiritual violence will become truly manifest in powerful ways when a cacophony of voices from varied communities join together, in love and power, to say "enough is enough." Such are the key ingredients of any effective social justice movement.

Moreover, whether we are policymakers, psychologists, educators, ministers, congregates, or community members from varied religious traditions, it is important that we remember the power in following principles of love and forgiveness. For those principles are at the very heart of so many of our religious and spiritual traditions. Living out those principles may very well mean the difference between death and life.

The nonviolent practice of speaking truth in the midst of loving dialogue holds the promise for a greater tomorrow for the queer community. And so, for the many who found themselves touched by the historic events in Lynchburg, Virginia, a catalyst of revived hope once fostered in the dreams and visions of Martin Luther King Jr., Mahatma Gandhi, and Jesus of Nazareth has been reborn. May that hope combine with social action to sustain the queer social justice movement. I hope that this chapter has served as an effective call to readers to "oppose the occupying power of evil and to place their lives in the stream of those working for change" (Smith, 1992, p. 6).

Note

1. In the fall of 1998, I preached my senior sermon at Columbia Theological Seminary in Decatur, Georgia. I was the first out queer person of any kind accepted into the institution in 1996. I was also the first out lesbian to receive a financial scholarship. I thought I had become accepted within this seminary community. My senior sermon called the church into accountability to love and support the most vulnerable: gay, lesbian, bisexual, and transgendered youth. The sermon, and myself, was met with bridled hostility outside of the seminary community. This same hostility manifested itself in varied ways within a community that I had considered safe and loving. In the end, love prevailed. However, in the midst of it all, I felt spiritual violence.

4

Genderism, Transphobia, and Gender Bashing

A Framework for Interpreting Anti-Transgender Violence

DARRYL B. HILL

Hate or bias crimes victimize an entire class of people because of their membership in a minority group (Herek, 1989). One hate crime rarely examined is violence against transgendered people. *Transgender* is an identity that has emerged in the past three decades. It refers to people who refuse to live up to society's expectations for gender. It is best understood as a "community" identity used by a collective of people who have personal identities as cross-dressers or transvestites (those who enjoy occasional or recreational cross-gender presentations); transgenderists (those who live a substantial part of their lives cross-gender); pre-, post-, and nonoperative transsexuals (those who desire to permanently alter their secondary sexual characteristics so as to live the remainder of their lives cross-gender); and intersexuals (those who have "mixed" genetic, anatomical, or hormonal indications of sex).[1]

The history of violence against these gender outlaws dates back to at least the early 1900s (even possibly as far back as the beginning of Christianity) (see Feinberg, 1996), when "men-women" and "women-men" were attacked for their lifestyles (e.g., Katz, 1976). Attacks continue to this day. As the list of murdered transgendered people in Canada and the United States grows, activists document the ongoing persecution of transgendered people across the world (Nangeroni, 1996; Nangeroni & Ryan, 1998), and widespread antipathy to the transgender community is apparent.

Documenting Anti-Transgender Violence

Although research is just beginning, the emerging picture is that transgender people are subject to widespread discrimination, hatred, and violence. But for all the literature suggesting violence against the transgender community (e.g., Brown & Rounsely, 1996), there are very little data on the nature and extent of these experiences. The empirical evidence available suffers from the same problems as research on antigay violence: a lack of uniform reporting, nonrandom samples, and flaws in survey construction, data analysis, and reporting (Berrill, 1990; Herek, 1989; Herek & Berrill, 1990). Research on anti-transgender violence is especially weak because it lacks a conceptual framework from which to understand the hate directed toward the community.

Interpersonal Violence

Up to this point, the job of documenting anti-transgender violence has been mostly left to informal conference reports (e.g., Witten, Eyler, & Cole, 1997) and some exploratory nonrandom studies. For example, Lombardi, Wilchins, Priesing, and Malouf (2001) distributed a questionnaire at meetings and events in the transgender community and through the World Wide Web. They found that 27% of the 402 transgender respondents had experienced violence, more than half the sample had experienced harassment or verbal abuse, and 14% had experienced either attempted rape or rape. These violence rates correspond to other nonrandom surveys of transgendered people that report that about half of the respondents have been victims of criminal violence (e.g., Tully, 1992). Similarly, a recent qualitative study of transgenderists in the United States found that a "substantial minority of respondents had experienced intimidation, harassment, and violence in public places" (Gagné,

Tweksbury, & McGaughey, 1996, p. 505). It is difficult, however, to discern whether these people are attacked because they are seen as transgendered women or ordinary women. Weinberg, Shaver, and Williams (1999), in a comparative study of male, female, and transgender sex workers, found that female transgender sex workers may be at no more risk of beatings and robbery than sex workers who are women or men; in fact, women sex workers were far more likely to have been raped than either men or transgender women. This also raises a question as to whether transgender men experience as much discrimination and violence as transgender women. Furthermore, due to their nonrandom samples, these studies only establish that some members of the transgender community experience violence and harassment and not that the transgender community is being targeted in particular.

More subtle forms of discrimination are just beginning to be documented by grassroots action groups and human rights organizations. One instance is "It's Time, Illinois!" (1998), part of the national "It's Time" transgender rights organizations documenting acts of discrimination and hate crimes against transgendered people. In 1997 in Illinois, this organization reported several acts of discrimination involving employment, finding housing or public accommodations, and civil rights violations, along with assaults and two murders. In Canada, research is beginning to document an oppressive climate for transgendered people. The Coalition for Lesbian and Gay Rights in Ontario (1997) reported that health care and social services such as Ontario hospitals, youth and women's shelters, and alcohol and drug treatment programs treat some transgendered people with contempt, ridicule, and disdain.

As with other forms of violence against minorities, it is likely that transgendered people are underreporting the violence to police. As noted by researchers documenting antigay violence, a climate of hostility "discourages individuals from disclosing their homosexual orientation and from reporting bias crimes motivated by antigay prejudice" (Herek, 1989, p. 949). Transgender people may not report crimes because of a lack of trust in the police and fears of additional harassment if their transgenderness is made public. A good illustration of potential underreporting is Devor's (1997) recent analysis of the lives of female-to-male transsexuals across North America. Although a majority encountered positive reactions to their coming out, Devor was suspicious of her respondents, concluding that they "appeared to favor memories of their successes over more unpleasant ones," leading them to underreport; she added, "However, abuse and harassment were also part of their reality" (p. 445). Feinberg (1996), a transgender activist who has documented the history of oppression experienced by transgender people the world over, affirmed Devor's suspicions:

> We face discrimination and physical violence. We are denied the right to live and work with dignity and respect. It takes so much courage to live our lives that sometimes just leaving our homes in the morning and facing the world as who we really are is in itself an act of resistance. (p. xii)

Indeed, leaving home and facing the world—"coming out"—is where many transgender people encounter society's anti-transgender beliefs. Brown and Rounsely (1996) suggested that transgender children experience taunting, teasing, and bullying at school. Many transgender teens, because they are different, may be the object of cruel jokes and physical and verbal violence.

However, anecdotal reports of derision might be somewhat exaggerated. Gagné et al. (1996) found that only a quarter of their sample experienced negative reactions to the first coming out. The overall positive tone to their experiences may be because many came out to people suspected to be supportive of their transgenderism, such as closer relatives or long-term friends. Their most unpleasant experiences involved coworkers and bosses, who were more likely to react with harassment, demotion, or termination. Also, even though Devor (1997) was suspicious of underreporting, she observed generally positive coming-out stories. Although parents often reacted initially with bewilderment and fear, they were eventually able to come to terms with their sons' transsexualism, a position greatly appreciated by their children. Some of Devor's respondents had even felt that there had been an improvement in the relationship. Other family, friends, acquaintances, classmates, or coworkers were generally supportive. Those friends estranged by the coming-out process were "retroactively discounted" (Devor, 1997, p. 435) as friends in the first place. However, lesbian acquaintances and less close coworkers and classmates tended to react negatively, characterizing transsexuals as delusional, traitors, or immoral, reacting with violent assaults.

The coming-out experiences of transgendered people are similar to those of gays and lesbians, but there are differences. For one thing, a transgenderist may come out many times—first as a cross-dresser, later as a transsexual or transgenderist, and even perhaps as gay, lesbian, or bisexual. Moreover, once a transgendered person has transitioned, their transgenderness may be more invisible, making it even more difficult to come out. In these two aspects, coming out as transgender is quite similar to coming out as bisexual (Fox, 1996). A further difference is that coming out as transgendered usually involves permanent changes to one's body, name, or pronouns. These changes are often quite demanding for families and friends but very important to the coming-out transgendered person because gender is largely validated by others (Gagné et al., 1996). Thus, although requests to use the new name and gender pronouns are often met with some mistakes and resistance, use of these social identifiers by family and friends may be necessary for self-acceptance.

Institutionalized Violence

The problem of anti-transgender violence is made even more serious due to the fact that it occurs in a culture that denigrates and devalues transgender lives. Transgender identities are challenged by the modern bureaucratic state (for voting, property ownership, and name changes), law (i.e., marriage, segregated jails), patriarchal power, and Christianity (Feinberg, 1992, 1996; Raymond, 1994; Rothblatt, 1995). Institutionalized violence is obvious in psychological and psychiatric discourses on transgenderism. Transgender identities are seen by psychological and psychiatric professions as disorders that are scorned and subjected to treatment (e.g., American Psychiatric Association, 1994; Burke, 1996; Lothstein, 1983). Mental health professionals pathologize transgender identities because they do not conform to the dominant identity paradigm in contemporary psychology (Hill, 2000). Psychological theories of transgenderism reinforce the notion that there are distinct sexes and genders, ignore the empirical complexity of sex and gender in the transgender community, and imply that those who transgress these rules are "to be spoken of, thought of, and treated as objects (pathological, rare, anomalous) rather than as persons with moral standing and agency" (Parlee, 1996, p. 639). Even though psychological theories of sex and gender are strikingly different from our everyday theories

(Stanley & Wise, 1990) or "situated knowledges" (Haraway, 1991) regarding gender, especially evident in the transgender community (Parlee, 1996), psychological theories have gone unchallenged.

Scientific discourses tend toward reproducing the legitimacy of their own positions at the expense of transgendered persons. This form of violence against the transgender community, then, is institutionalized violence. It is a violence legitimated by the social institutions of psychology and psychiatry, perpetuating misinformation and myths about gender identity and threatening transgender subjectivities.

Understanding Anti-Transgender Violence

Very little effort has been devoted to developing a conceptual framework for anti-transgender hostility that is grounded in the lived experience of transgendered people. In the only published work on this topic so far, Onken (1998) presented a conceptual understanding of antigay violence that he defined as violence against gay, lesbian, bisexual, intersexual, and transgendered people. He explored antigay violence using Van Soest and Bryant's (1995) model of violence from three different levels (individual, institutional, and structural-cultural), dimensions (interpersonal, intrapersonal, and collective), and types (omission, repression, and alienation). Onken's conceptualization is important for drawing parallels between the experiences of gay, lesbian, bisexual, intersexual, and transgendered people. He noted that they are oppressed by heterosexism and stigma, as well as regulated by moral and medical systems of belief and gender oppression. However, his analysis is primarily based on lesbian and gay experience. With the goal of respecting differences between transgender and lesbian, gay, and bisexual experiences, this chapter focuses on concepts that may specifically conceptualize anti-transgender violence: genderism, transphobia, and gender bashing.

Genderism

Genderism is a concept obviously inspired by feminist discourse on sexism. Sexism, as it is generally understood, is the negative evaluation of people based on their sex. Sexism and its supporting ideology, patriarchy, are the set of beliefs that justifies the subordination of women. Under patriarchy, women are dominated mostly in subtle forms of antipathy but sometimes viciously.

The parallel concept of "genderism" is an ideology that perpetuates the negative evaluation of people who present nondichotomous genders.[2] It is the system of beliefs that reinforces a negative evaluation based on gender nonconformity or an incongruence between sex and gender. It is the cultural notion that gender is an important basis by which to judge people and that nonbinary genders are anomalies. As such, transgender people are subordinated to nontransgender people as less normal and worthy. Like sexism and heterosexism, genderism is pervasive in our society, sometimes operating in subtle ways such as ignorance or misinformation about the transgender community. The very fact that most people are largely ignorant about transgendered people or that transgendered people are often marginalized as pathological is a testament to the genderism inherent in our society.

Transphobia

A closely related concept, a clear extension of the concept of homophobia, is *transphobia*. Homophobia is probably best understood as antigay prejudice, although it is commonly understood as fear, disgust, anger, discomfort, and aversion to homosexuals. Coined by Weinberg (1973), the term *homophobia* was used to refer to discomfort with traits or behaviors associated with gays or lesbians (often effeminacy in men or masculinity in women). Homophobia can result in self-loathing if homosexuals internalize societal attitudes (Meyer & Dean, 1998).

Transphobia has been defined by many (e.g., Bornstein, 1994; Califia, 1997; Feinberg, 1996), but the best definition is "a fear and hatred of changing sexual characteristics" (Wilchins, 1997, p. 230).[3] Some in the transgender community call this *genderphobia*, or a "fear and hatred of different genders" (Wilchins, 1997, p. 225; see also Feinberg, 1996, p. 116). Transphobia is the motivating force for negative reactions to transgendered people that involve fear and disgust in the observer. *Biphobia*, a fear of people who cannot be neatly categorized into binary sexuality categories (Ochs, 1996), is quite similar to transphobia. Whereas genderism is a broad societal attitude that subordinates transgender people and is most often manifest in institutional policies and cultural beliefs, transphobia is often more an intrapsychic or interpersonal phenomenon that is often manifest in the fear of personal acquaintances being transgendered or revulsion on learning one is transgendered or meeting a transgendered person.

Homophobia and transphobia are clearly related concepts. Because transgender people are, or are often perceived as, gay (Feinberg, 1996; Gagné et al., 1996), and gay persons may be gender transgressors, sometimes homophobia and transphobia are indistinguishable. It is truly difficult to determine if an effeminate gay man is feared or hated for his gender or sexuality. Thus, gays, lesbians, bisexuals, and transgendered people are not immune to either homophobia or transphobia (Califia, 1997).

Gender Bashing

Gay bashing refers to violence against another person because of the perception that the person is gay or lesbian. Gender bashing, the parallel concept in the transgender community, denotes the harassment, abuse, or assault of gender and sex nonconformists (Wilchins, 1997). Basically, genderism and transphobia are the attitudes, and gender bashing is the behavior. Genderism provides the negative cultural attitude; transphobia fuels the attitude with fear, disgust, and hatred; and gender bashing is the violent expression of these beliefs. Although genderism and transphobia often result in covert expressions of discrimination and antipathy, gender bashing is an overt expression of hostility.

Namaste (1996), in one of the few empirical studies on gender bashing, contended that much of the violence against sexual minorities is motivated by the "perceived transgression of normative sex-gender relations" (p. 221). The male who is derided by being called "faggot" and the female who is called "dyke " are labeled such because of their failure to fulfill their gender roles and not, in many cases, because of direct knowledge of their sexual orientation.[4] Common understandings collapse gender and sexuality such that gender nonconformity connotes sexual nonconformity. Because gay bashers may rely on gender cues to target victims, gay bashing and gender bashing are interrelated such that one could argue that transgenderists are being bashed because they are presumed gay or lesbian.

The issue of gender nonconformity and gay bashing is rather contentious. Herek (1990) agreed that gender and sexuality are distinct but closely related. Thus, homosexuality is often aligned with "abnormal" masculinity and femininity. Following Harry's (1982) finding that effeminate gay men were twice as likely to have been bashed, gays and lesbians may avoid certain stereotypical mannerisms or clothing styles, adopting gender conformity as a protective measure (Herek, 1989, 1990). Herek (1990) asserted that there are three consequences to the link between gender and sexuality: Gay people are stigmatized for both their sexuality and their gender, gender deviations justify further hostility toward homosexuals (see also Harry, 1990), and people who are gender violators are attacked for being gay. Overall, gender nonconformity and homosexuality put a person at a higher risk because perpetrators perceive such people as less likely to resist or report a violent attack (Harry, 1982, 1990).

Functions of Anti-Transgender Violence

The social function of anti-transgender violence parallels antigay violence. Herek (1992) believes that the function of antigay violence is to maintain or assert social identities. Herek (1990) has hypothesized that there are three main functions of antigay violence: value expressive, social expressive, and defensive. Value-expressive hostility helps attackers affirm important personal values through violence. By extension, this would mean that gender bashing helps attackers affirm their genderist and transphobic values. Social-expressive violence connotes that perpetrators use antigay violence to attain approval from, and solidarity with, peers. Accordingly, a gang of young men may affirm their social identities as masculine men by attacking a feminine man, or they may affirm their heterosexuality by attacking a masculine woman. The defensive function of gay bashing is to reduce the anxiety caused by unconscious psychological conflicts perhaps surrounding their latent homosexuality. Herek (1990) speaks to the defensive function of gay and gender bashing: "Anti-gay assaults ... may provide a means for young males to affirm their masculinity ... by attacking someone who symbolizes an unacceptable aspect of their own personalities (e.g., homoerotic feelings or tendencies toward effeminacy)" (p. 324). Thus, "Their brutal assaults on men whom they perceived as the antithesis of masculinity may have been an attempt to deny any trace of femininity in themselves" (Herek, 1992, p. 161).

Genderism and transphobia, often more subtle and covert processes, are likely far more pervasive than gender bashing. Still, genderism and transphobia create a generalized sense of inferior status akin to what others have called minority stress (DiPlacido, 1998) or a climate of fear (Herek, 1989). All this is especially troubling given that transgendered people are specifically protected in only a few jurisdictions in North America. Covert hatred toward the transgender community permeates our culture, and social institutions assault the transgendered person's self-concept, identity, and thoughts. The transgender community is only too aware of these conditions and how society controls and oppresses the lived experience of gender transgressors.

This is an appropriate time to begin a more in-depth scrutiny of anti-transgender violence and attempt a more sophisticated conceptual understanding of the processes at work. Researchers have begun to document the existence of a problem but clearly need to move beyond piecemeal studies of the problem. For systematic research to continue, however, we need a framework to conceptualize just what might be happening. A conceptual framework will assist researchers in formulating specific research strategies and emphasizing some of the more salient processes at work. The framework presented here identifies interpersonal and institutional violence at work against the transgender community. This violence is grounded in subtle forms of genderism and transphobia and ultimately expressed in gender bashing. This study presents an empirical exploration of the preceding conceptual framework for interpreting anti-transgender violence.

Method

This study involved in-depth interviews with 18 members of the transgender community in Toronto, Ontario. Participants ranged in age from 20 to 51 years. The average age was 38.8 years. To be eligible for this study, participants simply had to self-identify as transgendered. All participants described their sex at birth as male except one who was female. Almost half the participants described their current gender as either female or woman, a few as male or man. The majority of the sample identified as transsexual ($n = 11$, or 61%), followed by transgenderist ($n = 5$, or 28%), with most respondents endorsing multiple gender identities. The most common sexual orientation was straight or heterosexual ($n = 10$, or 56%), followed by bisexual (n = 5, or 28%) and lesbian, poly- or pan-sexual, queer, or gay (n = 6, or 33%), with some endorsing several categories. The ethnic background of participants was mostly European (n = 15, or 83%). Most of the sample described their family background as middle class (n = 12, or 67%), 4 (22%) had working-class backgrounds, and 1 (6%) was raised in an upper-class family. The majority of the sample had a college education or better. Most were employed in trades or technical-related fields, the computer industry, or in professions. These conditions netted most participants fair to above-average economic means.

The sample was obtained through convenience and snowball sampling techniques. Participants were recruited from personal contacts within the transgender community in Toronto and the referrals provided by these respondents. Advertisements on the Internet, in a cross-dressing social club's newsletter, and in several community organizations and businesses throughout Toronto netted the remaining respondents. Because this was not a large random sample, these experiences are not expected to generalize beyond this sample. Last, the researcher was not in a clinical or "gatekeeping" relationship with any participant.

The interviews were conducted as ethnographic interviews (Marshall & Rossman, 1989) or conversational encounters (Potter & Wetherell, 1987). Overall, the interviews documented the participants' life stories relevant to their gender, particularly how others reacted to their gender. From the start, the interviewer made it clear that although there were specific topics to address, the interview should be a friendly conversation whereby the interviewer and interviewee learned about each other's view of the subject. Appropriately, participants had considerable control over the flow and direction of the interview. As a result, the interview protocol was not standardized across participants. In fact, the interview protocol changed seven times throughout the study. The interview with the first respondent began with questions about how gender came to be an important issue in this person's life. Then, the interviewer probed with questions designed to elicit opinions on controversies in the literature. Subsequent interviews followed this basic format but increasingly relied on questions raised and positions taken by the participants themselves (Guba & Lincoln, 1989). In some cases, respondents were confronted with accounts provided by prior participants to solicit competing accounts (Potter & Wetherell, 1987). Because participants were not asked the same standard questions and were not considered representative of the population in general, percentage calculations for proportions of responses are inappropriate, so respondents were distinguished by minority and majority views.

Participants received transcripts of the interview so they could make changes if the transcripts did not communicate their position correctly, and although several sought clarification, none sent revisions. Participants selected their own pseudonyms.

Genderism, Transphobia, and Gender Bashing

The analysis of interview transcripts involved a four-part coding strategy. First, the participant's specific responses to questions were coded using a grounded theory approach (e.g., Glaser & Strauss, 1967; Rennie, Phillips, & Quartaro, 1988; Strauss & Corbin, 1994). Some theoretical discourses (e.g., feminist, lesbian and gay) implicitly assisted the interpretation of the interviews. The second stage of the analysis consisted of looking for common patterns among responses on a specific issue. In the third stage of analysis, differences among participant responses were identified. Respondents were then split into minority and majority clusters on each issue.

The results document how strangers on the street, coworkers, family, friends, teachers, spouses, and helping professionals demonstrated genderism, transphobia, and gender bashing. Although a minority of gender transgressors met with complete acceptance, a majority met with moral outrage, outright rejection, and, for a few, physical assault.

Cultural Values

A majority of respondents reported a generalized impression of genderism and transphobia in society. That said, it was difficult to discern from participant accounts when genderism was operating and when transphobia was at work. Perhaps the clearest representations of genderism were found in the observations of participants regarding portrayals of transgendered people in movies, on television talk shows, and in the news. As a result of media representations, respondents believed that society viewed transgenderism as "sick" (BC), "nuts" (Sherry Denise), an offense to Christianity

(Dawna), or a "horror" (Mildew). But society's revulsion was tinged with fascination because there was something about "crossing over boundaries that appeals to society" (BC). These more general observations reflect genderism, but probably both processes are at work supporting anti-transgender cultural values.

Participants received a wide range of responses to their gender. Sherry Denise found that some people reacted favorably and smiled, and others knew what was going on but ignored it. Some, such as Ken, who likes to wear a dress with nylons but no makeup on his face, were especially likely to draw negative reactions. Perhaps people on the street or in stores expect to encounter someone who is clearly one gender or the other, and when they cannot decide which gender the person is, they get uncomfortable. From the perspective of a long-time cross-dresser, Miqqi failed to understand all the negative reactions and found such genderism restrictive:

> If you're a cross-dresser, the thing that drives you absolutely crazy is why is it so terrible? What am I doing wrong? I'm not hurting anyone. I'm not bothering anyone. All I want to do is wear women's clothes and go for a bloody walk. And if I dress up at night and . . . put on my makeup and everything, and realize that I'm out of milk, I can't go to the corner store. And that's oppressive.

Respondents confirmed the concept of genderism as a general impression that society is not accepting of transgenderism.

In anticipation of the costs of being open about their gender expression, many respondents cross-dressed in private under the shroud of stigma and shame or adopted safety strategies to protect themselves in public. One common safety strategy was *passing*. Passing involves presenting clearly as one gender, erasing any trace of multiple or conflicting genders, and avoiding confrontation. Sherry recounted the reality of the situation:

> People on the street don't want to hear your explanation. . . . They just look at you. . . . Fact of the matter is you're going to be walking down the street and people are going to be pointing at you and saying, "That's a guy!" They don't want to hear why . . . to live as a woman successfully you have to fit in.

By clearly presenting as one gender, respondents were largely able to avoid offending transphobic and genderist cultural values.

Every once in a while, even the proficient passer will get read, just as nontransgendered people will be mistaken for the wrong gender. *Being read* means being correctly identified as transgendered. BC reported that being read can be threatening:

> Being read itself . . . is disconcerting. . . . It sort of jars one . . . makes you nervous or on guard because you have to kind of think, "Well, what if . . . they are like the 1% who actually does confront me?"

Having acknowledged the fear that comes along with being read, BC was also quick to point out that the fear, at least in her experience, is unfounded:

> At one time I would have believed that . . . if I was read in public that people would . . . point me out in the street and do that invasion of the body snatchers thing where they scream at you . . . but that doesn't happen. . . . When people do see you, they're . . . uncomfortable and they don't know what to say.

BC once had internalized transphobia but found that most people were uncomfortable rather than violent.

Enforcing the Gender Dichotomy

Passing was not an option when interacting with people who need to know about one's transgenderism. A majority of participants encountered institutionalized genderism and interpersonal transphobia when asking for assistance from medical, psychiatric, or psychological professionals. These health care providers expressed their lack of acceptance by providing inadequate health care, attempting to convert (cure), and forcing "either/or" decisions.

In a minority of cases, genderism and transphobia manifested themselves in inadequate health care. For instance, Melisa, a transgenderist, reported that her medical doctor prescribed estrogen to her and then sent her on her way. Her doctor failed to warn her of the possible negative health effects or order any endocrinological testing, accepted practices by medical practitioners. Melisa also found herself in another trap: Standards of care for the treatment of transsexuals prescribe psychological counseling, but she has been repeatedly refused psychotherapy.

Sarah did not have very positive experiences with medical practitioners either, and her experiences with a psychiatrist were no better. First, she was subjected to highly personal questions in front of a room of residents. Then, after a month of interactions, she confronted the psychiatrist who bluntly dismissed her desire for gender reassignment surgery:

> He said, "OK, well, it's like this. What we want to do is find out what triggers in you the feelings for wanting to be female so we can stop those triggers." This was the first time I realized that he did not want me to try cross living or being transsexual, like he wanted me to continue being male. . . . And I freaked all over him.

The psychiatrist failed to take her wishes seriously, rejected her most fundamental self-beliefs, and attempted to convert her to back to "male." This aspect of transphobia often permeates professional policies, procedures, and treatment, assaulting transgender people with a lack of respect.

A few participants felt that medical professionals were unfairly enforcing gender dichotomization by encouraging people to choose either one or the other gender and providing the medical technologies to make it happen. Dawna's perception was that the local gender identity clinic communicated its expectations for gender, and this, in turn, had a negative impact on the community. The gender identity clinic encouraged its male-to-female clients to make themselves as feminine as possible because "if you're not passable, then . . . things are going to happen." Dawna's point was that "the clinic unfortunately paints this picture that the world is out there waiting to expose us, ready to ridicule us, ready to . . . make our lives hell. And that's not necessarily true." This genderist attitude conveys the sense that transgender lives are very difficult unless they completely pass, a view that excludes and marginalizes those that do not present as clearly one gender or the other.

Another participant also observed genderism in the practices of the local gender identity clinic. Glen had heard that the local gender identity clinic was not enforcing gender dichotomization but, while participating in its program, found that the services were

> designed entirely by the professional community to force you into making an either/or decision. In other words, you will live your life either this way or that way. Now, the sad thing is . . . that they

say that they were posturing on the basis of being neutral, but how can anybody be neutral that sets up a room that has professionals in it that are constantly feeding you on the basis of making this either/or decision?

Glen felt they encouraged an either/or decision rather than a search for the right option for each person. To Glen, the medical establishment enforced gender dichotomization by offering to change sex, which only reinforced the presumed wall between the sexes. Glen's point was as follows:

The professional community, as we probably see it today, are working very hard to maintain [societal standards]. . . . They created transsexualism because what they couldn't deal with is the overlap in behavior of males with that of females and vice versa. . . . If they acknowledge the overlap, as I've come to understand in myself now and say I can wear whatever I want, then gender breaks down.

He saw dichotomization as endemic to the psychiatric profession. After all, they profit from the care and treatment of transgenderists, so they have a vested interest in maintaining dichotomization. So gender clinics do not help individuals become who they are; rather, they help the person become who professionals think they should be.

Ken also specifically criticized psychologists. After talking at length about the necessity of not enforcing dichotomized genders, Ken contended that

I think the psychological profession needs to be let in on the [transgender] culture. I think they have to be let in on the fact that there are differences out there. . . . In other words, they're not mixed up, they're just . . . evolving in a different way . . . as a culture. . . . As opposed to . . . "You can't do that, OK? You're either going to be one role or the other. Come on, make up your mind." You can't make up your frigging mind because your mind doesn't work that way.

His view was that psychology should understand transgender culture rather than force people to dichotomize gender. However, "either/or" choices preserve the culturally dominant binary gender system. In the case of society in general and people on the street, the influence is more subtle, but helping professions stress the practicality of conformity to binary genders, thus reinforcing genderist and transphobic values.

Coming Out

As participants told their family and friends about their trans-genderness, their stories became even more dramatic. Coming out as transgendered was a very significant event for a majority of participants. A minority of respondents had very positive reactions to their coming out, but in contrast to previous research, negative reactions were more common and contributed to a climate of hostility for transgendered persons. Much of the reactions that the participants received when telling family or friends about their gender suggest genderism. That is, by their reactions, which ranged from "standoffish" to complete prohibition, nontransgendered people imply that the state of transgender is devalued by society.

"Standoffish" Mode

A substantial minority of respondents had met awkward, or transphobic, reactions when discovered or coming out. Melisa found that people were surprised, did not know what to think, and freaked. For example, her coach at university was "very sympathetic and compassionate about my situation but . . . feels extremely awk-ward about it. And he's told me that." Sarah, Dawna, Zena, and Phyllis attributed the discomfort they have observed in others to a lack of knowledge about transgendered people.

Sherry reported a sense of discomfort among her coworkers. She transitioned from man to woman at work and everybody knew, and for the most part things went well:

> But there still is that distance. . . . You're fine at work and you can talk up close, but should you be walking to work and you're coming to somebody who's going home from work on the street, it's a little bit different. It's not . . . "I hate your guts," but it's maybe a standoffish mode. It's "Hi" and "I gotta go."

Several respondents perceived similar discomfort in others once their acquaintances discovered they were transgendered.

Are You Gay/Perverted/Crazy?

There is a world of difference between a fidgety awkward reaction and confrontations about your sexuality or sanity. The simple disclosure of one's transgendered life often elicited such transphobic reactions. Several respondents reported that the first impulse of many was to wonder if the transgendered person was gay (Ken, Sherry, Veronica). As Glen, a cross-dresser, told me, "The first question my mother asked me, 4 years ago when I told her, she said, 'Are you gay?' And I said, 'No.' She went, 'Whew.' Like she didn't care about the clothes so much." This question could be seen as motivated by a misunderstanding over the relation of sex, gender, and sexuality. What is more likely is that concerns about gayness are motivated by covert heterosexism or homophobia, emphasizing the implicit connection between transphobia and homophobia.

Many people confronted with a friend or kin who is transgendered saw transgenderism as a sexual fetish or perversion (Sherry, Phyllis, Zena). David, who had thought he was a transsexual and now is living as a man again, said that many people think it is a perversion or a form of insanity:

> I've only told a few people. And when I've told people the reaction has been quite negative . . . because people cannot handle it. And they think, "Oh, this person is mentally deficient." They just don't understand.

Two respondents, Melisa and Jenniffer, reported that they told people and were characterized as "monster" or "freak." Obviously, to some people, coming out as transgendered challenges their understanding of sex and gender and, by implication, their basic sense of humanness. This is transphobia at its most basic.

Shame

Genderism often manifested itself in the shame family and friends expressed. Several respondents were told by others that they were ashamed of their transgenderness (e.g., Mario, Betty). A good example is Jenniffer. After telling her parents she was transsexual, Jenniffer's parents told her that "they don't want to see me unless I'm dressed appropriately" and "they are ashamed of me because of my gender." Basic to the genderist attitude is the belief that there is something wrong with people who don't play by society's rules for gender.

Family members often tried to use shame as leverage to get the person to be ordinarily gendered. BC's mother would say things such as the following: "'What would your father think if he saw you like this?' and stuff like that. So . . . you just get a very clear message: This is not appropriate. Other people will disapprove of you. You better stop doing this."

Some parents distinguished between public and private cross-dressing. Sherry Denise reported that her mother "can't cope with it. When she comes over here, . . . I better not be wearing any of this stuff. . . . Or else I'm ostracized out of the family." She continues, "She doesn't mind so much that I do this, here in private. It's just that . . . she's afraid . . . people who know me . . . know her and she's going to be . . . asked a lot of embarrassing questions."

David had the experience of being shamed by his wife. He kept his transgenderism a secret until later on in his marriage. When he told her about his desires for cross-dressing, they sought counseling together. In this case, the shame of David's cross-dressing had interesting implications for his wife:

> [She] was like, "Don't tell anybody. Don't want anybody to know about this." I said, "Why?" "Well, they'll think I'm kind of, you know, there's something wrong with me because I'm with you, and they'll think I'm lesbian or whatever." She didn't want to be labeled that. So I said, "OK, I understand that. But respect me, too. Don't be telling other people because I know what the implications are." But of course as soon as you're separated, they tell everyone.

David's wife feared being labeled a lesbian, so she feared David's transgenderism. In other words, she was transphobic because she was homophobic.

Putting the Clamps Down

Perhaps the strongest indication of genderism and transphobia in participant accounts involved "putting the clamps down"—prohibitions against cross-dressing by family and friends. Glen reported his experience of prohibition:

> Until I was about 5 years old, I pretty well wore whatever I wanted to. But at 5 years old, my parents . . . suddenly put the clamps

down. . . . And at 5 years old, all of a sudden, my mother said, "You can't wear my clothes any more. You have to wear clothes like your father." That was very devastating to me.

Parental prohibition of cross-gender impulses and control of gender expression were fairly common in a minority of accounts. Sherry Denise's father found out about her wearing dresses as a boy and she received spankings, scoldings, and lectures during which Dad "almost got violent." Like Glen and Sherry Denise, Melisa was silenced, never being allowed to talk to her family about what was going on, even today as an adult woman. Glen found that his wife could not tolerate his cross-dressing:

> My wife knew about this beforehand. And before we got married, she said it was fine. And after we got married, traditionally as it always happens, "I don't want to see it any more."

Despite his wife's prohibition, Glen persisted in dressing, and the relationship ended in divorce.

At least one respondent had been prohibited from her gender expression at work. Three months after transitioning and living full-time as a woman, Dawna's employer demanded that she revert back to a "quasi-male figure" at work. They failed to understand what was going on, joked about it, and eventually threatened her employment. Dawna went to the Human Rights Commission and told them what had happened; the commission said she had a case. After being reinstated, she was allowed to dress the way she wanted, but "they have given me a kind of position where I'm isolated from a lot of people . . . from . . . my coworkers." Reflecting on the experience, Dawna concluded that

> what kind of differs us from the gay community is that . . . they're already integrated into society, but they just want recognition for being different. . . . Now . . . we already know we're different. Everybody knows we're different, but . . . we want to be fully integrated. People . . . aren't giving us that chance.

Coming out for Dawna meant being discriminated against at work, alienating her from her coworkers and boss.

In summary, respondents recounted several occurrences in which they felt threatened from society in general, strangers on the street, and friends and family. Ultimately, these experiences marked participants. A majority of respondents internalized the shame others extended to them (Betty, Miqqi, David, Sarah, and Glen), feared derision (BC), and felt alienated (Sherry, Ken, and Melisa) and vulnerable (Sarah, Veronica, and Betty). If they had transitioned full-time to the other gender, several reported that they would have been completely ostracized by their family and friends. These threats were targeted at their very sense of being, their identity as transgendered, the heart of their gender. Most disclosures to family met with initial wonderment, but the majority of participants received positive reactions from family, friends, and spouses. In the end, with understanding, patience, and communication, many of these relationships were strengthened.

Gender Bashing

Despite the obviously hostile cultural climate to transgenderists, only a few participants recounted being gender bashed. A few had had close calls. Betty had been seriously threatened but not assaulted. She was very distressed at the thought of being discovered:

> I was terrified to walk outside the door because I had friends who were going to kill me. I've had other, like friends, I could hear them on the telephone telling me . . . "Don't ever show your face around here. You're dead," and shit like that. . . . Like one guy was trying to get me to come with him . . . and then I found out that it was some guys at the other end, waiting for me. He was just bringing me over there to get my head kicked in and stuff like that.

Betty's wariness had protected her, but she remained feeling extremely vulnerable.

Some respondents were victims of physical abuse but not because of their gender. Mario's dad would beat him three or four times a week because he did not get good grades in school. As a child, Ken was assaulted fairly often, but he attributed this to the fact that he was not interested in the same things as other children. And Miqqi figured that kids liked to pick on him because he was Jewish and better off than other kids in the neighborhood.

A few participants, however, had been the focus of anti-transgender violence. Of all the participants, Zena probably experienced the most violence because of her feminine presentation. Like other participants, she was often teased as a young boy for being too feminine. She experienced a great deal of violence at the hands of her school friends, endured several sexual assaults, had been almost run over twice in the past two months and was harassed on the street. Zena attributed the violence to her femininity: "I was assaulted because I was female, feminine, I was female inside." Jenniffer, who had been gender bashed as a child, also inferred that it was her lack of gender conformity that they targeted:

> They see somebody that's visibly different and a minority . . . who is not supposed to fight back. They make a perfect target so they can belittle that person, make them look smaller, more insignificant and say, "Look, I am better because that person's a piece of shit," and they don't . . . have to worry about any retaliation because I'm not supposed to fight back because . . . I'm just one of those feminine little things.

This analysis directly supports the hypothesized function of gender bashing suggested by research on gay bashing. Attackers figured that because she was feminine, she would not fight back. In addition, her attackers bolstered their self-worth by denigrating her.

It is likely some respondents had been gender bashed but were unwilling to speak about such sensitive matters. As other researchers have found, they were more likely to recount positive experiences. Also, this study was probably biased toward respondents who were more successful at being out. Indeed, many respondents reported being successful at "fitting in" or "being secretive" to avoid discovery or attacks (e.g., Mario, Sherry, Miqqi, and Veronica). Especially fearful, closeted, or past victims of abuse may not have volunteered for this study for fear of maltreatment.

Toward the Future

Considering the small sample, quite a great deal of genderism and transphobia was evident in respondent accounts. A majority of respondents felt that cultural values supported transphobic and genderist attitudes, leading transgenderists to try to pass and fear being read. Most respondents encountered institutional forms of genderism and transphobia in the practices and ideology of the helping professions, which translated into inadequate health care, unwanted "cures," and the enforcement of binary gender ideology. A majority of respondents noted interpersonal forms of transphobia when they came out as transgendered. The most common reactions were being standoffish; characterizing transgenderists as gay, crazy, or perverted; and controlling transgender expression through shame or prohibition. These processes led to intrapsychic transphobia with effects such as internalized shame, fear, and alienation. With regard to gender bashing, fortunately for most, reality was not as bad as feared. Although there were very definite threats of violence, few had been physically assaulted because of their gender.

Obviously, this preliminary research provides only an initial conceptual framework for interpreting anti-transgender violence. Gay and lesbian discourse on coming out, homophobia, and gay bashing and feminist discourses on sexism were very closely aligned with the lived experiences of transgender participants. This is not entirely surprising, given that the transgendered community is familiar with gay and lesbian studies and has relied on the structures of this discourse to organize their reality. Work on the conceptual framework proposed here should continue. One interesting approach might be to explore whether gays, lesbians, and bisexuals are the victims of genderism, transphobia, and gender bashing. Also, researchers should document rates of genderism, transphobia, and gender bashing in a random representative sample using a standardized assessment tool. For example, the instrument designed by Herek and Berrill (1990) to assess gay bashing could be easily modified for research on anti-transgender violence. The conceptual framework and experiences of transgender people presented here should be helpful in designing such an instrument.

Even though the results of this study are preliminary, respondents' comments suggest several directions for professionals and the general public wishing to alleviate anti-transgender violence. Transgender activists have taken the lead, lobbying for basic human rights protection, protesting violence against transgendered people, and forming a coalition of gender-oppressed people challenging the institutional sources of gender violence. Many respondents advocated educating the public and mental health professionals on the experiences of the transgender community. Specifically, psychology should consider altering the dominant paradigm from which it studies identities, so that it can accommodate insights from the transgender community. This study's informants were simply living the variability of human experience, and denial and pathologization of this diversity are nothing short of violence. In the very least, as Devor (1995) has argued, if we do not acknowledge transgender subjectivities, we go against reality. I would add that psychologists need to account for transgender knowledge (increase our understanding of and sensitivity to the diversity of human experience and the knowledge of other communities and cultures) by seriously exploring gender identities beyond man and woman, accepting the many ways to be gendered.

Notes

1. Transgender is a debated identity both in terms of its meaning and who subscribes to the identity. *Transgender* was the preferred "umbrella" term for this community when the data for this study were collected (1996-1997) in Toronto. Recently, however, "trans" is probably now the more inclusive community identity. Like other social and collective identities, it has different meanings in different historical and cultural contexts.

2. I am partially indebted to one of my research participants, Melisa, for generating this understanding of genderism. Bornstein (1994, p. 74) provided the earliest published use of this concept, although she was not disposed to its use.

3. Nataf (1996) defined *transphobia* consistent with the definition of *genderism*: "the groundless fear and hatred of cross-dressers, transsexuals, and gender benders and what they do, resulting in denial of rights and needs, and violence" (p. 63).

4. Bornstein (1994) argued a somewhat unpopular but similar point: When a gay man is bashed on the street, it probably has more to do with his violation of gender rules than sexual rules. But Califia (1997) contended that this is misleading: Gays and lesbians are also bashed because of their sexual orientation.

5

Perceived Racism, Racial Environments, and Hate Violence Against Asian Americans

Research, Clinical Issues, and Prevention

ERIC L. KOHATSU

TOSHI SASAO

In a San Francisco housing project, a Vietnamese American male has racial epithets hurled at him and is struck on the head with a rock. The victim's father claims that family members have been harassed for the past six years because of their ethnicity.

—National Asian Pacific American Legal Consortium
(NAPALC, 1993, Appendix 2)

Three White tenants struck a middle-aged Chinese woman repeatedly while saying, "Bitch, f—k you, chink, I want to kill you. F—k you chink, go back to your country." Massachusetts.

—NAPALC (1995, p. 30)

A Chinese American male was brutally beaten on a public
street by an inebriated 27-year-old male who shouted, "I'll kill
you, you f—king chink!" The perpetrator told police upon
arrest, "I kicked that f—king gook's ass." The victim sustained
severe physical damage and has been rendered disabled, despite
numerous surgeries. (St. Louis, Missouri.)

—NAPALC (1996, p. 21)

As these documented cases reveal, racially motivated violence against Asians has become increasingly commonplace in the United States (U.S. Commission on Civil Rights, 1992). In addition, racial violence has been a consistent factor in the experiences, both in the present and historically, of all racial minority groups in the United States (Brown, 1991; Sue & Sue, 1999). Hate violence directed against individuals of color continues to occur in alarming numbers (e.g., L.A. County Human Relations Commission, 1995, 1996) despite the widespread problem of underreporting. Interpersonal violence that is racially motivated has become a serious social, psychological, and public health issue and deserves far greater attention from mental health professionals in terms of research and development of clinical interventions.

The focus of this chapter will be on racially motivated hate violence against Asian Americans. The first part will provide an overview of hate violence against Asian Americans in terms of the frequency and types of hate violence that Asian Americans have been subjected to in recent years. To provide a context for understanding racially motivated hate violence, we analyze current research on Asian American adults and adolescents regarding the racial environments in which they live and their perceptions of race, racial tension, and intergroup contact, as well as a model linking psychological well-being and perceived racial tension.

The second part will entail a critical review of the psychological effects of hate violence and proposed clinical interventions. As part of this section, an emphasis will be placed on the applications of racial identity theory in counseling Asian American victims of hate violence. The third part will focus on recommendations for prevention, as well as suggestions for future research.

The Root of the Problem:
Hate Violence, Racism, and Racial Environments

Little attention has been paid to the effects of hate violence on Asian Americans. Even though the reported rates of anti-Asian hate violence have risen dramatically in recent years (e.g., U.S. Commission on Civil Rights, 1992), the model minority myth continues to obscure this disturbing trend. That is, the prevailing notion that Asian Americans do not experience significant social problems, such as hate violence, prevents mental health professionals from giving this population the serious attention it deserves. Virtually no research has examined the effects of hate violence on Asian Americans or interventions for Asian victims of racially motivated hate violence. Because there is insufficient knowledge about the racial context in which intergroup relations take place for Asian Americans, the task of understanding, intervening, or preventing the effects of hate violence is more difficult. Before proceeding, the rates and types of racially motivated violence against Asian Americans need to be clarified.

Hate Crimes

Although the terms *hate crime* and *hate violence* have become common language in the United States, these terms are not synonymous and should be clearly defined. For the purpose of this chapter, the definitions used were developed by the National Asian Pacific American Legal Consortium. Hate violence is defined as

> any verbal or physical act that intimidates, threatens, or injures a person or person's property because of membership in a targeted group. That membership can be based on actual or perceived race, ethnicity, national origin, religion, gender, sexual orientation, or age. (NAPALC, 1994, p. 3)

However, hate crimes are violations of the criminal or penal statute and link racial hatred to criminal acts. Specifically, the L.A. County District Attorney's office classifies hate crimes as those cases in which the facts indicate that bias, hatred, or prejudice based on the victim's race, religion, ancestry, national origin, disability, gender, or sexual orientation are *substantial* factors in the commission of the offense. Evidence of such bias, hatred, or prejudice can be direct or circumstantial. It can occur before, during, or after the commission of the offense. (L.A. County Human Relations Commission, 1996, p. ii)

Hate crimes include verbal or written threats, harassment, graffiti, hate literature, vandalism, property damage, cross burning, phone threats, arson, and physical assaults, including attacks resulting in serious injury or death (Brown, 1991; NAPALC, 1994).

Given the relatively short period of formal documentation and the problems with underreporting, there exists no accurate account of the severity of hate violence against Asian Americans. Many cases of anti-Asian violence go unreported or, even if they are reported, are ignored by the public at large. As suggested by Delucchi and Do (1996), many communities are indifferent to Asian victims of racially motivated violence. From capstone events, such as the cases of Vincent Chin and Jim (Ming Hai) Loo, to more current acts of violence, the increasing rate of anti-Asian hate violence is clearly evident.

According to audits conducted by the National Asian Pacific American Legal Consortium (1996), there was a steady nationwide increase in *reported* anti-Asian hate violence incidences from 1993 to 1996. In 1993, there were 335 reported anti-Asian hate incidents, and 30 Asian Pacific Americans died as a result of this hate violence. Similarly, there were 452 reported cases in 1994 and 458 cases in 1995. Assaults were the most common form of hate violence in 1995, as was the case from 1993 to 1994. In 1996, there were 535 reported anti-Asian incidents, which represented a 17% increase from the previous year.

Reported forms of anti-Asian violence included assault, vandalism, homicide, harassment, and threats or intimidation (NAPALC, 1995). The NAPALC reports clearly documented that the most common form of hate violence against Asian Americans involved assault, which suggests that there has been a significant increase in physical violence against Asians. Given the recent Asian bashing centering on political contributions, the rates of anti-Asian violence will undoubtedly increase.

Furthermore, acts of anti-Asian hate violence took place in increasing numbers in homes, workplaces, and schools. From 1994 to

1995, there was an 80% increase in anti-Asian violence that took place in the homes of Asian Americans (NAPALC, 1995). Asian Americans who lived in public housing units were especially vulnerable to hate violence. From 1995 to 1996, there was a 117% increase in hate violence taking place in Asian American homes or workplaces.

A "local" analysis of hate crimes in Los Angeles County revealed some disturbing trends as well. For example, from 1987 to 1996, the percentages of reported hate crimes against Asians ranged from 9% to 19% of the total reported hate crimes (L.A. County Human Relations Commission, 1996). It is important to note that there were 80 reported hate crimes in 1992, the year of civil unrest in Los Angeles. Although it appears that the number of reported cases in L.A. County has slightly diminished from 1994 to 1996, the overall national rate of anti-Asian violence as discussed earlier continues to escalate.

These disturbing trends reflect the reality that hate violence against Asian Americans represents a significant social and mental health issue. Despite the growing number of organizations that offer assistance to victims (primarily legal) in many parts of the country, the field of psychology has been relatively slow to respond. That is, there has been no comprehensive effort on the part of psychologists to study the impact of these experiences on Asian Americans, devise clinical interventions to help in the recovery process, or implement psychoeducational programs to provide better coping strategies for victims and to prevent this violence from occurring.

To make matters worse, adequate research on perceptions of racism or quality of racial contact between Asian Americans and other racial minority groups has not been conducted. Therefore, the racial and cultural contexts in which Asian Americans function are not well understood. A brief review of current research examining the complexities of racial interactions and environments among Asian American adults and adolescents will now be presented.

Perceptions of Race and Quality of Racial Contact

Generally, psychologists have not systematically examined the effects of sociorace (i.e., psychological race) on the psychological functioning of Asian Americans. In addition, very little is known about the extent of racial stereotyping, racial contact, cultural knowledge, and emotional valence attached to stereotypes of other racial groups among Asian Americans (Kohatsu, 1997). Because researchers have not critically evaluated the complex ecological contexts in which racial contact takes place for Asian Americans, there is scant knowledge on the degree and quality of interracial contact of Asian Americans with Latinos, African Americans, and American Indians.

One of the least understood and most underused within-group variables in cross-cultural research that has tremendous potential with Asian Americans is racial identity theory. Briefly, racial identity development is a process by which members of oppressed groups overcome society's negative evaluation of their group and develop an identity with its roots in the culture and sociopolitical experiences of their ascribed group (Helms, 1995). A critical component in racial identity theory is understanding the process by which people of color overcome internalized racial stereotypes and negative self and own-group perceptions (Helms, 1995). Four racial identity statuses were proposed: *Conformity* refers to an individual who identifies with Whites/White culture, *dissonance* entails confusion about one's socioracial affiliation, *resistance* involves individuals immersing themselves in their own respective ethnic culture and rejecting Whites/White culture, and *integrative awareness* involves an integration of multiple cultural perspectives (Helms, 1995).

Several studies have examined perceived racism from Latinos and African Americans among Asian Americans from a racial identity perspective (e.g., Kohatsu, 1997; Kohatsu et al., 2000; Kohatsu et al., 1996). Racial identity theory (Helms, 1990) was used as a predictive framework in these studies to examine how cognitive (e.g., cultural knowledge), affective (e.g., comfort level), and behavioral (e.g., interracial contact) variables mediate racial perceptions and quality of racial contact of Latinos and African Americans with Asian Americans. Before highlighting these results, the extent of racial interaction with African Americans and Latinos will be discussed.

Asian Americans reported more negative personal experiences with Latinos than Latinos did of Asians (e.g., Kohatsu, 1997). Moreover, Asian Americans possessed greater knowledge of Latino sociopolitical history and attendance of Latino cultural events than did Latinos of Asian culture. Although Asian Americans did not socially interact with Latinos frequently, they still reported feeling comfortable interacting with Latinos and had a positive overall impression of Latinos.

Interestingly, the patterns of racial contact with African Americans among Asian Americans were similar to the patterns reported with Latinos. Asian Americans had moderate knowledge of African American culture and moderate racial contact with African Americans (Kohatsu et al., 2000). Yet, moderately high levels of perceived racism from African Americans were reported by Asian Americans. Given these patterns of racial knowledge and contact, the predictive utility of racial identity theory will now be examined.

Racial identity attitudes strongly predicted the extent of perceived interpersonal racism from Latinos (e.g., Kohatsu, 1997). Specifically, the more an Asian American subscribed to integrative awareness attitudes, the lower was the level of perceived racism from Latinos. In addition, the higher the level of resistance attitudes, the more Asian Americans perceived racism from Latinos. Furthermore, racial identity attitudes significantly predicted the comfort level among Asian Americans when interacting with Latinos. That is, the higher Asian Americans' level of resistance attitudes was, the lower was the reported comfort level in interacting with Latinos. Last, racial identity attitudes also predicted the extent of social interaction with Latinos. If an Asian American subscribed to either conformity or resistance attitudes, he or she would tend not to interact socially with Latinos.

Similar trends were found in analyzing the quality of racial contact with African Americans using racial identity theory (Kohatsu et al., 2000). For example, racial identity attitudes significantly predicted perceived interpersonal racism from African Americans. The more an Asian American subscribed to conformity attitudes, the higher was the level of perceived racism from African Americans. In addition, racial identity attitudes were strong predictors of an Asian American's overall impression of African Americans as a group. The more Asian Americans endorsed conformity and resistance attitudes, the more negative was the overall group impression of African Americans.

Although there is scant research on this topic, some empirical data exist that broaden our understanding of the complexities of racial environments and interracial contact among Asian American adults. Racial identity theory has proven useful in analyzing perceptions of racism and the quality of interracial contact among Asian Americans with African Americans and Latinos. Given the predictive power of racial identity, cross-cultural researchers would benefit from using this framework to further unravel the relationships between the three domains of intergroup contact (i.e., behaviors, attitudes, and emotions) to better understand how Asian Americans function in interracial situations. Recent research has also examined the complexities of racial environments in which Asian American adolescents function.

Asian American Adolescents and Perceived Racism

As noted earlier in this chapter, although racial violence against Asian Americans has been on the rise (U.S. Commission on Civil Rights, 1992), the "model minority myth" obscures the issues related to the psychological well-being of Asian American adolescents in school settings. Because the majority of Asian students in public schools are foreign born with limited English-language proficiency (LEP), the educational needs of these students are obvious and will likely continue with the influx of new immigrants into U.S. schools. ELP students often face the ridicule of their classmates for their accented English or anti-Asian sentiments through racial slurs or name-calling. According to the L.A. County Human Relations Commission (1989), some Asian immigrant students have been victims of racially motivated violence. Thus, the school environment where many adolescents spend their prime hours should be carefully examined to ensure the well-being of Asian American students.

School Environment and Psychological Well-Being. Sasao (1999) argued that, particularly for Asian American students, academic settings hold a number of important implications for their quality of life. First, the model minority myth has perpetuated the image of Asian "superachievers" in all areas of life, including social relationships and academic performance (e.g., Sue & Morishima, 1982; Toupin & Son, 1991). Nonetheless, many Asian students are not as happy or satisfied as White students or free from interpersonal and/or emotional problems (Sue & Okazaki, 1990). In fact, many Asian students express discomfort in situations demanding interpersonal fluency, such as in classrooms (Callo, 1973).

A second reason for the importance of investigating racial environments for Asian Americans is that educational attainment is highly valued and is often perceived as a vehicle for advancing and promoting social mobility (Sue & Morishima, 1982). Therefore, it can be argued that because of Asian Americans' strong personal investment in education, the campus environment becomes crucial to their optimal functioning in social relationships and academic performance.

Another rationale for a focus on Asian American students is the tremendous within-group diversity that currently characterizes the Asian American group. Asian Americans speak more than 30 different languages and bring with them a comparable number of distinct cultures (Asian Week, 1991). Therefore, the potential effects of diversity in an academic setting on the lives of various Asian subgroups are expected to vary considerably.

To understand how diversity influences quality of life among general student populations, including both "minority" and "non-minority" students, we used an ecological-contexualist framework in community psychology, which has proven helpful in previous work (e.g., Kelly, Azelton, Burzette, & Mock, 1994; Sasao, 1999; Sasao & Sue, 1993; Swarts & Martin, 1997). The ecological approach stresses the assessment of contextual variables that interact with the values, predispositions, and experiences of the populations involved. It also ensures that culturally anchored variables are considered in their unique environmental contexts such as campus communities. By using an ecological approach, then, the purpose of this study was twofold: (a) to assess the perception of racial/ethnic tension in 34 California public high schools and (b) to examine the impact of perceived racial tension on psychological well-being among Asian American adolescents.

Method

Sample Design and Respondent Characteristics

Data for the present study were part of a larger study that focused on the epidemiology and correlates of alcohol, tobacco, and other drug use (ATOD) among high school students in California (Sasao, 1999).[1] The sample consisted of both 9th- and 12th-grade students from 34 high schools in California. Students in these two grade levels were surveyed to examine the prevalence and incidence of ATOD use and their correlates. These two grades were chosen because they would allow for later comparisons with both the

California Student Substance Use Survey (Skager & Austin, 1994, 1996), which includes 9th graders, and the National High School Senior Survey ("Monitoring the Future 1995" (Johnston, Wadsworth, O'Malley, Bachman, & Schulenberg, 1997), which includes 12th graders. Schools selected (according to 1994-1995 California Basic Educational Data System [CBEDS] data) had at least 200 students of Asian ancestry in both 9th and 12th grades, and at least 25% of the total enrollment in those two grades was made up of Asians. As a result of this modified sampling procedure, 14,416 students participated in the survey: 7,943 ninth-grade and 6,473 twelfth-grade students. The sample represented a slightly higher percentage of females (53.1%) than of males (46.9%). Approximately one third of the sample were Asian, and the rest were White, African American, Latino, and mixed-race adolescents. The breakdown of the Asian ethnic groups indicated that there was not equal representation of all five Asian groups initially targeted. There was a large number of Chinese, Filipinos, and mixed-heritage Asian students in the sample. For the purpose of the present study, we focused our analyses on 6,021 self-identified single- and mixed-heritage Asian American adolescents.

Survey Instrument

The instrument, the 1995 SWRL Multiethnic Drug & Alcohol Survey, was a combined and modified version of the American Drug Abuse and Alcohol Survey (ADAS) and the Prevention Planning Survey (PPS). The survey instrument contained six major domains: (a) ATOD use, (b) peer drug associations, (c) parental/family variables, (d) mental health variables (e.g., depression, anger), (e) cultural identification, and (f) demographic information. The survey was translated and back-translated into Chinese, Korean, Vietnamese, and Spanish and modified where the wording was ambiguous.

Findings

Perceived Racial/Ethnic Tension on Campus

Students' perceptions of racial/ethnic tension on their high school campuses were assessed by three items using a 4-point Likert-type scale (4 = *very often*, 3 = *sometimes*, 2 = *not very often*, and 1 = *not at all*): (a) How often are you treated unfairly at your school

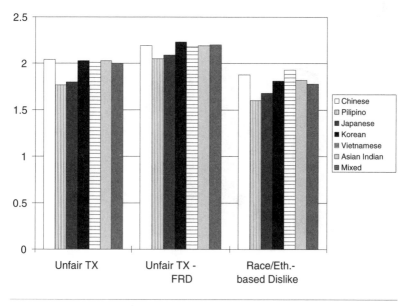

Figure 5.1   Perceived Racial/Ethnic Tension

because of your racial or ethnic background? (b) How often have you seen your friends treated unfairly at your school because of their racial or ethnic background? (c) How often do other students dislike you because of your racial or ethnic background?

Figure 5.1 shows the means of all three items by five racial categories. By far, the African American students showed the highest level of perceived racial tension on all three items, followed by the Asian American students, students of Hispanic background, students of mixed-heritage background, and White students; *omnibus* F (4, 13,470) = 357.98, $p < .001$. A priori multiple comparison of the means among these groups showed statistically significant differences between the White students and all the rest, indicating that non-White students' perceptions of race relations across 34 high school campuses were qualitatively different from those of White students. White students perceived significantly less racial tension on campus than did the minority students.

Similarly, Figure 5.2 depicts subgroup differences among seven Asian and mixed-heritage student groups. The Chinese students appeared to be higher in their perception of their own and friends'

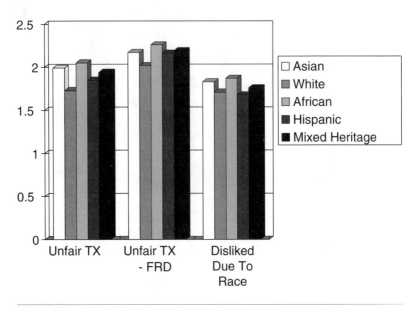

Figure 5.2   Perceived Racial/Ethnic Tension Among Asian American
Adolescents: A Subgroup Comparison

unfair treatment when compared to other groups ($p < .01$), whereas
the Vietnamese students were highest in perceptions of being disliked due to their race ($p < .01$). On the other hand, Filipino and
Japanese students perceived less racial tension than the other Asian
ethnic groups in the sample ($p < .01$).

As expected, the perception of race and ethnic relations on a
high school campus varies depending on to which racial or ethnic
groups the students belonged. Moreover, because of the significant
subgroup differences among the various Asian ethnic groups,
caution is necessary in generalizing these findings. That is, generalizing any research findings from one Asian ethnic group to all Asians
obscures important ethnic differences. Public policy decisions based
on this ethnic gloss then would not account for these significant
ethnic group differences.

To the extent that school ecology is assumed to affect the well-
being of Asian American students (Sasao, 1999), the next analysis
entailed testing a theoretical model linking ecological factors and
other theoretically driven variables to psychological well-being
measures. Figure 5.3 shows the results of a structural equation

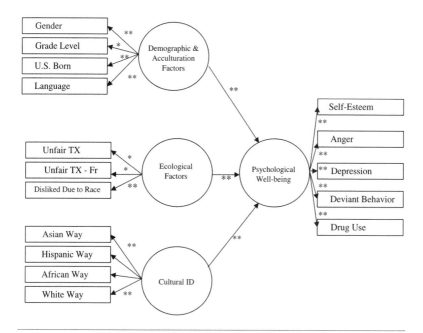

Figure 5.3   EQS Models Predicting Psychological Well-Being Among
Asian American Adolescents ($n = 4{,}704$)

NOTE: Comparative fit index (CFI) = .923.

$^{*}p < .05; ^{**}p < .01.$

model that attempts to explain the paths among ecological factors, demographic factors, and cultural identification indicators to five different but interrelated measures of psychological well-being.

This path model was empirically tested with all the Asian students as a group using the EQS (Bentler, 1995) structural equation modeling technique. All of the statistically significant paths are shown with either * or **. Goodness-of-fit indices indicate adequate model fit: comparative fit index (CFI) = .923, $\chi^2/df = 1.89$. The validity of the path model was further tested by performing a chi-square difference test in which the overall goodness of fit was compared with that of the correlation model. The test revealed no significant difference between these chi-square values, indicating that the initial path model was successful in accounting for the observed relationships between latent constructs. Results of this modeling showed that each set of factors (demographic/acculturation, ecological factors, and cultural identification measures) had a significant *independent* effect on the latent construct of psychological well-being measures.

Although this model, as in other previous research, demonstrates the importance of personal and acculturation factors, the effects of perceived intergroup relations on a school campus and those of cultural identification (being Asian and being White) contributed significantly to the overall model. The interpretation of these findings needs to be tempered, however, by the fact that racial/ethnic tension was measured by only three self-report items. Future model fit needs to include a more comprehensive set of perceived tension measures, including actual incidents of racially motivated violence on school campuses.

Given the complexities of race and racial interactions for Asian Americans, the next section of this chapter will discuss the psychological outcomes of hate violence, coping strategies used by victims, and preliminary recommendations and observations on clinical research and psychoeducational interventions for Asian Americans.

Clinical Issues

As alluded to earlier, there has been a dearth of research on the psychological effects of hate violence on Asian Americans (Dunbar, 1997). Therefore, little information exists on the psychosocial correlates of hate violence, adjustment processes, and coping resources and mechanisms used by Asian American victims and their families. Furthermore, there are scant data on the longstanding effects of hate violence on Asian American families (i.e., transgenerational effects of racial trauma) or on the individual victim. Although several psychologists have made important contributions to our understanding in this area (e.g., Chen & True, 1994; Dunbar, 1997; Loo, 1993; Nagata, 1993; Root, 1992), there is a vast gap in the knowledge and intervention base with this particular mental health issue. Despite this lack of information, an analysis and some preliminary recommendations regarding clinical implications for Asian American hate violence victims will be discussed next.

The posttraumatic stress disorder (PTSD) model is a useful tool to use in framing the psychological responses or outcomes (i.e., symptoms) to hate violence and the corresponding process of coping with that experience. Symptoms commonly experienced by hate violence victims include feelings of hopelessness, frustration, guilt, detachment/isolation, avoidance, shock, nightmares, numbness, paranoid-like guardedness, shame, fear, dysphoria, and disillusionment (Dunbar, 1997; Loo, 1993; Root, 1992). In addition, hate crime victims may exhibit denial or denigration of their racial group membership, demonstrate strong out-group prejudice, and show increased antisocial behavior (Kohatsu, Lum, Soudah, Luong, & Hah, 1995). According to Barnes and Ephross (1994), emotional responses experienced by hate crime victims in their sample included anger at the perpetrator, fear that family or self would be injured, sadness, suspiciousness of other people, and feeling bad about oneself. Thus, many of the symptoms experienced by hate violence victims closely parallel the PTSD symptom cluster. Dunbar (1997) proposed three distinct categories of affective responses to hate trauma: (a) anxiety/tension, (b) dysphoria/sadness, and (c) anger/aggression.

Moreover, researchers have not examined coping strategies used by Asian American victims of hate violence. However, Liu and Dunbar (1994) reported that for Asian Pacific Americans, greater in-group identity was related to a more active coping response to racial discrimination. Generally, much of the existing work suggests that coping responses used by hate violence victims also reflect similar strategies used by PTSD clients (e.g., Loo, 1993; Root, 1992). For example, avoidance, detachment, moving out of the neighborhood, and isolating oneself are some of the typical coping strategies used by hate crime victims and PTSD clients (Barnes & Ephross, 1994; Loo, 1993).

Treatment Issues

As noted previously, relatively few researchers have studied the issues involved in the treatment of Asian American hate crime or violence victims. Before reviewing a recently developed model of treatment for hate crime victims, several general comments will be made. First, as with individuals suffering from PTSD (whether by natural or intentional human design), a key factor in the recovery process rests on the hate violence victim's level of psychological functioning prior to the hate event. Personality style, coping strategies, and prior experiences of trauma affect the person's ability to recover from the hate trauma. Second, Dunbar (1997) suggested that the two primary intervention tasks in treating victims of hate crimes are reducing symptoms related to the hate crime event and facilitating the client's reestablishment of a healthy in-group identity. Third, a consistent theme in the research has been that the development of a strong and positive sense of oneself (i.e., racial identity) buffers a person of color from being victimized or participating in racial violence (Hill, Soriano, Chen, & LaFromboise, 1994; Hollinger, Offer, Barter, & Bell, 1994). Thus, in the treatment of Asian Americans victimized by hate violence, it is imperative that the individuals' racial identity be assessed and its reestablishment be supported (Kohatsu et al., 1995).

Recently, a model for treating hate crime victims was developed and has potential applications for working with Asian Americans (Dunbar, 1997). Dunbar (1997) proposed five phases of counseling:

1. Event containment and safety

2. Assessment of client-event characteristics

3. Addressing culture in the counseling relationship

4. Targeted symptom identification and reduction

5. Functional recovery and identity reformation

Briefly, in Phase 1, the primary concern of the therapist is to ensure that the client's safety is not threatened and that he or she is not engaging in any destructive behaviors (e.g., aggressive behavior toward others or oneself). It is critical that the therapist remain mindful of cross-cultural differences throughout the course of treatment. Phase 2 entails the clinician evaluating the hate crime experience, client symptoms, and available social support. An integral component of Phase 2 is to assess the frequency and quality of interracial contact that the Asian American individual had prior to the hate crime event.

In Phase 3, cultural issues should be dealt with as they affect the therapeutic relationship. Counselor race and racial identity, for example, are important factors that affect the counseling process and should be addressed continuously (Helms, 1995). Likewise, it is also critical that the counselor continually monitor the client's racial identity profile as counseling progresses. In addition, Dunbar (1997) suggested that clinicians monitor their own countertransference in working with hate violence victims because feelings of hopelessness or guilt may emerge.

Phase 4 involves incorporating a wide range of interventions to assist in the client's recovery from the hate violence experience. This model proposes that the clinician focus on tasks such as desensitizing the client to the hate event, reframing the meaning of the event for the client, and teaching anger management skills. Again, most interventions used in Phase 4 are widely used in the trauma and PTSD treatment approaches. Enhancing social support, desensitization (or progressive exposure to traumatic memories), cognitive reframing, and learning active mastery skills are some of the fundamental treatment approaches to trauma that can be applied to hate violence victims as well (Loo, 1993).

According to Dunbar (1997), Phase 5 entails "measuring and reinforcing symptom reduction and change, monitoring outgroup attitudes, promoting benign intergroup contact experiences, and targeting after-care goals" (p. 35). Furthermore, the clinician should focus on the impact of hate violence on the Asian Americans' level of racial and ethnic identity. Depending on which model of identity the clinician uses, it can help to map out the various ways in which an individual responds to these traumatic insults to the self. Helms's (1995) racial identity model, discussed earlier, has numerous applications for this phase of the counseling process with Asian American victims of hate violence.

Dunbar's (1997) model is extremely useful for clinicians and researchers in that it provides a structure by which to develop clinical interventions to assist clients in the recovery from a hate violence experience. This model certainly deserves greater scrutiny and research to test its validity. Nonetheless, several additions to Dunbar's model using racial identity theory will now be proposed.

Developing and maintaining a strong, integrated sense of oneself as an Asian American is one of the most critical components to prevent and treat hate violence (Hill et al., 1994). Kohatsu et al. (1995) proposed that racial identity theory can be used as a guiding framework for clinical interventions with hate violence clients and for developing psychoeducational programs. With regard to Dunbar's (1997) model, racial identity theory as a counseling intervention and educational tool should be consistently used throughout the course of treatment. Using racial identity theory is potentially useful for the following reasons.

Racial identity theory provides a structure by which one can begin to make better sense of racially motivated incidences. In other words, this theory can help Asian Americans to demystify the dynamics of race. On one level, rather than internalizing painful incidences dealing with race, racial identity theory can help individuals put such experiences into a more accurate and healthy perspective. Instead of making inaccurate and potentially damaging internal attributions about oneself, the locus of responsibility is placed on the external environment and its corresponding interpersonal (racial) dynamics. Thus, racial identity theory provides a useful framework for Asian Americans to interpret their racial experiences in a less damaging manner.

On another level, racial identity theory can help to diffuse the anger that many Asians may experience in the aftermath of hate violence in light of its potential interpretive power. Specifically, racial identity theory can provide a framework for understanding racial incidences and serve as a buffer against psychological trauma (Moore, Fried, & Costantino, 1991). An Asian American with adequate knowledge of racial identity theory can learn to recognize the motivations that underlie racial acts. As articulated in Helms's (1995) model, individuals who operate using different racial identity statuses will interpret and react to racial issues in fairly predictable ways. If an Asian American can understand this, then aspects of the hate experience can be framed in ways that enhance growth rather than promote self-destructive behaviors. Thus, she or he will possess a greater understanding of people's racial motivations and behavior patterns and, consequently, will be better equipped to cope with racial trauma.

Concomitantly, racial identity theory can help professionals to better understand how racism has affected the victim and how to intervene in the environment to promote more positive interpersonal interactions. More broadly, then, racial identity theory can be a useful diagnostic tool to assist one in analyzing and therefore demystifying racial interactions at the individual and group levels (Carter, 1995; Helms, 1990, 1995). Helms (1990, 1995) developed her racial identity interaction model based on four principles. She proposed that (a) the particular racial identity status from which individuals operate structures their reactions to other people and to environments, (b) people can form harmonious or disharmonious relationships with one another based on their racial identity statuses,

(c) reactions to race occur in the context of directly or vicariously experiencing interpersonal transactions, and (d) patterns of reactions can be classified according to their quality (Helms, 1995). Therefore, if one can interpret the racial dynamics in a given environment, then predictions could be made about people's behaviors. These racial predictions, based on racial identity theory, could then lead to improved ways of intervening in an environment to enhance racial interactions. In other words, if one could "diagnose" the kind of relationship(s) existing in a particular environment, then the existing racial dynamics could be better understood and consequently handled more effectively.

An implication of the research discussed earlier is that promoting more positive intergroup (i.e., racial) relations may be better facilitated by enhancing the Asian American individual's level of racial identity development (Kohatsu et al., 2000). Encouraging a deeper awareness of sociorace (Helms, 1994) and increasing an individual's positive assessment of his or her own group will likely help in promoting more positive attitudes, emotions, and behaviors toward other racial groups (Kohatsu, 1997). In conjunction, facilitating racial identity development may in turn result in the reduction of racism and prejudice and increase one's ability to function more effectively in a variety of cultural contexts (Kohatsu et al., 2000).

Suggestions for Future Violence Prevention Research and Practice

Given the research and clinical issues discussed previously, a few suggestions for future research and practice will now be presented.

First, although racially motivated violence against Asian Americans has not been widely studied, the experiences of Asian American adults and adolescents appear to confirm their perception of actual racial problems on campus and in their communities. Such empirical findings are important because many violence prevention or reduction programs target other racial groups to the exclusion of Asian Americans. Regarding adolescents, it could be argued that this negligence is often prompted by the fact that most Asian students in public schools are recent immigrants with limited language and social skills; this means that their input into any such prevention programs will be reflected less often. Perhaps conducting a comprehensive assessment of violence-related experiences among Asian American students and adults will be a positive step toward remedying the problem. Moreover, the knowledge base of the experiences of racism and its psychological impact on Asian Americans is quite limited and also needs to be addressed in future research.

Second, although ecological factors were found to be important in accounting for various measures of psychological well-being, other factors were also significant. Particularly, to the extent that four separate cultural identification measures showed significant paths to well-being measures in support of Oetting and Beauvais's (1990-1991) orthogonal identification theory, both researchers and practitioners (e.g., teachers and clinicians) must be aware of cultural values and beliefs that may not be related to what Trimble (1990-1991) calls "ethnic or racial glosses." Rather, this suggests that we need to emphasize the assessment of the "person-environment fit" for Asian American students in school settings.

Prevention

A powerful tool that can be used to reduce and prevent racial violence is psychoeducational programs. Although there are a number of avenues for prevention, for the purpose of this chapter, we will only highlight a few. First, it is critical to educate Asian Americans to respond to racism in a constructive manner. These educational programs should be implemented in arenas that will effectively communicate important information to the greatest number of people. For example, school organizations, community-based groups, and law enforcement agencies can provide training programs to help Asian Americans interpret racial events more accurately and constructively. As part of this educational effort, it may also be helpful to offer ongoing support groups for processing racial experiences. These support groups have proven useful in the past as a way for victims to cope with hate trauma (Loo, 1993).

Second, because aggressive behavior often takes place in school, experts on youth violence have recommended that school-based interventions be a primary focus for prevention (Guerra, Tolan, & Hammond, 1994). Classes on the psychology of race need to be made an integral part of the school curriculum. Many so-called "race educational programs" merely devote one or two sessions to the topic, which is a grossly insufficient approach. The topic must not be seen as merely the "theme for the day" because that would allow it to be too easily disregarded or dismissed (VanBebber, 1991). Ongoing racial education classes are necessary so that some of the issues and experiences of students can be brought out and dealt with in a growth-enhancing manner (Tatum, 1992).

Third, promoting education regarding race and racial identity should extend beyond the academic system to include the family and community (Kohatsu et al., 1995). These realms are interconnected and work in tangent together. For instance, race education should take place in families (Stevenson & Renard, 1993). Parents need to talk to their children about race and racial issues in a constructive way. Hence, Asian American adolescents will more likely venture into society being better equipped to deal effectively with racism. It is recognized that among many Asian American families, the shame of hate violence and the corresponding lack of understanding regarding racial dynamics make it more difficult to promote race education. Again, community organizations can help to coordinate these race education programs so that more Asian families are serviced.

Fourth, districtwide task forces could be used to educate people about racial identity by regularly conducting workshops and seminars (Kohatsu et al., 1995). The advantage of these task forces is that the most knowledgeable and best-trained experts in race relations can be part of these teams. These teams can go to different institutions to provide information via seminars, assemblies, and lectures and conduct hands-on workshops and training sessions on race and racism; therefore, no single facility would have sole responsibility for instituting its own race education program. A number of national Asian American organizations could coordinate efforts to introduce such programs to the various Asian communities in any given city.

Similarly, hate trauma response teams can also provide critical on-site services to assist Asians who have been victimized (Kohatsu et al., 1995). These response teams should comprise mental health professionals who have experience in working with Asian Americans and who are deeply aware of the psychological aspects of racism. In many Asian communities, mental health agencies have been developed to provide culturally specific (i.e., sensitive) services. It therefore makes sense to form these response teams from within these local Asian American agencies.

Conclusion

The context of racial interactions and racial environments for Asian Americans is complex and multifaceted. Much of the ecology of race for this particular group is not well understood. Nonetheless, racial identity theory can be a powerful tool to use in understanding the impact of racial interactions on Asian Americans, as well as providing a framework in counseling when working with Asian victims of hate violence. Undeniably, the basis of promoting more constructive interracial contact is through enhancing a more positive sense of one's racial identity. Integrating an understanding of racial identity into families, school curricula, and community organizations could move entire communities to achieve a more positive and constructive racial environment (Kohatsu, et al., 1995). In turn, people would be better equipped to deal with racial discord in a more productive manner. That, in the end, is our fundamental hope.

Note

1. The study was supported by a grant from the National Institute on Drug Abuse (R01 DA08269-02; Toshiaki Sasao, Ph.D., principal investigator).

Part III

Understanding and Dealing With Violence in Academic Settings

6

Developing Men's Leadership to Challenge Sexism and Violence

Working in University Settings to Develop "Pro-Feminist, Gay-Affirmative, and Male-Positive" Men

Tom Schiff

Several years ago, I reconnected with an old high school friend, a woman I had not seen in many years. Initially, I had met her as the girlfriend of one of my best friends. We were out having dinner together, catching up on each other's lives. I had been telling her how one of my areas of work, and a real passion for me, is working with men to challenge sexism, homophobia, and male violence. She looked me in the eye and said, "You know, I have a very specific memory of you from high school, which I think is quite fascinating in light of the work you now do." Her tone of voice indicated that there was some disparity between this memory and the current reality of my life. Always being amazed at how one's past can collide with the present, I swallowed hard and asked, "What is that memory?" She told me of a time she and I were talking at a party. Her boyfriend was not there for one reason or another. She was telling me about some conflict the two of them were having and how she felt he was being really sexist. According to my friend, at that point

I looked her in the eye and said, "You're right, he is being sexist." She was floored to think that a man was actually agreeing with her, especially considering this was one of my best friends. So she looked at me and asked hopefully, "Will you tell him that?" And without missing a beat, I quickly said, "Oh no, that's not my place or my business!"

I start this chapter on working within educational settings to develop men's leadership with that story because I feel it illustrates some critical points. First, there are many men in our communities who have a good, critical gendered analysis and pro-feminist perspective but for whom taking action feels inappropriate or, probably more often, inaccessible and/or frightening. Second, women have been asking men to join the struggle for gender equality and ending gender-based violence for many years. Sexism is literally killing thousands of women every year and, in a broader sense, killing the minds and spirits of women who are our mothers, grandmothers, sisters, daughters, lovers, friends, and neighbors. It is my business to challenge sexism, and it behooves all men committed to social justice to find ways to engage with our selves and other men to be allies to women.

Background

I am defining violence as "that which violates or causes violation, and is usually performed by a violator upon the violated" (Hearn, 1994, p. 735). This violation has become so commonplace that leaders such as the secretary of the U.S. Department of Health and Human Services, representatives of the Centers for Disease Control and Prevention, and a former surgeon general consider violence a major public health issue (Koop & Lundberg, 1992; Rosenberg, O'Carroll, & Powell, 1992; Shalala, 1993). Because roughly 90% of all violent crime in the United States is committed by men, it seems to follow that male violence is a major public health issue (Federal Bureau of Investigation [FBI], 1996).

Exactly what causes male violence is unclear. There continues to be discussion about whether male violence is learned behavior or if it is biologically based. For example, there is evidence indicating that high levels of testosterone may be linked to characteristics that tend to be precursors to violence, such as irritability, frustration, and impatience, and there may be links between violence and other biological and genetic conditions such as attention deficit disorder with hyperactivity and Asperger's syndrome (Miedzian, 1991). This does not, however, indicate a causal relationship. Although biology may lead to a predisposition to violence in some men, it is clear that violent behavior (and other behaviors) is probably more affected by the ways in which cultures shape and modify biological factors. This cultural intervention in the shaping of masculinity and male behavior (as well as femininity and female behavior) has long been supported by anthropologists such as Margaret Mead (1935). Cross-cultural studies indicate that in cultures where there tends to be less of a hierarchical gendered division of behavior and related beliefs about such division, there typically is less gender-based violence and greater gender equality (Sanday, 1990). The manner in which gender, gender relations, and thus masculinity are socially constructed is culturally dependent, and therefore so is the level of "permission" a society gives to men to be violent. Viewing this through the lens of U.S. culture, Miedzian (1991) stated that "as long as male behavior is taken to be the norm, there can be no serious questioning of male traits and behavior" (p. 12). This, of course, includes male violence.

A major factor that has been identified as contributing to male violence is male gender socialization. Many U.S. men seem to encounter numerous common experiences that teach them to be tough, dominant, repressive of empathy, hypercompetitive, emotionally absent, and violent (Brannon, 1976; O'Neil, 1990). Violence is one of the normative aspects of "hegemonic masculinity" (Connell, 1995). The social pressure to be "masculine" leads many men to be aggressive and/or violent because violence is associated with "manliness" (Groth, 1979; Mosher & Sirkin, 1984; Paymar & Pence, 1993; West, Roy, & Nichols, 1978). Gender socialization is a cornerstone of male violence and sexism as it serves to normalize violence and patriarchal beliefs and patterns. This involves exerting dominance and mastery over others while maintaining self-control and composure in all relationships, including sexual relationships. When there is a threat or perceived threat to their ability to control, many men respond with a wide range of coercive, abusive, and violent behaviors in an attempt to reclaim control and thus self-worth (Kivel, 1992; Paymar & Pence, 1993).

Given this background, it appears that effective prevention and intervention with men would involve an exploration and deconstruction of male socialization and the various meanings of masculinity. However, historically, violence programs have focused on risk reduction for potential victims. For example, college and university sexual assault and rape prevention programs have typically focused on training women to identify and reduce risk factors and situations. Although mixed-gender prevention education is provided on many campuses, the few empirical evaluations of single-sex programs seem to support the efficacy of a single-sex format for men (Berkowitz, Burkhart, & Bourg, 1994). However, this should in no way be seen as conclusive evidence because these findings are based on very few studies. Evaluation studies of specific violence prevention programs have shown that females tend to show more changes than males in knowledge and attitudes toward relationship violence after participation in mixed-group prevention programs (Berkowitz et al., 1994; Lavoie, Vezina, Piche, & Boivin, 1995) and that one-time workshops tend to be less effective than ongoing multidimensional efforts (Hausman, Spivak, & Prothrow-Stith, 1995). Yet, there seems to be little conclusive evidence about the long-term impact on behavior of any of these programs, although the last study cited does seem to support multilayered systemic interventions.

In the remainder of this chapter, I will highlight some important aspects of working with men within educational settings to develop their leadership in challenging sexism and violence. The suggestions I will put forth are based on more than 20 years of working with men in this arena. I will begin with a rationale for why it is important to work with men, define men's leadership, explore obstacles to developing men's leadership, and move into presenting a systemic model for framing this. The focus of this model is educational settings, although I believe some of this could be generalized to other settings as well.

Rationale for Developing Men's Leadership

There are four primary reasons why it is essential to develop men's leadership to challenge sexism and violence. First, men are the primary perpetrators of violence. Violence is a men's issue. As I stated earlier, roughly 90% of all violent crime in the United States is committed by men (FBI, 1996). This encompasses not only men's violence against women but also all violence, including racial, homophobic, religion-based, and other hate-based violence. Although this chapter is focused on men's violence against women, it is important to note that men also are the primary victims of violence. For example, the homicide rate for men is more than four times greater than the rate for women, and about 90% of the time the perpetrator is another man (FBI, 1996). As the last statistic points out, although most of the violence is committed against men, it is men who are committing this violence. When we turn to violence against women, the trend continues—this violence is male violence. For example, studies indicate that 1 in 12 college males have raped women (Koss, 1988). Please note the way in which I stated that "college males have raped women." Language is a powerful way in which we name and frame reality, and thus it is important to think carefully about how we discuss the dynamics of violence. A problem with the term *violence against women* is that it leaves out the primary active perpetrator—men. In grammatical terms, in the phrase "violence against women," women are the object, but there is no stated subject. In societal terms, the phrase, although certainly useful, objectifies women and allows men to remain invisible, and therefore men escape some of the responsibility and scrutiny we really need to own.

Second, men are friends and family members of victims and survivors of violence. This is a horrible position in which to find oneself. It is imperative for anyone in this position to find ways to understand the emotional responses that arise because how we respond can either help or hinder the other person's process of recovery and empowerment. Unless we can find constructive ways to help men deal with this secondary trauma, we have large numbers of men who are like the walking wounded, looking for any outlet for their feelings of powerlessness.

Third, men are victims of violence. As stated earlier, men actually are the primary victims of violence, but as a society, we have accepted this violence as "normal" to such a degree that it is often ignored and discounted. Therefore, we have few explicit resources for male victims of violence. In the work I do with young men, I continually hear reports of fights with peers and of physical, verbal, and psychological abuse from their parents, siblings, teachers, coaches, and others. We are teaching our young men that might makes right and that violence is an acceptable, perhaps even a valued form of male behavior. Thus, for many men who have been victimized, violence serves as a socially acceptable way to allay all the pain and hurt heaped on them as young men (Finkelhor, Hotaling, & Yllö, 1988; Sonkin, Martin, & Walker, 1985).

Fourth, men have much to offer as models and leaders in endeavors to challenge men's violence and men's violence against women. Many men care but do not know how they can take action. There is a need for role models and for peer and institutional supports to develop men's responses and leadership. One of the things I stress in my work is that men's leadership is a combination of taking responsibility and having response-ability. In other words, we need to own what part of ourselves can connect to other men around violence (and we ourselves may have been violent in our own past and present) while also finding ways to challenge ourselves and others to take action.

Defining Men's Leadership

Leadership is a topic that has been explored from many perspectives—business, sports, social change, politics, and more. In this model, leadership is viewed as having two primary components. One is the outward "activist" behaviors, things such as organizing events, building coalitions, conducting workshops, and so on. The second component is the personal part of leadership—connecting with other men, living by one's values, challenging sexism close to home, being a model in one's life, and so forth. The personal, political, and theoretical are brought together to foster male leadership that is pro-feminist, gay affirmative, and male positive.[1]

To fully develop pro-feminist, gay-affirmative, male-positive leadership, men must be willing to engage and deal personally and politically in each of the following areas: relationships with women and feminism, relationships with other men and homophobia, and our relationship with ourselves.

Relationships With Women and Feminism

Understanding feminist analysis and applying that to pro-feminist perspectives on men and violence is an essential ongoing step for those wanting to take leadership to challenge men's violence. Of course, as with any topic, we want to help develop critical thinking and not simply create unquestioning adherence to a particular perspective. After all, isn't an ability to see multiple perspectives a fundamental component of developing a multiculturally sensitive approach to violence prevention and to life itself, for that matter? Exploring the breadth of feminist thought is a formidable task, but because we are in the business of nurturing critical thinking skills, it does not feel like much of a stretch to expect this of our students.

What is undoubtedly the harder part of developing pro-feminist leadership is to examine our current and past relationships with women in our lives—mothers, sisters, friends, lovers, and so on—and how that affects our view of women. In our view of women, if we are truly honest in our self-reflection, we often find places that may feel dissonant with our feminist analysis. After all, we all grew up and live in a patriarchy. We are immersed in oppressive beliefs at a deep level.

Although some of this work can be done in mixed-gender groups, it seems much more appropriate for there to be spaces for men to be able to wrestle with these issues with other men in a safe but challenging environment. Just as there is a need to have some women's-only spaces, there also needs to be men's-only spaces that allow men to redefine "traditional" men's-only spaces.

Relationships With Other Men and Homophobia

Within that men's space and in our daily lives, we need to look at our relationships not only with women but with other men as well. How do we connect with other men? How do we advocate for men in a way that is caring and confrontive at the same time? How do we address homophobia in our selves, relationships, work, and culture? How do we reach across barriers that typically separate men—race, class, sexual orientation, and so forth?

Homophobia plays a key role in shaping heterosexual male sexuality and behavior. Many men feel a continual need to provide their credentials as "real men" and to prove their mastery as men; being gay does not fall into the category of "real man" (Blumenfeld, 1992; Stoltenberg, 1989). Interestingly, heterosexual sexual "competition" also can be seen as a form of expression of sexuality between men in an acceptable, socially sanctioned way, a form of homoerotic interaction (Sanday, 1990).

Homophobia, as a factor in the shaping of male identity and sexuality, starts at an early age. Young boys target other boys with homophobic comments, often not even knowing what the words mean. This behavior becomes part of the way in which we posture and jockey for a position in the male hierarchy. By the time young men enter high school, being called gay is considered the worst insult imaginable (American Association of University Women, 1993). Homophobia intersects with sexism and misogyny in many ways. One important way is that it helps reinforce hierarchical thinking about all relationships while establishing a system that not only values heterosexual men over women and gay men but also supports heterosexual men's violence against women and gay men. Homophobia is so deeply ingrained into so many men that it is crucial to address this overtly and fully to effectively challenge male violence.

Our Relationship With Ourselves

Throughout the process of figuring out where we stand in relation to women, feminism, other men, and homophobia, we also need to examine where we stand in relation to ourselves. How do I view myself ? What does it mean to me to be a man? Why am I doing this work? This last question is significant. Some men want to enter this work for their own healing—either from their own victimization or that of someone they know or, less commonly, healing from their own violence. None of these factors should exclude any man from wanting to do work to challenge sexism and violence, but it is critical to be aware of our underlying motivations. One's motivation and level of self-awareness have much to do with how this person can be most effective. Men who come from a place of wanting to place guilt or to shame others or to show they are better than others will at best be ineffective and potentially harmful. The most effective educators I have seen in this venue are men who have a good sense of themselves, can connect easily with other men because they understand the common experiences so many of us share, and have a true desire to create lasting change. One final note about one's motivation: A few years ago, I was telling a friend about an upcoming speaking engagement I had as a part of a university sexual assault awareness week. He jokingly said to me, "I guess you'll definitely get laid." It was funny because we both understood the context and just how ludicrous that statement was. However, I have seen men get involved in this work for just that reason—to impress women and get dates. They are not always even that overtly aware of this motivation, which translates to a generalized lack of self-awareness. The men who do this with cognizance are unusual, in my experience, and typically more easy to identify.

Men's lack of self-awareness, or the less common predatory motivation, can serve as an obstacle to gaining support for the development of pro-feminist, gay-affirmative, male-positive men's leadership. In the next section, other obstacles will be explored.

Obstacles to Developing Men's Leadership

Changing male leadership is not just about changing individual men. It is also about changing the environment, such as the educational setting in which they operate, so that this leadership can be nurtured and blossom. To transform our domains, we need to critically examine and be willing to change ourselves and our systems. However, before moving into a presentation of a systems model for supporting the development of pro-feminist, gay-affirmative, male-positive leadership, it is useful to examine some of the obstacles that often get in the way of effectively working with men around issues of violence.

Obstacles to working with men fall into three basic categories (see Figure 6.1). First, there appears to be a low investment by many men around issues of sexism, homophobia, and violence. This is usually wrapped in either apathy or fear and defensiveness. Violence against women is seen as a women's issue, and antigay violence is seen as a gay issue. In addition, our collective cultural denial and silence about the prevalence of these forms of violence, mixed with a lack of personal experience or knowledge, pervade many men's willingness to consider looking deeper into sexism, homophobia, and violence. This manifests itself in behaviors and attitudes that are reflected in the following commonly heard statements, all of which I have heard numerous times in both formal and informal educational settings:

"It's not a big deal."

"You're blowing this thing way out of proportion."

"It's not my issue."

"Other men do that, not me."

"I don't know anyone who has been harassed/beaten up/raped."

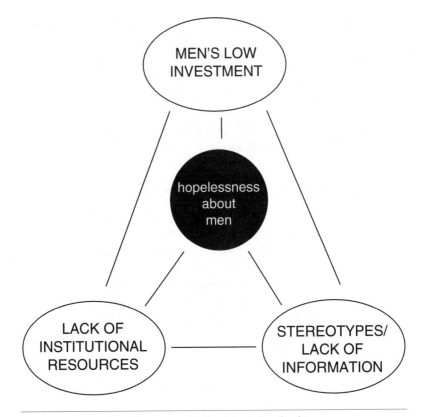

Figure 6.1   Obstacles to Developing Men's Leadership

Men's low investment in challenging sexism, homophobia, and violence also reflects a high level of fear and defensiveness. If we truly begin to explore the dynamics of sexism, we often fear we may discover that we have done and continue to do numerous sexist things ranging from the mild to the horrid. The potential guilt can be overwhelming and paralyzing. Compounding that is the fear of women's anger—anger that we fear may be targeted at us as individuals or as representatives of our gender.

An additional fear can be framed as a fear of upsetting social norms that implicitly and explicitly prop up sexism, homophobia, and violence as "normal" parts of the social fabric. These norms afford heterosexual men with a high level of social and economic privilege. To begin to overtly question sexism, homophobia, and violence means jeopardizing that privilege and, quite possibly, becoming a target of homophobia and violence. Thus, for many heterosexual men, it feels better or at least safer to remain silent.

The second set of obstacles is the dearth of accurate information about heterosexual men's experiences and perspectives. In the years I have been doing this work, I have heard quite a bit of this misinformation. Numerous stereotypes exist about these men that interfere with effective education. For example, it has not been uncommon to hear statements such as, "All men are rapists," "Men just don't care," or "They'll never change." Additional layers of misinformation exist when we factor in racial stereotypes, such as, "Latino men are more sexist" or "Black men more homophobic." These pieces of misinformation also are alarmingly common. They serve not only to reproduce racist ideologies, but they also can place a wedge between men trying to have productive dialogue about issues around sexism, homophobia, and violence.

As educators, if we approach men "armed" with misinformation and assumptions about their low investment, if we try to educate while stewing in our own unbridled anger, and if we try to impose answers and use guilt, there is a good chance that we will contribute to creating more division and defensiveness, thus setting up ourselves and the men with whom we hope to work for failure. Our assumptions about people have much to do with how we deal with them (e.g., if we expect a conflict, we are probably going to get one).

A third obstacle for effectively developing men's leadership to challenge sexism, homophobia, and violence is more systemic in nature. Typically, there is a low investment of institutional resources focused on developing this sort of men's leadership. Sexism and homophobia are seen as a "women's problem" or "gay issues," and men's violence just happens or is part of someone's individual pathology rather than a product of ongoing sociocultural dynamics. Therefore, priority services go to women and occasionally the gay communities. There should be a plethora of services offered to these groups, but if we do not also focus on heterosexual men, we are missing half the picture (Capraro, 1994).

These three obstacles—men's low investment, misinformation about men, and lack of institutional resources—can lead to feelings of hopelessness, frustration, anger, and fear. Often, when I am working with teachers, student development personnel, human service workers, or others who will be working with men, particularly young men, I ask them to think about their assumptions about men, violence, and change. I do a variety of different exercises to get people in touch with their feelings and thoughts. The responses I hear are remarkably similar everywhere I go. These responses typically do reflect hopelessness and thus resignation about effecting any real change. And the cycle continues.

A Systems Model for Developing Men's Leadership

I started by examining obstacles because the level to which these things exist often are indicative of where our systems reside in regard to developing pro-feminist, gay-affirmative, male-positive men's leadership. We need to know where we stand so that we can identify what we need to do to get where we want to go. As we start to assess our systems in relation to developing pro-feminist, gay-affirmative, male-positive male leadership, it is not uncommon to find many aspects of our systems that are predicated on a sense of hopelessness about heterosexual men. To create systems that sustain men's leadership in challenging sexism, homophobia, and violence, we need to transform the underlying base from one built on hopelessness to one built on hopefulness. A vision of hopefulness and belief in men requires bolstering by environments and structures that foster the development of loving, caring, nonviolent male heterosexualities. Creating these systems is a long-term process. What follows are some suggestions for putting such a system in place (see Figure 6.2). In addition, the assessment form (see Table 6.1) may serve as a useful tool in guiding your efforts.

Creating a Shared Vision

Shared vision is not something we agree to on a cognitive level and then it happens. It is something we have to share in our minds and our hearts. It is something we are enacting every day in everything we do because it is fully enmeshed in who we are. Shared vision is not imposed from "the top." It must be co-created through ongoing interactions and conversations that serve to enroll individuals into a collective agreement (Senge, 1990).

On the most fundamental level, creating a shared vision of pro-feminist, gay-affirmative, male-positive male leadership based on hopefulness requires answering just one simple question—what

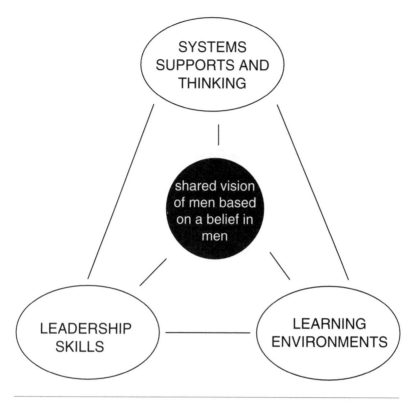

Figure 6.2   Systemic Strategies for Developing Men's Leadership

characteristics do we want to encourage men in this community to have? This is a simple question with no simple answer. Often when working with groups of educators, I ask them to think about two questions for the purpose of starting a conversation about how this vision will unfold. These two questions are as follows:

1. What characteristics of men you know would you like to encourage more men to have?

2. What are characteristics that you may not experience coming from men in your life that you would like to see more men display?

These two questions can lead to hours of dialogue, which is part of creating shared vision. As our vision gets clearer, we can begin to

(Text continues on p. 176)

Table 6.1   Organizational Self-Assessment Checklist for Developing
Men's Leadership

VISION

- Is there a vision of the characteristics we want to encourage men in our campus community to have?
- How does the conversation about this vision occur? With whom?

SYSTEMS SUPPORT AND THINKING

- Where do male students, faculty, staff, and administrators go for support?
- How are they supported?
- Who are mentors?
- How is supporting pro-feminist, gay-affirmative, male-positive male leadership part of appraisal systems?
- How is pro-feminist, gay-affirmative, male-positive male leadership supported by curricula?
- What activities are offered to support male leadership?
- What types of student organizations support male leadership?
- Are staff trained in this area? If so, how?
- Are there student-run workshops on issues of masculinities and male violence?
- How are rape and sexual harassment responded to? How is this communicated to the campus community?
- How is homophobia responded to? How is this communicated to the campus community?
- Are students involved in planning and visioning?
- What types of community education are used?
- How are needs of specific male communities addressed?
- How are systems regularly evaluated?
- How is the system structured to provide opportunities for members to uncover, examine, and reach consensus concerning underlying assumptions about men, sexism, homophobia, heterosexism, gender socialization, gender relations, sexuality, relationships, femininities, masculinities, and so on?

LEADERSHIP SKILLS

Do our male leaders have skills in the following areas?

- Group skills such as the following:
    Gatekeeping
    Meaning attribution
    Modeling of emotional expression
    Knowledge of group dynamics and development

- Cross-gender communication skills such as the following:
  Listening to women
  Taking responsibility for one's own feelings and behavior
  Recognizing the subtleties of sexism in language
  Recognizing the subtleties of sexism in interactions
  Being aware of how male privilege operates

- Caring confrontation skills:
  Holding people accountable for sexist, homophobic, and violent
      behavior and attitudes while supporting their desire to change
  Expressing compassion while upholding a standard of challenging
      sexism, homophobia, and violence
  Modeling assertiveness as opposed to aggressiveness

- Cross-cultural communication skills
- Community building
- Coalition
- Collaboration
- Consensus building

If they do not have these skills, how do we help develop them?

LEARNING ENVIRONMENTS

- Do our learning environments create safety by
  stating assumptions that reflect belief in men?
  emphasizing the importance of men's experiences?
  acknowledging discomfort, fears, defensiveness, and experiences?
  acknowledging and confront stereotypes about men?
  using inclusive language?

- Do our learning environments provide information that
  gives definitions of sexism, rape, sexual harassment,
      heterosexism, and homophobia?
  gives specific examples?
  uses specific language?
  uses facts such frequency of occurrence?
  examines differences in gender perceptions of sex, sexuality, and
      power or force?
  differentiates between legal and interpersonal harassment?
  explores the nuances of consent?
  explores the nuances of sexualities?

- Do our learning environments generate men's perspectives by
  differentiating between reactive and reflective perspectives?
  supporting and valuing expression of feelings, experiences, and
      questions?
  promoting constructive dialogue with women?
  promoting constructive dialogue between men?

(Continued)

Table 6.1   Continued

- Do our learning environments challenge men by
    emphasizing the need for courage to be honest with self, to
      stand up for beliefs?
    using language that puts men in active role (e.g., "a man who
      sexually harasses someone" or "men rape")?
    supporting questioning of self and each other?
    exploring how male violence and socialization hurt men?
    exploring relationships with women and feminism?
    exploring relationships with other men?
    exploring relationships with ourselves?
    expressing the belief that few people want to hurt another person?
    reinforcing that many of us have had an experience of intentional
      or unintentional violation of another person?
    discussing the dynamics of victimization?
    offering deeper experiences for men who are interested and
      invested in support (e.g., groups, cross-gender discussion,
      courses, student organizing)?

think about ways to reinforce those characteristics, which leads us
into systems support and thinking, leadership skills, and learning
environments.

Systems Support and Thinking

As we attempt to move toward our vision of male heterosexualities, it is critical to establish a foundation on which to build structures that support pro-feminist, gay-affirmative, male-positive
thinking and behavior. Too often, we hope that "men of good con-
science" will "do the work" and "spread the word." Without systemic institutionalization, those efforts quickly fall by the wayside
when that handful of committed men move on or burn out.

Once we are clearer about what our vision is, the first question
we need to ask is, "Are we committed to developing pro-feminist,
gay-affirmative, male-positive men's leadership?" If the answer is
yes, then we need to ask how the system is structured (or not) to provide opportunities for members to uncover, examine, and reach consensus concerning underlying assumptions about men, sexism,
homophobia, heterosexism, gender socialization, gender relations,
sexuality, relationships, femininities, masculinities, and so on. We
need to look at whether supporting pro-feminist, gay-affirmative,

male-positive male leadership is part of appraisal systems. We need to look at how pro-feminist, gay-affirmative, male-positive male leadership is supported by curricula, student organizations, and campus activities. We need to make sure faculty and staff are trained so that they have the skills to support men and serve as mentors. We need to make sure our campus has systems in place to effectively address and respond to incidents of rape, sexual harassment, relationship violence, homophobia, and other male violence. We need to make sure we have effective ways to communicate our responses to the campus community. Finally, we need to make sure our systems are regularly evaluated to ensure they are truly accomplishing what we want, which means having some baseline measurements for comparison. And this is by no means an exhaustive list.

Learning Environments

My framework on creating effective learning environments for working with men has been outlined elsewhere (Landis-Schiff, 1996). These strategies also are based on a belief in men and involve creating safety; providing accurate information about sexism, homophobia, and violence; generating men's perspectives that are truly well thought out; and challenging men to take the step(s). What I will offer in this section are some general thoughts on effective learning environments for working with men and a few descriptions of activities that can be used.

Often, our learning environments are in the context of a particular issue such as rape, sexual harassment, or relationship violence. It is in these environments that we can begin to develop leaders. We need to take advantage of these opportunities because some potential leaders will never rise to the surface if this environment is one that puts them off, uses shame and blame, or does not speak to them.

If we expect to challenge and end sexism and violence, we have to demonstrate ways of being in relationships that are not based on dominance, hierarchy, and asymmetry but instead are built on a foundation of connection, caring, and reciprocity. This involves accepting other perspectives and experiences while simultaneously finding ways to be ourselves and get our needs met.

There are four things I find useful in this process. First, as educators, we need to genuinely model full respect for all individuals, particularly those with whom we disagree. In this work and in other work I do around relationship violence, I often frame this belief or approach with the Hindi word *namaste,* which I take to mean "I honor the place in you where the universe resides." Second, when learner defensiveness takes the form of offensiveness—and it often does—I can either try to reframe what I am saying so as to not seem so dogmatic (even if I don't think I am being this way), or I can use what might be considered an Aikido approach (Crum, 1987). To me, this means not fighting or pushing back. It means just listening and recognizing the speaker's truth and perhaps his or her hurt. Third, I find it essential to validate learners' realities, as those realities are as valid as mine, while reframing or renaming the way we discuss an issue. When I train educators to work with men around sexism, homophobia, and violence, I often ask them to respond to some tough but typically provocative statements I have heard in classes and workshops. People have the opportunity to first express their emotional response to the statement. Then I ask them to try to find a point of agreement or validation. Imperative in that process is thinking about what could be underlying such statements. In the last part of this exercise, I have them offer another perspective. I call this the "good point and . . ." or the "yes and . . ." activity. In this way, we validate the learners' experiences while not compromising ourselves. Keep in mind that this is not merely a technique. Your point of agreement has to be genuine. Of course, there are also many times when this does not work, or it is not an option, and we have to take a firm stand and disagree with a statement to be a conscientious educator and advocate. Even then, there are many ways to disagree respectfully.

Let me illustrate these three points with an example. Discussions often arise that focus on appearance, attraction, and responsibility for statements and behavior. The text of an actual discussion is given below. The focus is whether individuals can bring harassment on themselves by their appearance and behavior.

> **Student:** Some girls dress in a way that you know they're asking for it.
>
> (Numerous "yeahs" from other, mostly male students)
>
> **TS:** So when a woman dresses in, let's say, a halter top and a short skirt, you find that attractive and provocative.
>
> **S:** Yeah! She wants to be looked at.
>
> **TS:** You know, I think what you're getting at here is really important. Most, if not all, of us want to be seen as attractive at

some point to certain other people, and we want to express our attractions to others. It's really an exciting part of life. So you see this girl and you find her attractive. So do you want to get to know her better?

S: Yeah, I guess so.

TS: So what do you think is going to work better, approaching her in a way that is respectful or in a way that may be unwanted by her and [make her angry]?

S: It depends on the girl.

TS: So how do you know?

All three of the above-described ways to engage are present in this example. First, I respected the student's reality by asking him questions so I could understand his perspective better. I never passed judgment on him. In fact, I let him know that I thought what he was saying was important. Second, I reframed a potentially confrontational statement to make it personally relevant to the student by saying, "So when a woman dresses in, let's say, a halter top and a short skirt, you find that attractive and provocative." This allowed any defensiveness to dissipate and engagement to continue. I did not force the discussion into a particular direction because the process took precedent over making a point. Third, I found a point of agreement with him and then reframed the issue as one of interpersonal interaction and communication. A deep discussion ensued focusing on individual styles for encouraging and discouraging attention from others, showing respectful and disrespectful ways to give attention to others, communicating one's needs, and taking personal responsibility for one's actions and statements.

One final way I find useful to engage learners is through the judicious use of playful, nontargeting humor. This not only shows you to be human, but it can serve to break the ice or make a point. In a similar discussion such as the one described earlier, my response was, "It's true, some women are looking for attention. However, as far as I know, there is no documented evidence of a direct connection between the eyes, genitals, vocal cords, and hands." This statement helped move the group into a discussion about why people respond to each other the way we do, which became intertwined with an exploration of gender differences in communication and expectations. Of course, one needs to gauge each group and one's own comfort before using a humor intervention.

There are numerous activities one can use to get at specific aspects of developing male leadership or challenging sexism, homophobia, and violence. One is called a stand-up activity. This involves reading statements out loud and having all the participants for whom that is true to stand in silence and notice how it feels and who else is standing with them. Processing occurs after all the statements have been read. Creighton and Kivel (1990) provided a good example of this for high school students in their book, *Teens Need Teens*. It is useful to customize a stand-up for each audience and to be focused on particular dynamics. For example, I have different variations I use if the focus is developing positive sexualities as compared to challenging violence. The purpose of this activity is to demonstrate the commonalties of experience of the participants and to name the high level of sexism and violence of which so many of us have firsthand knowledge. It is a great way to get discussion going on both an emotional and cognitive level.

Another useful technique is storytelling. I usually will share a story from my own life that exemplifies the focus I want them to take. Then I will ask them to think about experiences they have had and to tell their stories to each other. Stories might be focused on messages they got about being a man, messages they got about violence, or messages about sexuality. Whatever the case, it is typically a very evocative exercise. I find that after the storytelling and processing, it is useful to have a theoretical framework on which to build an understanding and connection to their emotional responses to the stories. For example, when I work with men about sexuality, I find it useful to frame their responses using the 5Cs model—control, conquest, competition, climax, and confusion (Landis-Schiff, 1996).

It is always important to ask about the implications of the stories, the framework, and the participants' experiences. I often talk about examples with which I am familiar, such as the infamous Lakewood, California, "Spur Posse" incidents. Most of the men with whom I work are familiar with this group of young men who received spoken support from their community for their efforts to have sex with as many women as possible. Many in the community rallied around these men (whose behavior included "allegedly" raping a 10-year-old girl and other young women and creating an environment of harassment and intimidation) and chastised the women who reported them. One father stated, "Aren't they virile specimens?" (Gross, 1993). I ask if they know about situations such as this, which are quite common, though not always to this degree.

If they do know about such situations, what do they do? Do they challenge it, participate, or passively collude?

Another activity related to the stand-up is specifically designed to get the participants to think about sexual assault. A series of statements are read out loud twice. The first time they are asked just to listen. The statements start with something, such as "talking to a woman you don't know just because you think she is attractive," and move in progression to "continuing to move forward sexually when you are getting told no." On the second reading, I ask men to stand when they think we have reached a gray area and to raise a hand when it becomes sexual assault. This exercise not only names specific sexual and violent behaviors, but it also allows for an examination of what is healthy, what is questionable, and what is violent. It is critical for new and old leaders to engage in that sort of examination.

Finally, we must ask what are the next steps each participant can and will take. Workshops are great for awareness building and even for motivating, but to get men to think about what else they can do and to publicly declare it is a powerful intervention in itself. This sort of intervention helps start or support continued individual and collective leadership development, so long as there is the systemic support to sustain it.

Leadership Skills

If we want to develop leaders, we have to help foster certain leadership skills that will enable these men to be effective in their endeavors. Because at some point they will probably conduct educational sessions with groups, they will need to have presentation skills and groups skills. If this work is being done with other men, then these leaders will need to know how to hold other men accountable for sexist, homophobic, and violent behavior and attitudes while supporting their desire to change. They will need to be able to express compassion while upholding a standard of challenging sexism, homophobia, and violence. Finally, they will need to be able to model assertiveness as opposed to aggressiveness. Of course, there are other, more "traditional" leaderships skills that we want to help nurture in these men—skills such public speaking, visioning, decision making, consensus building, and so on. All of this needs to be done in a way that connects them with other men rather than holding themselves out as better or more enlightened.

In addition, most effective pro-feminist, gay-affirmative, male-positive male leaders will also be working with women and women's groups. Therefore, they will need coalition-building skills and cross-gender communication skills. These skills include but are not restricted to listening to women, taking responsibility for one's own feelings and behavior, recognizing the subtleties of sexism in language, recognizing the subtleties of sexism in interactions, and being aware of how male privilege operates.

Leadership skills development cannot occur without systemic support. The key question to ask is the following: If the men with whom we are working do not have these skills, how do we help develop them, and how do we continue to support this development?

Conclusion

In this chapter, I have offered some models and ideas for developing men's leadership to challenge sexism and violence. As I stated earlier, little research supports the efficacy of prevention programs in reducing male violence. Clearly, more research needs to happen. This research should look not only at specific programs but also at how these programs target and affect specific male populations, using race, culture, class, religion, and other social identity markers as filters. Both short-term and longitudinal studies are needed. The particular model presented in this chapter is no different. Empirical research is needed to explore the validity of this model.

Furthermore, I believe that those of us interested in challenging sexism and male violence need to continue to approach this with a systemic perspective. We need to continue to develop our vision of a violence-free world, build systems that support our efforts, nurture present and future leaders, and create effective educational interventions.

Note

1. I choose to employ the term *pro-feminist* for men rather than *feminist* because I feel that feminism is an intellectual, political, or social movement that is about bringing women's experiences to the center of consciousness and analysis. It does not mean men are being kicked out of the center; it means we are being asked to share the center. I believe men can support this process, but it is not about us; therefore, I use the term *pro-feminist*.

7

Sexual Violence Against African American Women

*General and Cultural Factors
Influencing Rape Treatment and
Prevention Strategies in University Settings*

HELEN A. NEVILLE

MARY J. HEPPNER

LISA B. SPANIERMAN

Tamika, a 25-year-old college student, went dancing with a girlfriend as a way to relieve stress from schoolwork. It was near closing time, and Tamika wanted to use the restroom before driving home. On her way to the restroom, a male she dated a couple of times approached her and began to converse. She politely told him she was busy and that she could not talk to him then. He continued to talk while following behind her. Suddenly, he grabbed her arm and forced her into the men's restroom. He then shoved her into a stall. Yelling and cursing, he threatened to hurt her if she did not "give in." Tamika fought back, but he was too strong. After a struggle, he forced himself on Tamika; he raped her.

The above scenario is based on an interview we conducted as part of a larger study examining the postsexual assault recovery process of African American women college students. Unfortunately, Tamika's story is all too familiar to many women in the United States. Women across racial and ethnic backgrounds experience sexual violence at an alarming rate, including incest, sexual abuse, and rape. Incidences of sexual assault (attempted and completed rape) are particularly high. Studies indicate that between 14% and 25% of women in the United States will be raped sometime in their lifetimes (Kilpatrick, Edmunds, & Seymour, 1992; Koss, 1993; Koss, Gidyez, & Wisniewski, 1987; Wingood & DiClemente, 1998; Wyatt, 1992). When the offense is broadened to sexual assault, the prevalence rate significantly increases, especially for college-age women. For example, Koss and colleagues (1987) found that 50% of college women were survivors of sexual assault or rape. Historically, researchers suggested that African American women were more susceptible to being sexually assaulted than other racial and ethnic groups. However, more recent community studies suggest that the prevalence of sexual assault is comparable among African American and White American women (Winfield, George, Schwartz, & Blazer, 1990; Wyatt, 1992). In our own work, we have also found similar prevalence rates in a sample of African American and White American college students (Neville & Clark, 1997).

The trauma that Tamika, as well as many women who have been sexually assaulted, experienced has wide-ranging deleterious effects. In Tamika's case, several months after the incident, she reported feeling nervous, depressed, irritable, and guilty. Tamika's immediate and longer-term psychological and behavioral responses to the assault are within the normal range of reactions that many rape survivors report. Findings from retrospective and prospective studies consistently suggest that sexual assault survivors often suffer acute and/or chronic psychological, behavioral, social, and physical consequences (Neville & Heppner, 1999). For example, depression is a primary postrape symptom, with research suggesting that nearly

45% of rape survivors meet clinical levels of depression up to 1 month following the assault (Frank & Stewart, 1984). More recently, scholars have begun to conceptualize rape reaction in terms of post-traumatic stress disorder (PTSD), a cluster of three interrelated symptoms: reexperiencing the rape, avoiding feelings around the rape and/or numbing oneself, and having elevated arousal. In a prospective study, Rothbaum, Foa, Riggs, Murdock, and Walsh (1992) found that 94% of their sample met diagnostic criteria for PTSD at 1 week, and nearly 50% did at 3 months following the assault. Compared to women who have never been sexually assaulted, women sexual assault survivors also experience greater levels of sexual dysfunction, such as lack of desire or fear of having sex (e.g., Becker, Skinner, Abel, & Cichon, 1986); substance abuse (e.g., Kessler, Sonnega, Bromet, Hughes, & Nelson, 1995); and sexual risk taking, such as engaging in unprotected sex and subsequently having higher rates of self-reported HIV exposures (Wingood & DiClemente, 1998).

Although many of the large-scale rape studies include a sizable number of African American women in their sample, very few studies have analyzed race or ethnocultural variables. Initial research undertaking this task commonly has compared the postassault reactions of African American women with other racial and ethnic groups. Results from these studies are equivocal. For example, Williams and Holmes (1982) found a significant difference in the level of postassault distress among Black, Mexican, and White women, with Mexican women reporting the most distress and Black women the least. However, it is important to note that the overwhelming majority of women in their study, irrespective of race or ethnicity, experienced some degree of postassault distress. Other studies, including our own research, generally suggest that there is little difference in the psychological sequelae of rape between White women and women of color (e.g., Morelli, 1981; Neville, Heppner, Oh, Spanierman, & Clark, 2002; Wyatt, 1992). These findings are important in that they underscore that rape has at least a similar initial effect on women across racial lines. Rape is traumatic for most women. Regardless of race or class, survivors in general will experience some degree of acute or chronic disturbance. The degree of the disturbance, however, will be mitigated by a host of factors, including personal factors such as previous level of abuse and contextual factors

such as severity of rape (see Neville & Heppner, 1999). It is important to note, however, that more recent research has begun to examine cultural factors influencing the sequelae of sexual violence
against women across racial lines (e.g., Sorenson, 1996), and phenomenological inquiry with African American women sexual
assault survivors specifically has underscored the impact of sexual
violence on women's psychological and physical health (R. E. Davis,
1997; Pierce-Baker, 1998).

Although there has been a recent increase in the examination of
race and cultural issues related to the sexual violence against
women of color, there remains a dearth of theoretical and empirical
literature examining African American women rape survivors or
prevention and intervention efforts within African American communities. In this chapter, we discuss some of our research designed
to understand the factors related to the psychological sequelae of
African American women rape survivors as well as our efforts to
evaluate intervention programs to prevent sexual aggression against
women. Our intent is to explicitly examine both general and cultural
factors that may be related to the recovery process of women such as
Tamika. Specifically, our goal is to first provide a sociohistorical
context for understanding African American women's sexual
victimization in this country and then to describe a culturally
sensitive theoretical model designed to explicate the multiple factors
influencing rape treatment and intervention efforts. We also review
the treatment and prevention literature, noting the implications for
working with African American populations.

Sociohistorical Context of Rape

The intersection among race, gender, and class oppression has historically played a significant role in the circumstances and consequences of sexual violence against African American women (A. Y.
Davis, 1985). The importance of race-gender ideologies in legitimizing
the rape of African American women and these women's lack of
legal and social recourse emerge as central themes in reviews of the
sociohistorical context of rape of African American women (see A. Y.
Davis, 1985; McNair & Neville, 1996; Neville & Pugh, 1997; Wyatt,
1992). Essentially, the race-gender ideology of African American

women as Jezebels or as sexually loose, wanton, and lascivious has served several purposes, including the following: (a) to deny or minimize sexual assault (if a woman is always desirous of sex, then she cannot be raped, and if an assault were to occur, she cannot be injured) and (b) to justify limited legal sanctions against perpetrators of sexual violence against African American women. Historian Deborah Gray White (1985) poignantly described the restricted legal options for African American women rape survivors and the process of discounting Black women as legitimate victims:

> From emancipation through more than two-thirds of the twentieth century, no Southern white male was convicted of raping or attempting to rape a black woman. Yet the crime was so widespread that the staff of the National Commission on the Causes and Prevention of Violence admitted in 1969 that the few reported instances of the crime reflected not the crime's low incidence but the fact that "white males have long had nearly institutionalized access to Negro women with relatively little fear of being reported." Black women had almost as little recourse to justice when the perpetrator was black. When a black man raped a black woman police consistently reported the crime as "unfounded," and in the relatively few cases that reached the courts, the testimony of black female victims was seldom believed by white juries. (pp. 164-165)

These race-gender myths continue to affect the way in which sexual assault of African American women is evaluated within Black and White communities alike. For example, the Mike Tyson–Desiree Washington rape case stimulated much discussion within the Black community, with many individuals conjuring the image of the Jezebel to blame Desiree Washington for the crime. Empirical studies with primarily White samples also support the observation that African American women are to blame for the assault and/or are not psychologically injured by the crime. For example, Foley, Evancic, Karnik, King, and Parks (1995) found that college students perceived the effects of rape as less serious for African American women than for White women. Specifically, the perpetrator's behavior in a rape scenario involving a Black victim was more likely to be perceived as all right or as an act of love when compared to a White rape victim.

Culturally Inclusive Ecological Model
of Sexual Assault Recovery (CIEMSAR)

We originally developed the culturally inclusive ecological model of sexual assault recovery (CIEMSAR) to describe the differential short- and long-term outcomes of sexual assault (Neville & Heppner, 1999). One unique aspect of the CIEMSAR is its explication of ethnocultural factors potentially related to the recovery process for rape survivors. For the purposes of this chapter, we have slightly modified the model to provide a framework to describe systemic issues related to the incidence of rape, potential intervention avenues to prevent sexual assault or promote supportive environments for rape survivors, and treatment implications for survivors. It is important to note that although the model has implications for prevention and intervention efforts with perpetrators, the focus of the CIEMSAR is on enhancing the recovery process for rape survivors.

Our model is grounded in the ecological literature suggesting that human behavior is dynamic and results from the dialectic between persons and environments. Ecological models underscore that human behavior is multiply determined by interrelations between subsystems within a larger ecosystem. Bronfrenbrenner (1977) identified four major subsystems influencing human behavior:

1. microsystem, or the interpersonal interactions within a given environment, including work, school, and home;

2. mesosystem, which constitutes interactions between two or more microsystem environments, such as the relations between an individual's school and her or his work environment;

3. exosystem, which consists of linkages between subsystems that indirectly influence the individual, such as the police or health care systems' linkage with one's neighborhood; and

4. macrosystem, which includes the ideological components of a given society, including norms and values.

Specific components of the CIEMSAR model are presented in Table 7.1 and Figure 7.1 Consistent with many feminist scholars, we argue that sexual violence against women occurs in a specific socio-cultural context; that is, the values, customs, and norms of our society implicitly condone rape and promote faulty beliefs about the causes

Table 7.1   Factors Comprising the Culturally Inclusive Ecological
Model of Sexual Assault Recovery (CIEMSAR)

MICROSYSTEM/INDIVIDUAL

- Individual factors (e.g., previous abuse history, type and severity of sexual assault)
- Family, friends, peers (e.g., level of support)
- Police officers or mental health workers (e.g., level of support and/or assistance)
- Cultural factors on the individual level (e.g., racial identity development, race of perpetrator)
- Cultural factors on the microsystem level (e.g., racial and gender sensitivity of the specific police station or mental health agency)

MESOSYSTEM

- Police and family interactions and support
- Counselor and family interactions and support

EXOSYSTEM

- Police system (e.g., policies, organizational practices)
- Health care system (e.g., policies, organizational practices)
- Cultural factors (e.g., policies and practices toward racial minorities)

MACROSYSTEM

- Broad sociocultural context (e.g., rape-prone culture, level of rape myth acceptance)
- Cultural factors (e.g., cultural rape myths; rape myth acceptance within African American communities)

of rape. Consequently, our society supports a rape-prone culture. Although we believe that race, gender, and class hierarchies influence the incidence and consequences of sexual assault, general rape myths (i.e., false beliefs designed to blame women for rape) form the central macrosystem-level component discussed in the literature. We also argue that cultural rape myths (e.g., Jezebel), as discussed earlier, influence the context of sexual violence against all women on a macrosystem level.

These general and cultural rape myths affect the practices of other subsystems as well as individuals. For example, race-gender ideologies historically have influenced the treatment of rape cases of both African American men and women within legal and paralegal

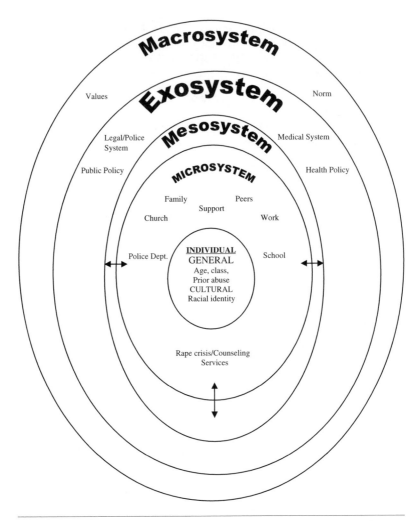

Figure 7.1   Culturally Inclusive Ecological Model of Sexual Assault
Recovery (CIEMSAR)

systems. The image of the Black male rapist served to legitimize the
lynching and tougher sentencing practices for African American
men "suspected" of having consensual or forced sexual relations
with White women (A. Y. Davis, 1985). Because of the historical mis-
treatment of African American men and women by the police and
judicial systems, especially around "alleged" rape cases, African

American rape survivors might be reluctant to report the crime to police for fear of not being believed or not wanting to assist in the imprisonment of African American males. In support of this observation, we found that African American women identified cultural barriers such as these as more important in not reporting the crime to police compared to White American women (Neville & Clark, 1997). The above discussion illustrates the complex interrelations among macrosystems, exosystems, and individual systems.

Microsystem-level components are also important in perpetuating both general and cultural rape myths in the recovery process of survivors. For example, the reactions of family, friends, and peer confidants influence a woman's recovery process. Research suggests that poor levels of social support (Moss, Frank, & Anderson, 1990) and negative or unsupportive responses such as blaming the survivor (Davis, Brickman, & Baker, 1991; Ullman, 1996) are related to increased psychological symptomatology. In Tamika's case, although she received emotional support from a few family members and friends, the friend she went dancing with was unsupportive. Her friend minimized her disclosure of the assault and continued to talk about her own concerns; at no point did the friend provide outward signs of support or concern for Tamika. Tamika also reported receiving "very unsupportive" responses from a police officer she reported the crime to and the rape crisis center staff. She commented that these negative reactions influenced how she perceived herself initially as a victim of a crime; she questioned if the rape was her fault.

Treatment Strategies

Women's postassault recovery process is influenced by multiple factors, including the circumstances of the assault, available social support, and material conditions. One of the factors within the control of mental health providers is providing effective counseling services. In this section, we thus focus on microsystem implications of the sexual assault recovery process—specifically, the effectiveness of mental health services provided to sexual assault survivors. We briefly review various treatment strategies that have been used to reduce rape symptom sequelae—including anxiety, depression, and sexual dysfunction—and disrupt avoidance patterns in female sexual assault survivors. Then, we discuss current thinking in treating sexual assault victims, focusing primarily on cognitive-behavioral techniques. Last, we point out ways in which cultural issues could be included in future treatment research.

Extensive reviews of the literature cite a variety of approaches to the treatment of sexual assault victims, including psychodynamic and cognitive-behavioral therapies (Foa & Rothbaum, 1998; Rothbaum & Foa, 1996). In her review of the literature, Koss (1993) noted several commonalties within many of these treatments, including "the avoidance of victim blame; a supportive, nonstigmatizing view of rape as a criminal victimization; an environment to overcome cognitive and behavioral avoidance; and information that the symptoms will improve" (p. 1066). Although some initial efforts have been made to evaluate treatments such as crisis, pharmacological, and psychodynamic interventions, little evidence supports the effectiveness of these interventions. Moreover, although African American women are represented in many of the samples, possible cultural differences treating women of color rarely have been addressed. In what follows, we review general ("colorblind") treatment approaches and then describe how these approaches can be expanded to include culturally relevant variables using multicultural counseling and therapy principles.

The bulk of the empirical treatment research has focused on general (colorblind) cognitive-behavioral interventions, especially exposure therapy, anxiety management training, or a combination of the two (see Foa & Rothbaum, 1998; Resick & Schnicke, 1993). Exposure techniques are often enlisted to activate and relive the trauma memory, which promotes recovery through confrontation rather than avoidance. An early form of exposure treatment with trauma victims is based on Wolpe's (1958) systematic desensitization. Early studies investigating general exposure therapies provide initial support of the effectiveness of the treatment (Frank & Stewart, 1984; Frank et al., 1988). However, findings from many of these earlier studies are problematic due to various methodological flaws such as lack of a clearly defined target treatment, random assignment, standardized measures, or blind evaluations. A more recent exposure treatment is eye movement desensitization and reprocessing (EMDR) (Shapiro, 1989), in which the assault survivor imagines a scene from the trauma while she is "tracking" the therapist's moving fingers. Some initial data support the effectiveness of EMDR in reducing PTSD symptomatology (Rothbaum, 1997).

Other recent forms of exposure therapy include prolonged imaginal exposure and in vivo exposure (Foa, 1997). Foa and Riggs (1993) purported that these techniques address the organization of trauma memories through reactivating and "reliving" the experience. In addition, Foa (1997) found that PTSD symptoms were markedly reduced in victims who received prolonged exposure (PE) treatment; her treatment program consists of the following four techniques: (a) education about common trauma reactions, (b) controlled breathing techniques, (c) repeated reliving of the trauma, and (d) in vivo confrontation with safe situations that remind the victim of the trauma. However, it is important to note that all patients are not suited for this type of intervention. For example, if a sexual assault victim is also a substance abuser, the substance abuse must be treated first. Thus, it is critical to perform a thorough, multidimensional assessment to determine if the treatment is appropriate (cf. Resick & Schnicke, 1993).

Another cognitive-behavioral therapy receiving attention in the literature is anxiety management training (AMT). This approach emphasizes breathing retraining, muscle relaxation, thought stopping, and other techniques to decrease overall anxiety levels and to increase coping skills of the client (Foa, 1997). A common form of AMT is stress inoculation therapy (SIT), originally applied to rape survivors by Kilpatrick, Veronen, and Resick (1982). In general, there is support for the effectiveness of SIT in reducing specific symptoms. Resick, Jordan, Girelli, Hutter, and Marhoefer-Dvorak (1988) found that SIT was effective in decreasing rape-related fear and PTSD symptoms immediately following SIT intervention with rape survivors (Resick et al., 1988) and at follow-up (Foa & Meadows, 1997).

A combination of exposure and AMT therapies is proving beneficial to treating rape victims (Rothbaum & Foa, 1996). Resick and Schnicke's (1993) cognitive-processing therapy (CPT) is a combination of these therapies. In their systematic work, they found that individual and group CPT was effective in significantly reducing a variety of postrape symptoms, including depression, anxiety, and PTSD symptomatology. Although the combined treatment approach seems effective, Foa and Meadows (1997) found that PE, SIT, and a combination of the two therapies produced similar improvement in PTSD symptoms. Thus, it appears that the combined approach may not be superior to either the independent exposure therapy or AMT approaches.

As noted earlier, absent from the empirical research in this area are discussions of cultural issues that may affect the therapy process. The general (colorblind) approaches described above can easily be extended to include cultural aspects using multicultural counseling and therapy (MCT) principles. Essentially, MCT is a metatheory designed to serve as a framework to help contextualize general therapy approaches, including cognitive-behavioral therapies (Sue, Ivey, & Pedersen, 1996). A core component of MCT is cultural identity development; that is, the saliency and importance of one's cultural identities (e.g., race, gender). The following queries are grounded in MCT principles and could aid future researchers to incorporate race and ethnocultural variables into their treatment protocols:

1. Does the racial makeup of group members affect the group therapy outcomes for African American women?

2. Do African American women find treatments that incorporate race and cultural issues more engaging, thus producing greater improvements than treatments that do not incorporate race or cultural issues?

3. What are the critical general and cultural within-group factors that might affect the effectiveness of specific types of treatments?

4. What role does the internalization of cultural rape myths play in the therapy process?

This latter point is of particular relevance; in our own work, we found that African American college women survivors identified cultural rape myths as the most important reasons they used to understand why they were assaulted, and they rated these myths as more meaningful than their White American counterparts. For example, Tamika felt as though the statement, "People think Black women are sexually loose," was "completely true" in helping her understand why she was attacked. Both Foa and Rothbaum (1998) and Resick and Schnicke (1993) included a segment on examining beliefs about the trauma in their treatments. Explicit examination of potential cultural rape myths could easily be included in such treatment interventions.

Prevention and Intervention Strategies

When one understands the trauma and psychological sequelae that are the result of sexual violence, effective prevention efforts become paramount. Designing interventions to stop sexual violence before it is perpetrated is a vitally important and yet highly complex effort. The complexity of this issue can be best seen through the ecological framework. The CIEMSAR provides a schema for understanding the various levels at which intervention is necessary. In this section, we describe a sexual violence prevention intervention ultimately aimed at changing macrosystem values but is manifested in changing the values and behaviors of the various environments in which potential rape survivors interact. We also briefly outline intervention research needed to influence multisystemic change.

Since Koss et al.'s (1987) pivotal findings that 50% of college women were victims of sexual abuse or rape and that, like Tamika, 84% knew their assailants, there has been a dramatic shift in our thinking about sexual assault prevention. Prior to this seminal study, the stereotype was that rapes were perpetuated by psychopathic individuals who hid in bushes and attacked unsuspecting young women. When this was the stereotype of rape, prevention efforts centered on self-defense training for women, increased lighting, emergency phones, and safety escort services. But with the Koss et al. findings, we have begun to understand that rape is grounded in a context of sexism, racism, and sociocultural mythology about rape. This mythology includes beliefs such as women enjoy rape. Thus, the past decade has witnessed a burgeoning of prevention efforts on college campuses. Unfortunately, the efficacy of these prevention efforts has rarely been evaluated, and when evaluations were done, they were collected immediately after the intervention. Research now indicates that changes evidenced immediately after an intervention tend to be short-lived and that attitudes tend to rebound to preintervention levels in the weeks following the interventions (Heppner, Good, et al., 1995; Heppner, Humphrey, Hillenbrand-Gunn, & Debord, 1995).

A rape prevention intervention that was aimed specifically at the macrosystems (changing attitudes in a rape-prone culture) was designed and implemented with a culturally diverse sample of university men and specifically examined a culturally specific intervention. This intervention built on earlier intervention research

(Heppner, Good, et al., 1995; Heppner, Humphrey, et al., 1995) that used the elaboration likelihood model (ELM) (Petty & Cacioppo, 1986) as the theoretical base. Briefly, ELM conceptualizes attitude change on a continuum, with the anchors being peripheral route processing and central route processing of the persuasive message. In peripheral route processing, participants attend to the superficial issues (e.g., attractiveness of the speaker), but in central route processing, participants attend to the central core of the message itself. The model suggests that when the participants find the message has low personal relevance to them, they tend to lack motivation to hear the message and feel that the message is of low quality and inappropriate to them. Their attitude change tends to be transitory and subject to counterpersuasion from their environment. Conversely, central route attitude change is based on the participant finding personal relevance in the message, thoughtfully evaluating the message, feeling motivated to listen, and subsequently demonstrating more stable attitude change. Central route processing is also more resilient to later counterpersuasion attempts and more able to influence actual behavior. Thus, the current intervention study was designed to foster central route processing by increasing the personal relevance and motivation of the participants. Specifically, we were interested in strengthening the personal relevancy of rape prevention programming with racially diverse men. To this end, we wanted to test if infusing culturally relevant content (e.g., including specific information about race-related rape myths, providing statistics on prevalence rates for both Blacks and Whites, and using Black and White speakers to discuss their sexual violence experiences in a cultural context) as opposed to using a generic ("colorblind") rape prevention program would increase the personal relevance of the message and thus encourage Black and, potentially, White men to process the message centrally.

To this end, we recruited both Black and White fraternity men to be part of three 90-minute sessions that were designed around altering cognitive, affective, and behavioral pathways to attitude change. More information concerning the intervention is available in Heppner, Neville, Smith, Kivlighan, and Gershuny (1999). Briefly, the cognitive component examined myths and facts about rape through use of the Myths and Facts Quiz. The affective component consisted of a panel of rape survivors and male allies talking about the lasting impact of the rape on their lives. The behavioral component taught skills through role-played scenarios on recognizing consent and coercion in a sexual situation and understanding what is helpful to do in supporting a friend who has been raped.

Each of the three modules in the culture-specific group had culture-specific form and content infused into the intervention. One of the two male facilitators was Black. Also, one of the rape survivor panelists, one of the male ally panelists, and one pair of role-players in the behavioral component were Black. In addition, specific culturally relevant content was included. For example, in the cognitive module, the incidence and prevalence figures for both Black and White populations were included, and race-related myths were included in the Myths and Facts Quiz. In the affective component, the panelists specifically discussed how race and culture might have played a role in the initial response and recovery process. In the behavioral change component, culture-specific information concerning the recovery process for Black and White women was infused. Thus, although being fairly subtle, we were interested in whether these attempts at cultural inclusion would increase the personal relevancy for Blacks in this condition.

This intervention was aimed at changing the value system within a specific environment, in that it was designed to get men together to examine institutional structures that create a rape-prone environment. Appeals were made to the leadership abilities of these men to help change the culture of fraternities that promote sexual coercion and violence. In contrast to previous interventions, the philosophy presented in this intervention was that these men were part of the solution rather than part of the problem. The intervention was aimed at empowering them to change their environment (e.g., know how to recognize coercion in sexual situations and stop their fraternity brothers from perpetuating this abuse). In essence, we were attempting to change the high-risk, rape-prone culture of a fraternity by appealing to influential individuals within that system.

In contrast to previous findings that have indicated a rebound of scores to preintervention levels for all participants, the current investigation found three different treatment responses. About a third of participants demonstrated the typical rebound pattern of scores, another third deteriorated, and another third improved, with their improvement remaining stable at 5 months. Those who improved were much more likely to have attended more of the presentation than those in the other two categories. In addition, Black students in the culturally relevant condition reported being more motivated and cognitively engaged in the intervention than their Black peers in the traditional colorblind intervention.

Thus, these results indicate a couple of important findings. First, it appears that a greater amount of training is more effective in producing long-term change. Although this has been the conjecture for years, this is the first study to empirically demonstrate this finding. In addition, it appears that Blacks in the culturally specific intervention did find the intervention to be more personally relevant to them and reported feeling higher levels of motivation to hear the message. This finding has several important implications. For example, this result suggests the need to carefully examine the relevance of rape prevention programming across the nation for racial and ethnic minority group members. If one of the goals of rape prevention is to design personally relevant interventions for all participants so they feel motivated to listen to and cognitively engage in the message, then attending to the unique contexts of the participants' lives seems warranted.

Although this intervention was specifically aimed at changing the rape-prone culture by getting men together to examine and change the overall structure, many other levels of intervention are also needed. For example, the individual perpetrator can be one source of intervention. Perpetrator programs that are aimed at increasing the individual's empathy or decreasing the individual's level of aggression are important individual efforts. Currently, programs aimed specifically at racial minority perpetrators, including African American men, are designed to take sociocultural issues into consideration such as race, ethnicity, and class (e.g., Jones, Winkler, Kacin, Salloway, & Weissman, 1998). White, Strube, and Fisher's (1998) findings, which underscore the relations between racial identity attitudes and rape myth acceptance such that greater internalization of a positive racial identity is related to lower acceptance of rape myths, have implications for scholars' work with African American men in this area.

Broadening intervention strategies, such as our university efforts, to other microsystem environments, including Black churches, police stations in predominantly Black neighborhoods, and community centers, may prove helpful. Intervening at this level can help alter patterns within the peer group and family that create environments in which sexual violence is tolerated and, in some cases, expected. The mesosystem is perhaps one of the most potentially fruitful intervention levels. At this level, interventions are designed to increase appropriate and supportive responses from family, work, and community interactions. For example, because African American women often rely on family support to assist with stress, greater inclusion of family in therapy interventions with rape survivors should be explored. Exosystem interventions are equally important, especially in changing the police and court systems to be more responsive to victims and more effective with perpetrators of sexual violence. What are needed are new evaluations of recent court cases involving the outcome of rape cases involving Black survivors. Special attention should be given to the quality of representation of the women. Such an examination will inform efforts to ameliorate potential systemic abuses in the criminal justice system. Finally, the macrosystem, in which we are attempting to change the ideological components of a society—in this case, the rape-prone culture in which sexual violence is seen as a normal end of a dating continuum—must also continue to be a critically important level of intervention. These interventions must include challenging both general and cultural rape myths.

Conclusion

Women of all racial and ethnic backgrounds are being sexually assaulted in the United States at an alarming rate. As in Tamika's case, such violence is traumatic and has significant psychological and behavioral consequences. Although there has been a substantial increase in the general literature on the causes and consequences of rape over the past two decades, there is a dearth of literature examining cultural factors related to the sexual assault of all women, especially African American women. Because of the psychological and social costs of this disturbing crime to all sectors of our society, it seems imperative that we investigate both general and cultural aspects of rape, including understanding (a) why rape occurs, (b) the most effective methods of preventing sexual violence, (c) the factors associated with negative and positive health outcomes for survivors, and (d) the most effective treatment modalities for women across racial and ethnic backgrounds. We presented the CIEMSAR to address the theoretical gaps in the literature. This culturally relevant model provides a framework to guide treatment and prevention research with African American women. According to this perspective, researchers should consider the multiple levels potentially influencing the incidence and sequelae of rape, including societal values about rape (i.e., macrosystem) and individuals' responses to rape survivors (i.e., microsystem). The central cultural variables to consider across subsystems and research foci (e.g., prevention, intervention research) are cultural rape myths (e.g., Black women as Jezebels). Further theoretical advancements are needed to identify other cultural variables related to specific subsystems; moreover, empirical research is needed to investigate the potential mitigating role of cultural variables in the sexual assault recovery process and in preventing sexual assault.

8

Preparing Teachers to Recognize and Confront Symbolic Violence in Bilingual Education

*Understanding and Dealing
With Violence Against Latino Youth*

María Torres-Guzmán

The preparation of teachers in a changing world and with a changing student population has been a topic of discussion for the past decade and a half. Many modifications in the preparation of teachers and in the teaching profession have occurred as a result. Nonetheless, some issues are not understood and need greater discussion. One such issue is the role of language as a tool for symbolic violence in everyday school life and how teachers can take an active role in confronting and bringing an end to this invisible form of violence. This chapter will discuss the concept of *linguicism,* the use of language as a tool for systematic disempowerment, and explore ways in which teacher preparation programs can begin to help teachers recognize and confront symbolic violence. A proposal and guiding principles for teacher preparation will be presented, along with case examples that illustrate the principles based on my many years of experience in bilingual/bicultural education teaching, teacher preparation and training, and research.

The aim in this chapter is also to begin the process of developing a critical understanding of linguicism within the context of teacher education. I will assert that, although the issues of language learning are most central to bilingual educators, issues of linguicism and other forms of oppression need to be recognized and confronted by all teachers. Indeed, it is asserted that widespread symbolic violence is perpetrated against Latino youth within the U.S. educational system. Although this chapter seeks to ask questions and foster understanding about this violence, it also proposes ways in which educators can effectively confront and deal with this unfortunate situation.

Linguicism and Symbolic Violence

The concept of linguicism was developed and introduced to the field of bilingual education by the Finnish educator Skutnabb-Kangas (1991), who defined linguicism in the Scandinavian countries as "ideologies, structures and practices which are used to legitimate, effectuate, and reproduce an unequal division of power and resources (both material and nonmaterial) resources between groups which are defined on the basis of mother tongues" (p. 42).

One of the central strategies of linguicism that Skutnabb-Kangas (1991) described within the Scandinavian context is applicable to the United States. The strategy is to restrict and redefine the concept of ethnicity as solely language based and grounded in deficit theory rather than one inclusive of culture, language, class, and power issues. Within the United States, this strategy appears when we examine how the needs of language minorities are treated within the context of general education as well as language programs such as bilingual education and English as a second language. Although there are many sociopolitical and cultural issues associated with ethnolinguistic populations, the tendency has been to highlight language because it is the most salient and visible difference between language minorities and immigrant and the general student population. It is much more difficult to translate cultural values, beliefs, standards of behavior, and judgment into needs for the development of instructional practices. Similarly, the isolated focus on language does not provoke or position educators to address power relationships associated with ethnicity, race, and class in the context of schooling. Consequently, the processes associated with language and culture are streamlined, trimmed, and simplified to justify the educational concern as centered on a lack of English proficiency. In other words, the use of the cultural heuristic of language for understanding inequalities and power relationships in the social organization of schooling is boiled down to a deficit conception of the child and his or her learning needs—it centers on the lack of ability to understand, speak, read, and/or write English.

Bilingual education, as a community response to the historical academic lag of language minority children, embodies more than language. Garcia (1998) characterized bilingual education in the following manner:

> In its initial stages ... some of [the] distinct features [of bilingual education] included a close correlation between language, culture, history, class, sociolinguistics, and multiethnic and racial commemoration. The empowering assets which bilingual education constituted at the outset promoted cultural and linguistic pride, avenues of hope for bilingual children to perform and complete school, and a determined sense that dreams [could] be realized. (p. 80)

Although the initial conception of bilingual education enjoyed support by the general public, and many restrictionist laws were done away with during the 1960s and 1970s, fierce debates about the effectiveness of the approach have been constant throughout the years. Garcia (1998) has the following to say about the effects of the debates:

> The relentless assault on bilingual education has diminished the supportive stance of bilingual teachers and generally sympathetic school administrators.... At present, the epistemology of bilingual education is associated with assisting bilingual children to join and participate in mainstream schooling activities.... The faster bilingual children learn English and become monolingual English speakers, the more success is attributed to bilingual education. (p. 80)

In other words, although bilingual education grew out of civil rights struggles that were comprehensive and counterhegemonic in nature, the contemporary general tendency is to define it as solely a language development program. Instead of viewing the child's native language[1] as an asset (that which the child brings with him or her), it is seen as a deficit (something to be done away with). The notion is that one language is better than two and that if you learn English, there is no room for the other language. A more sophisticated version of this notion is that if you know the common language of the world, English, you do not need to know any other language. Many of these assumptions are based on ignorance about the children, their languages, and their communities. They do not take into account the complex relationship between the linguistic, social, cultural, psychological, and cognitive growth of children. The attack on the community response of bilingual education has been similarly rooted in the strategies embodied in linguicism.

In the current movement to reinstate the restriction of languages other than English,[2] not only is the nature of the community response ignored and distorted, but the solutions to the academic lags of language minority groups are conceptualized from a dominant group perspective. The contemporary highly touted solution adopted in California after Proposition 227 in June 1998—sheltered English programs—are comparable to the solutions proposed during the 1940s Sri Lanka famine. A mass movement was organized to help the people of Sri Lanka. Tons of boxes of corned beef were collected and sent to them. Yet the people who were suffering from hunger rejected the corned beef. If they were hungry, how could this occur? The best explanation of what occurred is that those who wanted to help conceptualized the problem as a physical need (i.e., the need for food) and did not account for culture (the types of food, preparations, meanings, etc.), which is fundamental to how societies organize food intake. The helpers did not consult the people from Sri Lanka and were thus unable to conceptualize the solution to fit the problem the way the community saw it.

Similarly, sheltered English solutions conceive of learning the English language as the task, not the holistic education of language minority children. This kind of misfit between needs, as conceptualized by those in the community and those in power to enact educational policies, results in miseducation, as well as oppression.

Skutnabb-Kangas (1991) characterized linguicism as one of societies' modern forms of oppression, calling it structural and/or symbolic violence, which acknowledges that societal control mechanisms have evolved from physical to symbolic ones. For example, in the United States, we no longer tend to see physical punishment as an appropriate response to children speaking a language other than English. Now, subtle forms of shame and guilt are predominant

(Bourdieu, 1991). Some of these forms are direct situations children face in classrooms and schools where their language is negated, and some are found in public media displays and public campaigns such as those recently seen in California, Arizona, New York, Massachusetts, Colorado, and elsewhere. The forms of shame and guilt result from the historical discrimination and perpetuation of damaging misinformation and myths about the superiority and inferiority of certain languages and the status and value of the ethnic and cultural groups for which those languages are the means of communication.

There are many forms of symbolic violence. Many occur in the prevailing language education models in the United States. When children are systematically separated via language from their social group, symbolic violence occurs. In most schools, it happens when children are placed in "sink or swim" learning situations, meaning that all instruction is in English and little, if any, help or support is provided for nominal survival needs. The end result is that most language minority children end up miseducated as they simply "drown." Another form of symbolic violence occurs in the sheltered English programs of the type adapted within California after Proposition 227 in June 1998, in which the primary concern is how quickly the children learn English. Transitional bilingual programs—the federal government's preferred model—is not far behind in reflecting fundamental philosophical and practical pedagogical problems. The assumption of this model is that the child will be able to function academically in an all-English setting after 3 years of native language support and that the native language does not play a role in the education of children thereafter. None of these learning situations are the best for children. The solutions cannot rest on cleansing the child of the linguistic and cultural tools he or she possesses and through which he or she connects with significant adults. It must rest on building on what is known.

The results of two major studies show how significant the native language (what is already known) is, not only for learning the second language but also for academic achievement. Ramirez, Yuen, and Ramey (1991), in the most comprehensive governmentally funded study, demonstrated that children in programs that extended the use of the native language eventually facilitated these students to outperform their comparison peers. Thomas and Collier (1997), using a multidistrict sample of more than 45,000 students, found similar results. They compared the long-term educational outcome of a variety of well-implemented[3] programs. They found that although initial academic progress shows up in English-based language programs, the growth curve levels off by the third year. The academic growth of children in the native language-based programs initially is less than that in the English-based program, but in the long run, their educational progress far outweighs that of their peers in other programs. Furthermore, this research shows that the longer the use of the native language throughout the learning years, the better the students will perform academically.

The studies on cognition and bilingualism also speak to the benefits of bilingualism. Hakuta and Diaz (1984) showed that balanced bilinguals (meaning those individuals whose development of both languages are at par and at developmentally appropriate levels) outperform monolingual individuals in intelligence. Bialystok (1992) found that bilinguals outperform monolinguals in the display of efficient perceptual and linguistic strategies for the reconstruction of events. Bialystok (1987) and Ben-Zeev (1977) found that bilinguals are better judges of the correctness of grammaticality, and Genesee, Tucker, and Lambert (1975) found bilinguals to possess greater sensitivity as listeners.

Despite all the benefits of bilingualism, there is much resistance to teaching children in their own language and about their own culture. Schools give little importance to the native language beyond using it as a transitional tool to get students to the point where they can use the language of power—English. The result of this public rejection of bilingualism, at the school and societal levels, is that children themselves begin to reject their native language and culture. The misinformation and myths about the supposed superiority of English and the perpetuation of this symbolic, invisible violence against their language and, by extension, their families and culture result in groups of children that are unable to appreciate their language and culture. They cannot benefit from that which they know and own; schools do not build on the children's strength. Children develop negative attitudes toward their own language and those who speak it, including their own parents. Children are made to feel ashamed of their parents and origins. The victims of this invisible, symbolic assault are the children themselves, who end up feeling shameful of and guilty about their origins and internalizing the message that abandoning their language and culture opens the gates of access to the world of the majority. Thus, the invisible symbolic violent assault ends up being against their self-concept, identity, affects, and consciousness, consistent with the analysis of Wallace (1993; see also Chapter 2, this volume).

The societal messages of assimilation are not always overt; most of the time, the messages are subtle, pervasive, and systematic and thus difficult to pin down. Such is the nature of invisible violence. Thus, sometimes we must look at what does not happen rather than what does. The exclusion, absence, or lack of mention of a group in the curriculum is one of the ways in which the negative messages are communicated. Those who are invisible within the curriculum clearly are not of value; nor are their contributions significant. Within the curriculum, minority children tend to not find events, situations, or people with which to identify; they do not find a space in which to locate who they are. Within bilingual education, even when the native language is used, these messages come through because of such glaring deficits in the curriculum. The language of the child is not ascribed a value in itself because it is an instrument to transmit the same assimilationist message to the children that would otherwise be transmitted in English. The difference is that the process is a little less cruel, a little gentler, and more "civilized." This is important to understand.

The goal achieved through the use of symbolic violence, which was once achieved through the use of physical violence (i.e., corporal punishment for speaking a language other than English), is alienation of the children (and adults) from their own group. It is logical that if everything that is judged to be of value at school, everything rewarded with praise and good grades, and everything that leads to high-status positions (at school and outside) is associated with the language of power, then students will want to shift to it. If, at the same time, the minority language is not even accepted in school programming, then there is no reason for making an effort to learn it. To the contrary, identifying with the minority language is a source of shame and an acceptance of less power (Griego-Jones, 1994).

An example of what occurs among ethnolinguistic minority children was demonstrated by one of my university students. In her master's project, she documented how she came to understand her linguistic insecurities and how she came to doubt whether she could teach in her home language, which was not her dominant language. She was teaching in a dual-language setting at a middle school, and she saw similar negative feelings among students toward learning in Spanish. As she thought about her own attitudes, she realized that just as it had been necessary for her to pay attention to her own linguistic insecurities, she had to organize instruction in a way that helped students rethink their attitudes toward the language. She thus established a curriculum that was historically based; it made parallels between the language and cultural loss of the indigenous peoples of the Americas to Spanish and the threat of losing Spanish to English. It was also a curriculum that confronted their beliefs about the people who spoke Spanish; she dealt with their stereotypes of each other. She reported later how this emotive, historically based foundation provided students with the motivation to change their attitudes toward learning and studying Spanish. She recognized her internalization of linguicism and helped the students confront theirs in their own learning. She challenged their feelings of guilt and shame as well as their stereotypes of the speech communities that spoke the language. Since then, the students in this middle school have moved on to explore and voice their concerns, as well as use all the linguistic resources available to them. They have published at least two books of poetry and a play that focus on identity formation and pride of being Latinos. They became authors, using both languages in their writing.

One could say that the alienation students felt, individually and as a group, was embedded in the ethnolinguistic minority group's relationship to the dominant society in which they live. But this relationship does not have the same history for the different groups, even when they speak the same language. The group relationships of power differ from one Spanish-speaking country to the next and within each country from one class to the next. Yet, each of the countries of origin has similar relationships with the English-speaking world. Differentiating between Spanish-speaking groups permitted the teacher to deal with stereotypes more directly. But more important for this chapter is that one of the results of structural or symbolic violence is the inability to differentiate whether the messages many minority children (and adults) receive are their own or someone else's. They no longer recognize why these messages are given or where they are coming from.[4] The power messages become internalized (Fanon, 1966; Habermas, 1984). I contend that the internalization of these messages is embedded in another fundamental belief of U.S. society, that is, that sameness is equity. Children are taught the surface-level understanding of equity. They conclude that they have had the same opportunities as mainstream children because they have gotten the same teacher and the same curriculum. It is difficult for them to see the different starting points of those historically marginalized and oppressed versus those who have benefited from privilege and the oppression of others, as well as the continuing legacy that contributes to contemporary differences. Nor can they assume an equity position, like the teacher and the students in the middle school were able to by acknowledging the past and moving beyond it The contemporary belief that sameness means equity becomes the latest misinformation and myth spread by those who deny the historical legacy and contemporary facts of oppression. As a result of their miseducation, students come to believe that which we abhor when we hear it in deficit theories—that their poor performance must be their own fault. In other words, students believe they are just not as capable; that is why they do not do well. This is not referring to the surface statements about their beliefs in themselves but the deep internal messages to which they hold on to as if inherently part of their identity.

To confront linguicism and this system of beliefs, we must intercept the social messages that may impinge on students. The case of the unemployment strikes in France might be useful in thinking about how this can be done. The unemployed, those no longer actively seeking employment, and the never employed (those seeking employment for the first time or those on lifetime public subsistence) have come together in strikes against the government. This has been organized as a collective action that challenges the internalization of incompetence. The group argues that because the economic system needs a certain level of unemployment to function, they ought to be compensated for meeting such a need. They argue that they are a commodity and that just compensation is required. They are asking that the government attend to their minimal needs of survival. They are conscious about their situation—they make no bones about being the system's victims—but they are asking that the situation be recognized fundamentally differently so that their stake in the situation is considered and a mutually agreed-on solution can be found. They do not want to be victims; they want to be partners.

In a similar way, we need to figure out how to intercept linguicism in the United States and, if needed, begin to construct a new way of seeing what is occurring and find solutions that are more mutually agreeable. To do so, the public must become informed as to the values and benefits of bilingualism and bilingual education. We need to push for school districts to do a better job at documenting their successes (Brisk, 1998), and we need to learn how to counter the "sound bites" coming across in contemporary misinformation campaigns, spreading lies and distortions that frequently appear as public opinion. The danger of not doing so is a return to an era of legal and physical violence as a way of eradicating "other than English languages" in our nation's schools. Thus, I propose seven guiding principles for educators.

A Proposal for What Educators of English-Language Learners Need to Know: Seven Guiding Principles

Although I believe that all educators need to understand the complex relationships between culture, language, and learning, I will focus on what bilingual educators for this is where my expertise lies and for which I have the most experience as the coordinator of the Program in Bilingual/Bicultural Education at Teachers College, Columbia University. My experience with bilingual/bicultural education, developing and evaluating programs in urban schools, and with teacher preparation at a preservice and in-service level expands over two and a half decades.

I also focus on bilingual educators because, nationally, this field is among the top six with the greatest need for teachers (Haselkorn & Calkins, 1993; Recruiting New Teachers, 2000). There are also many more practicing bilingual teachers than there are certified teachers in the field (New York State, 1998). According to the National Commission on Teaching and America's Future (1996), teacher expertise is an essential factor for student achievement. This is critical because it frames the remarks I will make about the importance of preparing quality teaching staff.

Given that the numbers of language minorities and immigrants, in general, are increasing, particularly in inner-city schools, it is highly important that we attend to the recruitment of new teachers and the better preparation of practicing teachers. With respect to better preparing teachers, I do not solely mean certifying them. I would like to go beyond this to discuss that for which they need to be prepared. My assumption is that they cannot be prepared in traditional ways because what they will face in the classroom is not traditional. Garcia (1998) made the following point in this regard:

> The primary logic invoked in the preparation of bilingual teachers remains monolithic and traditional except for the provision of native language instruction in a language other than English. Most importantly, the philosophical formation of bilingual teachers remains positivistic and non-analytical. (p. 77)

How we should prepare teachers to work with children who are developing cognitively while learning a second language is an important question for teacher educators. Although there is a lot of conversation about teaching standards and accreditation of teacher education programs, many institutions are at a loss when it comes to preparing teachers to work with this student population. Those of us who have been preparing teachers who work with this student population and who have a historical sense that embodies the collective wisdom in the field need to come together to think carefully about a collective response that goes beyond a narrow focus on language acquisition. I offer the following as a proposal. It is not meant to be comprehensive, but it embodies some of my grounded thinking based on my experience and knowledge of bilingual teacher education and the field. My hope is that it will generate conversation and debate, given what is summarized in Figure 8.1 and what is articulated below as the seven principles.

Principle 1: Teachers need to be prepared to improve education.

There are two underlying assumptions associated with the first principle. First, language minority children need programs that consider the complexity of their linguistic, cultural, and social needs. Second, we know that the teaching staff can be the catalyst for changing the low quality of education these children have traditionally received. Language minority children, in large numbers, attend the lowest performing, lowest resource schools. These schools are also generally not the first pick of the better teachers. Thus, the quality of teaching staff assigned to the schools is far from the best. How do we change these conditions?

Many structural and organizational responses need to be put in place to make these schools more attractive to teachers. These issues must be attended to at the state and local levels and will take time to put in place. What I want to explore here is how to prepare the teachers for what they will face. Here, I am referring to transformative attitudes as a critical factor.

We need to prepare teachers to go to schools with the explicit goal of improving their conditions of work as well as the education the students receive. They must be ready to find ways of changing the traditional curriculum that is organized to transmit knowledge into a dynamic space for the creation of knowledge. They need to know how to do away with a curriculum in which children are viewed as having no need to be culturally and linguistically acknowledged (Garcia, 1998, p. 81). Teachers must be prepared to go beyond their role as technocrats. They must see that the teaching tasks traditionally organized around accountability and management schemes, as well as the theories in which these practices are grounded, are limited. Although they need to know the concepts and skills of their trade, teachers who are to improve education for language minorities must also assume an agency role.

As we think about how to do this, the most difficult challenge to teacher educators parallels the experience and challenges facing the teachers. How do we organize the knowledge, experience, skills, and attitudes of teachers and students in ways that do not reproduce the past, fostering binary categories of those deemed superior and inferior? How do we impress on the teachers the need to struggle against the ideology and culture of power when most teachers are not aware of its presence or underpinnings (Freire, 1970)? Even when we get teachers to understand the nature of traditional schooling ideology with implicit notions of superiority and inferiority, how do we engage them in ways to contest its operative dogma while they struggle to survive?

Coursework and fieldwork ought to be more intimately connected than what they are today. Coursework material about a particular student population, for example, is often focused on the story of decontextualized statistics. One cannot deny the power of presenting the conditions of education children face through statistics, as is common within the old paradigm of traditional teacher preparation. Yet this is not enough to prepare individuals for the reality they will face in the schools that embodies the facts of those statistics. For example, let's take the following facts (see Figure 8.1) about the conditions of education of the largest language minority group—Latinos.

- There are 18.8 million Latinos in the continental United States.
- 11 million of these report speaking Spanish at home.
- 50% live in central cities.
- The U.S. Latino population grew by 61% from 1970 to 1980, as compared to the 11% growth in the general population.
- Close to 200,000 people immigrate legally, and an estimated 200,000 immigrate illegally each year.
- In education, 40% leave school prior to high school graduation, 35% are held back at least one grade, 47% are overaged at Grade 12, and 70% attend segregated schools (up 56% from 1956).

Figure 8.1   Facts About the Education of Latinos

What can be constructed from these facts? These facts tell us that there are many Spanish-speaking Latinos, but it does not tell us anything about the diversity of cultures and histories with the group. The statistics tell us that the numbers are increasing, particularly in the inner cities. The statistics on immigration can lead to many interpretations, one of which is that the conditions of educational attainment are far from desirable. Although many teacher education students might advance their thinking by knowing these facts, this is not enough. We need to impress on teachers that teaching in traditional ways will render similar results from the past—as embodied in these statistics documenting the shortcoming of what has prevailed as teaching English language learners. If they do not look at the context of education and ways of improving teaching, they will not get beyond the statistics or produce better results to be codified in a future decade's statistical analysis of the problem. Students need to go beyond the bare numbers, receiving preparation by entering into the world of schools that have turned around the statistics for children from low-resource schools, providing a different kind of evidence that inspires hope.

The Program in Bilingual/Bicultural Education at Teachers College, Columbia University, for example, has established a Professional Development School relationship with one such school. Close to 10 years ago, the school, PS165, was under state review for low academic performance. The children were scoring in the lowest 10th percentile. Throughout the subsequent years, the school has undergone an incredible change. The program faculty members have been involved since the very beginning of this collective change process. The program has documented what is going on, placed student teachers in the school, and provided the teachers with different professional development activities. For the teacher preparation program, this school is the key to providing a context-embedded teacher education. It gives students a place to observe transformations while they occur, see teachers struggle with ideas, and experience the dynamism and hope that emanates from within its walls. It is an inner-city school with a high incidence of poverty and where there are many problems to solve on a daily basis. The importance of this school, however, is its willingness to take on the difficult task of improving education for all children. It is a setting that challenges and supports change. We encourage our students to observe in this school prior to their student teaching placement. In their student teaching placements, our students are supported and encouraged to experience change. Experiences, such as the ones our students have in this school, are necessary for the novice teachers to concretize their notions of change and to gain experience on how to work beyond the technocrat to become a change agent. In sum, teachers need to be prepared to improve education.

Principle 2: Teachers need to see themselves as competent and capable of changing learning environments.

My conversations with teachers have brought me to see the importance of empowering the self as a way of doing so with others. Many years ago, I was documenting the development of an alternative, bilingual high school (Torres-Guzman, 1992). This experience was critical to my understanding of the multiple meanings of the word *empowerment*. In subsequent years, various discussions with teachers have led me to understand how the feelings of competence and capacity relate to the process of empowerment. Teachers need to feel competent and capable to exercise leadership roles in schools and to take risks with their teaching as a way of enabling their students. Two different discussions revealed different aspects related to these feelings. In a dialogue with Korean bilingual teachers, I was reminded of the structural issues of symbolic violence related to resulting feelings of competence. The teachers identified what they saw as school and administrative structures that made their children and, consequently, the teachers appear incompetent. One of the factors was the importance placed on testing during early stages of English-language development. The teachers felt that the reliance on standardized tests in English at the end of the year made the teachers' efforts throughout the year appear as inefficient and ineffective. The administration, on receiving the test results, would focus on the task of raising test scores. This exacerbated the problem because the teachers felt they were then placed in a compromising position. They had to sacrifice their pivotal work in the native language for the sake of their evaluations and the garnering of a few incremental points on the test in English each year. This "catch-22" disturbed them and distracted them from engaging in more creative work with the children. They felt something needed to change, and I interpreted this as meaning that structures needed to change. Within the context of this current chapter's introductory analysis, this included a structure wrought with the perpetuation of symbolic violence. It did not acknowledge the work of the teachers, and the importance of their work was translated through the lens of the language of power.

Although I believe my interpretation at the time was adequate, it was a former pensive student who came into my office to share with me a situation she was thinking ever so deeply about that led to a different analysis. A factor she associated with teachers who resisted being involved in change was their self-concept; they did not see themselves as capable of making a difference or confident enough to show what they knew. They had no concept of themselves as agents of change or as teachers for social justice in education, and they did not have enough confidence to stand behind what they knew worked in producing positive academic outcomes. What she shared with me added a new layer to my interpretation of what the Korean teachers had been saying. Perhaps what they were saying was that they needed validation and affirmation of what they did. They wanted leadership that understood that language and cultural learning are a process that takes many years. They wanted their principal to know that children could not perform in English immediately in the same fashion as their native English-language peers. They also needed their principal to understand that in the world of bilingualism, where the context of language cannot be untangled neatly, teachers needed to spend time in language planning.

The former student stressed the need for teachers to learn how to cope with negative messages in school settings, surviving such hostile environments by actively reaffirming with each other the nature of the challenge, as well as their experiences of problem solving in the classroom, and sharing their creativity and risk-taking experiences among themselves. She proposed that teachers should support teachers, and subsequently, she began a teacher-initiated group that has been instrumental in transforming literacy instruction in her school. Helping teachers turn situations of negativity in hostile school environments into situations of active struggle in which they are agents of change and social activists for change, using their creativity, emerges as highly important for teachers to feel competent and capable of changing their learning environments.

> *Principle 3:* Teachers need to change the way they think about knowledge—about what is legitimate knowledge, cultural knowledge, and transformative knowledge—and learn how to use that which the child brings (lives, experiences, and learns at home) to the act of learning in the classroom.

Teachers tend to teach the way they have experienced teaching. Teaching is one profession all of us get to know as we are growing up, having been students ourselves. It is not like other professions that are not accessible to us for the accumulation of years of observational data. We all have memorable learning experiences associated with teacher role models. These experiences are critical to the individuals who go into teaching. They are key to the images they have of themselves as teachers. In stressful situations, teachers tend to resort to what they know and not to what they are taught in teacher education courses. Breaking away from past notions and patterns is a process that many prospective teachers need to engage in consciously. Many bilingual educators came to bilingual education because of what damage or benefit they have personally experienced as bilinguals (Lemberger, 1997). They believe that if they have experienced bilingualism, they are better prepared to deal with the issues of schooling that young bilingual children may be facing. Although this is a good start, there is a lot to be learned that goes beyond the individual experience of bilingualism. This is why they need to know about educational models of bilingualism, pedagogy, language development, the sociocultural aspects of bilingualism.

An incident that occurred a few years ago with one of our students illustrates this point. The student was placed in the first of two student teaching experiences. It was a monolingual setting. She found herself working with a child who did not understand what she was saying in English and decided to use his native language, which she also knew, to nudge him and advance his learning. The cooperating teacher, on hearing the use of the native language, turned to the student teacher and strongly impressed on her that the classroom was not bilingual (as if only in bilingual programs one would hear the native language spoken by the teacher). As a native speaker of the language that was banned from the classroom, the student teacher felt offended. She reacted as a speaker of the language normally would. The teacher, under the most generous of interpretations, was applying the pedagogical rule of language separation. Bilingual education theorists agree that language separation promotes greater complexity, depth, and subtlety in the uses of the languages involved. It also places the student in a greater need to learn the second language to function. But the rule of language separation within the bilingual education setting does not necessarily mean that the native language should be banned from the monolingual classroom or, for that matter, banned from the bilingual classroom. Nor does it justify such a strong negative message toward the language of the child in the classroom, regarding the forbidden, inferior language—as, through symbolic violence, damaging misinformation and myth about what is presumed superior and inferior is spread to that student. In thinking about the incident and what subsequently happened with the teacher and the supervisor (which could also be summed up as a negative experience for the student involving symbolic violence), I would assert that the interactions were plagued with ignorance, based on linguicism. The student teacher was in her first semester at the college. She did not have enough understanding of bilingualism and the societal issues involved. Had she been at the college longer and had she and the others involved known about bilingual education theory, perhaps a dialogue could have ensued about the role of the native language as a resource in the monolingual classroom, instead of creating a situation wrought with cultural conflict. The cooperating teacher and supervisor might have viewed the student teacher as an asset, and they could have taken advantage of her presence and knowledge. They could have approached the native language of the child as something to celebrate and to build on as a valid strength. They did not have enough transformative academic knowledge (Banks, 1993) to reframe the incident in a positive way.

The value of reframing situations is very critical and requires specialized knowledge. In the Columbia University Program in Bilingual/Bicultural Education at Teachers College, for example, the native language and the culture of the children are viewed as a resource and valued strength. We ask bilingual teachers to entertain the idea that the homes and communities from which their children come are valuable resources. Particularly, we want teachers in training to acknowledge how such personal and cultural knowledge can be a legitimate intellectual resource. Although it sounds easy, this is sometimes not as palpable as it may seem. The traditional perspective of education proposes that learning is a mental cognitive task. Thus, what teachers look for are the academic skills brought to school from the home.

A sociocultural perspective on learning proposes that learning is a social activity (Gonzalez, 1995; Mercado & Moll, 1997). We encourage the latter interpretation. The sociocultural interpretation of learning positions teachers to think about the social activities of the family and the community as sources of knowledge on which they can build. Teacher groups in Arizona and New York have based their curricular work on the assumption that the households of the children they teach can be resources for use in the classroom, if they take the time to know and understand them (Gonzalez, 1995; Mercado & Moll, 1997). Once the teachers interacted with the families of children and gained knowledge about what the children brought with them, they were able to explore how to integrate this personal and cultural knowledge into various aspects of the school curriculum.

In the supervised fieldwork in our program at Teachers College, one of the assignments is to do home visits. The students read about the "funds of knowledge" theory and how it has been implemented in Arizona and New York (Gonzalez, 1995; Mercado & Moll, 1997). Although one of our students, a Dominican, resisted the idea of going into the homes for a while, when she did visit, she was surprised by what she learned. In her words, she "was observing a lot of culture in this Dominican home." Although the mother was illiterate, there were a lot of things that she did in an expert way in the home that were translatable and could be transformed for school learning. The teacher was not only able to use the information gathered, but she was also able to get the mother to make a presentation to the children on that which she had expertise. After the visits, our student felt that she would never again be so blind to what children brought into the classroom. A visit to a humble home provided her with the path to understanding the richness of knowledge in homes and communities that could be useful to schools. It was not the "legitimized knowledge" that she could get from books or the curriculum. It was the knowledge that came from lived experiences within a cultural context. These were important because she felt that they could be used to validate and affirm the child and that the conceptually complex home knowledge could be used as a springboard to more complex and abstract work in school. In other words, cultural and personal knowledge could contribute to transformative knowledge.

Often, the teacher acquires learning theory and practice in a cumulative yet linear fashion. This mainstream academic knowledge is unpackaged and becomes a simple commodity; it is often neither questioned nor negotiated. Regardless of the children's needs and their background, these goods are translated into instruction and curriculum, whether in the first or second language. The children thus receive information already codified and constructed in traditional ways prior to the teacher having practical experiences in the school setting. Teachers need to understand how to break free from these traditional ways of seeing, learning, and knowing. Teachers need to change the way they think about knowledge— about what is legitimate knowledge, cultural knowledge, and transformative knowledge— and learn how to use that which the child brings (lives, experiences, and learns at home) to the act of learning in the classroom.

> *Principle 4:* Teachers who reflect on their own practice and do teacher research (as individuals and in groups) will find new ways of thinking about learning and knowledge and discover new ways of presenting content.

I have been involved in reflective teaching research for more than 15 years. My first experience was with a White working-class community in Michigan (Campbell, 1988). That experience taught me how much teachers in practice do know about their craft and how unlikely they are to voice what they know. The separation between who theorizes about education ("university folks") and who practices the craft ("classroom teachers") creates the impression that teachers are not experts and that their voice is of less importance. That has been changing in the past two decades. More and more teachers are writing about their experiences, and we are getting a better look at what happens in classrooms. However, teachers of language minorities are far from voicing what they know. One of my former doctoral students, Nancy Lemberger (1997), completed the first book that focuses on what bilingual teachers theorize about teaching in a bilingual setting. It is a real treasure and contribution to the field.

For more than a decade, I have been teaching a course that asks students to reflect on their teaching practices and those of others. At the same time, they are familiarizing themselves with the theories of teaching in culturally and linguistically diverse settings. I am not always successful in getting the class to do significant quality work within the semester, but what I can see when they do their master's projects is that they have received several messages: They must think about what they do, question what things mean, understand that theory is based on thinking about practice (that practice can be theoretical), and feel capable of thinking systematically and researching aspects of bilingual education theory.

Teacher inquiry is now the norm at our Professional Development School (PS165) in New York City. Each year, there is a presentation and acknowledgment of the research work in which the teachers are engaged; many have chosen to present portfolios in lieu of principal observations and evaluations. The first portfolio project I was involved with was important for my understanding of how to motivate teachers to engage in research and how the activity of teacher research was a vehicle for promoting teacher growth, as well as a way of grounding theory in practice. One of the former students of the program, a team teacher, and the computer teacher took a look at how three children differed in their transfer from Spanish to English. There was a child who was a model from the perspective of bilingual education theory—this was the child who was making the transfer beautifully. Both her first and second languages were developing at age and grade level. The other two children defied the theory because, in one case, the transfer into the second language was not occurring, although the child had, according to the theory, what it took—a strong foundation in the native language. In the other case, the child transferred completely to the second language, rapidly losing his ability to work or speak in his native language. The team collected data, analyzed them, and came to understand the phenomena of transfer between languages in a more complex way. Transfer, they concluded, was bidirectional. They were able to poke holes in the theoretical assumptions they were making about the children and how reality sometimes defied or confirmed theory, given the particular context of their classrooms. The computer teacher, who was not a bilingual teacher, learned a great deal about teaching language minorities and is now applying what he has learned about the ELL (English Language Learners) to the teaching of computer skills. Their growth as teachers was significant.

Within the Professional Development School, reflective practice is encouraged. Teachers are able to build on, test, and go beyond the theories they have learned; they are able to theorize about their practice and, above all, to improve on their teaching through meaningful research experiences. Thus, teachers who reflect on their own practice and do teacher research (as individuals and in groups) will find new ways of thinking about learning and knowledge and discover new ways of presenting content.

Principle 5: Teachers who know more than one language and are knowledgeable about language are better prepared for the students with whom they work.

Rosaldo (1989) challenged his own ability and accuracy, as a young anthropologist studying grief and headhunting rage behaviors, to make meaning of the observed behaviors in the ways these were understood by the Ilongots, the people he was studying. He proposed that he did not have the wisdom that comes from experiencing the phenomena of death and grief about which he was theorizing. There is something to be said about the added value of experience. My belief is that teachers often practice in a world where sounds are nonsensical and communication is wordless. Bilingual teachers must not only experience this world but also go beyond it. They need to have transformed the world of silence into one where sophisticated and subtle language forms can be evoked. Teachers need to understand how much sociocultural meaning is carried and constructed through language. They need to have the experiences that will help them reflect on how to provoke the students' thinking and guide them to find ways in which to express ideas and emotions in more than one language—the language of the children and the second language (Gibbons, 1993). The teacher must be competent enough to use both languages as a means of expression as well as an end. To masterfully manipulate more than one language takes many years of dedication and hard work. If the teacher is brought up with more than one language, this is already an advantage. But to know how to speak a language does not guarantee that the teachers' linguistic competence is at a level where they can teach or that they feel competent to do so, as was the case of the middle school teacher mentioned above.

I am literate in both Spanish and English, yet every single day I learn about language. The ongoing nature of language and world learning is not only applicable to students but also to teachers. Bilingual teacher education programs need to find ways of ensuring that teachers are minimally competent in the language(s) in which they will be teaching and that they have goals for developing their own language and sociocultural knowledge through literature groups, study abroad, and service work in the linguistic community they serve. To not do this is to exercise symbolic violence and disrespect the community of learners.

Principle 6: Teachers need to identify the roots of symbolic violence—not just in how they see the value of language and pedagogy but also in the nature of pedagogy itself.

Language often becomes symbolic to individuals and groups who speak it. The status of the language (and its speakers) in a school setting is important to recognize and confront. Whether it is the message of the teacher who banned Spanish in her monolingual classroom or the messages that come from the lack of using a language as a medium of instruction, children from both majority and minority language groups hear and internalize values regarding which languages are superior and powerful, as well as inferior and devalued. Children know that languages are not equally valued; they know the speakers of the minority language have less power, and they work at re-creating the power relations in their mini-society, the school.

Teachers need to be aware of what is happening in their schools, through their instruction and among their students. In a cooperative group in a two-way bilingual program, Perez and Torres-Guzman (1998) found that the asymmetry in power relations was re-created, even in favorable conditions. The two-way bilingual program is the model that includes both majority and minority children. Some premises that are made regarding cross-cultural experiences of heterogeneous linguistic groups, however, do not always prove themselves in practice. We found that majority-language males will tend to dominate the group, even on designated non-English days, if the task does not give the non-English speaker the advantage. It was not enough to designate a non-English speaker for leadership to counter this domination. Teachers cannot afford to stop their vigilance against the mechanisms of "isms" within groups that maintain White and male privilege or that reconstruct and reify the dominant social relationships of power.

Teachers need to learn how symbolic violence is re-created in their own schools and classrooms (Daarder, 1991; Garcia, 1998; Shannon & Escamilla, 1997) and ways in which to intervene. Teachers need to identify the roots of symbolic violence—not just in how they see the value of language and pedagogy but also in the nature of pedagogy itself. Pedagogy is needed that does not facilitate the perpetuation of symbolic violence.

Principle 7: Teachers need to break the isolation of the classroom by learning how to collaborate with other teachers.

Last, I want to share with you my experience with a group of middle school teachers whom I have worked with for the past decade and a half. This experience reflects how teachers need not engage in formal tasks such as research, as described above, to collaborate and learn from each other. Collaboration can take place through other kinds of activities that lead to meaningful dialogue among teachers. Through one such activity, I videotaped all the teachers teaching literature in this middle school (Torres-Guzman, 1998). They individually viewed the tapes, selected a problem they were grappling with, and chose a 5-minute segment that illustrated the problem. The group was to reflect collectively on the segment. On viewing her teaching, one of the teachers decided that she would share with the other teachers a particular segment that illustrated a problem of practice in the Spanish literature class. She was teaching a short story. The text, she felt, was linguistically complex and was difficult for the students. The difficulty of teaching this type of text, in addition, was exacerbated by the linguistic diversity and the variety of cultural experiences the students had among themselves.

The other teachers, when they saw the tapes, were both affirming and critical, but what was most telling about their dialogue was what happened when the teacher being viewed shared with others that she thought the text was too difficult for the linguistically heterogeneous class. She was moving toward eliminating difficult readings during the first semester. She felt a less difficult and more relevant book, such as one she had used at a subsequent time, would prove a better start for her students. The rest of the teachers disagreed strongly. They referred to the long-term benefit they had experienced in using such challenging texts. The teachers felt that the students were not the only ones to benefit; the teachers reaped the benefits also. The teachers had been able to engage in higher order thinking with these students during the subsequent literature classes. The struggle of teaching a "difficult" text early in the year had created better literature readers in both languages and created room from a variety of "cultural texts" in the long run because it pushed the students to go beyond what they knew. The teachers also felt that the initial readings would set the pace and the standards for the year. Expectations, they discovered, were established not just individually but collectively; they also demonstrated that higher expectations are established when there is a long-range vision for the curriculum.

Teachers need to break the isolation of the classroom not just by working together but by thinking more collectively about the teaching problems and situations they encounter. Teachers need to challenge the tendency to see problems from their perspective as individuals, moving on to look at their collective responsibility as teachers to share their views with each other and arrive at new understandings. Teachers need to break the isolation of the classroom by learning how to collaborate with other teachers.

Conclusion

This chapter has defined and discussed linguicism as it applies to language minority education and bilingualism. In addition, the chapter proposed that teacher education programs could help prepare teachers to intercept the negative societal messages around language and culture, specifically offering seven principles to guide teacher preparation and generate discussion about what is needed to effectively teach English language learners. The examples used were intended to promote discussion and dialogue. Individually, it is reasonable that someone will question the generalizable "interceptive" value of the examples provided. Collectively, however, the examples are compelling and push the field in a direction that is not debatable, as we need to better prepare teachers, bilingual and monolingual, to confront linguicism.

Bilingual teachers need to assert both the equal status of the languages and a critical perspective on pedagogy. Bilingual teacher education programs need to design programs that take up the task of recovering the possibility of becoming "a pedagogy of everyday life and struggle for agency" (Garcia, 1998, p. 80). But classroom teachers cannot do this alone. They need the structures of teacher education programs that prepare teachers who will not accept how things are and are willing to engage in change and become agents of change.

Bilingual teachers also need the support of general educators. Confronting linguicism is a task for all. The preparation of quality, critical teachers means developing knowledge about language minorities, recognizing and confronting negative attitudes toward minority languages and their speakers, and developing pedagogical competence that promotes positive change and the improvement of all students, not just the selected few.

Notes

1. *Native language* is a term used to refer to the heritage language of the child. It is often interchanged with terms such as the *child's first language*, the *dominant language*, and the *mother tongue*.

2. Affirmation of English as the primary goal of instruction occurred with the Californian vote in favor of Proposition 227. In a statewide proposition, the California electorate voted to eliminate instruction in the native language in favor of instructional methods using English as the medium of instruction. Since then Arizona has followed suit, and efforts to reverse bilingual education efforts have been ongoing in New York, Massachusetts, Colorado, and other states.

3. The criterion of "well-implemented" programs comes from the *Castañeda vs. Pickard* (1981) case, which measures the closing of the achievement gap between bilingual/ESL students and their peers in a 3-year period.

4. Skutnabb-Kangas (1991) proposed that this internalization is what Fanon (1966) called *colonized consciousness*.

Part IV

Understanding and Dealing With Youth Violence

9

African American
Adolescent Males Living
in Violent Communities

Coping With Interpersonal Assaultive Violence

ELIZABETH SPARKS

Since the early 1980s, there have been an increasing number of highly visible stories in the media about violent incidents involving young people in suburban, rural, and inner-city communities across the United States. Initially, most of these stories told of homicides among urban African American adolescents. More recently, they have reported on mass homicides perpetrated by White suburban/rural male adolescents and hate crimes perpetrated by young people targeting members of different minority groups. The stories of youth involvement in violence are indeed alarming, and the statistics that accompany them have caused many to believe that the words *youth* and *violence* are inextricably linked (Eron & Slaby, 1994). But this is not the case. After two decades of psychological research, we know that violence is not random, uncontrollable, or inevitable (Eron, Gentry, & Schlegel, 1994). Many factors, both within the individual and in the external environment, contribute to the development of violent behaviors in children and adolescents. And many of these factors are amenable to change. Evaluations of various violence prevention programs have shown that it is possible to bring about reductions in many of the problem behaviors that are associated with violence and aggression in youth. However, the effectiveness of these programs in reducing serious aggressive and violent behavior remains undetermined (Hammond & Yung, 1994). Violence prevention programs targeted for high-risk youth have increased in recent years, but despite their success, there has been very little reduction in incidents of violence at schools and in violence-provoking behavior that are particularly evident in inner-city schools and among ethnic minority adolescents (Centers for Disease Control and Prevention, 1992; Menacker, Weldon, & Hurwitz, 1990). Research has shown that African American male adolescents living in inner cities are at the highest risk, reporting levels of personal victimization and weapons carrying that far exceed those reported in national surveys (Menacker et al., 1990; Sheley, McGee, & Wright, 1992). There is clearly a need to better understand the experiences of interpersonal violence among African American male adolescents and to search for more effective ways of altering their vulnerability to victimization.

This chapter presents research that explores the coping processes used by African American male adolescents as they negotiate their social world and respond to aggressive provocation. The study takes the perspective that violent confrontations between peers are a relatively common occurrence among urban African American male adolescents and represent a significant source of stress (DuRant, Cadenhead, Pendergrast, Slavents, & Linder, 1994; Gibbs et al., 1989; Yung & Hammond, 1998). The study examined the coping processes used by these young men in violent encounters with peers and the socially constructed norms that govern their responses to interpersonal conflict. To present the context surrounding the experiences of interpersonal violence reported by the young men who participated in this study, I will briefly review some of the national statistics on youth involvement in violence.

National Statistics on Youth Involvement in Violence

Violence involving youth has dramatically increased over the past decade, and many young people have become victims and perpetrators of violent acts in schools and communities. The rates of youth violence began to rise in the late 1980s, and by 1991, federal crime statistics reported a 103% increase in the homicide rate among 15- to 19-year-olds for the 5-year period between 1985 and 1990 (Centers for Disease Control and Prevention, 1992). The problem of youth homicide is most acute among African American youth living in poverty. For males (ages 15-24 years old), homicide is the leading cause of death for this group (Cristoffel, 1990; Gibbs et al., 1989). A young African American male has a 1 in 21 chance of being killed prior to reaching age 25, and from 1978 to 1988, homicide accounted for 42% of all deaths for these young men (Hammond & Yung, 1993).

These statistics on homicide, however, represent only the tip of the iceberg. There are many more youth who become involved in nonfatal interpersonal assaultive violence between peers and who witness such violence. Many incidents of youth homicide began as arguments, increased in intensity over time, and ultimately turned into a lethal confrontation (Jenkins, 1995). Research examining violence in diverse groups of adolescents estimates that 3,273 deaths occur yearly because of interpersonal violence among youth, and each month, more than 28,200 students in secondary schools are physically attacked (Gorski & Pilotto, 1993). A recent survey conducted by Metropolitan Life Insurance (1999) found that one quarter of the 1,044 student participants had been victims of a violent act that occurred in or around school. One in eight of these same students reported that they had carried a weapon to school at some point during the previous year.

When these experiences are examined in low-income African American youth, the results reflect an even more serious problem. There can be no question that male and female African Americans of all ages are consistently overrepresented as the victims and perpetrators of interpersonal violence (Yung & Hammond, 1998). Studies report that from 32% to 37% of African American adolescents have been involved in a physical fight at school and that from 19% to 30% of these students have carried weapons (knife/gun) to school on at least one occasion (Cotton et al., 1994; Schubiner, Scott, & Tzelepis, 1993). The rate of exposure to violence for inner-city African American youth is striking and affects their quality of life (Schubiner et al., 1993).

Theoretical Perspectives on Stress and Coping

The study was informed by the work of Lazarus and Folkman (Lazarus, 1966; Lazarus & Folkman, 1984; see also Anderson, 1991; Myers, 1989). The cognitive theory of psychological stress and coping developed by Lazarus and Folkman (1984) suggests that the person and the environment are in a dynamic, mutually reciprocal, bidirectional relationship. *Stress* is defined as the psychological state derived from individuals' appraisals of their adaptation to the demands that are made of them. *Coping* is defined as the problem-solving efforts made by individuals when the demands of a given situation exceed adaptive resources (Lazarus, Averill, & Opton, 1974). A central feature of the model is the process of cognitive appraisal (Lazarus, 1966). A person's response to any stressor will be influenced by his or her appraisal of the situation and capacity to process the experience, attach meaning to it, and incorporate it into his or her belief system (Folkman, Lazarus, Dunkel-Schetter, Delongis, & Gruen, 1986).

Anderson (1991) built on this work and articulated a model that attempts to explain the connection between stress and coping for African Americans. This model is also interactional but hypothesizes an additional source of stress (termed *acculturative stress*) that is the result of efforts made by African Americans to adjust to the threats and challenges posed by the environment. According to Anderson, sources of stress, acculturative factors, and mediating factors interact to produce psychological and physical distress or adaptation in the individual.

Myers's (1989) model is similar to Anderson's (1991) model and describes the connection between stress and coping in African American youth. He suggested that African American youth develop a number of coping skills and adaptive behaviors to compensate for their marginal minority status in this society. This leads to their developing patterned sets of behaviors in response to the realities of inner-city life (Mancini, 1980; Myers & King, 1980). Myers (1989) claimed that African American youth not only grow up in an insidiously stressful environment, but they must also develop a repertoire of coping behaviors within a context that severely restricts their resources (e.g., few models of effective coping and social barriers that impede access to resources).

Thus, the theoretical perspective used in this study was based on a transactional model of psychosocial stress and coping. It was hypothesized that the stress associated with interpersonal assaultive violence would have a unique meaning to the study's participants because it occurred within a stressful environmental context where there are few external resources to assist with the coping process. It was also hypothesized that these young men have developed a patterned set of behaviors to respond to this stress.

Method

The participants in the study were 30 African American adolescent males, ages 13 to 19 years (mean age = 15.33), who were drawn from youth programs situated in three inner-city neighborhoods in a city in the Northeast. These were predominantly ethnic minority neighborhoods where a majority of the residents lived in families that had incomes at or below poverty level. Approximately 89% of the sample lived in one of these three neighborhoods; the other 11% lived in contiguous urban areas. Slightly more than one half of the participants (51.9%) were from one-parent homes, 40.7% were from two-parent homes, and 7.4% lived with other caretakers. Although the participants were unable to provide accurate information about parental income, 86% were from families in which at least one parent worked full-time.

Data were obtained from focus groups, individual interviews, and objective measures. The focus group questions were as follows:

1. What is the level of violence occurring in your neighborhood?

2. What do you think are some of the causes of this violence?

3. How do you think you should react (in public) when someone your own age confronts you?

4. Would this change at all if you were confronted in private (alone with the other person)?

5. How do you think others expect you to react in these situations (in public, in private)?

6. In general, how do you cope with the violence that you encounter on the streets? What "works" for you? What doesn't work?

7. Do you use any supportive resources to help you cope with this violence?

8. What do you think can be done to stop the violence?

The three objective measures were (a) the Experience and Exposure to Violence Questionnaire (Gladstein, Rusonis, & Heald, 1992), (b) the Cognitive Appraisal of a Violent Encounter Questionnaire (Folkman et al., 1986), and (c) the Ways of Coping Questionnaire (Folkman & Lazarus, 1985; Vitaliano, Russo, Carr, Maiuro, & Becker, 1985). The Experience and Exposure to Violence Questionnaire (Gladstein et al., 1992) was used to determine the extent to which a participant had been exposed to interpersonal assaultive violence. This 35-question inventory solicits information in three areas (the extent to which youth have been victims of crime, know victims, or have witnessed violent acts), and it provides a structured way of obtaining this information.

The Cognitive Appraisal of a Violent Encounter Questionnaire (Folkman et al., 1986) determines cognitive appraisals of a recently experienced violent incident or of a hypothetical violent situation (for those participants who had not recently experienced a violent incident). The questions focused on their primary (what is at stake in the encounter) and secondary appraisals (what can be done to prevent or overcome harm) of the incident. Participants responded on a 5-point Likert-type scale indicating the extent to which each stake was involved in their response to a violent encounter, along with their beliefs regarding what could be done to prevent or over-come the harm associated with the situation.

Finally, the Ways of Coping Questionnaire (WOCQ) (Folkman & Lazarus, 1985; Vitaliano et al., 1985) is designed to identify the thoughts and actions an individual has used to cope with a specific stressful encounter. The items on the WOCQ were designed to be answered in relation to a specific stressful encounter (termed the *focal encounter*). For this study, the focal encounter was presented to the participants, who were asked to think about a situation in which they either got into a fight with a peer or were involved in an inci-dent in which violence could have occurred. The WOCQ contains 66 items that describe a broad range of cognitive and behavioral strate-gies that individuals use to manage internal or external demands in specific stressful encounters. The individual responds to each item on a 4-point Likert-type scale, indicating the frequency with which each strategy was used: 0 = *does not apply and/or not used*, 1 = *used somewhat*, 2 = *used quite a bit*, and 3 = *used a great deal*. The WOCQ contains eight scales: Confrontative Coping, Distancing, Self-Controlling, Seeking Social Support, Accepting Responsibility, Escape-Avoidance, Planful Problem Solving, and Positive Reappraisal. Validity studies (Vitaliano et al., 1985) indicate that the WOCQ holds promise as a measure of a wide range of coping strategies, and the scales have respectable internal consistency (ranging from .61 to .79), reliability, and construct validity. In addition, it has been noted that the scales are generally not confounded by demographic differences. The WOCQ is considered to be a valuable measure of coping in response to environmental stressors.

The measures were administered orally during individual interviews, which made it possible to verify participants' comprehension of the questions.

Discussion of Results

Descriptive statistics were calculated for each of the measures, and *T* tests were used to identify any significant differences in coping processes between those participants who were direct victims of violence and those who were not.[1] A content analysis of the focus group data was conducted to identify the normative behaviors associated with interpersonal assaultive violence within the participants' peer culture.

Based on the responses to the Experience and Exposure to Violence Questionnaire, 76.7% had been direct victims of violence, 93.3% were indirect victims (witnessed violent acts), and 100% were personally acquainted with individuals who had been direct victims of violence. The most frequently endorsed category of victimization was "having your life threatened" (63%). Approximately one third of the participants had been robbed with a weapon and/or assaulted without a weapon, and less than one fourth had been knifed. More young men had witnessed incidents of violence than had been directly victimized, which is consistent with previous research (Gladstein et al., 1992; Metropolitan Life Insurance, 1999; Schubiner et al., 1993; Shakoor & Chalmers, 1991). The violent incidents most frequently witnessed were assaults either without a weapon (76.7%) or with a weapon (63.3%). Approximately one fourth of the young men had witnessed a murder at some point in their lives, and more than half (60%) had seen someone shot.

These findings suggest that a majority of the participants had been both direct and indirect victims of various types of violence. Although similar to prevalence rates found in other studies of inner-city children and adolescents (e.g., Gladstein et al., 1992; Fitzpatrick & Boldizar, 1993; Schubiner et al., 1993; Shakoor & Chalmers, 1991), the participants in this study had experienced somewhat higher levels of violence.

Cognitive Appraisals

The Cognitive Appraisal of a Violent Encounter Questionnaire was used to determine the participants' primary (what is at stake) and secondary (what can be done to prevent or overcome harm) appraisals in response to a fight (or a potential fight) with a peer. The experience of an actual or potential fight served as the focal encounter for this measure. The most frequently endorsed primary appraisal item suggested that the young men were concerned about harm to their own health, safety, and physical well-being (90%). The most frequently endorsed secondary appraisal items suggested that the young men felt the situation had to be accepted but that there was something that could be done to change it as a result of their own actions. The comments made by the participants during the focus groups and interviews provided further clarification of this finding. Most believed that they had to prepare themselves for a fight whenever a peer was threatening or intentionally provocative. The young men stated that the only thing they could do if a peer wanted to fight was to defend themselves and make every effort to come out of the altercation without serious injury.

This appraisal process, however, seemed to be a dynamic one for these young men. In the focus groups, the participants stated that when a peer confronted them, they would initially try talking with the other person in an effort to avoid a fight. At this point, the situation would be appraised as avoidable and was accompanied by the belief that it might be possible to change the situation through personal actions (e.g., talking or negotiating). If these efforts were unsuccessful, the young men would alter their appraisal, and the encounter would become unavoidable. The preferred behavioral response at this point in the encounter would be to fight to protect oneself from physical harm. Determining whether a violent encounter was avoidable or unavoidable seemed to shift during the course of an aggressive encounter. Although attributions may have influenced the appraisal process to some extent, these seemed to be less important to the initiation of a fight than were the intentions of the instigator. The participants insisted that they always tried to talk to the instigator first, resorting to fighting only when they felt that there were no alternatives.

Coping Processes

The results from the Ways of Coping Questionnaire suggested that participants used all of the eight possible coping processes in response to a violent altercation with a peer. The Confrontative Coping scale describes aggressive efforts to alter the situation and suggests some degree of hostility and risk taking. The Distancing scale describes cognitive efforts to detach oneself and to minimize the significance of the situation. The Self-Controlling scale describes efforts to regulate one's feelings and actions. The Seeking Social Support scale describes efforts to seek informational support, tangible support, and emotional support. The Accepting Responsibility scale acknowledges one's own role in the problem with a concomitant theme of trying to put things right. The Escape-Avoidance scale describes wishful thinking and behavioral efforts to escape or avoid the problem. Items on this scale contrast with those on the Distancing scale, which suggest detachment. The Planful Problem Solving scale describes deliberate problem-focused efforts to alter the situation, coupled with an analytic approach to solving the problem. The Positive Reappraisal scale describes efforts to create positive meaning by focusing on personal growth. It also has a religious dimension.

Five of the processes were used by almost all of the participants (96.7%–100%). These included confrontative coping, distancing, self-controlling, planful problem solving, and approach/avoidance coping. The other three coping processes were used by at least three fourths of the participants (73.3%–86.7%). These included accepting responsibility, seeking social support, and having positive reappraisal/spirituality.

Confrontative Coping

Almost all of the participants (96.7%) endorsed this coping process. The young men seemed to use aggressive efforts to alter the situation and made a plan of action that was followed during and after the fight. This problem-focused coping process involved both talking with a potential assailant in an effort to alter the course of events and fighting. For some participants, fighting involved the use of weapons, which they believed increased their physical safety. One young man stated,

> If a whole bunch of dudes be looking at you and you're strapped or whatever . . . you got your pistol or whatever. . . . And they try and come up to you and say something to you, and you pull out. . . . They're going to jack dog . . . they ain't going to come up. They ain't going to try nothing stupid. They going to jet, probably try something the next time. . . . That's worth it—at least you didn't get your life took then.

For others, fighting did not involve weapons. Regardless of their perspective about the use of weapons, the general sentiment among participants was that they must directly confront the situation to adequately cope.

Distancing

All of the young men (100%) indicated that they used this coping process to some extent in their efforts to deal with the emotions resulting from violent encounters. They attempted to regulate their own feelings and actions associated with the encounter by employing wishful thinking or behavioral efforts to escape or avoid emotional reactions. They also used cognitive efforts to detach themselves from the experience by minimizing the significance of the encounter. Many of the young men reported that they avoided thinking about fighting, preferring to just "chill out" and relax. One young man stated,

> You just don't think about it. It's just a part of life. If you thought about it everyday, you'd be a nervous wreck. You wouldn't go outside; you wouldn't do the things that you want to do. That's not a way to live—you can't live in fear.

Planful Problem Solving

Ninety-three percent of the young men endorsed this coping process. They described three different methods of dealing with a violent encounter with a peer: (a) preparing for the worst, (b) watching your back, and (c) avoiding enemies.

Preparing for the Worst. According to the participants, it is important to always be prepared for the worst whenever one engages in a fight with a peer. All of the participants hoped to come out of a fight without experiencing serious harm; however, they mentally prepared themselves to be shot or stabbed whenever they engaged in a fight. One young man stated it this way:

> See, you must always assume that the other person has a weapon. You must always assume that. You can't always think—well, I'll just fight him. That rarely happens.

Watching Your Back. A primary strategy discussed by the young men was the need to "watch your back" while on the streets. This strategy entailed either conducting a reconnaissance of the area to plan ahead for potential trouble or traveling with a group of known and trusted friends who would assist in a fight. Communication with strangers was generally avoided, and the participants reported that they preferred to stay by themselves (or with friends) most of the time. The young men felt they had to be mindful of potential dangers at all times and believed that their safety depended on an ability to successfully execute this strategy. One young man explained the strategy in this way:

> My antenna go up if a group comes on the street. I start thinking ahead. Like if you're walking by a whole group of guys, you just gotta think. You ain't going to walk in between all of them. You take like a scenic route or something. 'Cause if you walk straight through them, they'll start something. . . . But don't cross to the other side of the street because they might throw a rock at you. If you see them from far away and cross the street, then you can play it off. But if you cross the street from far away and see somebody else cross, you know something might be happening. You stop walking and pretend you've forgotten something—turn around.

The participants seemed to use a planned set of behaviors to manage potentially violent peer interactions. They reported that every African American adolescent male is familiar with this strategy and executes it whenever traveling alone.

Avoiding Enemies. The participants articulated an additional strategy that they believed increased their chances of avoiding or surviving a violent encounter with a peer. The young men made efforts to avoid making "enemies," who are defined as peers that harbor grudges because of something that was previously said or done. The young men identified a "code of conduct" that should be followed to avoid making enemies. It involved the notion of respect. Gaining respect from peers and treating others with respect were considered critically important. According to the participants, gaining respect was directly linked to positive self-esteem and social acceptance. The ultimate insult was being disrespected, which could occur as a result of such behaviors as excessive staring or making negative comments about another person's family. Disrespect was identified as one of the chief reasons for fighting. The participants articulated strategies that they used to help them avoid being disrespected (or disrespecting others). One such strategy was to establish at least acquaintance relationships with young men in their home communities. One young man stated,

> I make sure that I speak to everyone . . . even the guys that I know are in gangs. I try to mind my own business. That way, no one can say that I'm being disrespectful.

This socially constructed notion of respect was an important coping strategy within this adolescent peer culture. It contributed to the avoidance of violence by defining a set of normative behaviors that the young men used in their peer interactions. This "code of conduct," however, also had rules that defined the appropriate response when someone violated the code. It dictated that when a young man had been disrespected, he was required to make a direct response. Whether or not this response led to fighting seemed to be influenced by the appraisal process described earlier.

Positive Reappraisal/Spirituality

Eighty-six percent of the young men used positive reappraisal as one of their coping processes. They were able to interpret fighting in such a way that they found some positive meaning to these experiences. The young men believed that engaging in aggressive (verbal or physical) encounters with peers increased their self-awareness. They reported becoming more consciously aware of how they were perceived by peers and learned to present a confident, nonthreatening image to others. Some of the young men developed self-identities as leaders, which enhanced their ability to respond in a less reactive manner to provocation, thereby reducing their involvement in fighting. Even those who were able to successfully avoid fighting recognized that the external environment had some influence on the effectiveness of their behaviors; however, they chose to focus their attention on controlling their own behaviors, instead of reacting to the behaviors of others.

Finally, there were some young men who relied on their faith and belief in God to help them deal with peer violence. One young man expressed it this way:

> Yup, whatever happens, happens. That's what I figure. . . . If God wants me to die, I'm going to die regardless. If He don't want me to die, it ain't my time to go. . . . That's how I figure.

Self-Controlling and Escape-Avoidance Coping

These two coping processes were similar in the ways in which the young men discussed them in the focus groups. They were endorsed by approximately 98% of the participants. From their discussions, it seems as though the young men made efforts to maintain control over their emotions by finding cognitive and behavioral ways to avoid experiencing negative affects. They reported trying to keep their feelings to themselves most of the time. This was especially the case when they were dissatisfied with their performance during a fight. The young men also reported listening to music, playing sports, or relaxing with friends to get away from the thoughts and feelings associated with a fight.

Seeking Social Support

Approximately three fourths (76.7%) of the participants indicated that they sought out support when dealing with emotional reactions following a fight with a peer. Most stated that they preferred to talk with friends and very rarely spoke about violent incidents with counselors or other adults (including parents). Counseling was perceived as a supportive resource for others but not for themselves. Only one young man indicated that he had spoken with a counselor after being victimized; the other 29 reported never having spoken with a counselor specifically about their experiences with violence or their reactions to violent incidents. This finding is particularly noteworthy because all of the participants were involved in youth programs or psychotherapy at the time of the interviews.

Other supportive resources identified by participants included youth programs, which were generally perceived as "safe" places because they afforded teens an opportunity to be involved in interesting activities without the fear of violence. Other safe places included job sites and house parties with friends. School was viewed by some as a safe place, but for others, it was the site where most of their violent encounters with peers occurred.

Accepting Responsibility

Approximately three fourths of the participants (73.3%) indicated that they accepted some degree of personal responsibility for violent encounters, even though none identified themselves as instigators. The young men seemed to feel personally responsible for managing their behavior during a fight and accepted responsibility for maintaining their own safety.

Implications of the Study

The results of this study provide a picture of the coping processes used by African American adolescent males when dealing with interpersonal assaultive violence between peers. They illustrate the dynamic nature of these coping processes and the ways that social context influences attitudes toward and responses to violent provocation. The coping processes used by these young men are similar to those seen by Folkman and Lazarus (1985) in research with White middle-class adults. They found that individuals tended to use distancing, escape-avoidance, and self-controlling coping processes most often when a situation was perceived as being unavoidable. In situations perceived as being a threat to self-esteem, individuals were less likely to seek social support. The coping processes used by the African American adolescent male participants in this study were consistent with these theoretical predictions.

The "code of conduct" described by the adolescents in this study is quite similar to the process of violence described by Oliver (1994) in his ethnographic study of African American men. In general, Oliver found that these adult men had normative expectations of behavior that were used to determine whether violence was justified in a particular situation. For example, disrespect was identified as a serious rule violation that warranted a violent response, and self-defense was the justification for violence in situations when an antagonist made verbal or physical threats. Both Oliver's research and the results of current study suggest that there is a powerful relationship between normative expectations, situational definitions, and behavior that is involved in the interpersonal assaultive violence that occurs between African American males. It also seems probable that this relationship is firmly established by adolescence.

Conclusion: Implications for Violence Prevention

It is important that information about the cognitive appraisals and coping processes of African American adolescent males be incorporated into violence prevention efforts to increase their cultural sensitivity and relevance to the everyday lives of these young men. Violence prevention and treatment programs for adolescents vary on a number of dimensions; however, they are generally directed at changing either individuals or the systems and settings that influence behavior (Guerra, Tolan, & Hammond, 1994). At the level of primary prevention, most programs that focus on the individual attempt to build adolescents' skills in one or more areas (e.g., school achievement, social skills, social problem solving, social perspective taking, and impulse control). The evaluation data from these programs suggest that those promoting social-cognitive skills (including perspective taking, alternative solution generation, self-esteem enhancement, and peer negotiation skills) have the most impact (Guerra et al., 1994). By incorporating information about coping processes and the socially constructed norms that define "acceptable" behavioral responses to violent provocation, it should be possible to increase the applicability of the training provided in these programs to the everyday lives of African American male adolescents. Encouraging the young men to discuss these socially constructed norms might contribute to the development of a level of critical consciousness that would support active questioning of their adherence to these norms. It might also be helpful for programs to encourage the use of coping processes that support avoidance of aggressive behavior, such as distancing, self-controlling, and positive reappraisal. Although the young men in the study seem to use a number of different processes to cope with aggressive encounters with peers, it might be possible to influence their use of specific processes through feedback and training.

The results of the study also have implications for programming at the secondary prevention level, where the focus is on adolescents who have already exhibited heightened levels of interpersonal assaultive violence. They are useful in expanding our understanding of the lack of motivation and reluctance to participate in prevention programs that is typically seen with this population. Violence-prone adolescents may be referred for services, but they are often not interested in becoming involved in programs (Guerra et al., 1994). Similarly, Gladstein and colleagues (1992) found that even victimized African American adolescents rarely seek psychological help and may not even go to a doctor for medical assistance except when they have suffered grave injuries. There has been little research on the reluctance of African American adolescents to seek professional assistance after a victimization experience. Rode and Bellfield (1992) conducted a study with adolescents in Minnesota that may shed some light on this issue. They found that the majority of African American adolescents who responded to a health-related survey did not feel that adults (such as school personnel) cared about their welfare. Hammond and Yung (1994) suggested that such feelings might contribute to a reluctance to go to professionals for assistance with problems of any type. Although this is a plausible explanation, the results of the current study offer an alternative explanation. African American adolescent males who are involved in frequent violent encounters with peers may strongly adhere to the socially constructed norms governing responses to provocation. The appraisal process used by these young men may contribute to the belief that a violent response is necessary to ensure personal safety or maintain respect. Their adherence to this code of conduct leaves them with few, if any, nonviolent response options. They may also have a tendency to prefer coping processes that lead to avoiding social contacts when experiencing negative affect and holding themselves accountable for the outcome of a violent encounter, particularly when that outcome was not good. Thus, such a young man would be reluctant to participate in programs that characterize his style of dealing with interpersonal conflict as problematic, and he would also be reluctant to seek out professional assistance following victimization because of shame.

One way of addressing this problem is for providers to place an increased emphasis on the prereferral process and to take the necessary time to gain a thorough understanding of the appraisals made by these young men. This would also provide an opportunity for providers to explore the code of conduct ascribed to by the young men and to gently encourage them to expand their definition of "acceptable" behaviors. Clearly, this would be a challenge; however, many violence-prone adolescents are involved in institutional systems (such as the courts) where they are subject to external controls, which could be applied to increase compliance with prereferral efforts. Because adolescent males are more willing to discuss violent experiences with peers, a group modality may be an effective strategy for this prereferral process. There is, however, an important role for adults to play. The participants in the study reported that they needed adults who were willing to take the time to listen to their thoughts and who cared about them. Thus, whether a group or individual modality is used for these prereferral discussions, the goal would be to work with the young men to establish the type of therapeutic relationships that would facilitate a change in some of the attitudinal and cognitive barriers that interfere with their willingness to participate in violence prevention and treatment programs. As we develop a more comprehensive understanding of the process by which African American adolescent males learn the rules of conduct and normative expectations that govern their attributions and behaviors, as well as the ways they cope with interpersonal violence, we will be better able to increase the applicability of prevention efforts to their social context.

There is a need for additional research to further examine situational determinants and their influence on the socially constructed meanings of assaultive violence among African American adolescents. As Oliver (1994) suggested, research is needed to answer questions such as the following: (a) How do role orientations, drug involvement, social context, and third parties contribute to acts of interpersonal violence? (b) How do African American youth become socialized into street culture? To address these questions, we will need to conduct research that involves heterogeneous samples of African American adolescent males and females and employs both quantitative and qualitative methodologies.

As a final note, it should be pointed out that the chapter's focus on cognitive coping processes should in no way be seen as minimizing the complex nature of the etiology of interpersonal assaultive violence among African American adolescent males. There continues to be a crucial need for prevention efforts that address all of the factors found to be associated with violence among youth, such as difficult environmental conditions (e.g., housing, schools) in low-income communities, prevalence of severe and persistent poverty in African American families, high rates of community violence that many youth experience on a daily basis, and incidences of domestic violence and child abuse that affect the lives of many young people. To reduce the level of interpersonal assaultive violence among African American adolescent males, the nation must make a firm commitment to developing multifaceted approaches to prevention and intervention.

Note

1. The Experience and Exposure to Violence Questionnaire was used to determine participants' victim status. *Direct victims* were defined as those who reported they had personally experienced at least one violent act, *indirect victims* were defined as those who reported they had witnessed at least one violent act, and *nonvictims* were defined as those who reported they had never personally experienced or witnessed a violent act.

10

Conflict Resolution Approaches to the Reduction of Adolescent Violence

Collaborative Problem Solving, Negotiation, and Peer Mediation Initiatives

MARIA R. VOLPE

DELORES JONES-BROWN

Imagine the following scenario:

Lucas, a 13-year-old boy, is in the schoolyard playing basketball with his friends at lunchtime. Les, one of the other boys, yells out that Lucas's girlfriend doesn't like him as much as she likes Alex. Embarrassed at having been "dissed" in front of his friends, Lucas gets angry and says, "I've had it with you!" He throws off his jacket, runs toward Les, and immediately starts throwing punches. Within seconds, seven boys are embroiled in a fight. When separated by three of their teachers, the boys promise to get each other later. After school, on their way home, Les says to his buddies, "Watch my back." All keep looking over their shoulders as they walk down opposite sides of the street yelling words at each other, including, "You'd better watch your back," comments about each other's mothers, and so on.

As the "dissing" intensifies, Lucas feels that he has to be ready for tomorrow. In his own mind, he begins to ask how he can best protect himself. He thinks a knife would be a good idea because he could flash it to scare the other boys away the next time they approach him. That evening, he searches for a pocketknife and packs it with the things he will take to school tomorrow. At school the next day, when Les gives Lucas a dirty look, Lucas thinks that this is the beginning of a new round of exchanges. Lucas immediately thinks that he must "do something" to avoid appearing weak or looking like a "sucker." When Les steps closer to him, Lucas pulls his knife and lunges at Les with knife in hand. The result is a small wound that is not life threatening.

Nonetheless, police are called. Lucas is taken to the local precinct by the responding officers, a juvenile petition is filed against him, and he is released to his parents. Les is rushed to the local hospital by ambulance, treated, and released to his parents. The next day, Les and his friends begin to think about ways of getting back at Lucas and his crew—evening the score. They are determined to never be overpowered by Lucas again. Concurrently, Les asks himself why Lucas seemed to get so crazy about what he said because he was just kidding Lucas about his girlfriend. In fact, Les doesn't know anything about Lucas's girlfriend and fabricated the story about her interest in Alex "just because." School officials are left wondering how this violent incident could have been prevented or managed differently.

On a regular basis, we read or hear about a variety of situations similar to the one referred to in the aforementioned scenario in which young people such as Les, Lucas, and their friends find themselves engaged in a confrontation over some matter that they could have handled differently. For sure, the complexity of violent behavior has been well documented and is seldom the result of a single risk factor (Avakame, 1998; Felson & Messner, 1998; Tonry & Moore, 1998). Although it is not easy to dissect official crime data to identify specific *causes* of all violent crime, official statistics gathered during the mid-1980s through the early 1990s established that violence among youth exists at levels significant enough to be considered a serious problem (Cook & Laub, 1998; Zimring, 1998).[1] Youthful involvement in violence includes reports that 1 of every 4 or 5 serious crimes of violence and 1 of 10 homicides are committed by juveniles younger than age 18 (Cook & Laub, 1998, p. 27). In addition, an examination of police petitions and school disciplinary reports would confirm that the rate of juvenile involvement in less serious acts of violence, such as fights and simple assaults, far exceeds the official figures for their involvement in serious crime.

This chapter and the strategies that it suggests proceed from the assumption that a portion of violent crime, particularly assaults and many homicides, is rooted in some form of unmanaged or mismanaged conflict (Decker, 1996). Indeed, LeBoeuf and Delany-Shabazz (1997) noted that "delinquency and violence are symptoms of a juvenile's inability to handle conflict constructively. By teaching young people how to manage conflict, conflict resolution education can reduce juvenile violence in juvenile facilities, schools, and communities, while providing lifelong decision-making skills" (p. 1).

Although no one intervention approach is successful in preventing, reducing, and managing all youth violence, this chapter takes into account that a variety of violent acts involve learned behavior and, as in the opening scenario, have their origins in something as rudimentary as dirty looks, teasing, rumors, gossip, misperceptions, misunderstandings, or, in some instances, what may have been said, for example, about someone's mother. With proper attention, intervention, and training, such conflicts may easily (or not so easily) lend themselves to nonviolent conflict resolution efforts instead of solutions involving physically aggressive acts.

Because conflicts are a normal and constant part of human interaction, how they are dealt with is very important. Like adults, the ways in which young people address conflict situations vary greatly from individual to individual and situation to situation. However, given their immaturity, underdeveloped cognitive and social skills, and sensitivity to peer influences and perceptions, adolescents are particularly susceptible to using violent or otherwise maladaptive responses to conflict situations. In particular, youth whose lives are saturated with exposure to direct (as victims) and indirect (as observers) violent behavioral episodes are particularly susceptible to viewing such behaviors as normative responses to various life situations (Anderson, 1998; Decker, 1996). Preventing or reducing the use of violence as a primary means of resolving short-term disputes or long-term conflicts among young people requires that they learn effective nonviolent alternatives.

This chapter focuses on the youth violence "problem" as it can be addressed through conflict resolution alternatives. More specifically, it examines the use of three approaches: collaborative problem solving, negotiation, and peer mediation as they relate to the peaceful resolution of youth conflicts.

Youth Violence: An Overview

Magnitude of the Problem

National data on youth violence show that from late 1980 until roughly 1994, there was a sharp increase in juvenile violent crime arrests (Snyder & Sickmund, 1995), particularly murder, forcible rape, robbery, and aggravated assault. Over the next 5 years (1994-1999), juvenile arrests for these violent crimes declined 19% in comparison to only 6% for adults (Snyder, 1999). Despite the decline, juvenile arrest figures for incidents of serious violence remained 15% higher than they had been in 1989. According to the Federal Bureau of Investigation (FBI), in 1998 there were 2,100 juvenile arrests for murder and nonnegligent manslaughter, 72,300 for aggravated assaults, and 237,700 for other assaults (FBI, 1998). National statistics indicate that juveniles (those younger than age 18) are most likely to suffer and engage in violence during school, fall victim to violence during the 3 hours immediately following school, and suffer violence at the hands of someone known to them (Office of

Juvenile Justice and Delinquency Prevention [OJJDP], 1999; Snyder, Sickmond, & Poe-Yamagata, 1996). In 1991, for example, 56% of juvenile victimizations happened in school or on school property (Snyder & Sickmund, 1995).

Weapons, especially guns, have increasingly become a part of the destructive "conflict resolution" approaches adopted by youth in addressing even seemingly trivial disagreements (Fagan & Wilkinson, 1998). The highly publicized school shootings in Colorado, Arkansas, Kentucky, California, and elsewhere demonstrate how guns have contributed to the potentially lethal nature of disputes that originate in schools.

Although we currently live in a culture where all youth are overexposed to violent messages via various mediums, there is clear evidence that, in situations of conflict, poor and minority youth dealing with the stress of urban living are particularly vulnerable to violent behavioral adaptations as both victims and perpetrators (Anderson, 1998; Bruce, 2000; Decker, 1996; Fagan & Wilkinson, 1998; Lattimore, Linster, & MacDonald, 1997; Markowitz & Felson, 1998; Sampson & Wilson, 1995). Cook and Laub (1998) noted, for example, that "the epidemic of youth violence that began in the mid-1980s has been demographically concentrated among black male youths" (p. 27). In particular, they pointed out that "the homicide-commission rate for this group increased by a factor of about 4.5." Utilization of conflict resolution initiatives within schools and other community settings shows promise in turning the tide on the injury and loss of life among minority youth in urban settings. However, the school shooting incidents noted in the previous paragraph have demonstrated that problems of gun availability and youths' lack of skill in resolving disputes without resorting to violence cut across race, class, and ethnicity.[2]

Dealing Realistically With Youth Violence

Clearly, no single approach to managing youth conflict will prevent all violent incidents. Historically, research has shown that youth violence can be complex and extremely challenging to understand, predict, or explain, with some factors putting children at risk for violence long before adolescence (Coie & Dodge, 1998). Well-known explanations for youth violence range from social learning in violent households or communities (Anderson, 1998; Bursik &

Grasmik, 1993; Sampson, 1986a, 1986b; Sampson & Groves, 1989; Sampson & Wilson, 1995; Wolfgang & Ferracuti, 1967) and peer influence and misperceptions (see gang literature generally and Anderson, 1998; Fagan & Wilkinson, 1998; Farrington, 1998; Hagedorn, 1998) to inequities related to economic resources and the experience of various social injustices, including racism, sexism, and poverty (Anderson, 1998; Bruce, 2000; Messerschmidt, 1993; Sampson, 1986a, 1986b; Sampson & Groves, 1989; Sampson & Wilson, 1995). Conflict resolution initiatives operate on the premise that despite environmental constraints, there is a broad range of youth violence that can, in fact, be prevented or reduced with attention devoted to preparing young people to work through their differences and feelings in a constructive and nonviolent manner (Crawford & Bodine, 1996).

Difficulties Associated With Changing Behavioral Norms

The adoption of behavioral responses to conflict situations in which violence is the norm is problematic for both children and adults. The fact that arrests of juveniles amount to only 20% of all arrests for violent crimes (Cook & Laub, 1998) indicates that a significant number of adults also use violence as a means of addressing conflicts and, as noted previously, may supply the prototype for verbal or physically aggressive action in response to various situations. Such behavior patterns are learned over time, may become reflexive, and may be effective coping mechanisms in the eyes of the user. It is not surprising, then, that legal approaches to violence prevention and reduction that seek to eliminate illegal violent behavior through swift and certain punishment have proved to be, at best, marginally effective.[3] Punitive approaches do not necessarily take into consideration that in their attempts to cope with everyday situations, individuals, especially youth who may perceive themselves as possessing few other tools, may be resorting to violence as a means of self-protection.

Ongoing research by Anderson (1998), Jones-Brown (1996), and others (Decker, 1996; Lattimore et al., 1997) suggests that young people may turn to violent "self-help" as a means of avoiding potential victimization. For them, the use of violence can be both a convenient and effective means of achieving the self-protective goal. That is, fear-induced responses from others may coincide with the actor's wishes, or the injuring of opponents may produce their short- or long-term physical incapacitation.

Whatever the case, for the young persons who are victorious, the conflict is resolved, albeit perhaps temporarily. From their perspective, it is faster and easier to throw a punch or use a weapon than to engage in protracted verbal communication as a means of working out misunderstandings, expressing their feelings, or reconciling differing perspectives. For youth who lack any formal training or experience in the use of verbal skills, the use of violence is a convenient and readily available means of managing a situation.

Even acts of violence that appear to have purely materialistic goals (e.g., robbery) may be aimed at or indirectly achieve the goal of self-protection. As noted by a court-involved youth interviewed by the second author, by having the reputation of being a "stick-up kid" (robber), "people were afraid of me" and "usually left me alone."

Put another way, the successful use of violence to handle a situation often connotes that some meaningful damage has been done to the other side. In a culture where *winning* is valued, acts of violence suggest that a powerful means of dealing with one's situation has been used. Left to their own devices, what may come naturally to some young people is resorting to self-help through "reputation-building" or "face-saving tactics" of a dangerous and sometimes lethal nature. As the old saying goes, if the only tool one has is a hammer, everything looks like a nail. Hence, if the principal way one knows of managing conflict involves physical confrontation, every interaction has the potential of being managed through violent aggression rather than even-tempered verbal communication and creative conflict resolution processes.

The likelihood of youth conflicts culminating in physically violent confrontations is increased when the bigger picture of young people's lives includes distrust of police, teachers, and other authority figures (Jones-Brown, 1996; Rafky & Sealey, 1975; Rusinko, Johnson, & Hornung, 1978) that the larger society sees as positioned to help them resolve their conflicts. Often, the youth do not see these individuals as viable resources for resolving conflict. No matter how well intended these adults may be, they will not be called on to intervene, leaving the individual youngster to self-help or peer intervention as the primary or sole resource for resolving conflicts of any nature. In some communities, the relationship between police and young people is particularly precarious and awkward (Jones-Brown, 2000). Under these conditions, when formal conflict resolution programs in their schools or other community-based settings are not available, youth do not have recourse to intervention mechanisms or processes that enable them to resolve their differences constructively rather than destructively.

Conflict Resolution Efforts

A New Paradigm

In the not so distant past, multiple incidents of "youth violence," such as the situation illustrated in the opening section of this chapter, would be pegged as indicative of pathological or maladaptive behavior. More often than not, such behavior would be dealt with via formal punishment (school suspension and/or juvenile justice processing) aimed at *extinguishing* it. However, the rise in youth crime between the late 1980s and 1994 showed little promise for the explanatory power of the "individual malady" view of youthful behavior or the effectiveness of punitive approaches in curtailing such crime. In fact, some evidence suggests that the increased use of punitive measures, such as custodial confinement and waiving juvenile offenders to adult criminal court, has had the effect of making some juvenile offenders more violent. In recognition of the magnitude of the problem and the limitations of traditional methods of addressing it, policymakers, scholars, program administrators, school personnel, and parents have devoted countless hours and spent inordinate sums of money attempting to understand the causes of youth violence and ways to remedy it.

Across the nation, questions focusing on the who, what, when, where, and why of youth violence have been widely explored from many perspectives. In fact, the literature on youth violence is so vast that any inventory is daunting. Despite the complexity of youth violence and the reality that there are no magical formulas, easy solutions, or panaceas, intervention approaches, particularly the emerging conflict resolution initiatives, are gaining increased recognition and acceptance and are showing promise (e.g., see Lindsay, 1998).

A recent study of one of the oldest and largest school-based conflict resolution programs in the United States found that the greater the availability of widespread conflict resolution efforts, particularly at an early age, the more likely violence will be reduced (Aber, Brown, & Henrich, 1999). In one 8-year school-based study, the introduction of in-house dispute resolution training for teachers and students helped unseat fighting as the most frequent cause of suspensions (Dupper & Bosch, 1996). Overall, there are indicators that the increased use of systematic conflict resolution approaches in schools and community-based settings alone or in conjunction with other programs may be responsible for an appreciable portion of the decrease in juvenile crime that the nation has experienced since roughly 1995.

In 1998, the Conflict Resolution Education Network estimated that there were 8,500 school-based conflict resolution programs in operation throughout the United States (Filner, 1998, p. xiii). As the ever-expanding body of research indicates (e.g., see Aber et al., 1999), managing youth violence requires both proactive and responsive approaches. Ideally, all of this is best achieved by creating a culture of resolving conflicts creatively, with structures, policies, programs, and procedures in place to support and reinforce ways of peacefully working out differences.

With all of the efforts under way, there is indication that a *paradigm shift* is beginning to emerge when it comes to coping with juvenile violence. Previous reactive approaches focusing on pathology and punishment are being replaced with proactive conflict resolution approaches that recognize that young people benefit from learning ways of managing their own differences constructively. Central to these proactive approaches are processes that include negotiation and mediation, particularly peer mediation.

Conflict Resolution: An Umbrella Term

The term *conflict resolution*, which includes a diverse set of skills and processes, is both elusive and generic. It is often used differently and loosely without any agreed-on universal understanding. For instance, it can be used as some monolithic term that incorporates all intervention processes aimed at *ameliorating* conflict situations. As a result, very different processes are lumped together as if they all mean the same thing. An example would be someone asking, "How can conflict resolution be used to deal with XYZ conflict?" The term *conflict resolution*, as used in this example, suggests that there is some generic intervention approach that could be applied to any conflict.

As a result of the aforementioned vague conflict resolution landscape, there is confusion about what is meant by the term *conflict resolution*. For instance, it is not unusual to hear objections about its use because it suggests a sense of finality or closure, something that is often difficult, if not impossible, to achieve or even imagine in many conflict situations, particularly those that are of a deep-rooted nature. There are those who prefer other terms such as *conflict intervention, conflict management,* and *collaborative problem solving,* among others. Others choose to distinguish between the numerous distinct conflict resolution processes and identify them, such as *negotiation, mediation, facilitation,* or *conciliation.*

Most accurately, *conflict resolution* is an umbrella term that encompasses a wide range of conflict resolution processes from avoidance to annihilation. Although avoidance is preferred to annihilation, it is a risky way of resolving conflicts. Examples of avoidance as a means to handle a conflict include when a person does the following to someone else: walks away, ignores, hangs up the phone, refuses to meet, quits, or otherwise removes himself or herself from a scene. Depending on the situation, particularly if there are ongoing relationships, these avoidance tactics can set the stage for much frustration, tension, and the likelihood that a conflict will not only blossom but also ripen and grow because communication becomes limited or nonexistent. Avoidance requires good judgment, that is, knowing when it is prudent to quit, ignore, or withdraw from a situation. What is most important is teaching young people when avoidance is a viable and acceptable option in resolving some conflicts. For example, they could be taught that it is not always necessary to have the last word and that walking away from a situation is not a sign of weakness.

Conflict Resolution Continuum

Avoidance ◄·········· Collaborative Problem Solving Processes ·········► Annihilation

Risky

Negotiation
Mediation
Peer Mediation

Tragic

At the other end of the conflict resolution process continuum is annihilation, a tragic approach. When annihilation is used as a means of managing conflict situations that result in the fatal and permanent elimination of other parties, it is likely to result in condemnation of the person who uses it. Despite the reprehensiveness of this approach, it is not unusual to hear on a daily basis that a variety of conflict situations, even the seemingly insignificant, are managed by getting rid of the other party. As noted previously, it is no longer unusual to hear about school shootings that have their roots in complex unresolved conflicts. Various conflict resolution approaches can be used to help young people recognize and understand the strong, potentially negative consequences of adopting this approach to resolve their differences.

Both avoidance and annihilation create major challenges and damage opportunities for sustaining ongoing communication and relationships. For sure, if parties have no need to continue a relationship and find ways to avoid each other, avoidance can indeed be a viable means of resolving a conflict. However, when ongoing relationships are necessary or desired, avoidance and annihilation, each in their own way, prevent the possibility for communication and, by extension, the opportunity to work through differences.

As conflict resolution has gained popularity, it has often been used interchangeably with collaborative or cooperative problem-solving processes that emphasize "productive techniques to address conflict" (Yarn, 1999, p. 119). Central to such processes is the notion that underlying concerns will be identified and addressed so that more meaningful and lasting solutions will emerge. Fisher and Ury (1991) identified four principles that contribute to more effective conflict resolution, including separating people from the problem, focusing on interests rather than positions, inventing options for mutual gain, and using objective criteria.

Conflict resolution efforts focusing on young people from coast to coast vary widely. In fact, they are so eclectic that they are not always easy to identify. The approach to teaching and implementing these conflict resolution skills can also be quite varied. Some are taught as part of a distinct classroom curriculum or a separate program, whereas others are integrated into the entire school's operation (LeBoeuf & Delany-Shabazz, 1997). They are known by very different names, operate in markedly different settings, and use different approaches to prevent and respond to violence. They differ in length of time, intensity, and skills taught. It is not unusual to hear about conflict resolution skills workshops at athletic events or at after-school programs being referred to as conflict resolution or violence prevention programs. A few of the many initiatives developed by the Dispute Resolution Program (DRP) at the John Jay College of Criminal Justice illustrate this point. For instance, the DRP has conducted conflict resolution workshops at basketball events sponsored by the Urban Dove as part of a variety of school- and community-based programs featuring facilitated dialogues between police and young people organized by the Westside Crime Prevention Program, and as part of the GEAR UP summer program for middle school students sponsored by LaGuardia Community College.

Of the approaches devoted to conflict resolution skill building, the vast range of initiatives reflects many variables, including the philosophy of the program designers or administrators, resources available, cultural context, and youths' ages and their cognitive skill levels. Although there is no easy way to categorize the initiatives or the many hybrid forms that exist, generally speaking, conflict resolution initiatives tend to emphasize positive, constructive ways of preventing and managing conflict situations (Bodine & Crawford, 1998; Crawford & Bodine, 1996). Some initiatives are directed at enhancing the skills of the youth themselves so that they can become more proficient in their everyday lives, such as communication and negotiation skills; other initiatives are aimed at helping other youth intervene in conflict situations, such as peer mediation.

Despite the broad range of programs, three identifiable conflict resolution approaches are prevalent in the violence prevention initiatives: (a) generic conflict resolution with a focus on collaborative problem solving and communication skills, (b) negotiation, and (c) mediation. In many instances, these processes overlap, and the terms are used interchangeably. The next section describes how these concepts fit into the larger discussion.

Collaborative Problem Solving

Like conflict resolution, *collaborative problem solving* is another umbrella term. In the *Dictionary of Conflict Resolution*, collaborative problem solving is "used to describe dispute resolution processes or techniques that are neither adversary nor competitive" (Yarn, 1999,

p. 84). The *Dictionary* also notes that collaborative problem solving "requires parties to design a problem-solving strategy to reach decisions to which all parties can agree and, in the process, first come to agreement on the definition of problems at hand" (Yarn, 1999, p. 84). Central to this process is a pronounced emphasis on both nonverbal and verbal communication, including active listening and related skills such as paraphrasing, reframing, summarizing, reflection, and using "I messages" (rather than "you messages," which may create an accusatory atmosphere that breaks down the collaborative and problem-solving process).

Collaborative problem solving relies on the ability and willingness of the parties to share their concerns, identify problems, listen to each other, remain open-minded about possible options, and consider consequences. The term *collaborative problem solving* is widely used to refer to those instances when parties engage in efforts to address their concerns and relationships with the other side either directly or with the assistance of third parties. Synonymous with collaborative problem solving are efforts resulting in win-win rather than win-lose outcomes.

The objective of collaborative problem-solving approaches is to maximize the opportunities for youth to find ways of thinking about how they can work *with* the other side (rather than against them) by "making talk work." Individuals are expected to be active listeners who are able to hear what is being said and respond in a meaningful way. Indicators of collaborative problem solving include the use of methods that suggest sharing information, taking turns speaking, setting ground rules or norms for fostering fairness and respect, brainstorming, and emphasizing good listening.

Because basic collaborative problem-solving skills are not universally taught, it is not surprising that frustration over managing a variety of interpersonal or intergroup situations can lead to anger, frustration, and physical confrontation. Collaborative problem-solving skills provide individuals with constructive ways of expressing themselves and processing their concerns. Studies show that if problem-solving skills are taught at an early age, even preschool youngsters will be more likely to prevent serious problems later in life (Shure, 1999). In short, youngsters learn how to become creative problem solvers. Rather than assuming there is only one way to deal with a situation, they learn that there are other perspectives and that one has to be resourceful to meet one's needs in nonviolent and constructive ways.

Of significance, many approaches such as disciplinary programs that handle conflicts among young people do not embrace collaborative problem solving. If young people are expected to work out their differences but have recourse only to adversarial processes to air their concerns, it is unlikely that they will be able to think about working collaboratively with others. Adversarial processes pit parties against each other and result in win-lose outcomes that shut down opportunities for communication between them.

Problem Solving Through Negotiation

Negotiation is a basic conflict resolution process that enables the parties to address their concerns directly by communicating with others (e.g., see Raiffa, 1982). Through exchange of information, parties share their positions, discuss their interests, and explore their options. In the process of doing so, they are able to consider their perceptions about their concerns and reach an understanding between themselves. As is true of other conflict resolution approaches, central to negotiation skills training are good verbal and nonverbal communication skills (Yarn, 1999, pp. 314-319). The parties must find ways to express themselves in such a way to be understood and to listen to the other side to understand what is being said. The techniques include paraphrasing, reframing, summarizing, reflection, using nonaccusatory language such as "I messages," and paying attention to one's body language such as eye contact, hand gestures, facial expressions, and posture. For instance, a fidgety person or bored expression can significantly impede the ability of parties to talk to each other.

Although negotiation occurs routinely on a daily basis in a wide range of settings, it is only in the past two decades that experts have devoted considerable attention to the different approaches involving back-and-forth communication between disputing parties, particularly principled or interest-based negotiation (e.g., see Fisher & Ury, 1991). Here the focus is on striving to find the mutual interests of the parties involved in a conflict rather than on winning at any cost. Parties are encouraged to explore the underlying concerns to address the issues over which they differ.

Numerous initiatives have been developed that enable young people to learn and practice how to negotiate with others. Drawing from the popular best-seller, *Getting to YES: Negotiating Agreement*

Without Giving In (Fisher & Ury, 1991), one of the more widely known negotiation programs for middle school age students is the Program for Young Negotiators (PYN), founded in 1993. Much like the negotiation programs developed for adults, PYN provides children with an opportunity to learn negotiation and joint problem-solving skills in a school-based setting using a 10-module basic negotiation course format (Curhan, 1996). The students learn how to separate people from the problem, brainstorm options, and craft solutions for themselves.

One of the features of the PYN is that all students in a classroom are offered the negotiation skills training. This contrasts with many other programs in which only a selected group of students is taught a set of skills. The large-scale involvement of a school community in the program enables the schools to create a culture of negotiation and shared values around problem solving.

Research of school records shows that PYN does have a positive impact on students (Nakkula & Nikitopoulos, 1996). Those who are enrolled in PYN classes were involved in significantly fewer serious disciplinary problems than those who were not involved in PYN classes. As a schoolwide initiative, PYN "enables the integration of negotiation as part of the core curricula for the entire school population, thus creating systemic changes that impact teachers, students, parents and administrators" (see the PYN Web site at www.pyn.org/programs/pyn/index.html).

Mediation

Of the increasingly popular collaborative problem-solving approaches, mediation is the process capturing the most attention. Before focusing on the use of mediation in matters involving young people, a general understanding of mediation is important.

Mediation involves a third party who helps disputing parties to work through their concerns with the hope of reaching some understanding and perhaps even an agreement. Mediators assist in the exchange of information between the parties and provide them with an opportunity to craft their own solutions and move on. Unlike arbitrators or decision makers in adversarial processes, mediators do not make decisions for the parties. They simply assist the parties in communicating with each other and, if successful, in coming to some kind of agreement with each other.

Despite its growing name recognition, however, confusion exists over what mediation is and how it should be undertaken. It is not unusual for mediation to mean different things to different people (Yarn, 1999, pp. 272-284). For those outside the mediation field, it is common for mediation to be confused with terms such as *meditation* as well as other conflict resolution processes such as arbitration and adjudication, which involve third-party decision makers. Within the field of mediation, there is growing concern about what is being done in the name of mediation. Depending on the setting and the mediator's style, the mediation process can appear to be very different.

As mediation has evolved, distinctions have been made about different ways of doing it. Some of the more popular types are transformative mediation, facilitative mediation, and evaluative mediation (e.g., see Bush & Folger, 1994; Riskin, 1996). Each reflects different approaches as well as goals about what mediation should strive for, resulting in questions such as the following: Should transformation of the parties' actions or relationships be goals of mediation? Should interventions be restricted to facilitation of difficult conversations? Should assessments, or perhaps even advice, be provided? Depending on the setting in which mediators function, the various approaches may even be blended. Whatever approach they use, it is not unusual for mediators to feel very strongly about their method and style. To complicate matters, because mediation often occurs in private settings behind closed doors, disputing parties may not know what type of mediation style their mediators will use. As is true with any new intervention approach, there is a learning curve for consumers before a process is well recognized and understood.

Despite the variations in how mediators conduct their mediations, mediators' toolboxes are full of techniques and skills to help parties that are in fact recognizable to most other mediators. The tools they use to intervene are quite complex and varied, with strong emphasis on good verbal and nonverbal communication. Most important, mediators must be active listeners who can assist disputing parties by clarifying, reframing, reflecting, validating, and summarizing their concerns. Through their skilled communication efforts, mediators help the parties sort through their concerns and consider viable options. Equally significant is the need to pay careful attention to nonverbal communication. Like verbal communication, some nonverbal communication can be quite challenging because in some cultures, different meanings are attached to different forms of communication. For example, direct eye contact can be discouraged in some cultures because it is perceived to be disrespectful, or, alternatively, failure to make eye contact could be viewed as dishonesty.

Knowing what will work in heterogeneous communities in the United States can be immensely challenging because different groups bring different traditions and customs. Despite this variety, mediators need to find ways to show they are listening and acknowledging that what is being said is important. Mediation techniques involve the ability to manage an intervention process that, among other things, requires that they set the tone for the parties to work through their differences. Mediators usually do this, for example, by establishing ground rules at the outset. They share information about the mediation process, the mediator's role to assist, and the importance of the parties to share their perspectives and to consider creative ways of addressing their concerns.

Mediators also use a variety of other techniques to assist the parties, including the caucus. A caucus is an opportunity for the mediator to meet separately with the parties to find out if there are any additional concerns, cool off emotions, and generate and assess options.

For the mediation process to work, the parties need to trust the process and the mediators enough to stay at the table, talk about their concerns, narrow their differences, and, it is hoped, even reach consensus. In addition to all of the skills and techniques, the work at the table is often aided by some of the mediator's own personal qualities. Those that help to build trust include patience, persistence, optimism, sensitivity, resourcefulness, tolerance, and reputation.

Given the complexity of conflict situations, sometimes the outcome is resolution; sometimes it falls short for any number of reasons. Parties need to be ready, willing, and able for mediation to work. The less they are ready, willing, or able, the more challenging it is to work through differences. In some situations, mediation provides parties with the opportunity to air their concerns and to begin relationship building. The mediation process enables them to find ways to communicate with each other and relate to each other at their own pace.

Peer Mediation

Peer mediation programs enable young people to respond to conflict situations involving their peers in a variety of settings, including schools, community-based organizations, youth agencies, and juvenile justice programs (Lam, 1989).

The use of peer mediators in some settings may be the only effective way to resolve youthful conflicts, given the possibility of distrust for adult authority figures. Not unlike mediation in other contexts, peer mediation efforts reflect differing philosophies, training approaches, and programmatic models (see Youth in Action, 2000). Specific variations occur over criteria used to select mediators, the number of mediators used, whether the disputing parties are kept in joint session or met with separately, and the number of training hours. In some instances, the young people learn how to approach disputing parties who are fighting or arguing and ask them if they are interested in working out their differences. In other instances, the peer mediation sessions are convened after an incident has occurred. Despite the many variations, peer mediators help disputing parties share their perspectives, emotions, and options so that the parties themselves can find creative ways of dealing with their conflict situation. Like mediators in other settings, peer mediators do not make decisions for the parties.

Peer mediation and other related conflict resolution programs report positive results in addressing violence-related situations (Hechinger, 1994). They help to reduce suspensions, fights, disciplinary problems, and disruptive behavior and have been viewed as helpful in improving the school climate, increasing the youths' self-confidence, and enhancing communication skills (Jones & Bodtker, 1999). These outcomes have been evidenced at all grade levels. At an elementary school in Oakland, for instance, suspensions were cut 50-fold, and violence was substantially reduced by the mediation program (Massey, 1994, p. 1).

Moving Toward a New
Conflict Resolution Culture

Increasingly, conflict resolution efforts are being understood within a larger context of creating a new conflict resolution culture. For example, recent research on the Resolving Conflict Creatively Program (RCCP), one of the more successful school-based prevention programs initiated in New York City and widely replicated around the country, revealed that programs aiming to transform the school culture by teaching skills that foster a more peaceful environment are more effective than approaches that are confined to specific classes or program participants (Aber et al., 1999). Designed as a comprehensive approach to violence prevention, RCCP teaches conflict resolution skills as part of the classroom curriculum and provides teacher training, parent skill building, and peer mediation efforts.

One of RCCP's main features is the teaching of conflict resolution skills over a protracted period of time. This approach provides the participants with an opportunity to embrace values and practices underlying a peaceful school environment. In fact, the recent 2-year evaluation of nearly 5,000 RCCP students in 15 New York City elementary schools found that the students tended to be less hostile, were less likely to use aggressive means to handle their situations, and chose verbal over physical ways of working out a conflict (Aber et al., 1999).

Interestingly, the aforementioned RCCP research found that when teachers were committed to new programming, violence prevention and reduction of aggressive behavior were even greater. Given the widespread interest in finding better ways to reduce youth violence, attention must be given to, among other things, the significant role teachers and trainers play in implementing conflict resolution education. Their support and commitment to new educational programming are crucial in transforming the culture and climate of a school.

Challenges

Conflict resolution initiatives experience a variety of challenges. As has been pointed out by the aforementioned RCCP research, conflict resolution initiatives need a supportive culture and practitioners for them to work and succeed. Without values, perspectives, and leadership that encourage parties to work out their differences, tolerate diverse views, and provide opportunities for individuals to seek creative approaches, conflict resolution initiatives can be significantly hampered.

Another significant challenge focuses on the self-determination feature of many conflict resolution approaches such as mediation. According to the Model Standards of Conduct for Mediators (American Arbitration Association, American Bar Association, and Society of Professionals in Dispute Resolution, 1995), self-determination "requires that the mediation process rely upon the ability of the parties to reach a voluntary, uncoerced agreement. Any party may withdraw from mediation at any time." If parties resist working directly with the other side, look to others for decision making, or walk away from talking to the other side, collaborative conflict resolution initiatives such as mediation become very vulnerable and severely challenged.

Moreover, because the conflict resolution processes discussed in this chapter rely on the willingness of the parties to participate, anything short of full engagement by the parties may challenge the viability of the processes. There are different degrees of vulnerability for these processes. For instance, if parties so choose, they could easily engage in a "pretend game" by showing up and going through the motions of participating but not be sincere or serious about their participation. Their considerations and contributions during a conflict resolution process may not be genuine, realistic, or made in good faith.

When there is an imbalance of power between the parties, such as relationships between older and younger students and between teachers and students, the dynamics between the parties may be even more complicated. A bullying situation provides another illustration of when a person (i.e., the bully) may acquire a perceived upper hand by virtue of the intimidating tactics that he or she may have used in interacting with others. At the extreme end, without the parties' willingness to work with the process, any collaborative intervention process cannot occur.

There is also a challenge about what should be taught, where it should be taught, and how. For instance, Fagan (1998) pointed out that

> classroom instruction in conflict resolution skills is generally ineffective when practiced in the neutral, unemotional context of a classroom. . . . Adolescents should be taught negotiating and conflict avoidance skills under conditions that mimic the street, that is, under emotional states that stimulate unpredictable

behavior. Role-playing can help participants better understand the provocative and steering behaviors of bystanders and other third parties. Bystanders can also learn how their behavior can increase the risks of lethal violence for young men facing off on the street. (p. 2)

Merely training for the sake of training is insufficient. Considerable attention needs to be paid to how people, particularly young people, learn new ways of managing conflicts.

Summary

Collaborative conflict resolution processes provide constructive ways of preventing violence as well as creative ways of responding to many acts of violence when they occur. Without such efforts, what is more likely to occur than not are strained relationships and limited communication between parties, thereby potentially contributing to future acts of violence.

Reports on racial/ethnic disparity in the treatment of youth within the juvenile justice system suggest that it is particularly important to avoid scenarios such as the one between Les and Lucas because although the physical harm to Les was minimal, the criminal justice system contact for Lucas can have long-term negative consequences. According to a recent report issued by the National Council on Crime and Delinquency (Poe-Yamagata & Jones, 2000), if Lucas is African American, he is six times more likely to be incarcerated in a public facility than a White youth committing the same offense. If Lucas is Latino, he is three times more likely than his White counterpart to be incarcerated on a similar offense. A long-standing line of research documents that such initial incarceration may have its own long-term negative effects (e.g., recidivism and becoming more violent). In addition, because the scene creates a perceived need for retaliation or being on the defensive among the boys' friends, the ripple effects of this single, somewhat minor conflict may result in multiple physical injuries and multiple potentially long-term contacts with the juvenile and adult criminal justice system should those friends seek revenge. Given this context, the importance of making nonviolent modes of conflict resolution, such as those discussed in this chapter, available to youth in a variety of settings cannot be underemphasized. This is especially important for urban youth whose environment may be particularly challenging.

Notes

1. Although Zimring (1998) suggested that the youth violence problem may be somewhat overstated.

2. In 1983, the general violent crime arrest rate for Black youth was nearly seven times the rate for White youth. Between 1983 and 1992, the violent crime arrest rate for White youth increased by 82%, reducing the violent crime arrest rate for Black youth to five times that of Whites (Snyder & Sickmund, 1995, p. 6).

3. Criminologists have struggled to demonstrate empirically that individuals are deterred from conduct because of the threat or imposition of punishment. Some research suggests that individuals processed through the formal legal system become worse offenders after system contact, especially if the contact involves incarceration. This is said to be particularly so for juvenile offenders. Competing explanations for the recent national declines in crime include both claims that punitive legal measures and improved economic conditions are responsible.

Suggested Readings

Bodine, R., & Crawford, D. (1998). *The handbook of conflict resolution education: A guide to building quality programs in schools.* San Francisco: Jossey-Bass.

Crawford, D., & Bodine, R. (1996, October). *Conflict resolution education: A guide to implementing programs in schools, youth-serving organizations, and community and juvenile justice settings* (Program report). Washington, DC: U.S. Department of Justice, Office of Juvenile Justice and Delinquency Prevention and U.S. Department of Education, Safe and Drug-Free Schools Program.

Kenney, D., & Watson, S. (1998). *Crime in the schools: Reducing fear and disorder with student problem solving.* Washington, DC: Police Executive Research Forum.

Part V

Understanding and Dealing
With International Victims
of Violence and Torture

11

Political Torture in South Africa

Psychological Considerations in the Assessment, Diagnosis, and Treatment of Survivors

Ashraf Kagee

During the apartheid era in South Africa, White domination was maintained by violent suppression of any opposition to the government. A variety of laws passed by the Whites-only legislature bestowed on the police and military forces the power of unhindered persecution of members of the liberation movement and their sympathizers. Various methods were used to suppress opposition to the racist and undemocratic status quo. Thousands of activists were subjected to detention without trial, imprisonment, house arrest, exile, and banishment to remote rural areas and were banned from public appearances.

Not satisfied with simply silencing the calls for democracy and a nonracist dispensation, the authorities also engaged in more overtly violent means of suppressing the movement for liberation by inspiring terror in the population. From the 1950s to the early 1990s, residents of Black townships were victims of countless military and police campaigns, and key antigovernment political leaders were assassinated and incarcerated. Those who were captured not only languished in jail but were subject to inhumane treatment from the police and prison authorities. The torture of political activists was a widely practiced if unspoken method of repression.

This chapter examines the research on political torture with a specific emphasis on its psychological sequelae. It considers the practice of torture in several ways. First, torture is defined and described as a psychological stressor. Thereafter, its psychological sequelae are considered in tandem with the complex and sometimes problematic issues of diagnosis and assessment. Some coping mechanisms of survivors are identified and contextualized within the social, cultural, and political milieu. Finally, selected issues in the psychotherapeutic treatment of survivors are reviewed. The literature is not confined to research conducted in the South African geographical area because the effects of repression are considered generic regardless of national origin. However, the specific features of the South African context will be highlighted.

Torture Defined

Far from being a rare phenomenon in countries whose regimes maintain power by undemocratic means, it is estimated that between 5% and 35% of the world's 14 million refugee population has had at least one experience of torture (Basoglu, 1992). This estimate places current numbers close to 5 million people. As a beginning point, *torture* may be defined as

> any act by which severe pain or suffering, whether physical or mental, is intentionally inflicted on a person for such purposes as obtaining from him or a third person information or a confession, punishing him for an act he or a third person has committed or is suspected of having committed, or intimidating or coercing him or a third person, for any reason based on discrimination of any kind when such pain or suffering is inflicted by or at the instigation of or with the consent or acquiescence of a public official or other person acting in an official capacity. (United Nations, 1985)

Although the above definition captures the overt features of torture, it simultaneously omits several important nuances that characterize this form of repression. It may be argued that the ultimate goal of torture is not primarily to obtain information but to "destroy and crush the spirit and soul of opponents of the regime" (Kastrup,

Genefke, Lunde, & Ortmann, 1988). Taiana (1993) supports this view, noting from reports of former prisoners that although the interrogators already possessed the information they demanded, the torture of prisoners often continued. Consequently, this author proposed that the purpose of torture may be viewed more appropriately as the destruction of the identity, personality, and humanity of the victim. Genefke (cited in Ritterman, 1987) concurs with this view that the purpose of torture is to "destroy the victim's personality, to break down, to create guilt and shame, to assure that he will never again become a leader" (p. 44).

The demoralizing of individuals and, by implication, families and communities, makes it easier for regimes to assert control over society (Ritterman, 1987). In this way, physical and psychological means are employed to maintain political control in repressive societies. In light of these contentions, a definition of torture somewhat more tailored to its unspoken agenda may be "the deliberate infliction of pain by one upon another in an attempt to break down the will of the victim" (Stover & Nightingale, 1985, p. 4). Given this definition, some of the descriptive features of political torture are now outlined.

Somnier and Genefke (1986), on the basis of reports from patients, identified two categories of techniques employed in torture situations. These are weakening procedures, which are intended to teach victims to be helpless and create exhaustion, and personality-destroying techniques, which have the purpose of inducing guilt, fear, and the loss of self-esteem (Somnier & Genefke, 1986). These authors identified several ways to achieve these goals—namely, deprivation methods, constraint techniques, communication procedures, and pharmacological methods. Deprivation methods, such as solitary confinement, are used to decrease environmental stimulation. Constraint techniques with arbitrarily determined regulations and rules are used to structure the person's daily activities.[1] Communication procedures may take the form of countereffect techniques (Somnier & Genefke, 1986), in which the victim receives meaningless punishment that may continue whether or not he or she cooperates.[2] Pharmacology may also be misused for the purposes of torture (Somnier & Genefke, 1986). Its intended effects may be to blunt the senses by using neuroleptics and sedatives. Neuromuscular blocking agents may be used to paralyze fully awake prisoners to induce panic when it becomes impossible for the person to breathe. Victims are then only offered oxygen just prior to the point of suffocation.

Numerous specific forms of torture have been identified by several authors (e.g., Foster, Davis, & Sandler, 1987; Suedfield, 1990) from detainees' descriptive accounts. These include brutal beatings, electric shocks, *falanga* (beating soles of the feet), sham executions, witnessing others being tortured (such as family members), and being blindfolded during torture, which intensifies feelings of helplessness and increases the sense of unpredictability (Basoglu & Mineka, 1992).[3] Essentially, components of the torture process may involve taking someone into a totally controlling situation with an unknown time scale and complete unpredictability about what might ensue, issuing threats about unpleasant experiences that might occur, and reducing or preventing normal human interactions with others (Simpson, 1993).

In a study of experiences of 176 political detainees in South Africa, Foster et al. (1987) found that 75% were beaten, 79% were subjected to solitary confinement, 50% were forced to stand for long periods, 25% received electric shocks, 23% were subjected to prolonged interrogation, 21% were deprived of food, and 15% were deprived of sleep. Also common in this sample were threats, verbal abuse, and contradictory information and treatment. Simpson (1993) noted that receiving poor food, being exposed to extreme heat and cold, being forced to stand for prolonged periods, and being denied sleep and opportunities to exercise also contributed to general inhumane treatment. Moreover, these authors cited the torturers' severe and unpredictable anger as a further stressor.

The above evidence suggests that the aim of torture is not only to extract information but also to attack the identity and dignity of the victim (Somnier & Genefke, 1986) and to "create a new subject— broken down, never to regain a former self" (Taiana, 1993, p. 289). Further aims are to destructure families and terrorize entire communities by providing a public example of the horror of torture. Furthermore, families of detainees may be isolated if the larger community is made to fear association with them (Ritterman, 1987). The development of psychological reactions to the experience of torture may be a deliberate and desired effect on the part of the torturers because after their release from incarceration, it is expected that survivors will be less effective members of any opposition to the state (Simpson, 1993). Taiana (1993) argued that even the term *survivor* may be misleading in the case of political persecution because in many cases, the subject of torture is intended to survive and return to the community with an altered personality. The effects of political detention and torture are best considered multidimensionally. However, given the scope of this chapter, specific psychological sequelae are now discussed.

Psychological Sequelae of Torture

That undergoing a torturous experience would yield numerous somatic and psychological sequelae is not surprising. Several studies have been directed at itemizing and classifying the dimensions of torture sequelae. In terms of specific problems at release from detention, Foster et al. (1987) found that most political detainees experienced changes in their lives. In this study of 175 South African activists, the following symptoms were reported: 46% stated they grew easily tired, 39% stated they experienced problems relating to friends and family, 34% reported problems falling asleep, 33% reported having nightmares, 31% noted increases in irritability, 24% reported depression, 24% experienced concentration problems, 17% had memory problems, 13% reported fear and nervousness, 13% noted an increase in alcohol consumption, 11% complained of headaches, and 6% reported hyperactivity (Foster et al., 1987).

Browde (1988) found similar results in a group of 83 South African detainees who exhibited psychological symptoms. These included sleep disturbances (68%), impaired memory and concentration (65%), recurrent and intrusive recollections (43%), recurrent nightmares (30%), and symptoms of anxiety and depression (18%) (Browde, 1988). Friedlander (1986) studied a group of 28 South African detainees and also noted psychological concerns such as concentration problems (96%), disturbed sleep (88%), intrusive fearful thoughts about the future (73%), depression (69%), irritability (65%), and tension headaches (62%). Somnier and Genefke (1986) reported similar symptoms in their patients—specifically, headaches, impaired memory, impaired concentration, fatigue, nightmares, fear, anxiety, social withdrawal, and sexual disturbances. Similar effects are also noted in other studies such as anxiety combined with sleeping difficulties (Cathcart, Berger, & Knazan, 1979), changed identity (Ortmann & Lunde, 1988), and somatization

(Mollica, Wyshak, & Lavelle, 1987). Symptoms observed by Solomons (1989) include anxiety as a response to danger. This author further noted that the onset of anxiety is often delayed until the detainee is released from prison or the traumatic environment.

Findings by Paker, Paker, and Yuksel (1992) concur that a positive history of torture predicted higher scores on measures of anxiety, obsessive-compulsive symptoms, interpersonal sensitivity, paranoid ideation, anger, hostility, and phobias. Moreover, these authors noted that the presence of physical sequelae may serve as a constant reminder of the traumatic experience victims endured, thus helping to maintain the feelings of helplessness they experienced during torture. Basoglu and Mineka (1992) found psychological reactions following release to include hyperarousal, hypervigilance, startle responses, restlessness, increased auditory acuity, depersonalization, derealization, analgesia, and submissive behavior. Turner and Gorst-Unsworth (1990) also reported somatic symptoms such as hyperventilation and sexual dysfunction. Turner and Hough (1993) further noted the onset of hyperventilation syndrome (HVS) in torture survivors. Symptoms of this condition include breathlessness, sighing breathing at rest, fatigue, numbness, tingling of the hands, and blurred vision.

Many survivors have also reported sleep disturbance with nightmares, too little sleep, and daytime fatigue also reported (Astron, Lunde, Ortmann, Boysen, & Trojaberg, 1989). The findings of these authors suggest that previously healthy young persons subjected to extreme stress develop abnormal sleep patterns. Specifically, using polysomnographic recordings, Astron et al. (1989) found that patients' deep sleep was significantly reduced, that their total REM sleep was lower than that of the control group, and that the average number of awakenings per night was six compared with one in the control group. Moreover, patients reported unpleasant dreams and torture-related nightmares upon awakening from REM sleep. These findings concur with Solomons's (1989) observations that recurrent intrusive recollections of the traumatic event constitute major symptoms, which may occur in clear consciousness or in dreams. Symptoms such as sleep disturbance are understood as the person wanting to avoid the loss of control inherent in sleeping as well as being afraid of not waking up again (Solomons, 1989).

Helplessness and passivity are other characteristics associated with many who have experienced torture. The stunted capacity to engage in voluntary and informed decision making is seen as a result of induced suggestibility and compliance with external instructions characteristic of torture (Simpson, 1993). On a related note, learned helplessness (Seligman, 1975) takes effect when the victim is confronted with uncontrollable stress (Saporta & van der Kolk, 1992). The person's sense of self as competent and in control of his or her fate is severely challenged because the ability to escape or control the stress is curtailed. Because forms of torture are usually varied, unpredictability is maximized, and this in turn prevents the detainee from developing effective psychological defenses (Basoglu & Mineka, 1992).

Fears are especially common among victims and often are centered not only on the prospects of death, further torture, and pain but also on concerns about what might happen to one's family (Simpson, 1993). Vague threats in particular are considered the most effective in inspiring terror because they allow people to project their deep fears onto the range of possibilities. Concomitant subjective experiences include anxiety, dread, despair, and willingness to sacrifice long-term interests for relief from these fears (Simpson, 1993).

It is likely that psychological sequelae may be severe in torture victims because the traumatic event of torture may be incomprehensible to the victims. This may be the case because it violates basic assumptions about oneself and one's place in the world, as well as notions of personal safety, security, integrity, worth, vulnerability, and a view of the world as orderly and meaningful (Saporta & van der Kolk, 1992).

Depressive reactions as sequelae to torture have also been noted because torture is associated with loss, particularly of body parts, normal bodily function, health, work, status, family, and credibility (Turner & Gorst-Unsworth, 1990). Depression is therefore considered a common sequela and related to loss events.

Simpson (1993) identified several further negative experiences to which victims of torture may be subjected. Hope and emotions may be manipulated by promises of better treatment, which make the benefits for compliance seem greater than the benefits of silence or resistance.[4] The unpredictability of the interrogator's responses may take the form of anger disproportionately related to the subject's actions. Hence, a sense of unreality may ensue, with the person's higher functioning and ability to make decisions adversely affected. The monotony of prison, particularly solitary confinement, is considered to affect cognitive disturbances, disorientation, poor concentration, and disturbances in memory. The exhaustion suffered from receiving poor food, being exposed to heat and cold, being forced to stand for long periods, and being deprived from sleep often results in weakness, tiredness, and a decline in the person's physical and mental ability to resist. Finally, the humiliation of being confined to dirty surroundings, being restricted from maintaining personal hygiene, being subjected to insults and taunts, and being stripped naked is thought to have damaging effects on self-esteem, thus encouraging compliance (Simpson, 1993). Having acquiesced to the onslaught of the experience by, for example, divulging information about friends or comrades, it is also likely that many victims experience guilt and remorse about their so-called "weakness." This phenomenon is considered one of the more long-lasting effects of torture.

Many sequelae of torture may be considered pathological from a mental health perspective. However, as a protective measure, many victims may dissociate from the experience (Ritterman, 1987). Maintaining a form of psychological detachment from the experience may constitute a necessary survival tactic for torture victims. Psychic numbing is a further effect that constitutes a defense against overwhelming emotions to remove one's vulnerability to further pain and loss. However, if these coping mechanisms continue following the person's release, they become problematic.

Basoglu and Paker (1995) found that the trauma experienced following a torture experience may be a threshold rather than a cumulative phenomenon because beyond a certain threshold, increased duration and frequency of torture appear to have no additional impact. These authors suggested that a nonlinear relationship may exist between torture and its impact because the duration of torture was found to be unrelated to severity of stress.

Because the symptomatology secondary to the trauma of political detention and torture is broad, the clinical imperative is to employ assessment procedures that aid accurate diagnosis. Some issues surrounding the assessment of torture victims in a clinical setting are now addressed.

Assessment of Torture Sequelae

In the development of treatment strategies for torture victims, various psychometric measures have been used to assess the direct psychological consequences of torture experiences. Evidence found by Mollica and Caspi-Yavin (1991) suggests that assessment should be specific and concrete rather than open-ended. For example, if a complete list of torture experiences is presented to a patient for verfication or disputation, this conveys the fact that the interviewer is familiar with the torture situation, thus fostering a sense of connectedness and rapport. Such knowledge initiates a process of revelation that often does not occur when the interview comprises only open-ended questions. Many survivors thus appreciate knowing that the health care professional is aware of what they have suffered and is interested in eliciting information about their experiences as part of the process of assessment. Indeed, the successful use of checklists puts words around traumatic experiences and symptoms for the client (Mollica & Caspi-Yavin, 1991).

Another hallmark of the assessment process is the sometimes compromised accuracy of the survivor's story. It is not uncommon for tortured persons to constantly change the details of their reports of trauma. This may be due to their increased emotional arousal and possible concomitant use of hyperbolic descriptions, as well as impaired memory often due to psychiatric and neurological damage incurred in the torture situation. Moreover, a cultural norm of silence about the trauma, as well as coping mechanisms that employ strategies of denial and the avoidance of memories, may also account for some change in the details of the experience (Mollica & Caspi-Yavin, 1991).

Open-ended interviewing using free recall was shown to generate the greatest emotional distress while simultaneously limiting the accuracy of reporting (Tulving, 1983). Tulving (1983) also found that memory was best enhanced by using neutral retrieval cues such as reading to the survivor a list of possible events from a questionnaire. In this way, memory of the events is enhanced by more systematic history taking and interviewing. Mollica and Caspi-Yavin (1992) further noted that traditional clinical methods that ask torture survivors to tell their trauma story in their own words have frequently been found to be ineffective, although the reason for this has not been established.

Seemingly, rather than evoking further symptomatology in survivors, the assessment process has been shown to be perceived positively. Survivors reported appreciating the opportunity to provide information about their experience of torture as a testimony of their experiences to a concerned health care professional (Mollica & Caspi-Yavin, 1992).

Various psychometric instruments have been used in the assessment of torture sequelae. These include the Harvard Trauma Questionnaire (Mollica et al., 1992), the Hopkins Symptom Checklist, the Hamilton Rating Scales for Depression and Anxiety, and various structured diagnostic interviews (Kastrup & Vesti, 1995). Other instruments include the General Symptom Index (GSI), the Positive Symptom Distress Level (PDSL), the Exposure to Torture Scale (Basoglu & Paker, 1995), and the Positive Symptom Total (PST) (Paker et al., 1992), all of which have been shown to have high reliability. However, these authors also concede the need to develop additional standardized measures for use in work with torture victims. This view is also echoed by Mollica and Caspi-Yavin (1991), who noted that epidemiological assessments of patients and traumatized communities have been limited because few valid and reliable instruments for specifically measuring torture and its sequelae are available. These authors noted that early studies directed at the assessment of torture consisted of phenomenological descriptions of patient demographic characteristics, torture experiences, and the more immediate needs of the survivor.

The various scales developed to assess the effect of trauma suffered during torture, such as the Allodi Trauma Scale (Mollica & Caspi-Yavin, 1991), are specifically directed at obtaining an account of the survivor's experience. This may include arrest history and extent of physical torture, deprivation, sensory manipulation, psychological torture and ill treatment, and violence suffered by family members. Similarly, the Harvard Trauma Questionnaire (Mollica et al., 1992) was designed to empirically measure traumatic events and trauma symptoms of survivors, although this measure was specifically intended for Indo-Chinese patients. It elicits various symptoms related to historically accurate torture experiences and is derived from the *Diagnostic and Statistical Manual of Mental Disorders (DSM-IV)* (American Psychiatric Association, 1994) criteria for posttraumatic stress disorder and clinical experience with torture survivors.

The process of assessing torture experiences is not free of pitfalls. Mollica and Caspi-Yavin (1991) raised the clinical concern of the potential emotional arousal that may follow an assessment with torture survivors. This raises the ethical and therapeutic issue of whether instruments should be used prior to or after the initial interview. If administered later in the course of therapy, the therapeutic interventions may reduce the symptomatology of post-traumatic stress disorder, which may render the instrument less sensitive. Mollica et al. (1992) also noted the diverse geopolitical backgrounds of survivors, which require assessment instruments sensitive to a wide range of traumatic events and experiences.[5]

The use of categorical variables has also been criticized in some studies of torture assessment scales (Paker et al., 1992). A categorical variable (e.g., tortured or not tortured) may lead to a loss of information regarding the subjective meaning of the experience. Such an approach has been criticized for its failure to acknowledge the complexity of the torture context by simply reducing the experience to two objectively defined and discrete variables. For example, Basoglu and Paker (1995) noted that what is perceived and defined as torture varies widely across contexts and cultures and even from person to person. By implication, then, different people's subjective appraisal of a single traumatic experience may differ in terms of the degree of stress it evokes. A partial indicator of such a differential appraisal may be a victim's prior vulnerability to traumatic stress (Basoglu & Paker, 1995).

Other factors to consider in the psychological assessment of torture victims relate to the context of the assessment process. The fact that anxiety and other symptomatology are evoked in survivors by tactile, auditory, and visual signals analogous to the torture situation implies the need for sensitivity on the part of psychological examiners (Somnier & Genefke, 1986). For example, a panic reaction may ensue from a door slamming, or a visit to a small room or elevator may be reminiscent of the prison cell. Moreover, being confronted with equipment or even taking a test may make the person recall the context of the interrogation and arouse stress-related symptoms.

In the clinical treatment of torture survivors, one of the aims of assessment is to render accurate diagnostic impressions of clients who have had experiences of torture in prison. Some of the controversies around diagnostic dilemmas are now expounded.

Issues in the Diagnosis of Torture Survivors

Given the broad spectrum of symptomatology displayed by many torture victims, the diagnostic category of posttraumatic stress disorder (PTSD) (American Psychiatric Association, 1994) has been closely associated with torture sequelae (e.g., Friedlander, 1986; Solomons, 1989). However, from both a clinical and an ideological perspective, this diagnostic category is permeated with several problematic dimensions.

Mollica and Caspi-Yavin (1991) cautioned that torture research is still in its infancy, and for its advancement to occur, researchers must "avoid the uncritical use of ready-made constructs such as the *DSM-III-R* diagnosis of PTSD" (p. 586). Priebe and Bauer (1995) expressed the concern that the *DSM-IV* (American Psychiatric Association, 1994) definition of PTSD does not include those forms of psychological torture in which the physical integrity of the sufferer is not threatened. Foster (1989) noted that while the PTSD diagnosis has utility, it does not sufficiently distinguish between natural and human-designed traumatic events because both of these are included under the same label. Moreover, this author warned that PTSD runs the risk of "'medicalizing' or 'pathologizing' what is fundamentally a social and political situation" (Foster, 1989, p. 30). Allodi (1991) concurred with this view in that a complex politico-historical problem may be reduced to an individual psychological cluster of symptoms. Basoglu (1992) extended this argument, noting that by medicalizing the sequelae of basic human responses to political oppression, the focus is shifted away from human rights and the prevention of torture to the objectifying and politically neutral diagnostic categories of modern medicine.

Simpson (1995) noted that in the development of the diagnostic category of PTSD, the authors of the *DSM-IV* failed to consult with practitioners who provided services to survivors of torture and political violence. Furthermore, not all survivors of torture demonstrate the symptoms of PTSD and therefore may not be diagnosed as such. There is thus an implicit danger of underdiagnosis of significant posttraumatic pathology. A consequence of this might be that a patient would be denied much-needed treatment if the diagnosis were too strictly and intensively applied (Simpson, 1995). Moreover, the symptomatology displayed by this group of clients is often the result of the deliberate induction of the disorder.

Basoglu (1992) noted a dilemma inherent in the diagnosis of torture victims. On one hand, the experience of torture is an extraordinary life experience capable of causing in any person a wide range of physical and psychological suffering and disability. On the other hand, the psychological reactions that ensue are normal responses to abnormal life-threatening situations. For this reason, it is questioned whether survivors should be stigmatized by medical and psychiatric diagnoses and treatment (Basoglu, 1992). In the same vein, and in an effort to resist unnecessarily pathologizing the torture survivor, Mollica and Caspi-Yavin (1991) argued that this group of patients does not have psychological disorders but instead exhibits normal psychological responses to life-threatening situations.

Foster et al. (1987) took issue with the use of a unitary syndrome such as PTSD, stating that a noxious stressor such as torture may produce separable disorders dependent on several factors. These may include the precise nature of the stressors involved, the existence of resilience and support, and individual differences in coping. This view is echoed by Simpson (1995), who noted that victims may instead experience generalized anxiety disorder (GAD), disorders of extreme stress (not included in the *DSM*), and partial PTSD (i.e., severe symptoms of PTSD without fully meeting the criteria as delineated in the *DSM-IV*). On the other hand, this author noted the success of PTSD as a diagnostic category in identifying a recurrent cluster of symptoms that predicts the prognosis and course of a disorder. Moreover, successful diagnosis helps in selecting therapies that are likely to demonstrate efficacy.

Mollica and Caspi-Yavin (1991) further cautioned that the relationship between the concept of the torture event and its symptomatology is fraught with complexity. By simply applying the diagnosis of PTSD, it may be difficult to capture the reality of the torture experience and the related onset of a disorder. Factors to be considered may include events unique to the torture experience and to the person's culture.

Given that the diagnostic process is not one free from complexity, researchers must approach the issue in a critical and cautious manner. Although in many cases diagnosis is appropriate, it is simultaneously imperative to examine the resilience of survivors and the ways in which coping is enhanced.

Coping Factors

It is erroneous to convey the impression that everyone who has been detained and abused emerges psychologically impaired. Indeed, large numbers of activists have been released with their resolve and commitment intact and even strengthened. However, the coping ability of many detainees rests on the convergence of several factors. These include the psychological stability of the individuals prior to the traumatic experience, the duration and severity of the abuse they endured, the availability of supportive relationships following release, and the internal appraisal these individuals are able to make of the experience (Dowdall, 1992).[6] Moreover, according to stress inoculation theory (Meichenbaum, 1985), when someone has handled previous similar stressors, he or she may be equipped with enhanced coping skills and greater confidence. On the other hand, for a competent person who faces extreme trauma and has trouble coping, the impact may be much worse.

Some symptoms also serve adaptive functions and help the person survive (Simpson, 1995). For example, in repressive societies, the symptom of hypervigilance may be an adaptive response. Hence, it may be better viewed as a characteristic sequela to the torture experience but not necessarily a symptom. Moreover, victims often suffer from symptoms such as denial and numbness, given the reluctance of others to hear and acknowledge their accounts of the torture experience. Paradoxically, however, people under severe stress have an enhanced need for support from others, and hence a strong support system may have the effect of lessening the effects of the trauma while simultaneously aiding psychological healing (Simpson, 1993).

Foster et al. (1987) cited the notion of a "hardy personality" (p. 163) in determining the level of resistance to stress in the case of survivors of torture. This concept consists of three essential components: commitment, control, and challenge. Commitment refers to an overall sense of belief in one's political agenda. Control implies a tendency to believe and act as if one could influence the course of events, and challenge is based on the notion that change rather than stability is a normative way of life. Challenge therefore involves being ready to respond to the unexpected (Foster, 1987).

Basoglu and Paker (1995) found that a longer stay in prison constituted a protective factor against some symptomatology. This phenomenon may be explained by the availability of opportunities for emotional support from comrades in prison who have also undergone traumatic experiences. Moreover, survivors of trauma were able to transform their captivity into a meaningful experience by continuing their political struggle in prison while incarcerated. Basoglu and Mineka (1992) concurred that the availability of support from other inmates who had similar experiences to survivors aided their recovery process from the effects of torture. One important coping strategy noted by these authors was the collective hunger strike that increased solidarity among prisoners and simultaneously attracted media attention, thereby exerting pressure on the government.

It is evident that the onset of symptomatology in survivors of torture is mediated by factors that are both interpersonal and intrapersonal. Clearly then, the victim's subjective appraisal of the experience warrants careful assessment to diagnose the presence of adverse reactions. Moreover, from a clinical perspective, the treatment of victims of torture is an ethical and professional imperative.

Treatment of Torture Survivors

That psychotherapy is an effective antidote to the psychological sequelae of torture stems from the idea that a therapeutic context provides a safe and predictable environment for the traumatized client. This safety and predictability may serve to counteract the effects of the unpredictability and unavailability of safety signals in the torture setting (Basoglu & Mineka, 1992). A characteristic of successful therapy with political activists in South Africa was the extent to which practitioners affirmed their strengths and political commitment (Browde, 1988). This strategy resisted undermining the political struggle by focusing only on damage and sympathy for the victim, which would have contributed to an appraisal of torture based on pessimism and despondency. As an extension of this approach, the goal of therapy may be to invert an introspective and self-absorbed process of psychological distress into one of shared social concern (Ritterman, 1987). Ritterman (1987) proposed that the perspective of the client as psychologically damaged may be challenged in the context of a new message—namely, that the social system that exerts hegemony over the individual is instead damaged. Furthermore, Basoglu and Mineka (1992) suggested that the therapeutic experience leads to a transformation of the survivors' negative self-perception, as well as the negative evaluation of their helpless behavior during the period of torture.

In psychotherapy with torture victims, Lunde and Ortmann (1992) proposed three essential stages: contact, cognitive, and emotional stages. The contact stage, possibly the most important of the three, occurs initially when the client tests the credibility of the therapist. Hence, any indication by the therapist of loyalty to an opposing ideology may be met with suspicion by the client and thus constitutes an impediment to therapeutic joining. This implies that the clinician's ideological positioning is an important indicator of a sound therapeutic alliance.

Kastrup and Vesti (1995) concurred with the importance of this initial stage of trust building. These authors suggested that practitioners often have to suspend their professional neutrality by explicitly condemning torture as an illegal and criminal activity that can never be condoned. Whittaker (1988) cautioned that practitioners must be wary of sounding like the torturer or police interrogator when they question or probe the client.

During the cognitive stage, the survivor is asked to recount the details of the torture experience. The therapy is directed at helping the survivor understand the real aim of torture and that all responsibility and guilt should be placed on the torturers and the repressive political system. In this stage, it is pointed out that it is beyond human capability to hold out on information while simultaneously enduring immense physical pain (Somnier & Genefke, 1986). Hence, the victim cannot be held responsible for her or his actions (e.g., of divulging information) while undergoing torture. In this manner, the vicious circle of guilt- and fear-inducing thought and emotional patterns is halted.

During the emotional stage, the therapist encourages the torture survivor to act out negative repressed emotions such as anger and hatred. Here the trauma is confronted with the aim of an abreactive experience in which tension and anxiety are released (Kastrup & Vesti, 1995). These two phases of therapy combine to help restore the person's identity, place the torture experiences in the past rather than the present, and focus on planning for the future (Lunde & Ortmann, 1992). Considered necessary for the emotional processing of the experience of trauma is an explanation of the experience (Basoglu & Paker, 1995). Consequently, therapeutic interventions are directed at bringing to the survivor's awareness the fact that torture is a political phenomenon and that his or her responses are normal reactions to an abnormal situation.

During reintegration, an additional phase identified by Kastrup and Vesti (1995), survivors begin to understand their ordeal and that they are healthy human beings exposed to abnormal and criminal circumstances. Part of the understanding process focuses on the fact that because the sequelae of torture are predictable, "the aim of the torturers was to change them as persons and make them function on a lesser level of fulfillment than before the torture" (Kastrup & Vesti, 1995, p. 350).

In terms of the efficacy of therapy with torture victims, findings indicate that the highest rate of success can be expected with this group compared with political exiles or relatives of activists murdered in detention (Cienfuegos & Monelli, 1981). Whittaker (1988) speculated that the clients' ideological and political commitment and level of social support may be directly related to their psychological recovery from torture. However, he offered the dubious proposition that "there is general agreement . . . that the effects of torture cannot be 'cured'" (Whittaker, 1988, p. 277). Nonetheless, these perspectives support the need for therapy to emphasize the political and social context of repression and to facilitate in the client an understanding of the trauma in terms of this broader context. Although the efficacy of psychotherapy for this population has yet to be demonstrated, successful treatment may occur when victims report a significant reduction in symptomatology and an improvement in various dimensions of living, such as work, family life, and social and recreational activities (Whittaker, 1988). Among the various forms of psychotherapy, group therapy in particular is thought to provide opportunities for mutual sharing and to convey an understanding in survivors that others are also struggling to reach their own understandings about their experiences (Turner & Gorst-Unsworth, 1990).

Political and Social Dimensions

Although a focus on the psychological sequelae of political torture is essential, such an emphasis is not free from criticism. Foster (1989) cautioned that by simply concentrating on individual symptomatology, detention and torture may be seen as unitary and depoliticized events. Dowdall (1992) argued that because torture is an instrument of power, it "cannot be understood separately from the historical, political and economic context of power relations" (p. 452). Indeed, the practice of torture often has widespread repressive effects on communities, even before anyone is detained (Turner & Gorst-Unsworth, 1990). Hence, in reducing the sequelae of torture only to individual effects, one may lose sight of its political and social dimensions. Detainees who are viewed as psychologically damaged are then subjected to secondary dependence on mental health practitioners, a perspective that sustains a "passivity model of victimology" (Foster, 1989, p. 32). Moreover, employing the psychological term *coping* to describe a reaction to stress implies a notion of adaptation rather than resistance to this overt form of repression.

An alternative view using social identity theory (Tajfel, 1978) considers torture and detention in terms of intergroup rather than individualistic or interpersonal relations. The relationship between torture victim and perpetrator is one better characterized by antagonistic social organizations (Foster, 1989)—namely, the state versus the liberation movement—with opposing ideologies.

Social and political effects of detention may include the effects on state officials when detainees tried to persuade them about their stand against apartheid. At the level of community, family and friends have rallied to support victims, and thus a broader effect may be social mobilization of people against detention and torture and hence against apartheid (Foster, 1989). Coupled with this, Gibson (1989) proposed that detention and torture are phenomena better viewed as extensions along the continuum of political oppression, which encompasses class, race, and gender discrimination.

Clearly, detention and torture are political phenomena because they are "designed to quell, contain and eradicate democratic opposition" (Foster et al., 1987, p. 154). Torturers are indelibly part of an ideological system with a common enemy and shared values and goals. The notion that their victims are enemies of the state and opposed to their own values and morality fuels the belief that they deserve ill treatment in prison. Hence, torturers often believe that their duty is to obey orders and serve their country by their actions (Basoglu & Mineka, 1992). Rather than viewing this form of repression through the optic of individualism, Basoglu and Mineka (1992) proposed a holistic model, which conceptualizes the effects of torture at the individual, communal, and social tiers.

Conclusion

The study of torture and its sequelae signals a commitment to the treatment of survivors inspired not only by scientific inquiry but also by a dedication to human rights. This review examined the phenomenon of torture through the prism of psychological discourse. Given the fact that the human experience does not neatly fall into clearly dichotomized disciplinary boundaries, it is thus necessary to conceptualize the experience of survivors within a broader paradigm that encapsulates the political and social nature of torture and abuse.

Research directed at the phenomenon of political torture and its sequelae is still in its infancy. Consequently, the methodological rigor of many studies cited in this chapter may be enhanced. Despite this, the body of research directed at the sequelae of torture has burgeoned in recent years. However, several silences in the literature may also be observed. Although cursory attention has been directed at sexual violence in captivity, seemingly scant regard has been given to the interplay of gender dynamics within the torture context. The added vulnerability of female detainees who are invariably at risk of sexual violation in addition to other forms of torture has not been examined in the mainstream psychological literature.

Although the short- and medium-term effects of torture have been well documented, its long-term sequelae warrant deeper investigation. Many activists who were detained and subjected to torture during the protest movements of the 1950s and 1960s in South Africa have not had the opportunity to seek and obtain psychological help. Hence, studying the long-term effects of torture is an area where further research may be an important contribution.

That the subjective experience of torture differs from person to person is a significant phenomenological point. It is well documented that the appraisal of the torture experience depends to an extent on the level of commitment and ideological conscientization of the victim. The impact of the level of political involvement on the intensity of symptomatology displayed by survivors is another area where an empirical analysis may advance the knowledge base in this area. Finally, in terms of the treatment of survivors, whether a cathartic experience in the therapeutic context exacerbates symptomatology secondary to torture or reduces it constitutes an area for further research.

By directing research and clinical expertise at the survivors of political torture, applied psychology may make an important contribution to the area of human rights. Indeed, because the field of counseling psychology has evolved for the service of so-called "normal" people who have problems in living, its contribution to the area of torture sequelae, as well as its prevention, holds considerable potential.

Notes

1. The prisoner is usually closely supervised, and many insignificant details are controlled. Violation of rules is used as an excuse to punish the victim. The prisoner may also be provided impossible choices and may be made to act against his or her ideology and ethics. In this way, victims are exposed to a pseudo-choice between alternatives in which they either submit to further torture or cooperate with the torturer's demands, thereby compromising their ideological values and consequently their integrity (Fischman & Ross, 1990).

2. Any response from the prisoner then becomes the pretext for renewed and continuous torture; ultimately, the person's ability to fight back decreases, and he or she learns to be totally helpless. The double-bind technique is another example of exposure to ambiguous situations and contradictory messages designed to induce confusion. For example, a prisoner may be violently tortured by state personnel of low rank and then interrogated by an officer of high rank in an atmosphere of friendliness and tranquility.

3. These authors describe an example in which a blindfolded person was made to stand on a table, told he was at a window high above the ground, and given a push. In reality, he was only a few feet from the ground. In another example, a restrained blindfolded detainee was given an object and told it was a bomb that would explode a few minutes after his captors left. It transpired that this was not the case, and the object did not explode.

4. For example, in manipulating the victim, an interrogator may pretend the prisoner has been betrayed by comrades, thus compounding the experience of confusion.

5. This has relevance in the South African context, where a negotiated settlement was reached between the former apartheid government and the liberation movement. Although many in South Africa have viewed this transition as desirable, survivors of torture may experience a sense of betrayal that their abusers have not been appropriately punished for their crimes.

6. If the survivor has a coherent ideological way of making sense of the experience, this may act to boost resilience (e.g., recognizing the long-term value of social and political change resulting from efforts of political activism).

12

Despair, Resilience, and the Meaning of Family

Group Therapy With French-Speaking African Survivors of Torture

HAWTHORNE E. SMITH

For 7 years, the Bellevue/New York University Program for Survivors of Torture has provided comprehensive, multidisciplinary health and mental health services for survivors of torture and refugee trauma from throughout the world. In the context of our treatment philosophy, *refugee* refers to immigrants who have come to the United States seeking asylum from persecution in their homelands as well as to those who have received official refugee status from the U.S. government. One of the Bellevue program's highly successful therapeutic interventions has been an ongoing support group for African survivors from French-speaking countries.

This chapter provides a description of the overall context in which psychological treatment with clients who have suffered such extreme and targeted social violence takes place. Therapeutic issues that have frequently been identified as being salient in individual therapy with survivors of torture and refugee trauma are detailed. In addition, treatment priorities that are becoming increasingly clear from therapeutic work and supported by the growing body of psychological literature are explored. These insights, priorities, and techniques have been instrumental in the formation and facilitation of the African group.

A detailed description of group functioning and processes will follow, including creative adaptations to the "traditional" group psychotherapy model that have been used to create a more cultur-ally syntonic therapeutic experience for survivors from Africa. In addition, issues of concern for therapists engaged in this type of work (such as "burnout" and secondary traumatization) will be addressed.

Contextual Factors

To facilitate understanding of the group therapy treatment, we must first discuss contextual factors. These include the psychological consequences of refugee trauma, the psychological consequences of torture, and a description of the client population.

Psychological Consequences of Refugee Trauma

When presenting information regarding clinical work with survivors of torture and refugee trauma to groups of students, trainees, or fellow mental health professionals, I have found it useful to engage them in a brief exercise before moving onto the more didactic material. I ask each member of the audience to write the "five most important things in the world" to them. These should be five precious things that "make life worth living" in an emotional sense. I wait a couple minutes, and then I collect the papers.

Without divulging names or identifying who wrote what, I read through some of the responses. Often, audience members will write down the names of family members or loved ones. They may name a relationship itself, such as marriage. Some respondents may men-tion material things and possessions, whereas others describe aspi-rations (i.e., obtaining an advanced degree), passions (i.e., playing or enjoying music), achievements (i.e., professional success), or a general sense of well-being (i.e., good health).

After reading through a number of these responses, I rip all of the papers to shreds. I ask the audience to imagine for a moment that all of these precious things have been taken from them through violent means and that they are currently powerless to reclaim any of them. Contrived theatrics aside, this symbolizes the situation that survivors of torture and refugee trauma who are now living in exile are facing.

Many of the clients we see at the Bellevue/NYU clinic have witnessed their spouses being raped and/or killed. Many families have been separated, and clients are not aware if their spouses, significant others, siblings, parents, or children are still alive or where they may be. The longing, insecurity, doubt, and possible guilt feelings can be overwhelming. I am reminded of one client who only has an old, fading snapshot of his then newborn son. This pains him greatly, as he has never seen his son in person due to his exile, and the client can only imagine what his now 7-year-old son is like. All too often, clients are not even able to contact the families that they have left behind because they fear the reprisals that may befall their loved ones if the government, or other forces, learned that there is ongoing correspondence between them.

These survivors and refugees have generally lost most, if not all, of their worldly possessions. This not only includes material things but also applies to self-esteem, dreams, aspirations, feelings of emotional and physical security, and a sense of personal control (Fischman, 1998; Silove, Tarn, Bowles, & Reid, 1991). Survivors of torture who are living in exile as refugees are coping with multilevel stressors that serve to reinforce and complicate their ability to adapt emotionally.

Members of this population have survived situations of violence, general social upheaval, and/or civil war in their countries. Significant numbers have been tortured and possibly imprisoned, and many may have lost family members in the conflict. They have lived as fugitives in their own country and escaped from their native lands under harrowing circumstances. They have been subjected to harsh living conditions in refugee camps and/or detention centers, including those in the United States, where asylum seekers are often held for months while their cases are being adjudicated (Fischman, 1998; Keller, Eisenman, & Saul, 1996).

All of these events precede the clients' resettling in their new "host" country, with the forced adaptation this entails. Some survivors have stated that "exile is the most painful form of torture" (Fischman & Ross, 1990, p. 139). The clients we see at Bellevue are confronted with navigating New York City, with all of its size, speed, complexity, and potential meanness. It is a situation that can be intimidating and disempowering on multiple levels.

Imagine being a well-trained professional with an advanced education and finding yourself in a situation where you are functionally illiterate as you struggle to learn the language of your new host nation. Imagine being a person of formerly significant social stature who is currently not allowed to earn a living or is working "off the books" in a menial, almost slave-labor job. Imagine the sense of social isolation as you are cut off from your loved ones and placed in an alien cultural milieu where you are no longer sure of the social norms, without the ability to fully express yourself or understand others. Such are some of the multifaceted emotional stressors that feed into the disempowerment and psychological distress that refugees who are living in exile are grappling with on a daily basis.

The multiple losses, social dislocation, feelings of fear, inadequacy, and disempowerment combine with cultural and linguistic barriers to form a difficult psychological reality for people living in exile as refugees. Among this refugee population, however, exists an unfortunately large segment of the population who have been subjected to torture. For these survivors of torture, the difficult realities that affect refugees in general are superimposed on the detrimental psychological effects of the torture experience itself.

Psychological Consequences of Trauma

The context of torture and the subsequent psychological repercussions have been widely examined in the psychological literature (see Kagee, Chapter 11, this volume). Several "official" definitions of *torture*, from organizations such as the United Nations and the World Medical Association, differ slightly in their wording. It is widely accepted, however, that the practice of torture is designed to purposely inflict intense physical and emotional pain, with the ultimate goal of breaking the will and spirit of the person, as well as the community, upon whom the torture is being inflicted (Chester & Holtan, 1992; Fischman, 1998; Silove et al., 1991).

Survivors often experience physical, cognitive, and psychological sequelae from torture experiences. These sequelae result from the purposeful effort by the torturers to destroy the very things that make the victims human. Some of the forms of physical torture that our clients have suffered, which have been widely reported in human rights literature, are beatings, burning with cigarettes, application of electrical shocks, forced standing or exercising, starvation, prevention of urination and defecation, *falanga* (beating the soles of the feet), needles under fingernails or toenails, being cut with a knife, the "aeroplane" (suspension from a rod by hands and feet), and rape (Goldfield, Mollica, Pesavento, & Faraone, 1988; Keller et al., 1996).

These practices can exact a severe physical toll on the victim. Some survivors manifest chronic head pain, scars or bruises, and joint discomfort, and they run the risk of acquiring infectious diseases such as tuberculosis, malaria, and intestinal parasites due to the poor sanitary conditions of their prisons or refugee camps (Chester & Holtan, 1992; Goldfield et al., 1988). Despite this, many survivors report that the emotional and psychological wounds are the most painful and, generally, the longest lasting effects.

Torturers take special care to inflict the most psychological damage possible through methods as diverse as sensory and social deprivation, response conditioning, and the use of pharmacological agents. Mock executions and forcing prisoners to witness other victims being tortured or killed are common practices among torturers. Victims are often placed in no-win, "double-bind" situations in which they are faced with impossible choices. Victims are left to feel inadequate, powerless, and confused. They are often led to believe that they are the ones guilty for inflicting pain on themselves and others (Somnier & Genefke, 1986).

Many of the psychological and cognitive symptoms experienced by survivors of torture are related to posttraumatic stress disorder (PTSD), as defined in the fourth edition of the *Diagnostic and Statistical Manual of Mental Disorder* (*DSM-IV*) (American Psychiatric Association, 1994). Torture survivors clearly fit the definition of people who have been exposed to catastrophic (traumatic) events. In fact, research has shown that PTSD symptoms are more severe for people who have suffered a trauma that has been inflicted by other human beings than those who have survived accidents or natural disasters (Vesti & Kastrup, 1991).

The psychological reactions of torture survivors can be partially demystified by examining the symptomatology of posttraumatic stress. The symptoms of PTSD fall into three categories:

1. *Intrusive symptoms:* The trauma is rexperienced by the torture survivor. Symptoms may include intrusive thoughts, "flashbacks," and nightmares related to the torture experience.

2. *Symptoms of avoidance:* Survivors become mistrustful and emotionally detached from other people, perhaps becoming emotionally "numb," losing interest in pleasurable activities, and denying connections between their experience and their current functioning.

3. *Symptoms of increased arousal:* Survivors exhibit an exaggerated startle response, difficulty sleeping and concentrating, cognitive deficits, hypervigilance, and increased irritability.

These PTSD symptoms may coexist with other mental health and medical disorders and are often misdiagnosed as such. Major depression, pervasive anxiety, panic attacks, phobias, personality disorders, dissociation, and substance abuse are some of the psychological disorders that may stem from the trauma experience or may be superimposed on the posttraumatic stress (Zohar, Sasson, Amital, Iancu, & Zinger, 1998). These potentially comorbid factors add complexity to the diagnostic picture. The situations faced by survivors of torture who are living as refugees are unique and complex, and in some ways, the label of *posttraumatic stress disorder* may be inadequate.

We have discussed how refugees who have survived traumatic events are buffeted with a continuous series of assaults on their psychological and emotional integrity. Consequently, the *post* in posttraumatic stress disorder can be misleading. Clients are not just reacting to an isolated traumatic experience from the past; they are reacting to a constant stream of emotional and cultural challenges that are potentially traumatizing by themselves. These stressors work to keep the clients' experience of trauma very much alive in the present.

It has been argued that stimuli reminiscent of the trauma become generalized and can evoke psychological responses long after the trauma has passed (Gurris, 2001; Mollica et al., 2001; Randall & Lutz, 1991). Such recurrent and reinforcing stressors have been referred to in the literature as different entities from "classic" PTSD and given names such as "complex-PTSD syndrome" (Herman, 1992) and "ongoing traumatic stress disorder" (Elsass, 1997; Straker, 1987).

PTSD can also carry the stigmatizing notion that there is something inherently wrong psychologically with the client. Survivors are often portrayed as having a psychological "disorder," which works to further disempower them and may lead some potential clients to refrain from seeking the services that they need. The distinction between normalizing and pathologizing the reactions of survivors is currently being debated within our program and within the field of psychology itself (Randall & Lutz, 1991; Yehuda & McFarlane, 1995).

Description of Client Population: Historical and Contemporary Influences

A large proportion of the clients we see in the Bellevue program come from countries in Africa. It is reported that 21 of the 43 countries emerging from large-scale violence between 1989 and 1999 were in Africa (United States Committee for Refugees, 2000). Recent figures show that 6 of the top 10 nations, in terms of generating refugees, hosting refugees, and having people internally displaced within their borders, are in Africa (United Nations High Commissioner for Refugees [UNHCR], 1995). A complex combination of factors has led to the widespread political, environmental, and economic turmoil that is forcing so many of Africa's sons and daughters to flee and seek asylum elsewhere.

It should not be news to the readers that Africa has a rich history of statecraft, scholarship, innovation, intercontinental trade, religion, and philosophy that dates back to antiquity. The historical positivity and genius of Africans and African culture are often ignored or forgotten, as well as the continuing impact of colonialism and Europe's underdevelopment of Africa. Unfortunately, the deluge of information regarding contemporary distress, deprivation, warfare, and brutality feeds into continued negative perceptions and stereotypes of Africa as a backward, unenlightened, or savage place.

The question often becomes a stigmatizing, "What is wrong with Africa?" as opposed to clinically assessing the following question: "What sorts of resilience and coping mechanisms must a people use to survive such harsh life conditions?" The contemporary oppressive circumstances and conditions vary from country to country and conflict to conflict. The complicated realities in Africa are reflected in the Bellevue African group membership's diversity, both demographically and psychologically.

Group members have come from 17 different countries, which speaks to the widespread turmoil in present-day Africa. Many group members have been victimized because of their ethnicity.

Some of this ethnic strife dates back at least to 1884-1885, when Africa was effectively partitioned by European colonial powers into spheres of influence. The partition was based on the political realities of the European states and had little to do with the realities of what was transpiring between and among African peoples (Afigbo, Ayandele, Gavin, Omer-Cooper, & Palmer, 1986a).

In some cases, functioning nations were divided among colonial entities, whereas other African peoples who had been mortal enemies for centuries were placed within the same colonies (which later became nation-states). The aftereffects of this partitioning are still being felt (Afigbo, Ayandele, Gavin, Omer-Cooper, & Palmer, 1986b). These political/ethnic divisions have affected many of our program's clients such as the Diollas from the Casamance region of Senegal; the Hutus and Tutsis from Rwanda, Burundi, and the Democratic Republic of Congo; the Bamilekes from Cameroun; and the Soninkes from Mauritania, to name a few.

Group members come from diverse social classes and educational backgrounds. There are group members from the elite or professional rungs of society (e.g., journalists, lawyers, physicians, and university students) who were persecuted due to their political activities such as advocating for human rights. There are also group members who have never spent a single day in a formal classroom, such as the "Haritans," who have escaped slavery in Mauritania.

Group members also come from diverse religious backgrounds. Religion has also become an active fault line that has caused ruptures in many African nations. Issues around religion continue to fuel social upheaval and the persecution of religious minorities in countries such as Nigeria, Sudan, and Cote d'Ivoire. As such, issues around religion and spirituality are often quite salient for group members.

Another reality facing some clients is that economic and environmental factors have led to greatly increased numbers of displaced people and refugees crossing borders in search of food (Akinsulure-Smith & Smith, 1997; Renner, 1996). These massive population movements have served to further destabilize neighboring countries. One of the harsh economic realities in the developing world is that particular ethnic groups, as well as immigrants and refugees from neighboring countries, are often scapegoated for the economic difficulties that a developing nation may be experiencing, which may have contributed to elevated levels of ethnic and nationalist fervor. This has affected our clients coming from refugee camps in diverse countries such as Guinea, Senegal, Gambia, Djibouti, South Africa, and the former Zaire.

The price for these violent implosions is paid in blood, tears, and suffering by ordinary people. Our program's clients are often just folks who may just have happened to be of the wrong race, ethnic group, or religion. Maybe they were speaking out for justice and equality. Maybe they were at the wrong place at the wrong time. Maybe there was guilt by association. Whatever the cause, they have all experienced the extreme psychological pain of torture and continue to face the multifaceted stressors of living in forced exile. This is the context in which members come to the African group.

Treatment Techniques and Priorities

In the previous section, psychological consequences and symptoms of torture and refugee trauma were discussed, including the diagnosis of PTSD. Clinicians should keep in mind that the effects of torture and refugee trauma may present themselves physically, cognitively, behaviorally, and/or emotionally. Given the recurrent stressors a survivor is facing and the complex psychological reactions related to their experiences, some insights in terms of engaging this population in therapy are warranted. The following themes have proven to be important in our work at the Bellevue program.

Emotional Safety

One of the factors that has become evident in our work with torture survivors is that fostering a feeling of emotional safety is of paramount importance. This finding has been echoed throughout the psychological literature, where developing a therapeutic relationship of confidence and trust with torture survivors has been described as being the first priority in treatment (Fischman & Ross, 1990; Keller et al., 1996; Silove et al., 1991; Somnier & Genefke, 1986; Vesti & Kastrup, 1991).

This is particularly important for torture survivors who have been so severely traumatized in their past. Many of the survivors we treat at Bellevue have been tortured by people in uniform within institutional settings. Some clients have arrived at the hospital for their first visit; have seen the crowds of people, including armed police officers and hospital security agents; have become overwhelmed; and have turned right around and gone home. It is important to try to diminish the negative institutional transference that may exist for the clients so that they may more readily engage in their treatment (Fischman & Ross, 1990).

When clients are coming to Bellevue for their first appointments, I always try to meet them right at the front door of the hospital. As I greet them and show them the way to our clinic, I try to normalize their emotional reactions to the hospital environment, which can be confusing and intimidating for anyone who arrives for the first time. I accompany the clients as they register and deal with the hospital bureaucracy, often serving as interpreter and facilitator for the clients. Through this process, the clients may sense that they have an ally, and a trusting relationship may begin to germinate.

It is also important to remember that many survivors have been tortured in conjunction with being interrogated for information by powerful others. This is of crucial therapeutic importance, particularly during the initial interview, as there is a significant danger of retraumatizing the client if the therapist strictly adheres to his or her usual information-gathering techniques. It is counterproductive to insist on "uncovering the whole story" if the client is emotionally unprepared to do so (Silove et al., 1991).

Clients may be resistant or reticent about sharing their stories for several reasons. Clients may fear that they will not be believed or may be so ashamed of their experiences that they are reluctant to reveal them. Clients may be vacillating somewhere between the intrusive and avoidant responses that accompany posttraumatic stress disorder, or it may be that they have not yet reclaimed the ability to fully trust another human being (Chester & Holtan, 1992). For all of these reasons, it is imperative for the clinician not to engage in an "interrogation" of the client. The need for client safety far outweighs the therapist's need to complete the necessary forms and paperwork during the initial intake.

During the first session, it may be helpful to engage the client in "anticipatory guidance," by which the therapist explains some of the common and expected symptoms that someone in the client's situation may experience. The therapist may also describe some of the recovery processes and the resources that the particular program can offer the client (Fischman, 1998). During this phase, clients should also be enlisted as active participants in prioritizing their needs and desires. Clients are encouraged to help in deciding the ways in which therapeutic resources will be used. This is an important first step in empowering clients in the relationship, which is another important treatment priority. Yet, empowering clients constitutes a broad aim within itself, worthy of discussion.

Empowering the Client

Torture survivors who are living in exile have been violently and purposefully disempowered on multiple levels. Survivors may see themselves as being helpless, unworthy, or less than human as consequences of the torture experience itself. They have also been forcibly removed from their familial and social support systems, as well as the cultural and linguistic contexts in which they feel comfortable operating. These factors, in addition to possible professional devaluation and survivor's guilt, work to disempower clients in complex ways (Keller et al., 1996; Silove et al., 1991).

Elevating the client in terms of the therapeutic relationship, helping him or her to realize that it is a relationship between two human beings—not just an authoritative helper and helpless victim—is a process that helps the client to find his or her voice in the relationship. One valuable way that clients can be empowered in the therapeutic relationship is by clinicians taking a "collaborative" rather than an "expert" stance. This is consistent with considerations offered by Wallace in Chapters 1 and 2 of this volume.

Therapists need to be flexible in their own conceptualization of the therapeutic relationship. We have already discussed how engaging torture survivors in helping to determine their own therapeutic priorities and needs serves to empower them. This is particularly salient because "traditional" psychotherapy is an alien, or perhaps stigmatized, notion to many of our clients from continental Africa (Akinsulure-Smith & Smith, 1997).

To insist that clients learn and internalize the cultural expectations and norms of "traditional" (read: "Western") psychotherapy places an additional cultural boundary in front of them. Clients are already struggling to traverse many cultural and linguistic barriers, and giving them an additional hurdle, one more context in which they are unsure of the "proper" behaviors, serves to further disempower them. Engaging clients in a more collaborative stance helps to give them an increased sense of personal control.

Another technique that helps therapists to empower the clients in the relationship is to allow them to teach the therapist about their homeland, their culture, and other salient historical and/or social issues. Of course, it helps when the therapist has some knowledge about the country and situation from which the survivors have fled. This is a way of letting the clients know that their past experiences exist on the therapist's cognitive "radar screen." However, a balance can be struck whereby the clients can share and broaden the therapist's contextual understanding of their history and culture. This is another therapeutic interaction that allows the clients to feel that their knowledge, experiences, and insights are valued.

This type of exchange also models for the clients that they are respected as human beings who have something valuable to offer. This works to counter the belief among some survivors that they are powerless shells of their former selves, with nothing positive to share with anyone. As clients gain more confidence that they are being listened to and respected in the relationship, the resistance to engaging in the therapeutic process decreases (Akinsulure-Smith, Smith, & Van Harte, 1997).

Forming an Alliance

Creating an environment in which the clients feel emotionally safe and empowered are crucial elements of forming a therapeutic alliance. However, some other aspects of forming an alliance may be unique to working with torture survivors who are living in exile. These are techniques, or therapeutic roles, that have proven to be effective in our work at Bellevue Hospital.

Our psychological work takes place within the context of a multidisciplinary treatment team. Psychologists work collaboratively with primary care physicians, psychiatrists, social workers, and activity therapists. Whenever possible, the psychologist and primary physician both meet with the client initially. This is to give the client the sense that we are working as a coordinated team and to decrease the number of times a client may feel compelled to describe the details of the torture. This also models that our program provides diverse resources.

Describing psychological therapy as part of a "resource" model may help to take away some of the fear, misconceptions, or stigma regarding therapy that clients may harbor initially. Portraying ourselves as resources for the client also helps to empower the client in the relationship. I try to avoid asking a client, "How may I help you?" This simple question may be understood in the dichotomous context of the "all-powerful helper" and "helpless victim," which would be disempowering. Rather, I try to express my queries so that clients feel that they have choices and control. "How may I be of service to you?" seems to be a more effective way of asking the initial question. This is reminiscent of what Wallace cites in Chapter 1 of this volume with regard to the concept of accompanying or working alongside clients, as described in the writing of Comas-Diaz, Lykes, and Alarcon (1998).

Another unique aspect of forming a therapeutic alliance with survivors of torture living in exile is that the boundaries and parameters of being a psychotherapist are often stretched. At Bellevue, one way we have come to conceptualize our expanded role is as an "accompanier" (Keller et al., 1996). This is one treatment approach used in our program that seems to help engage the clients in a meaningful therapeutic relationship. Therapy does not simply consist of a 45- to 50-minute clinical hour, after which the clients are not seen until the following week. As previously mentioned, therapists are sometimes enlisted to help the clients navigate the hospital bureaucracy and may function as translators and advocates for the clients within the hospital system.

Members of our staff have written numerous psychological and medical affidavits attesting to the physical and psychological evidence regarding our clients' claims for political asylum in the United States. As a therapist, I have been called several times to testify at Immigration and Naturalization Service court proceedings on behalf of clients. At times, clients have asked us to verify their identity and program participation because they often lack their "official" papers from their home country. This has helped clients to receive work authorization papers, register in schools, take GED exams, or sit for the SATs, with the hope of going on to college.

These treatment priorities and techniques have been supported by the positive reactions of the clients to our treatment programs. The therapeutic relationships that develop are usually complex and profound. By empowering our clients and listening to their insights, we have been able to develop therapeutic interventions that are increasingly culturally syntonic and effective for our client population. Beyond the critical techniques during the initial intake process, individual sessions, as well as establishing emotional safety, empowering clients, and forming alliances, the African group experience itself is one such culturally syntonic and effective intervention.

The African Group

The genesis of the African group, our initial concerns in launching the group, the treatment goals we formulated, and the group process and development deserve discussion to adequately convey the nature of this treatment experience. At the same time, clinician concerns around potential vicarious traumatization and burnout deserve attention because they are important elements for the success and sustainability of the African group.

Genesis of the Group

The original idea for starting the African group stemmed from being involved in individual therapy with several clients from Africa. By listening to their needs, desires, and insights and sharing this knowledge with other psychologists engaged in similar work, we had an idea that began to take root. Dr. Yael Kapeliuk and I shared the perception that beyond posttraumatic stress disorder symptomatology and depression, the major complaint from our French-speaking African clients was that of social isolation.

It is important to understand that Africa is a diverse and complex continent, with thousands of ethnic groups and languages (there are more than 400 languages spoken in Nigeria alone), but one can still identify aspects of larger "pan-African" cultural norms that are found among the peoples of the African continent and its Diaspora. Examples of these pan-African norms are the importance placed on social and collateral ties and the central role that the extended family plays in an individual's sense of belonging. In fact, in times of emotional distress, it is far more likely that an individual from Africa will seek guidance from members of the extended family, particularly elders, rather than seek outside assistance from a mental health professional (Akinsulure-Smith et al., 1997).

Another of the pan-African cultural norms is that of hospitality and openness, in which strangers, foreigners, and those who are not capable of supporting themselves are usually taken in and cared for. I have been the beneficiary of such hospitality when living in and traveling throughout Africa. Consequently, one of the major cultural difficulties that African immigrants report facing in the United States is the perceived lack of hospitality and the lack of communal support. Many African clients complain about "Western" society in terms of clichés such as, "It's every man for himself," "It's a dog eat dog world," and of course, "Time is money."

Dr. Kapeliuk and I believed that for clients who were suffering from social isolation and who were deprived of culturally syntonic coping mechanisms, a supportive group in which collateral ties would be fostered would be a positive psychological intervention. We considered the importance that is placed on the extended family in the pan-African context. We strove to create an environment that might not seem as foreign as individual psychotherapy to our African clients—a place where a sense of family could be reformulated psychologically. Our hypothesis was that African clients might be more likely to engage effectively in supportive therapeutic work in a context that seemed more aligned with the ways they might have dealt with significant stressors in their cultures of origin.

Initial Concerns

To prepare for launching the group, Dr. Kapeliuk and I searched the literature for insights on running groups with survivors of torture living in exile. To our dismay, not much had been written on the subject. We found one article that described a time-limited group for survivors from Central and South American countries (Fischman & Ross, 1990). Even though there were significant differences between the group described in the article and the group we were proposing at Bellevue, we were encouraged to see that treatment results supported the contention that an increased sense of community and belonging does foster individual healing in survivors. We were, nevertheless, concerned that we were venturing into relatively uncharted therapeutic waters.

Another significant concern was the potential for retraumatizing group members. We anticipated that there would be initial resistance to sharing with strangers in a relatively open forum. From the very first session, a consensus was developed among group members and clinicians that the group would be a safe place where clients could share their trauma experiences but that it was by no means obligatory to do so.

From that time on, group members engaged in conversations that often focused more on support and adaptation rather than deep emotional exploration. There have been sessions where particular members may have experienced an emotional trigger of some sort, which has led them to share some of their traumatic past in the group. On these occasions, the group has provided a safe holding environment.

There were also initial concerns about the heterogeneous nature of the group. The proposed group would be of mixed gender, with people from many African nations who may be Islamic, Christian, members of other faiths, or nonreligious. The group's two cotherapists would be, respectively, from the United States and Israel, male and female, Black and White, Catholic and Jewish. We were concerned that politics, prejudices, and other social schisms may stand in the way of forming a cohesive group. As we moved ahead with our work, we learned that many of the issues that concerned us as we began the group actually proved to be sources of strength.

The mixed-gender composition of the group led to profound discussions of traditional gender roles in pan-African culture and how these roles affected coping strategies. Men seemed to be more comfortable focusing primarily on logistical, problem-solving techniques while minimizing or trying to ignore the associated feelings and emotions. Women were more likely to focus on their emotional reactions, sometimes to the detriment of their decision-making abilities. The group process served as a model of a more holistic coping strategy that incorporated both cognitive and emotional strengths. Male and female group members spoke of valuing this new experience and encouraged each other to internalize the more holistic coping style.

It has become apparent that spirituality and religion are generally important coping mechanisms for African survivors of torture. The multireligious composition of our group has not led to any friction. In areas of Africa where religion has not become overtly politicized or linked with the ruling hierarchy, there is a long history of religious tolerance. Muslims and Christians have often lived side by side in the same villages for centuries. Group members seem to be comfortable in carrying forth this tradition of tolerance. They generally speak of "spiritual" matters and find consensus in the need for faith in whichever form it may take.

In terms of potential political schisms, clients are carefully screened before being referred to the group to make sure that they were not involved in repressive activities themselves. Some clients have expressed initial concern about meeting other people from their country, in case they are government spies or because of some other dangerous element. There has only been one occasion when it appeared that a political issue might arise, but group members worked hard to make sure that politics did not adversely affect the group functioning.

On that one occasion, two group members saw the president of a West African nation from diametrically opposite positions. To a male member of the group, this president was directly responsible for his torture, exile, and the death of two of his family members. To a woman in the group who had been tortured and raped in a neighboring country, it was only because of an intervention by this president that she was able to escape her country alive. To one person, he was the devil; to another, a savior.

These two survivors were able to express within the group that it was not important which side of the conflict they were on; the important thing was that they were all human beings. As sons and daughters of Africa who had all suffered horribly, the political details were inconsequential. The group members stated that they were all family, and it was now time to move forward.

This notion of family is an important one. Even as Dr. Kapeliuk and I conceived of the group as becoming an "extended family" in a psychological sense, we never labeled it as such for group members. We allowed group members to create their own group identity. Over time, the members began referring to the group as "the family." It seemed that we had been on target in terms of creating a culturally syntonic intervention for our African clients.

The psychological literature shows that diagnostic and treatment strategies must be in sync with cultural norms to be effective (Akinsulure-Smith et al., 1997; Fischman, 1998). Therefore, to become even more effective, we have allowed the group to evolve into something a bit different than the "traditional" group psychotherapy models about which we had learned in graduate school.

Treatment Goals

Two of the primary goals that we identified for the French-speaking African group were that clients would feel supported and that their sense of social isolation would decrease. In individual therapy, clients often reported feeling "lonely," "all by themselves," or that "nobody could understand" their problems. The group would strive to support these clients in multifaceted ways. It was hoped that clients would come to learn that they were not alone in terms of their torture experiences or in terms of the challenges facing them as they attempted to adapt to life in the United States.

Another major goal of the African group, which is consistent with the treatment priorities discussed earlier, has been to empower the client. The literature has shown that survivors who are able to regain a sense of purpose in their lives, perhaps by feeling useful in helping other people, have shown overall improvement in their psychological functioning (Fischman, 1998; Fischman & Ross, 1990). The African group was conceptualized with the hope that clients would begin to see that they are more than people who are needy. In an emotional sense, they would come to realize that they are people who are needed as well. We get a clearer view of the question posed earlier: What sorts of resilience and coping mechanisms must a people use to survive such harsh life conditions?

In a long-term, ongoing group, it was hoped that group members would be able to model for one another that progress was possible and that progress has indeed been occurring. The social reinforcements would work in multiple directions, serving to create an environment where clients could begin to feel hopeful again.

An example of this multidirectional reinforcement was when a new client from a Central African nation joined the group and attended his first session. The other members attending had been in the group anywhere from 4 to 18 months. The new client presented as being depressed. At first, he would barely make eye contact and was hesitant to speak. On two occasions, he even put his head down on the table. Group members greeted him and talked about what the group was like, as well as various ways they felt it had helped them.

The group members then began to catch up with one another and discuss various issues regarding adaptation to life in the United States. The new client began to gain interest in the conversation and started speaking up. He shared that he was often afraid to go out into his Harlem neighborhood. He admitted that he was supposed to have come to the group the previous week but had gotten hopelessly lost on the subway. The other group members, who had been in the United States for considerably longer than the new client, engaged him around his experiences.

They shared stories about when they first arrived in the United States. One client talked about taking the wrong train and ending up in Coney Island and not knowing enough English to ask anyone how to get home. Another talked about being afraid to leave his Bedford-Stuyvesant apartment for his first 6 months in the country. He had seen many American movies with Stallone, Schwarzenegger, and the like, and when he saw kids on the street corners wearing big, bulky "South Pole" and "Polar Bear" winter coats that were popular at the time, he thought they were all "muscle men" like in the movies.

The group members told these stories about unpleasant, scary, or disempowering events with unabashed humor and openness. Group members shared their vulnerability in an adaptive way, and everyone, including the new client, was laughing. It was the first time I had ever seen him smile, including all of the individual sessions we'd had to that point.

This interaction was powerful in three respects. By coming into contact with people who have encountered the same difficulties he was currently facing and seeing that they had learned to better navigate their environment, the new client was able to see that progress was possible. Second, it was beneficial for the senior group members to be able to express and share painful incidents in a way that diminished their impact, by placing them firmly in the past—a past they could now laugh about. Third, this interaction was empowering for senior members, many of whom were in the middle of the asylum application process, which can drag on for months or even years. Some of these clients had previously expressed feeling stuck, as if they were not making any progress. By meeting the new client, they saw a reflection of themselves a few months back. It helped clients realize that they had been making steady progress, even in the midst of feeling stuck.

Group Processes and Development

The African group is different from traditional group psychotherapy in several ways. The traditional group model states that the therapeutic work goes on during sessions, and outside contacts among group members are discouraged, if not forbidden. In direct contrast, outside client contacts are allowed and even encouraged in the African group.

During our initial group sessions, members made it clear that they desired a way of being able to converse with each other between group meetings. On further exploration, members spoke to feelings of loneliness, particularly at night. They said that it would be nice to hear a friendly voice when you needed it, as opposed to waiting a few days until you can see your "family" in the group. Group members and clinicians decided that an exchange of phone numbers would be allowed among group members.

This intervention has paid several dividends. One client expressed it this way: "Sometimes when you feel sad, just having the numbers is enough. You don't even have to call. But you know someone that cares about you is just a phone call away. It makes it easier to cope with life's struggles." Clients have cooperated and accompanied each other to social service agency appointments and have helped each other in finding work.

Another difference between the African group and a more structured group model is that there is no predetermined content area for the African group. As mentioned previously, group members may choose to share their previous trauma experiences, but the group focuses on many diverse areas. Sometimes the group focuses on concrete logistical issues, philosophical issues, social support, adaptation issues, and, occasionally, issues regarding crisis intervention.

In terms of concrete issues, group members often share insights or vent frustrations regarding employment problems, immigration concerns, health issues, and social services in general. Group members have gone so far as to help find or even provide emergency shelter for members who have lost their place to stay. This would be frowned upon in more traditional therapy. Clients help each other navigate the hospital system so that members can access the medical care that they need, often by acting as interpreters or showing new members where to find particular clinics or offices. Members help each other by providing guidance in terms of how they have navigated particular situations in the past, and they support each other when progress is slow and frustration levels are high.

The philosophical group discussions are especially fascinating and rewarding. Group members share insights and proverbs from their homelands to help illuminate complicated issues. Group members have discussed the relative merits of "forgiveness" versus "forgetting" in terms of recovering from their trauma. They have explored the thin line between fear and wariness and how it affects one's ability to navigate their new and sometimes threatening environment. Group members have also broached the subject of positive self-concept and the importance of valuing one's personal character above and beyond one's troubling circumstances. In terms of gender roles, the group has grappled with the question of whether it is culturally appropriate for an African man to cry, particularly in public. It should be noted that in the aftermath of this discussion, men have cried in the group on a couple of different occasions, and the group proved to be a safe place for them to do so.

Group members have discussed the frustrations of wanting to change the world but feeling powerless to do so. They have discussed the need to look at change and progress gradually. Over time, they have developed a list of the things required for a person to change the world (and adapt to difficult circumstances). The necessary ingredients they have identified are wisdom, courage, and hope. They have spoken about how it is necessary to have all three of these traits, as any combination of two will still be insufficient.

Group members frequently struggle with feelings of hopelessness, shame, and/or survivor's guilt. These painful feelings are often brought up in group sessions, as members strive to cope with this tormenting emotional baggage. One way that group members have made sense of these feelings and have supported each other is to view these painful emotions as an intended part of the torture experience. It has been shown that being able to place the burden of responsibility on the torturers for the current distress is an adaptive step on the way to recovery (Fischman & Ross, 1990; Somnier & Genefke, 1986). Group members have stated that by giving in to the feelings of guilt and hopelessness, they are giving power back to the torturers. They feel that fighting against these painful emotions and overcoming them is like fighting against the torturers, denying them their victory.

Sometimes the group has served a primarily social function. The group has had a picnic in Riverside Park, where friends and family of group members were welcome. The picnic was a big success. It felt good as a therapist to see group members laughing, eating, listening to music, and enjoying themselves in a context of positivity and familial support. I was particularly struck when I saw the group member from Central Africa, who had seemed so scared and depressed a few short months before, laughing, telling jokes, and playing with the children of another group member.

When Dr. Kapeliuk had to take extended time off from the group, group members prepared food, sang songs, and presented original poetry at her farewell party. This was partially a social gathering, but it also served an important therapeutic purpose. The African group is ongoing, so there is some client attrition as people move to other towns or take on jobs that preclude their regular group attendance. At these times, it is important for members to reflect on the meaning of being able to say a positive au revoir (good-bye) and how it relates to many of the losses they have already endured.

As refugees who have been so brutally uprooted from their homes and families, they are painfully aware that people are not always able to say good-bye to their loved ones. Even though good-byes are always painful, each positive good-bye that they are able to express is valuable. In a psychological sense, saying "au revoir" to family members from the group is an opportunity for survivors to find an adaptive way to process some of the unresolved feelings they may hold regarding the good-byes they never got to say in the past to people they have loved.

Recently, the group engaged in a "Ceremony of Remembrance and Thanksgiving" for those members who have lost family members, do not know the whereabouts of family members, or are separated from family members and friends. Group members offered prayers and songs from their various religious, spiritual, and ethnic backgrounds. Group members spoke about the need for continued courage and mutual support to surmount the challenges they face. They also expressed appreciation for all the blessings they have received, despite their troubled situations.

As previously mentioned, the group often focuses more on adaptation than emotional exploration. Adaptive defenses are supported, not dismantled.

As always, special care is taken that group members are not retraumatized by the therapeutic work. We have found it to be important to end sessions, particularly those that have been emotionally charged, in a way that leaves the clients feeling empowered and supported. It is helpful for the clinician to be able to sum up what has transpired in the group in a way that focuses on the wisdom that was shared and the courage that was displayed and, most importantly, engenders continued hope for the future.

Perhaps one last example will more fully demonstrate how the group can be helpful for a survivor of torture in distress, even in times of acute crisis. A group member who was in the midst of his asylum process learned that his brother had been killed in their homeland. It was a political murder, perhaps in retribution for the previous political activities of the client. The client became despondent, hopeless, and depressed. The entire multidisciplinary team was alerted, and when the client expressed some passive suicidal ideation, he was admitted to an inpatient unit for a couple of days.

When I first spoke with the client before he was hospitalized, he asked me to let the other group members know what had happened. On his release from the hospital, group members mobilized themselves and called him periodically to check in. Some group members who were especially close to him would go to visit and ask if he had eaten that day. If the client had not eaten, they would prepare food. They spent extended periods of time with him, just "keeping company."

In the months that followed, the client's emotional state improved. He was no longer suicidal, and he became less dysthymic. He began to reclaim some of the buoyant personality he had displayed before his brother's murder. He received his political asylum and has been planning for the future, working a temporary job, and looking for permanent work since then. When the client describes his experience, he expresses appreciation to the entire treatment team at Bellevue, but he saves his most profound thanks and praises for his "family" in the group, who helped see him through his darkest time. He says that it was invaluable to know that even when coping with the acute pain of losing his blood brother, he had some very real "family" here to look out for him.

Vicarious Traumatization and Clinician Self-Care

There is no question that working with this population is emotionally challenging and that strong countertransferential feelings do arise (Fischman, 1998; Keller et al., 1996). Clinicians must make a concerted effort to take care of themselves emotionally to minimize the potential effects of vicarious traumatization and "burnout."

The stories that these clients recount are harrowing, and sitting in the room with someone who is manifesting such acute emotional pain is potentially overwhelming, even for an experienced clinician. As therapists, we are exposed to the details and bear witness to the aftereffects of the most heinous, inhumane, and brutal acts that human beings willfully perpetrate on one another. It is not easy work.

One important way in which clinicians can help themselves to cope with these challenges is to make sure that they function as a *conduit*, not as a container. Therapists must find adaptive ways to process the content they are confronted with and the emotional reactions they experience. It is important to find time to engage in activities that you find pleasurable. Identifying ways to sublimate these emotions through creative and cathartic outlets such as singing, dancing, writing poetry, playing music, painting, exercising, or going to shows is valuable. Of course, engaging in therapy for one's own emotional needs is of the utmost importance.

If clinicians contend with the feelings that come with this difficult work without having positive emotional outlets, they will function like the proverbial sponge that gets filled up, becomes saturated, overflows, and becomes ineffective. This sort of "burnout" claims many clinicians who otherwise could have contributed valuable therapeutic services to a population in need.

Clinicians involved in this work receive additional support through frequent and multifaceted supervision. In addition to individual supervision, the Bellevue program provides biweekly clinical case conferences, wherein clinicians share insights and experiences while supporting each other emotionally and professionally. As with our clients, it is important to break through the feelings of being isolated and unappreciated with regard to our own experiences.

One lesson I learned in supervision is particularly salient in terms of not burning out on this work. I remember it was after I'd had the initial intake session with the Central African client I have discussed before. He was extremely depressed and withdrawn that first day. His face bore the physical scars of his torture. He was tearful and his problems seemed overwhelming. I was struggling to make an emotional connection with him but felt that I was just babbling useless words. I felt totally ineffective.

As I shared this with my supervisor, he asked me to fully describe how I had been feeling during the session. I explained that

I'd felt lost, powerless, unsure of what to say or do, clumsy, and stupid, and I had a desire to flee from the session. My supervisor put these feelings in a new context for me.

He told me that as clinicians in this work, sometimes we need to give ourselves "permission not to know." We cannot and should not expect to have answers or be able to "save" people all of the time. That is not even our true therapeutic role. Often, just being there, listening, and being a supportive person in the room with the client are exactly what is needed and all that can be expected.

He then portrayed my feelings during the session in a different light. He saw me as being extremely empathic with my client and actually feeling a lot of what he brought into the room: sadness, helplessness, a sense of being lost and not knowing what to say, and a desire to flee. My supervisor helped me to see that I had not been completely ineffectual. In fact, I'd been right on target in an emotional sense. The subsequent history with this client has shown that our relationship developed in a very positive therapeutic way. My supervisor had been right. Words of wisdom were not necessary that first meeting. Just being there with my client in a real emotional sense was exactly what was needed.

This lesson is very important for clinicians who want to engage in clinical work with torture survivors. What we hear is often overwhelming, and we are not going to have any easy answers. The work can be painful, and progress often comes slowly.

We must realize that we cannot "save" everybody. In fact, we cannot really "save" anybody. The most we can hope for, and the most we can expect of ourselves, is to help place people in a context where they can strive to save themselves. As clinicians, we have to give ourselves "permission not to know," or we run the risk of placing undue pressure on ourselves because of unrealistic expectations.

Conclusion

This chapter has been written to provide clinicians with an understanding of the overall context in which psychological treatment with survivors of torture from Africa takes place. It has been designed to shed light on the multifaceted stressors that these clients are facing and to illustrate ways that their incredible emotional strengths can be used to foster healing and growth. By providing psychologists with a model and guide for doing this challenging work, it is my hope that this will help facilitate further creative formulations of strategies and techniques in the psychological treatment of survivors of torture from throughout the world.

In terms of my continuing personal investment in this work, I have come to realize that even though I am exposed to some of the worst behaviors that mankind is capable of, I also bear witness to the miraculous resilience of the human spirit. I am blessed to work with people who have somehow found the strength to continue "fighting the good fight." They continue in the struggle to defend their humanity against seemingly insurmountable odds, and their progress helps reaffirm my faith that healing is possible. These ordinary people, heroes and "she-roes," one and all, empower me to continue with my own personal and professional struggles. When I look into their eyes, I see the endless possibilities for spiritual growth and emotional redemption in all of us.

References

Chapter 1

Canon, K. (1995). *Katie's canon: Womanism and the soul of the Black community.* New York: Continuum.

Ellison, R. (1952). *Invisible man.* New York: Random House.

Fanon, F. (1963). *The wretched of the earth.* New York: Grove.

Fanon, F. (1967). *Black skin, white masks.* New York: Grove.

Foucault, M. (1979). *Discipline and punish.* Harmondsworth, UK: Penguin.

Freire, P. (1970). *Pedagogy of the oppressed.* New York: Continuum/Seabury.

Freire, P. (1995). *Pedagogy of hope: Reliving pedagogy of the oppressed.* New York: Continuum.

Greene, M. (1988). *The dialectic of freedom.* New York: Teachers College Press.

Heyward, C. (1993). *When boundaries betray us: Beyond illusions of what is ethical in therapy and life.* San Francisco: Harper.

hooks, b. (1995). *Killing rage: Ending racism.* New York: Henry Holt.

Ivey, A. E. (1995). Psychotherapy as liberation: Toward specific skills and strategies in multicultural counseling and therapy. In J. G. Ponterotto, J. M. Casas, L. A. Suzuki, & C. M. Alexander (Eds.), *Handbook of multicultural counseling* (pp. 53-72). Thousand Oaks, CA: Sage.

Kenan, R. (1995). Introduction. In W. E. B. Du Bois, *The souls of Black folk* (pp. xxxi-xi). New York: Signet Classic/Penguin.

Melville, H. (1952). Benito Cereno. In *Selected writings: Complete short stories.* New York: Modern Library. (Original publication 1856)

Sedgwick, E. K. (1990). *Epistemology of the closet.* Berkeley: University of California Press.

Storey, J. (1994). Structuralism and poststructuralism: Introduction. In J. Storey (Ed.), *Cultural theory and popular culture: A reader.* New York: Harvester/Wheatsheaf.

Taylor, C. (1994). The politics of recognition. In A. Gutman (Ed.), *Multiculturalism: Examining the politics of recognition.* Princeton, NJ: Princeton University Press.

Wallace, B. C. (1991). *Crack cocaine: A practical treatment approach for the chemically dependent.* New York: Brunner/Mazel.

Wallace, B. C. (1993). Cross-cultural counseling with the chemically dependent: Preparing for service delivery within our culture of violence. *Journal of Psychoactive Drugs, 24*(3), 9-20.

Wallace, B. C. (1994, February). *How to avoid engaging in violence in psychotherapy: considerations of race and gender.* Paper presented at the annual Winter Roundtable on Cross-Cultural Counseling, Teachers College, Columbia University, New York.

DEALING WITH VIOLENCE

Wallace, B. C. (1995). Women and minorities in treatment. In A. M. Washton (Ed.), *Psychotherapy and substance abuse*. New York: Guilford.
Wallace, B. C. (1996). *Adult children of dysfunctional families: Prevention, intervention, and treatment for community mental health promotion*. Westport, CT: Praeger.

Chapter 2

Barret, K. (1993). Attitudinal change in undergraduate rehabilitation students as measured by the Attitudes Toward Disabled Persons Scale. *Rehabilitation Education*, 7(2), 119-126.
Berrill, K. T. (1992). Antigay violence and victimization in the United States: An overview. In G. M. Herek & K. T. Berrill (Eds.), *Hate crimes: Confronting violence against lesbians and gay men* (pp. 19-45). Newbury Park, CA: Sage.
Blank, H. R. (1957). Psychoanalysis and blindness. *Psychoanalytic Quarterly, 26*, 1-24.
Blumenfeld, W. (1997). *Adolescence, sexual orientation, and identity: An overview* [Online]. Available: www.edu/edu/ericcass/diverse/docs/overview.htm
Bongar, B., Berman, A. L., Maris, R. W., Silverman, M. M., Harris, E. A., & Packman, W. L. (Eds.). (1998). *Risk management with suicidal patients*. New York: Guilford.
Braithwaite, D. O. (1985, November). *Impression management and redefinition of self by persons with disabilities*. Paper presented at the annual meeting of the Speech Communication Association, Denver, CO.
Buck v. Bell, 274 U.S. 200 (1927).
Bulletin #97-BF-GX-K022. (1998, January 23-24). Presented at the symposium, Working With Crime Victims With Disabilities, Arlington, VA.
Carter, R. T. (2000). Reimagining race in education: A new paradigm from psychology. *Teachers College Record, 102*(5), 864-897.
Cass, V. C. (1979, Spring). Homosexuality identity formation: A theoretical model. *Journal of Homosexuality, 4*(3), 219-235.
Cass, V. C. (1996). Sexual orientation identity formation: A Western phenomenon. In R. P. Cabaj & T. S. Stein (Eds.), *Textbook of homosexuality and mental health* (pp. 227-251). Washington, DC: American Psychiatric Press.
Cholden, L. (1954). Some psychiatric problems in the rehabilitation of the blind. *Bulletin of the Menninger Clinic, 18*, 107-112.
Cohn-Kerr, N. (1961). Understanding the process of adjustment to disability. *Journal of Rehabilitation, 27*, 16-18.
Coleman, E. (1981-1982). Developmental stages of the coming-out process. *Journal of Homosexuality, 7*(2-3), 31-43.
Connors, R. E. (2000). *Self-injury: Psychotherapy with people who engage in self-inflicted violence*. Northvale, NJ: Jason Aronson.
Davis, F. (1961). Deviance disavowal: The management of strained interaction by the visibly handicapped. *Social Problems, 9*, 120-132.
Denning, P. (2000). *Practicing harm reduction psychotherapy: An alternative approach to addictions*. New York: Guilford.
Diamond, K. E. (1994a). Evaluating preschool children's sensitivity to developmental differences in their peers. *Topics in Early Childhood Special Education, 14*, 49-63.
Diamond, K. E. (1994b). Factors in preschool children's social problem-solving strategies for peers. *Early Childhood Research Quarterly, 9*(2), 195-205.
Díaz, R. M. (1998). *Latino gay men and HIV: culture sexuality and risk behavior*. New York: Routledge Kegan Paul.

Doddington, K. (1994). Are attitudes toward people with learning disabilities negatively influenced by charity advertising? An experimental analysis. *Disability & Society, 9*, 207-222.

Dunn, M. E. (1975). Psychological intervention in a spinal cord injury center: An Introduction. *Rehabilitation Psychology, 22*, 165-178.

Eliason, M. J. (1996). An inclusive model of lesbian identity assumption. *Journal of Gay, Lesbian, and Bisexual Identity, 1*(1), 3-19.

Emmons, R. A. (1999). *The psychology of ultimate concerns: Motivation and spirituality in personality.* New York: Guilford.

Evans, J. H. (1976). Changing attitudes towards disabled persons: An experimental study. *Rehabilitation Counseling Bulletin, 19*(4), 572-579.

Falek, A., & Britton, S. (1974). Phases in coping: The hypothesis and its implications. *Social Biology, 21*, 1-7.

Ferguson, P. M. (1994). *Abandoned to their fate: Social policy and practice toward severely retarded people in America, 1820-1920.* Philadelphia: Temple University Press.

Fichten, C. S., Lennox, H., Robillard, K., Wright, J., Sabourin, S., & Amsel, R. (1996). Attentional focus and attitudes towards peers with disabilities: Self focusing and a comparison of modeling and self-disclosure. *Journal of Applied Rehabilitation Counseling, 27*(4), 30-39.

Fink, S. L. (1967). Crisis and motivation: A theoretical model. *Archives of Physical Medicine and Rehabilitation, 48*, 592-597.

Gallagher, H. (1985). *FDR's splendid deception.* New York: Dodd Mead.

Goffman, E. (1963). *Stigma: Notes on the management of spoiled identity.* Englewood Cliffs, NJ: Prentice Hall.

Hafferty, F. W. (1994). Decontextualizing disability in the crime mystery genre: The case of the invisible handicap. *Disability & Society, 8*(2), 185-206.

Handler, E. (1994). Medical students' and allied health care professionals' perceptions toward the mentally retarded population. *Journal of Developmental & Physical Disabilities, 6*(3), 291-297.

Hastorf, A. H., Wildfogel, J., & Cassman, T. (1979). Acknowledgment of handicap as a tactic in social interaction. *Journal of Personality and Social Psychology, 37*(10), 1790-1797.

Helms, J. E. (1995). An update of Helms' White and people of color racial identity models. In J. Ponterotto, J. M. Casas, L. A. Suzuki, & C. M. Alexander (Eds.), *Handbook of multicultural counseling* (pp. 181-198). Thousand Oaks, CA: Sage.

Herek, G. M. (1996). Heterosexism and homophobia. In R. P. Cabaj & T. S. Stein (Eds.), *Textbook of homosexuality and mental health* (pp. 101-113). Washington, DC: American Psychiatric Press.

Horowitz, C. (1998, November 9). Village people. *New York*, pp. 28-33, 88.

Joseph, J., Breslin, C., & Skinner, H. (1999). Critical perspectives on the transtheoretical model and stages of change. In J. A. Tucker, D. M. Donovan, & G. A. Marlatt (Eds.), *Changing addictive behavior: Bridging clinical and public health strategies,* pp. 160-190. New York: Guilford.

Kiesler, C. A. (2000). The next wave of change for psychology and mental health services in the health care revolution. *American Psychologist, 35*(5), 481-487.

Kleck, R. E. (1968). Physical stigma and nonverbal cues emitted in face-to-face interaction. *Human Relations, 21*, 19-28.

Kleck, R. E., Ono, H., & Hastorf, A. H. (1966). The effects of physical deviance upon face-to-face interaction. *Human Relations, 19*, 425-436.

Klinger, R. L., & Stein, T. S. (1996). Impact of violence, childhood sexual abuse, and domestic violence and abuse on lesbians, bisexuals, and gay men. In R. P. Cabaj & T. S. Stein (Eds.), *Textbook of homosexuality and mental health* (pp. 801-818). Washington, DC: American Psychiatric Press.

LaPlante, M. P. (1997). *The context of employment statistics and disability: Data needs, employment statistics, and disability policy* [Online]. Available: http://dsc.ucsf. edu/reps/forum2/present.html

LaPlante, M. P., Carlson, D., Kaye, S., & Bradsher, J. E. (1996). *Families with disabilities in the United States* [Online]. Available: http://dsc.ucsf.edu/reps/families/ index.html

LaPlante, M. P., Kennedy, J., Kaye, H. S., & Wenger, B. L. (1995). Disability and employment. *Disability Statistics Abstracts, 11* [Online]. Available: http://dsc. ucsf.edu/abs/ab11txt.html

Levine, M. P. (1998). "It's raining men": The sociology of gay masculinity. In M. P. Levine (Ed.), *Gay macho: The life and death of the homosexual clone* (pp. 10-29). New York: New York University Press.

Linton, S. (1998). *Claiming disability: Knowledge and identity.* New York: New York University Press.

Livneh, H. (1986). A unified approach to existing models of adaptation to disability: Part 1. A model of adaptation. *Journal of Applied Rehabilitation Counseling, 17,* 5-16, 56.

Livneh, H., & Antonak, R. (1990). Reactions to disability: An empirical investigation of their nature and structure. *Journal of Applied Rehabilitation Counseling, 21*(4), 13-21.

Marlatt, G. A. (Ed.). (1998). *Harm reduction: Pragmatic strategies for managing high-risk behaviors.* New York: Guilford.

McAfee, J. K. (1995). Training police officers about persons with disabilities. *Rase: Remedial & Special Education, 16*(1), 53-63.

McClean, V. (1997). African American men and nonrelational sex. In R. F. Levant & G. R. Brooks (Eds.), *Men and sex: New psychological perspectives* (pp. 205-228). New York: John Wiley.

Miller, W. R. (1995). Increasing motivation for change. In R. K. Hester & W. R. Miller (Eds.), *Handbook of alcoholism treatment approaches: Effective alternatives* (2nd ed., pp. 89-104). Boston: Allyn & Bacon.

Miller, W. R. (Ed.). (1999). *Integrating spirituality into treatment: Resources for practitioners.* Washington, DC: American Psychological Association.

Miller, W. R., Brown, J. M., Simpson, T. L., Handmaker, N. S., Bien, T. H., Luckie, L. F., Montgomery, H. A., Hester, R. K., & Tonigan, J. S. (1995). What works? A methodological analysis of the alcohol treatment outcome literature. In R. K. Hester & W. R. Miller (Eds.), *Handbook of alcoholism treatment approaches: Effective alternatives* (2nd ed., pp. 12-44). Boston: Allyn & Bacon.

Miller, W. R., & Rollnick, S. (1991). *Motivational interviewing: Preparing people to change addictive behavior.* New York: Guilford.

Mills, J., Belgrave, F. Z., & Boyer, K. M. (1984). Reducing avoidance of social interaction with a physically disabled person by mentioning disability following a request for aid. *Journal of Applied Social Psychology, 14*(1), 1-11.

Olkin, R. (1999). *What psychotherapists should know about disability.* New York: Guilford.

Pfeiffer, D. (1995). An annotated bibliography of selected works in disability studies published during 1994 and not previously noted. *Disability Studies Quarterly, 15,* 75-80.

Pitman, J. A. (1994). Students' familiarity with and attitudes toward the rights of students who are disabled. *Journal of Applied Rehabilitation Counseling, 25*(2), 38-40.

Prochaska, J. O., & DiClemente, C. C. (1982). Transtheoretical therapy: Toward a more integrative model of change. *Psychotherapy: Theory, Research, and Practice, 18,* 276-288.

Prochaska, J. O., DiClemente, C. C., & Norcross, J. C. (1992). In search of how people change: Applications to addictive behaviors. *American Psychologist, 47,* 1102-1114.

Scheerenberger, R. C. (1983). *A history of mental retardation*. Baltimore: Brooks.

Scofield, M. E., Pape, D. A., McCracken, N., & Maki, D. R. (1980). An ecological model for promoting acceptance of disability. *Journal of Applied Rehabilitation Counseling, 11*(4), 183-187.

Scrivner, R. (1997). Gay men and nonrelational sex. In R. F. Levant & G. R. Brooks (Eds.), *Men and sex: New psychological perspectives* (pp. 229-256). New York: John Wiley.

Seligman, M. E. P., & Csikszentmihalyi, M. (2000). Positive psychology: An introduction. *American Psychologist, 55*(1), 5-14.

Shontz, F. C. (1965). Reactions to crisis. *The Volta Review, 67*, 364-370.

Sue, D. W., Carter, R. T., Casas, J. M., Fouad, N. A., Ivey, A. E., Jensen, M., LaFrombosie, R., Manese, J. E., Ponterotto, J. G., & Vazquez-Nutall, E. (1998). *Multicultural counseling competencies: Individual and organizational development*. Thousand Oaks, CA: Sage.

Sullivan, A. (1999, September 26). What's so bad about hate? *The New York Times Magazine*, pp. 50-57, 88, 104, 112-113.

Thompson, T. L. (1982). Disclosure as a disability-management strategy: A review and conclusions. *Communication Quarterly, 30*, 196-202.

Thompson, T. L., & Seibold, D. R. (1978). Stigma management in *normal*-stigmatized interactions: Test of the disclosure hypothesis and a model of stigma acceptance. *Human Communication Research, 4*, 231-242.

Trickett, E. J., Watts, R. J., & Birman, D. (Eds.). (1994). *Human diversity: Perspectives on people in context*. San Francisco: Jossey-Bass.

Troiden, R. R. (1989). The formation of homosexual identities. In G. Herdt (Ed.), *Gay and lesbian youth* (pp. 43-73). New York: Harrington Park Press.

Vargo, J. W. (1978). Some psychological effects of physical disability. *American Journal of Occupational Therapy, 32*(1), 31-34.

Wallace, B. C. (1991). *Crack cocaine: A practical treatment approach for the chemically dependent*. New York: Brunner/Mazel.

Wallace, B. C. (1996). *Adult children of dysfunctional families: Prevention, intervention, and treatment for community mental health promotion*. Westport, CT: Praeger.

Wallace, B. C. (2000). A call for change in multicultural training at graduate school of education: Educating to end oppression and for social justice. *Teachers College Record, 102*(6), 1086-1111.

Wallace, B. C., & Ayeboafo, N. K. (2001, April). *A cultural presentation for the re-spiritualization of humankind*. Workshop presented at Govinda's Cultural Arts Center, Philadelphia.

Warren, F. (1985). A society that is going to kill your children. In H. R. Turnbull III & A. P. Turnbull (Eds.), *Parents speak out* (2nd ed.). New York: Macmillan.

Wells, S. (1999). The health beliefs, values, and practices of gay adolescents. *Clinical Nurse Specialist, 13*(2), 69-73.

White, R. W., Wright, B. A., & Dembo, W. (1948). Studies in adjustment to visible injuries: Evaluations of curiosity by the injured. *Journal of Abnormal and Social Psychology, 53*, 13-28.

Chapter 3

A brief sample of Jerry Falwell's toxic rhetoric. (1999, October 22-24). In *Soulforce Journey to Lynchburg* [Press packet]. (Available from Soulforce, Inc., P.O. Box 4467, Laguna Beach, CA 92652)

Branch, T. (1988). *Parting the waters: America in the King years 1954-63*. New York: Simon & Schuster.

Meeks, W. A. (Ed.). (1989). *The HarperCollins Study Bible: New revised standard version*. New York: HarperCollins.

Merton, T. (Ed.). (1964). *Gandhi on non-violence: A selection from the writings of Mahatma Gandhi*. New York: New Directions Publishing Corporation.

Night, V., & North, D. K. (1998). I am not ashamed. On *I am not ashamed* [CD]. David North and the Gospel Celebration Singers. Hyattsville, MD: DNY Music Enterprises.

Smith, C. M. (1992). *Preaching as weeping, confession, and resistance: Radical responses to radical evil*. Westminister, UK: John Knox.

Soulforce, Inc. organization backgrounder. (1999, October 22-24). In *Soulforce journey to Lynchburg* [Press packet]. (Available from Soulforce, Inc., P.O. Box 4467, Laguna Beach, CA 92652)

White, M. (1994). *Stranger at the gate: To be gay and Christian in America*. New York: Simon & Schuster.

Chapter 4

American Psychiatric Association. (1994). *Diagnostic and statistical manual of mental disorders* (4th ed.). Washington, DC: Author.

Berrill, K. T. (1990). Anti-gay violence and victimization in the United States: An overview. *Journal of Interpersonal Violence, 5,* 274-294.

Bornstein, K. (1994). *Gender outlaw: On men, women, and the rest of us*. New York: Routledge Kegan Paul.

Brown, M., & Rounsely, C. A. (1996). *True selves: Understanding transsexualism for families, friends, co-workers, and helping professionals*. San Francisco: Jossey-Bass.

Burke, P. (1996). *Gender shock: Exploding the myths of male & female*. New York: Anchor.

Califia, P. (1997). *Sex changes: The politics of transgenderism*. San Francisco: Cleis.

Coalition for Lesbian and Gay Rights in Ontario. (1997). *Systems failure: A report on the experience of sexual minorities in Ontario's health-care and social-services systems*. Toronto: Author.

Devor, H. (1995, November). *The fallacy of duality in conceptualizations of sex, gender, and sexuality*. Plenary speech given at the 38th annual meeting of the Society for the Scientific Study of Sexuality, San Francisco.

Devor, H. (1997). *FTM: Female-to-male transsexuals in society*. Bloomington: Indiana University Press.

DiPlacido, J. (1998). Minority stress among lesbians, gay men, and bisexuals. In G. M. Herek (Ed.), *Stigma and sexual orientation: Understanding prejudice against lesbians, gay men, and bisexuals* (pp. 138-159). Thousand Oaks, CA: Sage.

Feinberg, L. (1992). *Transgender liberation: A movement whose time has come*. New York: World View Forum.

Feinberg, L. (1996). *Transgender warriors: Making history from Joan of Arc to RuPaul*. Boston: Beacon.

Fox, R. (1996). Bisexuality in perspective: A review of theory and research. In B. Firestein (Ed.), *Bisexuality: The psychology and politics of an invisible minority* (pp. 3-50). Thousand Oaks, CA: Sage.

Gagné, P., Tweksbury, R., & McGaughey, D. (1996). Coming out and crossing over: Identity formation and proclamation in a transgender community. *Gender & Society, 11,* 478-508.

Glaser, B. G., & Strauss, A. L. (1967). *The discovery of grounded theory: Strategies for qualitative research*. Chicago: Aldine.

Guba, E. G., & Lincoln, Y. S. (1989). *Fourth generation evaluation*. Newbury Park, CA: Sage.

Haraway, D. (1991). *Simians, cyborgs, and women: The reinvention of nature*. New York: Routledge Kegan Paul.

Harry, J. (1982). Derivative deviance: The cases of extortion, fag-bashing, and shakedown of gay men. *Criminology, 19*, 251-261.

Harry, J. (1990). Conceptualizing anti-gay violence. *Journal of Interpersonal Violence, 5*, 350-358.

Herek, G. M. (1989). Hate crimes against lesbians and gay men. *American Psychologist, 44*, 948-955.

Herek, G. M. (1990). The context of anti-gay violence: Notes on cultural and psychological heterosexism. *Journal of Interpersonal Violence, 5*, 316-333.

Herek, G. M. (1992). Psychological heterosexism and anti-gay violence: The social psychology of bigotry and bashing. In G. Herek & K. T. Berrill (Eds.), *Hate crimes: Confronting violence against lesbians and gay men* (pp. 149-169). Newbury Park, CA: Sage.

Herek, G. M., & Berrill, K. T. (1990). Documenting the victimization of lesbians and gay men: Methodological issues. *Journal of Interpersonal Violence, 5*, 301-315.

Hill, D. B. (2000). Categories of sex and gender: Either/or, both/and, and neither/nor. *History and Philosophy of Psychology Bulletin, 12*(2), 25-33.

"It's Time, Illinois!" (1998). *Discrimination and hate crimes against transgendered people in Illinois*. Oak Forest, IL: Author.

Katz, J. (1976). *Gay American history: Lesbians and gay men in the U.S.A.* New York: Avon.

Lombardi, E. L., Wilchins, R., Priesing, D., & Malouf, D. (2001). Gender violence: Transgender experiences with violence and discrimination. *Journal of Homosexuality, 42*, 89-101.

Lothstein, L. M. (1983). *Female-to-male transsexualism: Historical, clinical, and theoretical issues*. Boston: Routledge Kegan Paul.

Marshall, C., & Rossman, G. B. (1989). *Designing qualitative research*. Newbury Park, CA: Sage.

Meyer, I. H., & Dean, L. (1998). Internalized homophobia, intimacy, and sexual behavior among gay and bisexual men. In G. M. Herek (Ed.), *Stigma and sexual orientation: Understanding prejudice against lesbians, gay men, and bisexuals* (pp. 160-186). Thousand Oaks, CA: Sage.

Namaste, K. (1996). Genderbashing: Sexuality, gender, and the regulation of public space. *Environment and Planning D: Society and Space, 14*, 221-240.

Nangeroni, N. (1996). Transgender '95: A new day dawns. *Sojourner: The Women's Forum, 21*(6), 9-10.

Nangeroni, N., & Ryan, R. (1998). Trans-actions: News & notes from the gender frontier. *Transgender Tapestry, 83*, 9-11.

Nataf, Z. I. (1996). *Lesbians talk transgender*. London, UK: Scarlet Press.

Ochs, R. (1996). Biphobia: It goes more than two ways. In B. Firestein (Ed.), *Bisexuality: The psychology and politics of an invisible minority* (pp. 217-239). Thousand Oaks, CA: Sage.

Onken, S. J. (1998). Conceptualizing violence against gay, lesbian, bisexual, intersexual, and transgendered people. *Journal of Gay & Lesbian Social Services, 8*(3), 5-24.

Parlee, M. B. (1996). Situated knowledges of personal embodiment: Transgender activists' and psychological theorists' perspectives on "sex" and "gender." *Theory & Psychology, 6*, 625-645.

Potter, J., & Wetherell, M. (1987). *Discourse and social psychology: Beyond attitudes and behavior.* Newbury Park, CA: Sage.

Raymond, J. G. (1994). *The transsexual empire: The making of the she-male.* New York: Teachers College Press.

Rennie, D. L., Phillips, J. R., & Quartaro, G. K. (1988). Grounded theory: A promising approach to conceptualization in psychology? *Canadian Psychology, 29,* 139-150.

Rothblatt, M. (1995). *The apartheid of sex: A manifesto of the freedom of gender.* New York: Crown.

Stanley, L., & Wise, S. (1990). Method, methodology, and epistemology in feminist research process. In L. Stanley (Ed.), *Feminist praxis* (pp. 3-19). New York: Routledge Kegan Paul.

Strauss, A., & Corbin, J. (1994). Grounded theory methodology. In N. K. Denzin & Y. S. Lincoln (Eds.), *Handbook of qualitative research* (pp. 273-285). Thousand Oaks, CA: Sage.

Tully, B. (1992). *Accounting for transsexualism and transhomosexuality: The gender identity careers of over 200 men and women who have petitioned for surgical reassignment of their sexual identity.* London, UK: Whiting & Birch.

Van Soest, D., & Bryant, S. (1995). Violence reconceptualized for social work: The urban dilemma. *Social Work, 40,* 549-557.

Weinberg, G. (1973). *Society and the healthy homosexual.* New York: Anchor.

Weinberg, M. S., Shaver, F. M., & Williams, C. J. (1999). Gendered sex work in the San Francisco Tenderloin. *Archives of Sexual Behavior, 28,* 503-521.

Wilchins, R. A. (1997). *Read my lips: Sexual subversion and the end of gender.* Ithaca, NY: Firebrand.

Witten, M., Eyler, A. E., & Cole, S. (1997, June). *Violence within and against the trans-gender community: Preliminary results of the University of Michigan Medical Center Comprehensive Gender Services Program longitudinal study on violence in the trans-gender community.* Paper presented at the biannual meeting of the International Congress on Sex and Gender, King of Prussia, PA.

Chapter 5

Asian Week. (1991). *Asians in America: 1990 census.* San Francisco: Author.

Barnes, A., & Ephross, P. H. (1994). The impact of hate violence on victims: Emotional and behavioral responses to attacks. *Social Work, 39,* 247-251.

Bentler, P. M. (1995). *EQS structural equation program manual.* Encino, CA: Multivariate Software.

Brown, S. L. (1991). *Counseling victims of violence.* Alexandria, VA: American Association of Counseling and Development.

Callo, M. J. (1973). Culture shock: West, East, and West again. *Personnel & Guidance Journal, 51,* 413-416.

Carter, R. T. (1995). *The influence of race and racial identity in psychotherapy: Toward a racially inclusive model.* New York: John Wiley.

Chen, S. A., & True, R. H. (1994). Asian/Pacific Island Americans. In L. D. Ebron, J. H. Gentry, & P. Schlegel (Eds.), *Reason to hope: A psychosocial perspective on violence and youth* (pp. 145-162). Washington, DC: American Psychological Association.

Delucchi, M., & Do, H. D. (1996). The model minority myth and perceptions of Asian-Americans as victims of racial harassment. *College Student Journal, 30,* 411-414.

Dunbar, E. (1997). *Counseling practices to ameliorate the effects of discrimination and hate events: Toward a model of assessment and intervention.* Unpublished manuscript, University of California, Los Angeles.

Guerra, N. G., Tolan, P. H., & Hammond, W. R. (1994). Prevention and treatment of adolescent violence. In L. D. Ebron, J. H. Gentry, & P. Schlegel (Eds.), *Reason to hope: A psychosocial perspective on violence and youth* (pp. 383-403). Washington, DC: American Psychological Association.

Helms, J. E. (1990). *African American and White racial identity development.* New York: Greenwood.

Helms, J. E. (1994). Racial identity in the school environment. In P. Pedersen & J. C. Carey (Eds.), *Multicultural counseling in schools: A practical handbook* (pp. 19-37). Boston: Allyn & Bacon.

Helms, J. E. (1995). An update of Helms's White and people of color racial identity models. In J. G. Ponterotto, J. M. Casas, L. A. Suzuki, & C. M. Alexander (Eds.), *Handbook of multicultural counseling* (pp. 181-198). Thousand Oaks, CA: Sage.

Hill, H. M., Soriano, F. I., Chen, S. A., & LaFromboise, T. D. (1994). Sociocultural factors in the etiology and prevention of violence among ethnic minority youth. In L. D. Ebron, J. H. Gentry, & P. Schlegel (Eds.), *Reason to hope: A psychosocial perspective on violence and youth* (pp. 59-97). Washington, DC: American Psychological Association.

Hollinger, P. C., Offer, D., Barter, J. T., & Bell, C. C. (1994). *Suicide and homicide among adolescents.* New York: Guilford.

Johnston, L. D., Wadsworth, K. N., O'Malley, P. M., Bachman, J. G., & Schulenberg, J. E. (1997). *Smoking, drinking, and drug use in young adulthood: The impacts of new freedoms and new responsibilities.* Mahwah, N.J.: Lawrence Erlbaum.

Kelly, J. G., Azelton, L. S., Burzette, R. G., & Mock, L. O. (1994). Creating social settings for diversity: An ecological thesis. In E. J. Trickett, R. J. Watts, & D. Birman (Eds.), *Human diversity: Perspectives on people in context* (pp. 424-451). San Francisco: Jossey-Bass.

Kohatsu, E. L. (1997, April). *Predicting interpersonal racism among Latinos using racial identity theory.* Paper presented at the 77th annual convention of the Western Psychological Association, Seattle, WA.

Kohatsu, E. L., Dulay, M., Lam, C., Concepcion, W., Perez, P., Lopez, C., & Euler, J. (2000). Using racial identity theory to explore racial mistrust and interracial contact among Asian Americans. *Journal of Counseling and Development, 78,* 334-342.

Kohatsu, E. L., Hah, M., Lum, J., Luong, T., Soudah, C., Clemons, J., Vasquez, E., Motoike, J., & Lau, S. (1996, August). *Predicting racial mistrust between Asians and Latinos using RIT.* Poster presented at the 104th annual convention, American Psychological Association, Toronto, Canada.

Kohatsu, E. L., Lum, J., Soudah, C., Luong, T., & Hah, M. (1995, May). *Using racial identity theory as an intervention for racially motivated violence.* Paper presented at the Violence Prevention Coalition conference, Los Angeles.

L.A. County Human Relations Commission. (1989). *Hate crime in Los Angeles County in 1989: A report to the Los Angeles County Board of Supervisors.* Los Angeles: Author.

L.A. County Human Relations Commission. (1995). *Hate crime in Los Angeles County in 1995: A report to the Los Angeles County Board of Supervisors.* Los Angeles: Author.

L.A. County Human Relations Commission. (1996). *Hate crime in Los Angeles County in 1996: A report to the Los Angeles County Board of Supervisors.* Los Angeles: Author.

Liu, J. F., & Dunbar, E. (1994, August). *The experience of social group conflict for Asian-Pacifics: Relating conflict type and cultural identification to coping responses.* Paper presented at the annual convention of the Asian American Psychological Association, Los Angeles.

Loo, C. M. (1993). An integrative-sequential treatment model for posttraumatic stress disorder: A case study of the Japanese American internment and redress. *Clinical Psychology Review, 13,* 89-117.

Moore, L. V., Fried, H. J., & Costantino, A. A. (1991). Planning programs for cultural pluralism: A primer. In H. E. Cheatham & Associates (Eds.), *Cultural pluralism on campus* (pp. 117-135). Baltimore: American College Personnel Association.

Nagata, D. K. (1993). *Legacy of injustice: Exploring the cross-generational impact of the Japanese American internment.* New York: Plenum.

National Asian Pacific American Legal Consortium (NAPALC). (1993). *Audit of violence against Asian Pacific Americans: Anti-Asian violence, a national problem* (1st annual report). Washington, DC: Author.

National Asian Pacific American Legal Consortium (NAPALC). (1994). *Audit of violence against Asian Pacific Americans: Anti-Asian violence, a national problem* (2nd annual report). Washington, DC: Author.

National Asian Pacific American Legal Consortium (NAPALC). (1995). *Audit of violence against Asian Pacific Americans: Anti-Asian violence, a national problem* (3rd annual report). Washington, DC: Author.

National Asian Pacific American Legal Consortium (NAPALC). (1996). *Audit of violence against Asian Pacific Americans: Anti-Asian violence, a national problem* (4th annual report). Washington, DC: Author.

Oetting, G. R., & Beauvais, F. (1990-1991). Orthogonal cultural identification theory: The cultural identification of minority adolescents. *International Journal of the Addictions, 25,* 655-685.

Root, M. P. P. (1992). Reconstructing the impact of trauma on personality. In L. Brown & B. Ballou (Eds.), *Personality and psychopathology: Feminist reappraisals* (pp. 229-265). New York: Guilford.

Sasao, T. (1999). Campus diversity and well-being: A community psychological perspective. *Educational Studies, 41,* 61-83.

Sasao, T., & Sue, S. (1993). Toward a culturally anchored ecological framework of research in ethnic-cultural communities. *American Journal of Community Psychology, 21*(6), 761-783.

Skager, R., & Austin, G. (1994). *A statewide survey of drug use among California students in Grades 7, 9, and 11.* Sacramento, CA: Office of the Attorney General.

Skager, R., & Austin, G. (1996). *A statewide survey of drug use among California students in Grades 7, 9, and 11.* Sacramento, CA: Office of the Attorney General.

Stevenson, H. C., & Renard, G. (1993). Trusting ole' wise owls: Therapeutic use of cultural strengths in African-American families. *Professional Psychology: Research and Practice, 24,* 433-442.

Sue, D. W., & Sue, D. (1999). *Counseling the culturally different: Theory and practice* (3rd ed.). New York: John Wiley.

Sue, S., & Morishima, J. (1982). *The mental health of Asian Americans.* San Francisco: Jossey-Bass.

Sue, S., & Okazaki, S. (1990). Asian-American educational achievement: A phenomenon in search of an explanation. *American Psychologist, 45,* 913-920.

Swarts, J. L., & Martin, W. E. (Eds.). (1997). *Applied ecological psychology for schools within communities: Assessment and intervention.* Mahwah, NJ: Lawrence Erlbaum.

Tatum, B. D. (1992). Talking about race, learning about racism: The application of racial identity development theory in the classroom. *Harvard Educational Review, 62,* 1-24.

Toupin, E. S. W. A., & Son, L. (1991). Preliminary findings on Asian Americans: "The model minority" in a small private East Coast college. *Journal of Cross-Cultural Psychology, 22,* 403-417.

Trimble, J. E. (1990-1991). Ethnic specification, validation prospects, and the future of drug use research. *International Journal of the Addictions, 25*(2A), 149-170.

U.S. Commission on Civil Rights. (1992). *Civil rights issues facing Asian Americans in the 1990s.* Washington, DC: Government Printing Office.

VanBebber, L. J. (1991). Integrating diversity into traditional resident assistant courses. In H. E. Cheatham & Associates (Eds.), *Cultural pluralism on campus* (pp. 89-116). Baltimore: American College Personnel Association.

Chapter 6

American Association of University Women. (1993). *Hostile hallways: The AAUW survey on sexual harassment in America's schools.* Washington, DC: American Association of University Women Educational Foundation. (ERIC Document Reproduction Service No. ED 356 186)

Berkowitz, A. D., Burkhart, B. R., & Bourg, S. E. (1994). Research on college men and rape. In B. Berkowitz (Ed.), *Men and rape: Theory, research, and prevention in higher education* (pp. 3-19). San Francisco: Jossey-Bass.

Blumenfeld, W. J. (1992). *Homophobia: How we all pay the price.* Boston: Beacon.

Brannon, R. (1976). The male sex role: Our culture's blueprint of manhood, and what's it done for us lately. In D. S. David & R. Brannon (Eds.), *The forty-nine percent majority: The male sex role.* Reading, MA: Addison-Wesley.

Capraro, R. L. (1994). Disconnected lives: Men, masculinity, and rape prevention. In B. Berkowitz (Ed.), *Men and rape: Theory, research, and prevention in higher education* (pp. 21-33). San Francisco: Jossey-Bass.

Connell, R. W. (1995). *Masculinities.* Berkeley: University of California Press.

Creighton, A., & Kivel, P. (1990). *Teens need teens: A workbook for adults who work with high school students on dating and domestic violence prevention.* Oakland, CA: Battered Women's Alternatives.

Crum, T. F. (1987). *The magic of conflict.* New York: Touchstone.

Federal Bureau of Investigation (FBI). (1996). *Uniform Crime Reports: Crime in the United States.* Washington, DC: Author.

Finkelhor, D., Hotaling, G. T. & Yllö, K. (1988). Breaking the cycle of abuse: Relationship predictors. *Child Development, 59,* 1080-1088.

Gross, J. (1993, March 29). Where "boys will be boys," and adults are befuddled. *New York Times,* pp. A1, A13.

Groth, A. N. (1979). *Men who rape.* New York: Plenum.

Hausman, A. J., Spivak, H., & Prothrow-Stith, D. (1995). Evaluation of a community-based youth violence prevention project. *Journal of Adolescent Health, 17*(6), 353-359.

Hearn, J. (1994). The organization(s) of violence: Men, gender relations, organizations, and violences. *Human Relations, 47*(2), 731-754.

Kivel, P. (1992). *Men's work: How to stop the violence that tears our lives apart.* New York: Ballantine.

Koop, C. E., & Lundberg, G. D. (1992). Violence in America: A public health emergency. *Journal of the American Medical Association, 267*(22), 3075-3076.

Koss, M. P. (1988). Hidden rape: Sexual aggression and victimization in a national sample of students in higher education. In A. W. Burgess (Ed.), *Rape and sexual assault* (Vol. 2). New York: Garland.

Landis-Schiff, T. (1996). Sexual harassment: Why men don't understand it. *Initiatives, 57*(2), 15-25.

Lavoie, F., Vezina, L., Piche, C., & Boivin, M. (1995). Evaluation of a prevention program for violence in teen dating relationships. *Journal of Interpersonal Violence, 10*(4), 516-524.

Mead, M. (1935). *Sex and temperament in three primitive societies.* New York: McGraw-Hill.

Miedzian, M. (1991). *Boys will be boys: Breaking the link between masculinity and violence.* New York: Doubleday.

Mosher, D. L., & Sirkin, M. (1984). Measuring macho personality constellation. *Journal of Research in Personality, 18,* 150-163.

O'Neil, J. M. (1990). Assessing men's gender role conflict. In D. Moore & F. Leafgren (Eds.), *Problem solving strategies and interventions for men in conflict.* Alexandria, VA: American Association for Counseling and Development.

Paymar, M., & Pence, E. (1993). *Education groups for men who batter: The Duluth model.* New York: Springer.

Rosenberg, M. L., O'Carroll, P. W., & Powell, K. E. (1992). Let's be clear: Violence is a public health problem. *Journal of the American Medical Association, 267*(22), 3071-3072.

Sanday, P. R. (1990). *Fraternity gang rape: Sex, brotherhood, and privilege on campus.* New York: New York University Press.

Senge, P. M. (1990). *The fifth discipline.* New York: Currency Doubleday.

Shalala, D. E. (1993). Addressing the crisis of violence. *Health Affairs, 12*(4), 30-33.

Sonkin, D., Martin, D., & Walker, L. (1985). *The male batterer: A treatment approach.* New York: Springer.

Stoltenberg, D. (1989). *Refusing to be a man: Essays on sex and justice.* New York: Meridian.

West, D. J., Roy, C., & Nichols, F. L. (1978). *Understanding sexual attacks.* London: Heinemann.

Chapter 7

Becker, J. V., Skinner, L. J., Abel, G. G., & Cichon, J. (1986). Level of postassault sexual functioning in rape and incest victims. *Archives of Sexual Behavior, 15,* 37-49.

Bronfrenbrenner, U. (1977). Toward an experimental ecology of human development. *American Psychologist, 32,* 513-531.

Davis, A. Y. (1985). *Violence against women and the ongoing challenge to racism.* New York: Kitchen Table.

Davis, R. C., Brickman, E., & Baker, T. (1991). Supportive and unsupportive responses of others to rape victims: Effects on concurrent victim adjustment. *American Journal of Community Psychology, 19,* 443-451.

Davis, R. E. (1997). Trauma and addiction experiences of African American women. *Western Journal of Nursing Research, 19,* 442-465.

Foa, E. B. (1997). Trauma and women: Course, predictors, and treatment. *Journal of Clinical Psychiatry, 58*(Suppl. 9), 25-28.

Foa, E. B., & Meadows, E. A. (1997). Psychosocial treatment for posttraumatic stress disorder: A critical review. *Annual Review of Psychology, 48,* 449-480.

Foa, E. B., & Riggs, D. S. (1993). Post-traumatic stress disorder in rape victims. In J. Oldham, M. B. Riba, & A. Tasman (Eds.), *American Psychiatric Press review of psychiatry* (Vol. 12, pp. 273-303). Washington, DC: American Psychiatric Press.

Foa, E. B., & Rothbaum, B. O. (1998). *Treating the trauma of rape: Cognitive-behavioral therapy for PTSD.* New York: Guilford.

Foley, L. A., Evancic, C., Karnik, K., King, J., & Parks, A. (1995). Date rape: Effects of race of assailant and victim and gender of subjects on perceptions. *Journal of Black Psychology, 2*(1), 6-18.

Frank, E., Anderson, B., Stewart, B. D., Dancu, C., Hughes, C., & West, D. (1988). Efficacy of cognitive behavior therapy and systematic desensitization in the treatment of rape trauma. *Behavior Therapy, 19,* 403-420.

Frank, E., & Stewart, B. D. (1984). Depressive symptoms in rape victims. *Journal of Affective Disorders, 1,* 269-277.

Heppner, M. J., Good, G. E., Hillendbrand-Gunn, T. L., Hawkins, A. K., Hacquard, L. L., Nichols, R. K., Debord, K. A., & Brock, K. J. (1995). Examining sex differences in altering attitudes about rape: A test of the elaboration likelihood model. *Journal of Counseling and Development, 73,* 640-647.

Heppner, M. J., Humphrey, C. F., Hillenbrand-Gunn, T. L., & Debord, K. A. (1995). The differential effects of rape prevention programming on attitudes, behaviors and knowledge. *Journal of Counseling Psychology, 42,* 508-518.

Heppner, M. J., Neville, H. A., Smith, K., Kivlighan, D. M., & Gershuny, B. S. (1999). Examining immediate and long-term efficacy of rape prevention programming with racially diverse college men. *Journal of Counseling Psychology, 46,* 16-26.

Jones, R. L., Winkler, M. X., Kacin, E., Salloway, W. N., & Weissman, M. (1998). Community-based sexual offender treatment for inner-city African American Latino youth. In W. L. Marshall, Y. M. Fernandez, S. M. Hudson, & T. Ward (Eds.), *Sourcebook of treatment programs for sexual offenders* (pp. 457-476). New York: Plenum.

Kessler, R. C., Sonnega, A., Bromet, E., Hughes, M., & Nelson, C. B. (1995). Posttraumatic stress disorder in the National Comorbidity Survey. *Archives of General Psychiatry, 52,* 1048-1060.

Kilpatrick, D. G., Edmunds, C. N., & Seymour, A. K. (1992). *Rape in America: A report to the nation.* Arlington, VA: National Victim Center.

Kilpatrick, D. G., Veronen, L. J., & Resick, P. A. (1982). Psychological sequelae to rape: Assessment and treatment strategies. In D. M. Doleys, R. L. Meredith, & A. R. Ciminero (Eds.), *Behavioral medicine: Assessment and treatment strategies* (pp. 473-497). New York: Plenum.

Koss, M. P. (1993). Rape: Scope, impact, interventions, and policy responses. *American Psychologist, 48,* 1062-1069.

Koss, M. P., Gidyez, C. A., & Wisniewski, N. (1987). The scope of rape: Incidence and prevalence of sexual aggression and victimization in a national sample of higher education students. *Journal of Consulting and Clinical Psychology, 55,* 162-170.

McNair, L. D., & Neville, H. A. (1996). African American women survivors of sexual assault: The intersection of race and class. *Women and Therapy, 18,* 107-118.

Morelli, P. (1981). *Comparison of the psychological recovery of Black and White victims of rape.* Paper presented at the annual Convention of the Association for Women in Psychology, Boston.

Moss, M., Frank, E., & Anderson, B. (1990). The effects of marital status and partner support on rape trauma. *American Journal of Orthopsychiatry, 60,* 379-391.

Neville, H. A., & Clark, M. (1997). *Postsexual assault processes: An investigation of general and culture-specific factors among Black and White college students.* Unpublished manuscript, University of Missouri–Columbia.

Neville, H. A., & Heppner, M. J. (1999). Contextualizing rape: Reviewing sequelae and proposing a culturally inclusive ecological model of sexual assault recovery. *Applied and Preventive Psychology, 8,* 41-62.

Neville, H. A., Heppner, M. J., Oh, E., Spanierman, L. B., & Clark, M. (2002). *General and cultural factors influencing Black and White college students' recovery from rape.* Manuscript submitted for publication.

Neville, H. A., & Pugh, A. O. (1997). General and culture-specific factors influencing African American women's reporting patterns and perceived social support following sexual assault: An exploratory investigation. *Violence Against Women, 3,* 361-381.

Petty, R. E., & Cacioppo, J. T. (1986). *Communication an persuasion: Central and peripheral routes to attitude change.* New York: Springer.

Pierce-Baker, C. (1998). *Surviving the silence: Black women's stories of rape.* New York: Norton.

Resick, P. A., & Schnicke, M. K. (1993). *Cognitive processing therapy for rape victims: A treatment manual.* Newbury Park, CA: Sage.

Resick, P. A., Jordan, C. G., Girelli, S. A., Hutter, C. K., & Marhoefer-Dvorak, S. (1988). A comparative outcome study of behavioral group therapy for sexual assault victims. *Behavior Therapy, 1*(9), 385-401.

Rothbaum, B. O. (1997). A controlled study of eye movement desensitization and reprocessing in the treatment of posttraumatic stress disordered sexual assault victims. *Bulletin of the Menniger Clinic, 61,* 317-334.

Rothbaum, B. O., & Foa, E. B. (1996). Cognitive-behavioral therapy for posttraumatic stress disorder. In B. A. van der Kolk, A. C. McFarlane, & L. Weisaeth (Eds.), *Traumatic stress: The effects of overwhelming experience on mind, body, and society* (pp. 491-509). New York: Guilford.

Rothbaum, B. O., Foa, E. B., Riggs, D. S., Murdock, T., & Walsh, W. (1992). A prospective examination of post-traumatic stress disorder in rape victims. *Journal of Traumatic Stress, 5,* 455-475.

Shapiro, F. (1989). Efficacy of the eye movement desensitization procedure in the treatment of traumatic memories. *Journal of Traumatic Stress, 2,* 199-223.

Sorenson, S. B. (1996). Violence against women: Examining ethnic differences and commonalties. *Evaluation Review, 20,* 123-145.

Sue, D. W., Ivey, A., & Pedersen, P. (1996). *A theory of multicultural counseling and therapy.* Pacific Grove, CA: Brooks/Cole.

Ullman, S. E. (1996). Social reactions, coping strategies, and self-blame attributions in adjustment to sexual assault. *Psychology of Women Quarterly, 20,* 505-526.

White, A. M., Strube, M. J., & Fisher, S. (1998). A Black feminist model of rape myth acceptance: Implications for research and antirape advocacy in Black communities. *Psychology of Women Quarterly, 22,* 157-175.

White, D. G. (1985). *Ar'n't I a woman? Female slaves in the plantation South.* New York: Norton.

Williams, J. E., & Holmes, K. A. (1982). In judgment of victims: The social context of rape. *Journal of Sociology and Social Welfare, 9,* 154-169.

Winefield, I., George, L. K., Schwartz, M., & Blazer, D. G. (1990). Sexual assault and psychiatric disorders among a community sample of women. *American Journal of Psychiatry, 147,* 335-341.

Wingood, G. M., & DiClemente, R. J. (1998). Rape among African American women: Sexual, psychological, and social correlates predisposing survivors to risk of STD/HIV. *Journal of Women's Health, 7,* 77-84.

Wolpe, J. (1958). *Psychotherapy by reciprocal inhibition.* Stanford, CA: Stanford University Press.

Wyatt, G. E. (1992). The sociocultural context of African American and White American women's rape. *Journal of Social Issues, 48,* 77-92.

Chapter 8

Banks, J. A. (1993). The Canon debate, knowledge construction, and multicultural education. *Educational Researcher, 22,* 8-14.

Ben-Zeev, S. (1977). The influence of bilingualism on cognitive strategy and cognitive development. *Child Development, 48,* 1009-1018.

Bialystok, E. (1987). Words as things: Development of word concept by bilingual children. *Studies in Second Language Learning, 9,* 133-140.

Bialystok, E. (1992). Selective attention in cognitive processing: The bilingual edge. In R. J. Harris (Ed.), *Cognitive processing in bilinguals.* Amsterdam: North Holland.

Bourdieu, P. (1991). *Language and symbolic power.* Cambridge, UK: Polity.

Brisk, M. E. (1998). *Bilingual education: From compensatory to quality schooling.* Mahwah, NJ: Lawrence Erlbaum.

Campbell, D. (1988). Collaboration and contradiction in research and staff development project. *Teachers College Record, 90,* 85-98.

Castañeda v. Pickard, 648 F. 2nd 989 (5th Cir. 1981)

Daarder, A. (1991). *Culture and power in the classroom: A critical foundation for bicultural education.* West Port, CO: Bergin & Garvey.

Fanon, F. (1966). *The wretched of the earth.* New York: Grove.

Freire, P. (1970). *Cultural action for freedom.* Cambridge, MA: Harvard Educational Review.

Garcia, H. (1998). Bilingual education and the politics of teacher preparation. *Cultural Circles, 2,* 75-90.

Genesee, F., Tucker, G. R., & Lambert, W. E. (1975). Communication skills in bilingual children. *Child Development, 46,* 1010-1014.

Gibbons, P. (1993). *Learning to learn in a second language.* Portsmouth, NH: Heinemann.

Gonzalez, N. (1995). The funds of knowledge for teaching project. *Practicing Anthropology, 17*(3), 3-6.

Griego-Jones, T. (1994). Assessing students' perceptions of biliteracy in a two-way bilingual classroom. *Journal of Educational Issues of Language Minority Students, 13,* 79-93.

Habermas, J. (1984). *The critical theory of Jürgen Habermas* (T. McCarthy, Ed.). Cambridge, UK: Polity.

Hakuta, K., & Diaz, R. (1984). The relationship between bilingualism and cognitive ability: A critical discussion and some new longitudinal data. In K. E. Nelson (Ed.), *Children's language* (Vol. 5, pp. 319-344). Hillsdale, NJ: Lawrence Erlbaum.

Haselkorn, D., & Calkins, A. (1993). *Careers in teaching handbook.* Belmont, MA: The Recruiting New Teachers, Inc.

Lemberger, N. (1997). *Bilingual education: Teachers' narratives.* Mahwah, NJ: Lawrence Erlbaum.

Mercado, C. I., & Moll, L. C. (1997). The study of funds of knowledge: Collaborative research in Latino homes. *CENTRO Journal of the Center for Puerto Rican Studies, 9* (9), 26-42.

National Commission on Teaching and America's Future. (1996). *What matters most: Teaching for America's future.* New York: Author.

New York State Board of Regents and the New York State Education Department. (1998). *New York's commitment: Teaching to higher standards.* Albany, NY: Author.

Perez, B., & Torres-Guzman, M. E. (1998, April). *Access to language and literacy in two-way bilingual programs.* Paper presented at the annual meeting of the American Educational Research Association, San Diego, CA.

Ramirez, J. D., Yuen, S. D., & Ramey, D. R. (1991). *Executive summary, final report: Longitudinal study of structured English immersion strategy, early-exit and late-exit transitional bilingual education programs for language minority children* (U.S. Department of Education Contract No. 300-87-0156). San Mateo, CA: Aguirre International.

Recruiting New Teachers, Inc., Council of the Great City Schools, and Council of the Great City Colleges of Education. (2000). *The urban teacher challenge: Teacher demand and supply in the Great City Schools* [Online]. Available: www.cgcs. org/reports/2000/RNT-0101.pdf

Rosaldo, R. (1989). *Culture of truth: The remaking of social analysis*. Boston: Beacon.

Shannon, S. M., & Escamilla, K. (1997). *Mexican immigrants in U. S. schools: Targets of symbolic violence*. Manuscript submitted for publication.

Skutnabb-Kangas, T. (1991). Multilingualism and the education of minority children. In O. Garcia & C. Baker (Eds.), *Policy and practice in bilingual education: Extending the foundations*. Bristol, PA: Multilingual Matters.

Thomas, W. P., & Collier, V. (1997). *School effectiveness for language minority students* (NCBE Resource Collection Series No. 9). Washington, DC: National Clearinghouse for Bilingual Education.

Torres-Guzman, M. E. (1992). Stories of hope in the midst of despair: Culturally responsive education for Latino students in an alternative high school in New York City. In M. Saravia-Shore & S. F. Arvizu (Eds.), *Cross-cultural literacy: Ethnographies of communication in multiethnic classrooms* (pp. 477-490). New York: Garland.

Torres-Guzman, M. E. (1998). Language, culture, and literacy in Puerto Rican communities. In B. Perez (Ed.), *Literacy in diverse communities*. Hillsdale, NJ: Lawrence Erlbaum.

Wallace, B. C. (1993). Cross-cultural counseling with the chemically dependent: Preparing for service delivery within our culture of violence. *Journal of Psychoactive Drugs, 24*(3), 9-20.

Chapter 9

Anderson, L. P. (1991). Acculturative stress theory of relevance to Black Americans. *Clinical Psychology Review, 11*, 685-702.

Centers for Disease Control and Prevention (CDC). (1992). Behaviors related to unintentional and intentional injuries among high school students—United States, 1991. *MMWR, 41*, 760-765, 771-772.

Cotton, N., Resnick J., Browne, D., Martin, S., McCarraher, D., & Woods, J. (1994). Aggression and fighting behavior among African-American adolescents: Individual and family factors. *American Journal of Public Health, 84*(4), 618-622.

Cristoffel, K. K. (1990). Violent death and injury in U.S. children and adolescents. *American Journal of Disadvantaged Children, 144*(6), 697-706.

DuRant, R. H., Cadenhead, C., Pendergrast, R. A., Slavents, G., & Linder, C. W. (1994). Factors associated with the use of violence among Black adolescents. *American Journal of Public Health, 84*(4), 612-617.

Eron, L. D., Gentry, J. H., & Schlegel, P. (Eds.). (1994). *Reason to hope: A psychosocial perspective on violence and youth*. Washington, DC: American Psychological Association.

Eron, L. D., & Slaby, R. G. (1994). Introduction. In L. D. Eron, J. H. Gentry, & P. Schlegel (Eds.), *Reason to hope: A psychosocial perspective on violence and youth* (pp. 1-22). Washington, DC: American Psychological Association.

Fitzpatrick, K. M., & Boldizar, J. P. (1993). The prevalence and consequences of exposure to violence among African-American youth. *Journal of American Academy of Child and Adolescent Psychiatry, 32*(2), 424-430.

Folkman, S., & Lazarus, R. (1985). If it changes, it must be a process: A study of emotion and coping during three stages of a college examination. *Journal of Personality and Social Psychology, 48,* 150-170.

Folkman, S., Lazarus, R., Dunkel-Schetter, C., Delongis, A., & Gruen, R. (1986). Dynamics of a stressful encounter: Cognitive appraisal, coping, and encounter outcomes. *Journal of Personality and Social Psychology, 50*(5), 992-1003.

Gibbs, J. T., Brunswick, A., Connor, M., Dembo, R., Larson, T., Reed, R., & Solomon, B. (Eds.). (1989). *Young, Black and male in America: An endangered species.* New York: Auburn House.

Gladstein, J., Rusonis, E., & Heald, F. (1992). A comparison of inner-city and upper-middle class youths' exposure to violence. *Journal of Adolescent Health, 13,* 275-280.

Gorski, J., & Pilotto, L. (1993). Interpersonal violence among youth: A challenge for school personnel. *Educational Psychology Review, 5,* 35-61.

Guerra, N. G., Tolan, P. H., & Hammond, W. R. (1994). Prevention and treatment of adolescent violence. In L. D. Eron, J. H. Gentry, & P. Schlegel (Eds.), *Reason to hope: A psychosocial perspective on violence and youth* (pp. 383-403). Washington, DC: American Psychological Association.

Hammond, W. R., & Yung, B. (1993). Psychology's role in the public health response to assaultive violence among young African-American men. *American Psychologist, 48*(2), 142-154.

Hammond, W. R., & Yung, B. R. (1994). African Americans. In L. D. Eron, J. H. Gentry, & P. Schlegel (Eds.), *Reason to hope: A psychosocial perspective on violence and youth* (pp. 105-118). Washington, DC: American Psychological Association.

Jenkins, P. (1995). Threads that link community and family violence: Issues for prevention. In T. Gullotta, R. Hampton, & P. Jenkins (Eds.), *When anger governs: Preventing violence in America* (pp. 33-45). Thousand Oaks, CA: Sage.

Lazarus, R. S. (1966). *Psychological stress and the coping process.* New York: McGraw-Hill.

Lazarus, R. S., Averill, J. R., & Opton, E. M., Jr. (1974). The psychology of coping: Issues of research and assessment. In G. V. Coeho, D. A. Hamburg, & J. E. Adams (Eds.), *Coping and adaptation* (pp. 249-315). New York: Basic Books.

Lazarus, R. S., & Folkman, S. (1984). *Stress appraisal and coping.* New York: Springer.

Mancini, J. K. (1980). *Strategic styles: Coping in the inner city.* Hanover, NH: University Press of New England.

Menacker, J., Weldon, W., & Hurwitz, E. (1990). Community influences on school crime and violence. *Urban Education, 25,* 68-80.

Metropolitan Life Insurance. (1999). *Violence in America's public schools: Five years later.* New York: Louis Harris and Associates.

Myers, H. F. (1989). Urban stress and mental health in Black youth: An epidemiological and conceptual update. In R. Jones (Ed.), *Black adolescents* (pp. 123-152). Berkeley, CA: Cobbs & Henry.

Myers, H. F., & King, L. M. (1980). Youth of the Black underclass: Urban stress and mental health. *Fanon Center Journal, 1*(1), 1-27.

Oliver, W. (1994). *The violent social world of Black men.* San Francisco: Jossey-Bass.

Rode, P., & Bellfield, K. (1992). *The next generation: The health and well being of young people of color in the Twin Cities*. Minneapolis: Urban Coalition of Minneapolis.

Schubiner, H., Scott, R., & Tzelepis, A. (1993). Exposure to violence among inner-city youth. *Journal of Adolescent Health, 14*, 214-219.

Shakoor, B. H., & Chalmers, D. (1991). Co-victimization of African-American children who witness violence: Effects on cognitive, emotional and behavioral development. *Journal of the National Medical Association, 83*(3), 233-238.

Sheley, J., McGee, Z., & Wright, J. (1992). Gun-related violence in and around inner city schools. *American Journal of Diseases of Childhood, 146*, 677-682.

Vitaliano, P. P., Russo, J., Carr, J., Maiuro, R. D., & Becker, J. (1985). The Ways of Coping Checklist: Revision and psychometric properties. *Multivariate Behavioral Research, 20*, 3-26.

Yung, B. R., & Hammond, W. R. (1998). Breaking the cycle: A culturally sensitive violence prevention program for African-American children and adolescents. In J. R. Lutzker (Ed.), *Handbook of child abuse research and treatment* (pp. 319-340). New York: Plenum.

Chapter 10

Aber, J. L., Brown, J., & Henrich, C. C. (1999). *Teaching conflict resolution: An effective school-based approach to violence prevention*. New York: National Center for Children in Poverty.

American Arbitration Association, American Bar Association, and Society of Professionals in Dispute Resolution. (1995). *Model standards of conduct for mediators*. Washington, DC: Author.

Anderson, E. (1998). The social ecology of youth violence. In M. Tonry & M. Moore (Eds.), *Youth violence* (pp. 65-104). Chicago: University of Chicago Press.

Avakame, E. (1998). How different is violence in the home? An examination of some correlates of stranger and intimate homicide. *Criminology, 36*(3), 601-632.

Bodine, R., & Crawford, D. (1998). *The handbook of conflict resolution education: A guide to building quality programs in schools*. San Francisco: Jossey-Bass.

Bruce, M. (2000). Violence among African Americans: A conceptual assessment of potential explanations. *Journal of Contemporary Criminal Justice, 16*(2), 171-193.

Bursik, R., & Grasmik, H. (1993). *Neighborhoods and crime*. New York: Lexington Books.

Bush, R. A. B., & Folger, J. (1994). *The promise of mediation: Responding to conflict through empowerment and recognition*. San Francisco: Jossey-Bass.

Coie, J. D., & Dodge, K. A. (1998). The development of aggression and antisocial behavior. In W. V. Damon & N. Eisenberg (Eds.), *Handbook of child psychology: Vol. 3. Social, emotional, and personality development* (5th ed., pp. 779-861). New York: John Wiley.

Cook, P., & Laub, J. (1998). The unprecedented epidemic in youth violence. In M. Tonry & M. Moore (Eds.), *Youth violence* (pp. 27-64). Chicago: University of Chicago Press.

Crawford, D., & Bodine, R. (1996, October). *Conflict resolution education: A guide to implementing programs in schools, youth-serving organizations, and community and juvenile justice settings*. Washington, DC: U.S. Department of Justice, Office of Juvenile Justice and Delinquency Prevention, and U.S. Department of Education, Safe and Drug-Free Schools Program.

Curhan, J. (Ed.). (1996). *Young negotiators: Teachers' manual.* Cambridge, UK: Program for Young Negotiators, Inc.

Decker, S. (1996). Deviant homicide: A new look at the role of motives and victim-offender relationships. *Journal of Research in Crime and Delinquency, 33*(4), 427-449.

Dupper, D., & Bosch, L. (1996). Reasons for school suspensions: An examination of data from one school district and recommendations for reducing suspensions. *Journal for a Just and Caring Education, 2,* 140-150.

Fagan, J. (1998, January). Adolescent violence: A view from the street. In *NIJ research preview* (pp. 1-2). Washington, DC: U.S. Department of Justice: Office of Justice Programs.

Fagan, J., & Wilkinson, D. L. (1998). Guns, youth violence, and social identity in inner cities. In M. Tonry & M. Moore (Eds.), *Youth violence* (pp. 105-188). Chicago: University of Chicago Press.

Farrington, J. (1998). Predictors, causes, and correlates of male youth violence. In M. Tonry & M. Moore (Eds.), *Youth violence* (pp. 421-475). Chicago: University of Chicago Press.

Federal Bureau of Investigation (FBI). (1998). *Crime in the United States: Uniform crime reports.* Washington, DC: U.S. Department of Justice.

Felson, R., & Messner, S. (1998). Disentangling the effects of gender & intimacy on victim precipitation in homicide. *Criminology, 36*(2), 405-424.

Filner, J. (1998). Foreword. In R. Bodine & D. Crawford, *The handbook of conflict resolution education* (pp. xiii-xvi). San Francisco: Jossey-Bass.

Fisher, R., & Ury, W. (with Patton, B.) (Eds.) (1991). *Getting to yes: Negotiating agreement without giving in* (2nd ed.). New York: Penguin.

Hagedorn, J. (1998). Gang violence in the postindustrial era. In M. Tonry & M. Moore (Eds.), *Youth violence* (pp. 365-419). Chicago: University of Chicago Press.

Hechinger, F. (1994). Saving youth from violence. *Carnegie Quarterly, 39*(1), 1-5.

Jones, T. S., & Bodtker, A. M. (1999). Conflict education in a special needs population. *Mediation Quarterly, 17*(2), 109-124.

Jones-Brown, D. (1996). Race and legal socialization. *Dissertation Abstracts International, 57*(11A), 4942. (UMI No. 9711474)

Jones-Brown, D. (2000). Debunking the myth of Officer Friendly: How African American males experience community policing. *Journal of Contemporary Criminal Justice, 16*(2), 209-229.

Lam, J. A. (1989). *The impact of conflict resolution programs on schools: A review and synthesis of the evidence.* Amherst, MA: National Association for Mediation in Education.

Lattimore, P., Linster, R., & MacDonald, J. (1997). Risk of death among serious young offenders. *Journal of Research in Crime and Delinquency, 34*(2), 187-209.

LeBoeuf, D., & Delany-Shabazz, R. V. (1997, March). *Conflict resolution fact sheet.* Washington, DC: Office of Juvenile Justice and Delinquency Prevention.

Lindsay, P. (1998). Conflict resolution and peer mediation in public schools: What works? *Mediation Quarterly, 16*(1), 85-99.

Markowitz, F., & Felson, R. (1998). Social-demographic attitudes and violence. *Criminology, 36*(1), 117-138.

Massey, S. (1994, February 2). Schools find pupil mediators cut violence. *Wall Street Journal,* p. 1.

Messerschmidt, J. (1993). *Masculinities and crime.* Lanham, MD: Roman & Littlefield.

Nakkula, M., & Nikitopoulos, C. (1996). *Preliminary evaluation findings for the fall 1995 implementation of the Program for Young Negotiators.* Cambridge, MA: Graduate School of Education, Harvard University.

Office of Juvenile Justice and Delinquency Prevention (OJJDP). (1999, July). *Report to Congress on juvenile violence research*. Washington, DC: U.S. Department of Justice.

Poe-Yamagata, E., & Jones, M. (2000). *And justice for some*. Washington, DC: Youth Law Center.

Rafky, D., & Sealey, R. (1975). The adolescent and the law: A survey. *Journal of Crime and Delinquency, 21*(2), 131-137.

Raiffa, H. (1982). *The art and science of negotiation: How to resolve conflict and get the best out of bargaining*. Cambridge, MA: Harvard University Press.

Riskin, L. (1996). Understanding mediators' orientations, strategies, and techniques: A grid for the perplexed. *Harvard Negotiation Law Review, 1*(7).

Rusinko, W., Johnson, K., & Hornung, C. (1978). The importance of police contact in the formulation of youths' attitudes toward police. *Journal of Criminal Justice, 6*, 53-67.

Sampson, R. (1986a). Crimes and cities: The effects of formal and informal social control. In A. Reiss Jr. & M. Tonry (Eds.), *Communities and crimes* (pp. 271-311). Chicago: University of Chicago Press.

Sampson, R. (1986b). Neighborhood family structure and the risk of personal victimization. In J. Byrne & R. Sampson (Eds.), *The social ecology of crime* (pp. 25-46). New York: Springer-Verlag.

Sampson, R., & Groves, W. B. (1989). Community structure and crime: Testing social disorganization theory. *American Journal of Sociology, 94*, 774-802.

Sampson, R., & Wilson, W. J. (1995). *Toward a theory of race, crime and urban inequality in crime and inequality*. Stanford, CA: Stanford University Press.

Shure, M. (1999). *Preventing violence the problem-solving way*. Washington, DC: U.S. Department of Justice, Office of Justice Programs, Office of Juvenile Justice and Delinquency Prevention.

Snyder, H. (1999, December). *Juvenile arrests 1998*. Washington, DC: U.S. Department of Justice, Office of Justice Programs, Office of Juvenile Justice and Delinquency Prevention.

Snyder, H., & Sickmund, M. (1995). *Juvenile offenders and victims: A focus on violence* (Statistics summary). Washington, DC: U.S. Department of Justice, Office of Juvenile Justice and Delinquency Prevention, National Center for Juvenile Justice.

Snyder, H., Sickmund, M., & Poe-Yamagata, E. (1996). *Juvenile offenders and victims: 1996 update on violence*. Washington, DC: U.S. Department of Justice, Office of Justice Programs, Office of Juvenile Justice and Delinquency Prevention.

Tonry, M., & Moore, M. (Eds.). (1998). *Youth violence*. Chicago: University of Chicago Press.

Wolfgang, M., & Ferracuti, F. (1967). *The subculture of violence: Toward an integrated theory of criminology*. London: Tavistock.

Yarn, D. (1999). *Dictionary of conflict resolution*. San Francisco: Jossey-Bass.

Youth in Action. (2000, March). *Want to resolve a dispute? Try mediation*. Washington, DC: Office of Juvenile Justice and Delinquency Prevention.

Zimring, F. (1998). *American youth violence*. New York: Oxford University Press.

Chapter 11

Allodi, F. A. (1991). Assessment and treatment of torture victims: A critical review. *Journal of Nervous and Mental Disease, 179*, 4-11.

American Psychiatric Association. (1994). *Diagnostic and statistical manual of mental disorders* (4th ed.). Washington, DC: Author.

Astron, C., Lunde, I., Ortmann, J., Boysen, G., & Trojaberg, L. (1989). Sleep disturbances in torture survivors. *Acta Neurologica Scandanavica, 79,* 150-154.

Basoglu, M. (Ed.). (1992). *Torture and its consequences: Current treatment approaches.* Cambridge, UK: Cambridge University Press.

Basoglu, M., & Mineka, S. (1992). The role of uncontrollable and unpredictable stress in post-traumatic stress responses in torture survivors. In M. Basoglu (Ed.), *Torture and its consequences: Current treatment approaches* (pp. 182-225). Cambridge, UK: Cambridge University Press.

Basoglu, M., & Paker, M. (1995). Severity of trauma as predictor of long-term psychological status in survivors of torture. *Journal of Anxiety Disorders, 9,* 339-550.

Browde, S. (1988). The treatment of detainees. In *Proceedings of the 1987 National Medical & Dental Association (NAMDA) annual conference.* Cape Town, South Africa: NAMDA.

Cathcart, I. M., Berger, P., & Knazan, B. (1979). Medical examination of torture victims applying for refugee status. *Canadian Medical Association Journal, 121,* 179-184.

Cienfuegos, J. A., & Monelli, C. (1981). The testimony of political repression as a therapeutic instrument. *American Journal of Orthopsychiatry, 53,* 43-51.

Dowdall, T. (1992). Torture and the helping professions in South Africa. In M. Basoglu (Ed.), *Torture and its consequences: Current treatment approaches* (pp. 452-471). Cambridge, UK: Cambridge University Press.

Fischman, Y., & Ross, J. (1990). Group treatment of exiled survivors of torture. *American Journal of Orthopsychiatry, 60,* 135-142.

Foster, D. H. (1989). Political detention in South Africa: A sociopsychological perspective. *International Journal of Mental Health, 18,* 21-37.

Foster, D., Davis, D., & Sandler, D. (1987). *Detention and torture in South Africa: Psychological, legal and historical studies.* New York: St. Martin's.

Friedlander, R. (1986). *Stress disorders in former detainees in South Africa.* Paper presented at the World Psychiatric Association Regional Symposium, Copenhagen.

Gibson, K. (1989). Children in political violence. *Social Science and Medicine, 28,* 659-667.

Kastrup, M., Genefke, I. K., Lunde, I., & Ortmann, J. (1988). Coping with exposure to torture. *Contemporary Family Therapy, 10,* 280-287.

Kastrup, M., & Vesti, P. (1995). Treatment of torture survivors: Psychosocial and somatic aspects. In J. R. Freedy & S. E. Hobfoll (Eds.), *Traumatic stress: From theory to practice* (pp. 339-363). New York: Plenum.

Lunde, I., & Ortmann, J. (1992). Sexual torture and the treatment of its consequences. In M. Basoglu (Ed.), *Torture and its consequences: Current treatment approaches* (pp. 310-329). Cambridge, UK: Cambridge University Press.

Meichenbaum, D. (1985). *Stress inoculation training.* New York: Pergamon.

Mollica, R. F., & Caspi-Yavin, Y. (1991). Measuring torture and torture-related symptoms. *Psychological assessment: A Journal of Consulting and Clinical Psychology, 3,* 581-587.

Mollica, R. F., & Caspi-Yavin, Y. (1992). Overview: The assessment and diagnosis of torture events and symptoms. In M. Basoglu (Ed.), *Torture and its consequences: Current treatment approaches.* Cambridge, UK: Cambridge University Press.

Mollica, R. F., Caspi-Yavin, Y., Bollini, P., Truong, T., Tor, S., & Lavelle, J. (1992). The Harvard Trauma Questionnaire: Validating a cross-cultural instrument for measuring torture, trauma, and post-traumatic stress disorder in Indochinese refugees. *Journal of Nervous and Mental Disease, 180,* 111-116.

Mollica, R. F., Wyshak, G., & Lavelle, J. (1987). The psychosocial impact of war trauma and torture on Southeast Asian refugees. *American Journal of Psychiatry, 144,* 1567-1572.

Ortmann, J., & Lunde, I. (1988, August). *Changed identity, low self-esteem, depression, and anxiety in 148 torture victims treated at the RCT: Relation to sexual torture.* Paper presented at the WHO Workshop on Health Situation of Refugees and Victims of Organized Violence, World Health Organization, Gothenburg, Sweden.

Paker, M., Paker, O., & Yuksel, S. (1992). Psychosocial effects of torture: An empirical study of tortured and non-tortured political prisoners. In M. Basoglu (Ed.), *Torture and its consequences: Current treatment approaches* (pp. 72-82). Cambridge, UK: Cambridge University Press.

Priebe, S., & Bauer, M. (1995). Inclusion of psychological torture in PTSD criterion A. *American Journal of Psychiatry, 152,* 1691-1692.

Ritterman, M. (1987). Torture: The counter-therapy of the state. *Family Therapy Network, 11,* 43-47.

Saporta, J. A., & van der Kolk, B. A. (1992). Psychobiological consequences of severe trauma. In M. Basoglu (Ed.), *Torture and its consequences: Current treatment approaches* (pp. 151-181). Cambridge, UK: Cambridge University Press.

Seligman, M. (1975). *Helplessness: On depression, development, and death.* San Francisco: Freeman.

Simpson, M. (1993). Traumatic stress and the bruising of the soul: The effects of torture and coercive interrogation. In J. P. Wilson & B. Raphael (Eds.), *International handbook of traumatic stress syndromes.* New York: Plenum.

Simpson, M. (1995). What went wrong? Diagnostic and ethical problems in dealing with the effects of torture and repression in South Africa. In R. J. Kleber, C. R. Figley, & B. P. R. Gersons (Eds.), *Beyond trauma: Cultural and societal dynamics.* New York: Plenum.

Solomons, K. (1989). The dynamics of post-traumatic stress disorder in South African political detainees. *American Journal of Psychotherapy, 43,* 208-217.

Somnier, F. E., & Genefke, I. K. (1986). Psychotherapy for victims of torture. *British Journal of Psychiatry, 149,* 323-329.

Stover, E., & Nightingale, E. (1985). *The breaking of bodies and minds.* New York: Freeman.

Suedfeld, P. (1990). *Psychology and torture.* New York: Hemisphere.

Taiana, C. (1993). Confession and its twin, torture: Re-thinking the therapeutic alliance. In I. Lubek, R. van Hezewijk, & G. Tolman (Eds.), *Trends and issues in theoretical psychology.* Chateau de Bierville, France: Springer.

Tajfel, H. (1978). *Differentiation between social groups.* London: Academic Press.

Tulving, E. (1983). *Elements of episodic memory.* New York: Oxford University Press.

Turner, S., & Gorst-Unsworth, C. (1990). Psychological sequelae of torture: A descriptive model. *British Journal of Psychiatry, 157,* 475-480.

Turner, S. W., & Hough, A. (1993). Hyperventilation as a reaction to torture. In J. P. Wilson & B. Raphael (Eds.), *International handbook of traumatic stress syndromes.* New York: Plenum.

United Nations. (1985). *United Nations Convention Against Torture and Other Cruel, Inhuman or Degrading Treatment or Punishment,* G.A. Res. 39, GAOR Suppl. (No. 51) at 197, U.N. Doc. A/39/51.

Whittaker, S. R. (1988). Counselling torture victims. *The Counseling Psychologist, 16*(2): 272-278.

Chapter 12

Afigbo, A., Ayandele, E., Gavin, R., Omer-Cooper, J., & Palmer, R. (1986a). *The making of modern Africa: Vol. 1. The nineteenth century.* Essex, UK: Longman.

Afigbo, A., Ayandele, E., Gavin, R., Omer-Cooper, J., & Palmer, R. (1986b). *The making of modern Africa: Vol. 2. The twentieth century*. Essex, UK: Longman.

Akinsulure-Smith, A., & Smith, H. (1997, February). *Africans in America: Cultural and environmental considerations for psychotherapy*. Symposium conducted at the 14th annual Teachers College Winter Roundtable on Cross-Cultural Psychology and Education, Teachers College, Columbia University, New York.

Akinsulure-Smith, A., Smith, H., & Van Harte, E. (1997, April). *Psychotherapy with Africans in America*. Symposium conducted at Perspectives on Black Psychology: Past, Present, and Future, Pace University, New York.

American Psychiatric Association. (1994). *Diagnostic and statistical manual for mental disorders* (4th ed.). Washington, DC: Author.

Chester, B., & Holtan, N. (1992). Working with refugee survivors of torture. *Western Journal of Medicine, 157*, 301-304.

Comas-Diaz, L., Lykes, M., & Alarcon, R. (1998). Ethnic conflict and the psychology of liberation in Guatemala, Peru, and Puerto Rico. *American Psychologist, 53*, 778-792.

Elsass, P. (1997). *Treating victims of torture and violence: Theoretical, cross-cultural, and clinical implications*. New York: New York University Press.

Fischman, Y. (1998). Metaclinical issues in the treatment of psychopolitical trauma. *American Journal of Orthopsychiatry, 68*(1), 27-38.

Fischman, Y., & Ross, J. (1990). Group treatment of exiled survivors of torture. *American Journal of Orthopsychiatry, 60*(1), 135-142.

Goldfield, A., Mollica, R., Pesavento, B., & Faraone, S. (1988). The physical and psychological sequelae of torture: Symptomatology and diagnosis. *Journal of the American Medical Association, 259*(18), 2725-2729.

Gurris, N. (2001). Psychic trauma through torture: Healing through psychotherapy? In S. Graesner & N. Gurris (Eds.), *Standing at the side of torture survivors: Treating a terrible assault on human dignity* (pp. 29-56). Baltimore: Johns Hopkins University Press.

Herman, J. L. (1992). *Trauma and recovery: The aftermath of violence—From domestic abuse to political terror*. New York: Basic Books.

Keller, A., Eisenman, D., & Saul, J. (1996). *Bellevue/NYU Human Rights Clinic in-service training*. New York: Bellevue Hospital.

Mollica, R., Sarajlic, N., Chernoff, M., Lavelle, J., Vukovic, I. & Massagli, M. (2001). Longitudinal study of psychiatric symptoms, disability, mortality, and emigration among Bosnian refugees. *Journal of the American Medical Association, 286*(5), 546-554.

Randall, G. & Lutz, E. (1991). *Serving survivors of torture*. Washington, DC: Association for the Advancement of Science.

Renner, M. (1996). *Fighting for survival: Environmental decline, social conflict, and the new age of insecurity*. New York: Norton.

Silove, D., Tarn, R., Bowles, R., & Reid, J. (1991). Psychosocial needs of torture survivors. *Australian and New Zealand Journal of Psychiatry, 25*, 481-490.

Somnier, F., & Genefke, I. (1986). Psychotherapy for victims of torture. *British Journal of Psychiatry, 149*, 323-329.

Straker, G. (1987). The continuous traumatic stress syndrome: The single therapeutic interview. *Psychology in Society, 8*, 48-78.

United Nations High Commissioner for Refugees (UNHCR). (1995). *The state of the world's refugees, 1995*. New York: Oxford University Press.

United States Committee for Refugees. (2000). *World Refugee Survey*. Washington, DC: Author.

Vesti, P., & Kastrup, M. (1991). Psychotherapy for torture survivors. In M. Basoglu (Ed.), *Torture and its consequences: Current treatment approaches* (pp. 349-362). Cambridge, UK: Cambridge University Press.

Yehuda, R. & McFarlane, A. C. (1995). Conflict between current knowledge about posttraumatic stress disorder and its original conceptual basis. *American Journal of Psychiatry, 152*(12), 1705-1713.

Zohar, J., Sasson, Y., Amital, D., Iancu, I., & Zinger, Y. (1998). Current diagnostic issues and epidemiological insights in PTSD. *CNS Spectrums: The International Journal of Neuropsychiatric Medicine, 3*(7, Suppl. 2), 11-14.

Index

About the Editors

Barbara C. Wallace, Ph.D., is Associate Professor of Health Education within the Department of Health and Behaviors Studies, Teachers College, Columbia University. She is a New York State Licensed Psychologist. She specializes in the treatment of those presenting chemical dependency and histories of sexual abuse, physical abuse, emotional abuse, domestic violence, and HIV/AIDS. She not only maintains a private practice and specializes in the treatment of those in recovery from chemical dependency and various forms of trauma, abuse, and violence but also provides spiritual counseling, couples counseling, and same-sex relationships counseling. Dr. Wallace has presented regionally, nationally, and internationally, specializing in "training the trainers," or training other practitioners who can implement those techniques she has pioneered and refined in her frontline work (in the trenches, so to speak) with those impacted by the multiple epidemics involving drugs, HIV/AIDS, family trauma, and social and personal forms of visible and invisible violence. She has developed a reputation for being an especially dynamic presenter, covering topics such as the following: chemical dependency treatment, relapse prevention for a range of problem behaviors, trauma resolution for survivors of multiple forms of abuse, multicultural competency and diversity training, violence prevention and intervention, and social action for social justice. Her work reflects a deep-rooted commitment to social justice and ending the oppression of all humankind.

Dr. Wallace is the author of numerous journal articles, articles in community-based publications, and several book volumes: *Crack Cocaine: A Practical Treatment Approach for the Chemically Dependent* (1991), *The Chemically Dependent: Phases of Treatment and Recovery* (1992), and *Adult Children of Dysfunctional Families: Prevention, Intervention, and Treatment for Community Mental Health Promotion* (1996). She is currently working on two books and several papers and chapters in edited books, reflecting her current research in the areas of addiction treatment, methadone to abstinence treatment outcome, multicultural counseling, and multicultural competence training.

A native of Philadelphia, she traveled for the first time in the summer of 1999 to her spiritual home in Africa and rejoined her ancestral, indigenous Akan family through sacred ritual in the mountains of Larteh, Ghana. On January 6, 2000, in the presence of clan elders, sponsors, several chiefs, numerous priests, and loving family members, Dr. Wallace was enstooled as the Asona Aberadehemaa—being named Nana Ohemaa Agyiriwah. In Philadelphia, she serves the Asona Aberade Shrine as Queen Mother, also providing guidance and counseling within this context.

Robert T. Carter, Ph.D., is a Professor of Psychology and Education, Chair of the Department of Counseling and Clinical Psychology, and Director of Training of the Counseling Psychology Program at Teachers College, Columbia University. He is known internationally for his work on Black and White racial identity. He has published in the areas of psychotherapy processes and outcome, career development, cultural values, racial identity issues, educational achievements, and equality in education through the lens of racial identity. He has been retained to consult on organizational, legal, and educational issues associated with race and diversity. He also is the Conference Director for a national conference known as the Teachers College Winter Roundtable on Cross-Cultural Psychology and Education.

Dr. Carter authored *The Influence of Race and Racial Identity in Psychotherapy: Towards a Racially Inclusive Model* (1995); coedited (with Chalmer E. Thompson) *Racial Identity Theory: Applications for Individuals, Groups and Organizations* (1997); coauthored (with D. Sue, J. M. Casas, M. J. Fouad, A. Levy, M. Jensen, R. LaFromboise, J. Manese, J. Ponterotto, and J. Vasques-Natall) *Multicultural Counseling Competencies: Individual Professional and Organizational Development* (1998); and is Series Editor for the *Discussions From the Roundtable—The Counseling Psychologists and the Roundtable Book Series on Multicultural Psychology and Education*. He is coeditor for the special issue of the Teachers College Record on Multicultural Education (Spring 2000).

Dr. Carter is also a legal consultant. He works with organizations and individuals on issues such as organizational development, teacher training, desegregation, racial discrimination, cross-cultural adoption, and biracial custody. He is a Fellow in the American Psychological Association (Division 17, Counseling Psychology, and Division 45, Society for the Study of Ethnic Minority Issues) and former Chair of the Fellowship Committee for Division 17. He has also served on the editorial boards of *The Counseling Psychologist*, *Journal of Counseling and Development*, *Journal of Counseling Psychology*, and *Journal of Multicultural Counseling and Development*. He is Editor-Elect of *The Counseling Psychologist* (2003-2008).

About the Contributors

Vanessa Alleyne is a doctoral candidate in the Department of Clinical and Counseling Psychology at Teachers College, Columbia University. She is currently on internship at Kings County Hospital Center, Brooklyn, New York. Her research is in the area of addition, treatment motivation, and racial identity.

Madonna G. Constantine, Ph.D., is an Associate Professor of Psychology and Education in the Department of Counseling and Clinical Psychology at Teachers College, Columbia University. Her primary research interests are in the area of multicultural counseling competence and multicultural training and supervision. She has numerous publications related to her research interests, and she currently serves as an associate editor of the *Journal of Multicultural Counseling and Development.*

Edward Dunbar, Ph.D., is a practicing psychologist in Los Angeles and an Associate Clinical Professor at UCLA. He has consulted to state and county agencies in the analysis of hate crime trends, trained school mental health staff in bias victim intervention, and testified on legislation to strengthen the sentencing for capital crimes against women, gays, and lesbians. He is also active in the study of human rights attitudes and ethnic bias in Eastern Europe. He treats victims of workplace harassment, hate violence, and sexual assault. His current areas of research address clinical aspects of racism, analysis of hate crime offenders, and individual difference factors of ethnic bias.

Reverend Karla Fleshman is an ordained minister within the Universal Fellowship of Metropolitan Community Churches (UFMCC). She is the founding pastor of Imago Dei Metropolitan Community Church (MCC). The mission of Imago Dei MCC is that of a loving, diverse Christian community of gay, lesbian, bisexual, transgendered, and heterosexual allies providing transforming worship and small-group experience empowering people for ministry within our church and our world. Her mission echoes with that of the church; she is also a licensed social worker with a history of working within the HIV infected/affected community.

Mary J. Heppner, Ph.D., is Associate Professor in the Department of Education and Counseling Psychology and Assistant Director at the Career Center, University of Missouri at Columbia. Her research interests are in the areas of career development and vocational behavior and in sexual violence prevention. She is the coauthor of a recent text titled *Career Counseling: Process, Techniques and Issues,* as well as numerous journal articles. She recently won the 1999 Kemper Award for Outstanding Teaching from her university as well as the 1999 Early Scientist/Practitioner Award from Division 17 (Counseling Psychology) of the American Psychological Association.

Darryl B. Hill, Ph.D., is Assistant Professor of Psychology at Concordia University, Montreal, Quebec. He teaches courses on the social psychology of sex and gender and studies "trans" issues, gender identity, and self theory.

Delores Jones-Brown, Ph.D., is Associate Professor in the Department of Law and Political Science, John Jay College of Criminal Justice of the City University of New York. She conducts research in the area of African American youth and their involvement in the criminal justice system, violence prevention, and varied interventions against violence for youth.

Ashraf Kagee, Ph.D., is a fellow of the Solomon Asch Center for Study of Ethnopolitical Conflict at the University of Pennsylvania and a researcher in the Department of Psychology at the University of Stellenbosch, South Africa. Dr. Kagee's research interests include stress and trauma, psychology and human rights, and the interface between psychology and public health.

Richard Keller, M.A., is an advanced Ph.D. student in counseling psychology at Teachers College, Columbia University. His research interests focus on disability issues, and his clinical experience reflects work with the population at large. In addition, he has been the Director of the Office of Access and Services for Individuals With Disabilities at Teachers College since 1996. That office seeks to level the playing field for all individuals with disabilities at Teachers College. Mr. Keller is a person who lives with a disability and has been involved with the disability rights movement for the past 12 years.

Eric L. Kohatsu, Ph.D., is Associate Professor of Psychology at California State University, Los Angeles. His research interests include racial identity theory and its applications, Asian American mental health, racism and prejudice, cross-cultural counseling, research methodology, spiritual issues, and alternative approaches to healing. He also directs the Center for Cross-Cultural Research at California State University, Los Angeles.

José E. Nanin, Ed.D., is Assistant Director of the HIV Training Institute at the New York City Department of Health and adjunct faculty at Teachers College, Columbia University. He has developed several training curricula on HIV, sexuality issues, and behavior change counseling. His current interests include investigating the impact of burnout on HIV service providers as well as assessing factors that affect human sexuality development.

Helen A. Neville, Ph.D., is Associate Professor in the Department of Educational and Counseling Psychology and the African American Studies Program at the University of Illinois at Urbana-Champaign. Her research interests focus on general and culture-specific aspects of the stress and coping process, primarily among African American populations. Her work also examines effectiveness of social awareness interventions and, more recently, colorblind racial attitudes. She has received several local and national awards for her work with students, including the Kenneth and Mamie Clark Award for Outstanding Contribution to the Professional Development of Ethnic Minority Graduate Studies from the Student Affiliate Group of the American Psychological Association.

Toshi Sasao, Ph.D., is a community psychologist and Associate Professor of Psychology in the Department of Psychology and Graduate School of Education at International Christian University, Tokyo. He also directs the American Studies Program at the same institution. In addition, he teaches graduate-level courses in community psychology at the University of Tokyo Graduate School, Chuo University Graduate School, and Ochanomizu Women's University, all in Tokyo. His research interests include promoting the well-being and preventing mental health problems among adolescents, especially in multicultural contexts.

Tom Schiff, Ed.D., is a health educator at the University of Massachusetts in Amherst. Among his foci are men's health and violence prevention. In addition, he has over 20 years of experience as an educator, counselor, trainer, and consultant with an emphasis on organization development and human relations. He has a particular expertise in working with men on issues of abuse, violence, sexual harassment, sexism, and homophobia. He happy to discuss this chapter (and more) and can be reached at tschiff@uhs.umass.edu.

Hawthorne E. Smith, Ph.D., is a psychologist with the Bellevue/NYU Program for Survivors of Torture and the Coordinator of Direct Services for Nah We Yone, Inc. (a nonprofit organization working primarily with refugees from Sierra Leone). He holds a Ph.D. in counseling psychology from Teachers College, Columbia University, a master's degree in International Affairs from the Columbia University School of International and Public Affairs, and an advanced certificate in African Studies from Cheikh Anta Diop University in Dakar, Senegal.

Lisa B. Spanierman, Ph. D., is Assistant Professor in the Department of Educational and Counseling Psychology at the University of Illinois at Urbana-Champaign. Her research interests are in the areas of multiculturalism, specifically focusing on race and racism, psychological costs of racism to whites, and career development. She has presented her research at local and national conferences.

Elizabeth Sparks, Ph.D., is Associate Professor in the Counseling, Developmental and Education Department at Boston College. Prior to her academic career, she worked for 17 years as a practicing clinician in various community-based settings, such as child welfare agencies and juvenile courts. She currently teaches courses on multicultural issues in counseling, psychopathology, and clinical supervision. She also maintains a private psychotherapy practice. Her research interests stem from her clinical career in community mental health and focus on interpersonal assaultive violence among African American youth, psychotherapy with at-risk youth, psychotherapy with women of color, and issues in multicultural training and supervision.

María Torres-Guzmán, Ph.D., is Associate Professor of Bilingual Education in the Department of International and Transcultural Studies at Teachers College, Columbia University. She is also

Coordinator of the Program in Bilingual/Bicultural Studies, engaging in teacher preparation, training, and research.

Maria R. Volpe, Ph.D., is Professor of Sociology and Director of the Dispute Resolution Program at John Jay College of Criminal Justice, City University of New York, and serves as Convener of the CUNY Dispute Resolution Consortium. She is an international leader in dispute resolution; has lectured and written extensively about dispute resolution processes, particularly mediation; and has been widely recognized for her distinguished career in the field of dispute resolution. She is a past-president of the International Society of Professionals in Dispute Resolution (SPIDR). Her current research focuses on police mediation and the dispute resolution process in educational settings.